S. C. Breyfogel

Landmarks of the Evangelical Association

S. C. Breyfogel

Landmarks of the Evangelical Association

ISBN/EAN: 9783337153786

Printed in Europe, USA, Canada, Australia, Japan

Cover: Foto ©ninafisch / pixelio.de

More available books at **www.hansebooks.com**

LANDMARKS

OF THE

EVANGELICAL ASSOCIATION,

CONTAINING

ALL THE OFFICIAL RECORDS OF THE ANNUAL AND GENERAL CON-

FERENCES FROM THE DAYS OF JACOB ALBRIGHT

TO THE YEAR 1840;

AND THE PROCEEDINGS OF THE EAST PENNSYLVANIA CONFERENCE

TOGETHER WITH IMPORTANT EXTRACTS FROM THE TRANS-

ACTIONS OF THE GENERAL CONFERENCE FROM

1840 TO THE PRESENT TIME.

BY

· S. C. BREYFOGEL.

A. D. 1800-1887.

READING, PA.:

EAGLE BOOK PRINT, 542 PENN STREET.

———

1888.

TO THE REMNANT

OF THAT

NOBLE COMPANY OF THE FATHERS

WHOSE GODLY LIVES AND HEROIC DEEDS HAVE MADE

THE RECORD OF THESE PAGES POSSIBLE,

AND TO THE

𝔜oung 𝔐en in the 𝔐inistry

WHOSE PIETY, LEARNING, AND DISINTERESTED DEVO-

TION MAKE THEM WORTHY SUCCESSORS OF THE

MIGHTY MEN OF THE PAST, THIS VOLUME

IS AFFECTIONATELY INSCRIBED.

PREFACE.

A familiar acquaintance with the past leads to a truer appreciation of the present and a more intelligent apprehension of the future. Prompted by such a motive, the compiler of this work, now offered to the Church, frequently consulted the official records during the time when he was honored with the secretaryship of his Conference. Because of the discoveries which rewarded every research, and on account of the trains of thought which these pages of the past awakened, casual and desultory inquiries soon grew into a delightful and systematic study, and from a perusal for personal information the plan widened into an effort to share with others the knowledge of these old doings which lay entombed within the musty records of the years gone by.

Up to the year 1874 the present work is a translation, inasmuch as the minutes prior to that date were recorded in German. To make these translations from German script was singularly difficult. The peculiar phraseology of the past and the time-honored expressions which have the twofold sanction of age and continued use are retained, often at the expense of awkwardness in the English construction. In a word, equivalent renderings rather than rhetoric, and conciseness of statement in preference to style, have been the constant aim. There could have been greater condensation of the transactions by avoiding repetition of expressions, but upon close inspection it will readily appear that the plan pursued secures a more complete connection of events, an item of no small importance to one who is a student of historic sequence, as well as an observer of facts. The monotony which is necessarily connected with a repetition of terms has been relieved, as far as was consistent with conscientious exactness and a faithful presentation of the old and the new ways of doing things.

Transactions affecting the *personnel* of the Conference, boundaries, church affairs, education, finance, missionary appropriations, etc., are not found upon the earlier records in the systematic and convenient form in which they appear in this volume; on the contrary, they lie scattered in unclassified groups. In later years, when the committee reports on moral questions become voluminous, and the resolutions of one year contain repetitions of former deliverances, the repetitions are omitted and the language condensed.

This publication includes all the official Annual and General Conference proceedings of the entire Association prior to the year 1840. Subsequent to this period the scope of the book narrows down to the proceedings of the East Pennsylvania Conference, interleaved with important extracts from the transactions of the General Conference.

Special attention is directed to the alphabetical roll of preachers and to the table of statistics. Nothing like the former appears upon the records, and before the year 1861 there is only a fragmentary and unsystematic attempt to compile statistics. No means have been left unemployed, both of scrupulous research and repeated revision, to make these lists so accurate and reliable, that those who call here for information may do so with the fullest confidence. Thoroughness has been the persistent aim of the undertaking. For its imperfections of statement the indulgence of the reader is solicited.

To the brethren in the ministry, for their cheerful and ready assistance, as well as for their kind words of encouragement, the compiler is under many obligations. In the preparation of the copious index, Rev. J. H. Shirey rendered valuable assistance. Other quiet and helpful hands were constantly extended to lighten the task and hasten its completion.

The East Pennsylvania Conference possesses a striking and impressive individuality, which a careful analysis of her proceedings and an impartial study of her spirit will reveal. Her history is the history of the Evangelical Association during the greater part of the first half of this century; her spirit of self denial and heroic energy is the spirit of her founders, our fathers. For the many days of pains-taking labor spent upon the pages now ready, it will be a rich compensation, if the apostolic spirit of the early days will return more fully upon us through the study of these Evangelical Landmarks.

CONTENTS.

THE EARLY DAYS.

1800–1826.

"We have heard with our ears, O God, our fathers have told us what work thou didst in their days, in the times of old."— PS. XLIV: 1.

The origin of the Evangelical Association and the proceedings of the Conferences of Evangelical preachers, from A. D. 1800 to 1813.   Recorded by

GEORGE MILLER, *Elder.*

––––––––

At the Conference session, held at New Berlin, Pa., June 7–11, 1819, it was resolved that the proceedings compiled by George Miller, as well as all the subsequent transactions of the Conference up to date, be inscribed in a suitable conference record, to be procured for this purpose.   This was done by

JOHN DREISBACH,
Presiding Elder.

JANUARY 31, 1820.

THE EARLY DAYS.

1800.

The Lord our God, who always imparts sufficient light to men to work within them a good will and purpose, also bestows the power to do of his good pleasure and doubtless enables every one who wills, to perform his commandments and to become a diligent co-worker in the kingdom of grace according to the ability that has been given him.

Moreover Christ the Shepherd and Bishop of all souls gathers and edifies his church in manifold ways, but more especially through such who are faithful fellow-workers with his grace, whom he enlightens and sancti-fies by his Holy Spirit. And whenever in the past the needs of Christendom have required it, he has, in various ways through his wise Providence, caused anew the revival of true godliness by means of his devoted servants. We therefore accept as a gift from the Lord, that which he has wrought through his servant Jacob Albright, the Evangelical preacher; for we perceive that it has pleased the Lord to work, and spread abroad his knowledge through the counsel and direction of this godly man.

Under the direction of this devout preacher, various persons united themselves, in the year of our

Lord 1800, to pray with and for each other, in order that they might be saved from sin and flee from the wrath to come. In order to begin and carry out this good and momentous work, they decided to spend each Sunday in social prayer, and to set apart every Wednesday evening for prayermeeting. Studiously and with diligence they sought to avoid everything evil and sinful and to do all manner of good as far as God gave them strength and ability. The number of those disposed to attend such meetings soon increased and the work grew from year to year, as the records will show. This was the origin of the united Evangelical Association, the operations of which at first extended throughout the Counties of Berks and Northampton in the State of Pennsylvania. Because of their peculiarly earnest manner in worship, and more especially because Jacob Albright, by the grace of God, was the instrumental cause of their solemn union, they were at first called "*The Albrights*," by other Christian denominations.

1801.

In the year of our Lord and Saviour Jesus Christ 1801, the Association added only a few to its number. Several persons sought and found grace unto the pardon of their sins, so that they knew and were assured that God was their reconciled Father through Jesus Christ.

1802.

During this year about twenty persons united with

the Association. Among them was a young man named John Walter, who entered the work of the ministry as a preacher on probation under the direction of the Rev. Jacob Albright.

1803.

The membership now numbered forty, the most of whom were converted. John Walter had grown in grace and continued in his determination to be a co-laborer in the work of spreading the knowledge of God. Abraham Liesser, another young man, entered the work as preacher on probation under the direction of Albright. During this year the Association resolved to introduce and establish an ecclesiastical organization, and accordingly elected Jacob Albright to the office of Elder among them. He was consecrated, that is ordained, by the other preachers in a suitable manner, by the laying on of hands, and thereby authorized to administer all the affairs belonging to a Christian Church, and to exercise the duties and offices belonging to an Evangelical preacher. With one accord they chose the Holy Scriptures as their rule of faith and conduct. A written license was granted to Albright by which the Association recognized him as a genuine Evangelical preacher, and authorized him to appoint other competent persons as co-laborers. This license was given under the following title and form:

"*From the Elders and Brethren of his Congregation of Christian Evangelical Friends.*

We, the undersigned, as Evangelical Christian Friends, recognize and declare Jacob Albright to be a genuine

Evangelical preacher in word and in deed, and a believer (confessor) in the universal Christian Church and the communion of saints. To this we testify as brethren and elders of his congregation. Given in the State of Pennsylvania on the 5th day of November, 1803. Subscribed by John Walter and Abraham Liesser together with fourteen other persons."

1804.

In this year the total membership of the Evangelical Association was sixty, the greater number of whom professed to have experienced a change of heart. The circuits were confined mainly to Berks and Northampton counties, but the preachers extended their operations into Northumberland and Centre. The traveling preachers were Jacob Albright elder, and John Walter and Abraham Liesser preachers on trial. Alexander Jimeson was newly received on trial. The salary of the preachers was raised by voluntary contributions and amounted to $15.30 for each. John Walter received permission to collect special contributions for the purpose of purchasing a horse ; he secured $37.33.

1805.

The membership of the Evangelical Association reached a total of seventy-five persons during this year. The traveling preachers were Jacob Albright elder, John Walter in full connection, and Alexander Jimeson continued on trial. George Miller was newly received on trial. Abraham Liesser died during the year. The fields of labor remained the same as last year. Efforts were made to establish new circuits in the counties of Dauphin and Lancaster. Jacob Albright and John Walter received equal shares from the general collections for salary. In addition to his salary Walter was permitted to collect the extra sum of $18.67 for the purpose of purchasing a horse. The friends raised $66.67 for Alexander Jimeson as salary, besides giving him permission to collect $69.33 wherewith to purchase a horse.

1806.

In 1806 the work spread in the counties of Northumberland, Centre, and Dauphin. The total membership was 120. Three traveling preachers served the appointments. They were Jacob Albright elder, and John Walter and George Miller in full connection. Alexander Jimeson located during the year on account of family concerns. The contributions for salary were divided in equal shares among Albright, Walter, Miller, and Jimeson, with the exception that an extra sum was allowed to the last named to satisfy him for his services, after which he returned to his former avocation. The brethren resolved to receive no more preachers on probation who are not satisfied with an equal share of the general salary fund. It was also decided to create a new fund to be called *Briefschaft Steuer*, the object

---

*Near the close of each conference year, the preachers—usually the duty of the junior preacher on the circuit—solicited extra contributions with which to supply deficiencies in salary and assist the poor of the church. This collection was called the *Briefschaft Steuer*, and will be designated hereafter in these pages as the Subsidiary Collection.—S. C. B.

of which was to meet the incidental expenses of the traveling preachers and to assist the poor of the Association.

A suitable license was given to each of the preachers. The society authorized the appointment of local preachers. In consequence of this, Charles Bisse, Jacob Phillips, and Solomon Miller received license during the year as local preachers. It was resolved that hereafter regular *Annual Conference* sessions be held, to consist of the foremost members of our Evangelical Association, but more especially of our preachers, who are to be concerned to promote the general welfare of the Association by their counsel and their united action.

1807.

The First Annual Conference.

The first regular Annual Conference session of the Association was held at Muehlbach, Dauphin (now Lebanon) Co., Pa., on the 15th and 16th of November, 1807. The session was opened with a season of prayer during which we implored the divine blessing upon our transactions. Our membership had now reached a total of 220, nearly all of whom professed conversion. The following were the traveling preachers: Jacob Albright elder, and John Walter and George Miller in full connection. John Dreisbach and Jacob Frey were newly received on trial. The local preachers were Charles Bisse, Conrad Phillips, and Solomon Miller. The class leaders and exhorters present numbered twenty, making a total attendance of twenty-eight.

Jacob Albright was elected *Bishop* and George Miller, *Elder* by a majority of votes. The Conference appointed Jacob Albright to prepare and publish a brief compendium of church rules—a Discipline—for the instruction and edification of the societies. The fields of labor were then assigned to the preachers, after which the session closed with prayer.

1808.

The membership of the Association was not reported. There was, however, an increase in number. Besides Albright there were five traveling preachers: Geo. Miller elder, John Walter and John Dreisbach in full connection, and Jacob Frey continued on trial. John Erb was newly received on trial. The general salary fund was equally divided among the traveling preachers. The subsidiary collection, which amounted to $44, was distributed among J. Albright, G. Miller, and A. Jimeson. The revered Jacob Albright died during this year, between Easter and Whitsuntide, [May 18th, 1808.]

1809.

The Second Annual Conference.

In April of 1809 the second regular Annual Conference was held in Albany Twp., Berks Co., Pa. The session was opened with prayer for the divine blessing to rest upon the transactions. The membership of the Association was reported to be 426. One preacher was expelled on account of immoral conduct. The traveling preachers on record were George Miller elder, John Walter and John Dreisbach in full connection, and John Erb on trial. Matthew Betz and Henry Niebel were newly received on trial. John Walter and John Dreisbach were elected to the office of Elder and afterwards ordained as such. After the circuits had been arranged the preachers were appointed to their various fields.

Geo. Miller was directed to travel and to preach as much as his health would allow. He was also instructed to write upon such subjects as might prove edifying to the Association. Owing to the failing health and early decease of Albright, the preparation of Articles of Faith and of a Discipline was accomplished by Geo. Miller. The Conference instructed the latter to publish the work at his own expense. It was resolved that the official documents of the Association shall hereafter be published under the title of "The so-called Albrights." John Dreisbach was instructed to publish for the use of the Association a small catechism which he had translated from the English. The Conference gave John Walter $42.72 out of the subsidiary collection, for the purchase of a horse. The session closed with prayer.

BOUNDARIES.

Northumberland, Centre, and Mifflin counties were organized into a field to be known as Northumberland Circuit. The counties of Berks, Dauphin, Lancaster, Bucks, and Northampton were formed into a field called Schuylkill Circuit.

Northumberland Cir.—John Walter and John Erb.
Schuylkill Cir.—John Dreisbach, Mat- thew Betz and Henry Niebel, (who entered active work in the Fall of the year.)

1810.

The Third Annual Conference.

President, George Miller.
Secretary, John Dreisbach.

The Conference of 1810 convened near Muehlbach (now Millbach), Dauphin (now Lebanon) Co., Pa. The sessions continued from the 18th to the 20th of April. After the usual devotional exercises, Geo. Miller was elected chairman and J. Dreisbach secretary. The conduct of the preachers and the condition of the circuits were investigated. Geo. Miller located on account of his enfeebled health. The following were the preachers according to their station and order: elders, G. Miller, J. Walter, and J. Dreisbach; received into full connection and ordained (to the office of deacon), J. Erb and M. Betz; on trial, H. Niebel; newly received on trial, Michael Becker and David Yerlitz. There were ten local preachers in the Association.

Five new classes were organized, 78 persons converted, and 114 newly received into the church during the past year. The whole number of members reported at this session was 528, nearly all of whom professed conversion. John Walter was instructed to publish a small hymn book which he had compiled for the use of the Evangelical Association. It was also resolved that the Biography of Jacob Albright, composed by George Miller, be published at the expense of the traveling preachers. The Conference determined that an attempt should be made to hold two campmeetings, one on Northumberland Circuit to begin on May 30th, and the other in the month of October on Schuylkill Circuit. The salary received by a traveling preacher was $30. The subsidiary collection amounted to $30.80, which was distributed among Geo. Miller, John Walter, John Dreisbach, John Erb, Matthew Betz, and widow Maria Griffesin. It was made obligatory upon the traveling preachers to render at the next session of the Conference an accurate account of all their receipts and expenditures. The Conference resolved to hold its next annual session on Schuylkill Circuit, eight days before Easter.

APPOINTMENTS.

Schuylkill Cir.—John Walter, Henry Niebel, and Michael Becker.

Northumberland Cir.—John Driesbach and David Yerlitz.

To organize a new circuit—John Erb and Matthew Betz, with the understanding that J. Walter and J. Dreisbach shall relieve them by exchanging circuits during a part of the year. George Miller was appointed to travel throughout the conference district, as his strength would allow, to visit the friends, and to write a book which might prove useful to the membership.

Conference closed with prayer and an expression of unanimous approval of the foregoing minutes. As a token of our willingness to fulfill our calling, serve our appointments, and comply with our duties, as set forth in our Church Discipline and in the Holy Scriptures, we subscribed our names. Signed:—George Miller, J. Dreisbach, M. Betz, D. Yerlitz, J. Walter, J. Erb, H. Niebel, and M. Becker.

1811.

The Fourth Annual Conference.

President, Geo. Miller.

Secretary, John Dreisbach.

This session of the Conference was held near Muehlbach, Heidelberg Township, Dauphin Co., Pa., April 9–11, 1811. The Conference was opened with prayer. Geo. Miller was elected chairman, and J. Dreisbach secretary. The conduct of the preachers and the condition of the circuits were investigated. The following were the preachers in active service: elders,—G. Miller, J. Walter, and J. Dreisbach; in full connection,—J. Erb, M. Betz, and H. Niebel; on trial,—M. Becker and D. Yerlitz; newly received on trial,—Leonhart Zimmerman. The number of local preachers was twelve. The work of the Association was extended during the past year. Fourteen new classes were organized and a new field of labor formed, called Franklin Circuit. The brethren reported 72 conversions and 112 accessions, thus increasing the entire membership to 740.

The highest salary received was $45.56; the average, $29.33; the total, $283. The subsidiary collection amounted to $51.97, which was divided among J. Walter, J. Erb, H. Niebel, M. Becker, and a poor man named Samuel Kupper. The traveling preachers were instructed to organize catechetical classes on their circuits.

Schuylkill Cir.—J. Walter, M. Betz, and D. Yerlitz.
Northumberland Cir.—J. Erb and L. Zimmerman.

Franklin Cir.—J. Dreisbach, H. Niebel, and M. Becker.

Geo. Miller was instructed to travel and preach throughout the conference district, as his strength would permit, and to contribute with his pen whatever might conduce to the upbuilding of the church. The Conference adjourned to meet on Northumberland Circuit on the first Thursday after Easter, 1812. The minutes were signed by nine brethren.

1812.

The Fifth Annual Conference.

President, George Miller.
Secretary, John Dreisbach.

The session of 1812 was held on the 2d and 3d of April, in Buffalo Valley, Union Co., Pa., within the bounds of Northumberland Circuit. The Conference was opened with prayer, after which G. Miller was elected chairman, and J. Dreisbach secretary. The conduct of the traveling preachers was investigated. John Erb was ordained Elder, and Henry Niebel, Deacon. Robt. McCray, Michael Deibler, Abraham Huth, John Buechwalter, and Frederick Shauer were newly received as preachers on trial. G. Miller, J. Walter, and J. Dreisbach were elected a committee to station the preachers.

*The statistics reported at this session are the following:

	Newly Converted.	Newly Received.	Whole No. of Members.
Schuylkill Cir........	49	64	295
Northumberland Cir...	93	109	353
Franklin Cir.........	18	29	113
	202	160	761

*The general collections for salary amounted to $344.96; the subsidiary collection, to $113.68. The general salary fund and a part of the subsidiary collection were distributed among the traveling preachers. †The balance of the latter was divided among such as were in need. The preachers in charge were instructed to render to the next annual session a correct account of and proper information concerning the subsidiary collections gathered on their circuits, and also to secure subscribers to the fund. The Conference ordered that three campmeetings be held during the ensuing year: one on Northumberland Cir., May 22d; another on Schuylkill Cir., Aug. 21st; and the third on Franklin Cir., Sept. 24th. George Miller having written a tratise entitled "*Unterweisung zum Wahren und Thatigen Christenthum*," the manuscript was submitted to several elders and deacons for inspection. In the event of their approval it was to be published.

It was resolved that efforts be made to purchase lots and erect dwelling houses on Schuylkill and Northum-

*Here we find, for the first time in the records of the Conference, the statistics of the different circuits.

Hereafter these items will not appear on the record of each session but the summary statistics of each year may be found in their appropriate places in the Tables of Statistics.

†At least three needy persons, not preachers, received support.

berland Circuits for the families of poor itinerant preachers. The execution of the project was submitted to the elders and trustees of these circuits, with instructions that the funds bequeathed to the Association for the purpose shall be applied in equal portions.

APPOINTMENTS.

Franklin Cir.—J. Walter and D. Yerlitz.

To organize a new Circuit—J. Dreisbach and R. McCray.

Lancaster Cir.—J. Erb and M. Deibler.

York Cir.—M. Betz and M. Becker.

Schuylkill Cir.—H. Niebel and A. Huth.

Northumberland Cir.—L. Zimmerman, J. Buechwalter, and F. Shauer.

Geo. Miller was appointed by the Conference to devise a plan of episcopal church government, and to travel throughout the conference district to the extent of his ability. Each preacher received his license and each gave the other information concerning the most important affairs on the different circuits. The session closed with the usual resolution pledging the members to diligence and fidelity.

1813.

The Sixth Annual Conference.

President, George Miller.

Secretary, John Dreisbach.

On the 21st of April, 1813, the members of Conference assembled in Buffalo Valley, Pa., Northumberland Circuit, and continued in session three days. The proceedings were opened with prayer and supplication for the divine blessing. G. Miller was elected chairman, and J. Dreisbach, secretary. Two preachers were expelled from the Association on account of immoral conduct. G. Miller and J. Erb located on account of bodily infirmities. M. Betz and H. Niebel were ordained to the office of Elder; D. Yerlitz and L. Zimmerman to the office of Deacon. Abraham Buchman, John Kleinfelter, John Stambach, Adam Henig, Jacob Kleinfelter, and John Walter, Jr., were newly received on trial. A committee, consisting of G. Miller, J. Walter, and J. Dreisbach, was appointed to assign the different circuits to the preachers. The highest amount of salary received by a traveling preacher was $64.81.

APPOINTMENTS.

Schuylkill Cir.—J. Walter, Jacob Kleinfelter, and J. Walter, Jr.

Northumberland Cir.—M. Betz, R. McCray, A. Buchman, and J. Stambach.

Franklin Cir.—H. Niebel and M. Deibler.

York Cir.—L. Zimmerman and F. Shauer.

To organize a new Circuit—J. Dreisbach and A. Henig.

To organize another new Circuit—D. Yerlitz and John Kleinfelter.

Geo. Miller and J. Erb promised Conference to attend the extra meetings and to travel as much as God would grant them strength. The former promised also to complete the supplement to our Church Discipline provided God give him grace to do so. The preachers received their licenses and gave their successors a list of appointments, the class books, and correct information concerning the state of affairs on their respective fields. With a resolution of consecration to the service of God and of reliance upon him the Conference adjourned.

1814.

The Seventh Annual Conference.

President, John Dreisbach.

Secretary, Henry Niebel.

3

The session of 1814 was held on the 13th, 14th, and 15th of April, in Buffalo Valley, Pa., within the bounds of Northumberland Circuit. The Conference was opened with the usual religious exercises. J. Dreisbach was elected chairman and H. Niebel, secretary. A preacher on trial was deposed from the ministry. J. Walter located for this year on account of bodily infirmities. Matthew Betz died during the past year. F. Shauer, A. Buchman, A. Henig, and J. Stambach were ordained to the office of Deacon. Thomas Bruer, Michael Walter, and Henry Stauffer were newly received as preachers on trial. The Conference elected John Dreisbach to the office of Presiding Elder for a period of four years. A committee, consisting of G. Miller, J. Dreisbach, and H. Niebel, was elected to assign to the preachers their fields of labor.

It was resolved that during the ensuing year camp-meetings be held on Union, Bedford, York, and Schuylkill Circuits. G. Miller, J. Walter, and J. Erb promised Conference to travel according to their strength and to be co-laborers on the circuits. The preachers received their licenses and gave their successors all necessary information concerning their respective fields of labor, after which the session closed in the usual manner.

APPOINTMENTS.

CONFERENCE DISTRICT—*J. Dreisbach, P. E.*

Union Cir.—H. Niebel and John Kleinfelter.

Bedford Cir.—D. Yerlitz and Michael Walter.

York Cir.—J. Stambach and T. Bruer.

Franklin Cir.—F. Shauer.

Somerset Cir.—A. Buchman and Jacob Kleinfelter.

Lancaster Cir.—L. Zimmerman and H. Stauffer.

Schuylkill Cir.—A. Henig.

1815.

The Eighth Annual Conference.

President, Henry Niebel.
Secretary, John Kleinfelter.

The members of Conference assembled near Strasburgh, Pa., on York Circuit, April 4th, 1815, and continued in session three days. The session was opened with the usual devotional exercises. H. Niebel was elected chairman, and John Kleinfelter, secretary. D. Yerlitz located on account of family concerns. H. Niebel was elected to the office of Presiding Elder. The newly elected deacons, John Kleinfelter, Jacob Kleinfelter, and T. Bruer were ordained. David Thomas, John Dehoff, and Jacob Bruer were newly received as preachers on trial. H. Niebel, J. Erb, and L. Zimmerman were appointed to assign the circuits to the preachers. The highest salary received by a traveling preacher was $89.67. It was resolved that campmeetings be held during the coming year on Union, Centre, York, and Lancaster circuits.

J. Erb and D. Yerlitz promised Conference to travel as their strength would allow and to assist upon the circuits. Each preacher received his license, and gave to his successor the classbooks and all necessary information. The Conference closed with the usual resolution, and the minutes were subscribed by the preachers present.

APPOINTMENTS.

CANAAN DISTRICT.—*J. Dreisbach, P. E.*

Franklin Cir.—T. Bruer and J. Dehoff.
York Cir.—A. Buchman and D. Thomas.

Union Cir.—J. Stambach and Jacob Kleinfelter.

Lancaster Cir.—John Kleinfelter and J. Bruer.
Schuylkill Cir.—L. Zimmerman.

SALEM DISTRICT.—*H. Niebel, P. E.*

Centre Cir.—F. Shauer and H. Stauffer.
Somerset Cir.—A. Heulg and M. Walter.

1816.

The Ninth Annual Conference.

President, John Dreisbach.

Secretary, Henry Niebel.

Conference convened in Dry Valley, Pa., Union Circuit, on June 11th, 1816, and continued its sessions until June 13th. The transactions were preceded by the customary religious exercises. J. Dreisbach was elected chairman, and H. Niebel, secretary. The conduct of the preachers was investigated. A deacon and a local preacher were deposed from the ministry. A. Buchman, T. Bruer, and H. Stauffer located on account of bodily infirmities. The superannuated and worn out preachers were J. Walter and J. Erb. During the past year George Miller died. L. Zimmerman, and F. Shaner were ordained to the office of Elder, and M. Walter, D. Thomas, J. Dehoff, and Solomon Miller, to the office of Deacon. The following were received on trial: John Fruch, Philip Schmidt, Moses Dehoff, Adam Ettinger, John Shilling, Benjamin Ettinger, John Rickel, Andrew Wolf, and Fred. Kaltreiter. The committee elected to station the preachers consisted of J. Dreisbach, H. Niebel, and L. Zimmerman. The highest salary received was $92.48.

It was resolved that hereafter itinerant preachers shall receive annually in addition to their salary an allowance of $56 for clothes, provided the Conference find itself able so to do. At this time there were 41 local preachers in the Association.

The Conference appointed J. Dreisbach and H.

Niebel to secure a printed form of license for preachers, J. Dreisbach promising to procure a suitable conference seal. These two brethren were also instructed to unify and edit our Discipline and to compile a good and suitable collection of hymns. It was unanimously agreed that local preachers who have stood their probation for six years shall, upon the recommendation of twelve itinerant preachers, be ordained. The Conference elected a Chief Book Commission, empowered to superintend for the Evangelical Association the printing establishment and book bindery with all their appurtenances, as long as the Conference shall see proper. The commission was instructed to hold an annual meeting for consultation in order to secure proper management, and also to make a correct annual statement of all the publishing interests. This first Book Commission consisted of J. Dreisbach, H. Niebel, Solomon Miller, A. Ettinger, Dan'l Bertolet, P. Breidenstein, and Chr. Spengler.

It was resolved that the next General Conference be held on Union Circuit, October 14th, 1816. The delegates appointed to constitute that body were: J. Dreisbach, H. Niebel, J. Walter, L. Zimmerman, J. Erb, J. Stambach, John Kleinfelter, S. Miller, J. Dehoff, D. Thomas, A. Ettinger, and J. Fruch.

J. Dreisbach, Jac. Kleinfelter, and H. Niebel were instructed to visit A. Henig and F. Shauer on their fields of labor during the year. Each preacher received his license and gave his successor all needed information. The Conference adjourned with prayer and the customary resolution of sanction to the proceedings and of diligence in the work.

APPOINTMENTS.

CANAAN DISTRICT—*J. Dreisbach, P. E.*

Franklin Cir.—J. Bruer and F. Kaltreiter.

York Cir.—L. Zimmerman and A. Ettinger.

Lancaster Cir.—D. T h o m a s and A. Wolf.

Schuylkill Cir.—J. Frueh and B. Ettinger.

Lake Mission—Jac. Kleinfelter.

SALEM DISTRICT—*H. Niebel, P. E.*

Union Cir.—John Kleinfelter and M. Dehoff.

Columbia Cir.—P. Schmidt.

Centre Cir.—J. Stambach.

Bedford Cir.—J. Dehoff and J. Shilling.

Somerset Cir.—M. Walter and J. Rickel.

Canton Mission—A. Henig.

Scioto Mission—F. Shauer.

1816.

The General Conference.

President, John Dreisbach.

Secretary, Henry Niebel.

The General Conference of the Evangelical Association convened in Buffalo Valley, Union Co., Pa., on the 14th day of October, 1816, and continued in session until the 17th. J. Dreisbach was elected chairman, and H. Niebel, secretary. Solomon Miller was elected general book agent, and H. Niebel, assistant.

It was resolved to meet in Social Conference with the United Brethren in Christ, at Conococheague, Maryland, on Feb. 14th, 1816; the object of this conference being an attempt to unite the two denominations, if such be the will of God. The delegates chosen to represent the Evangelical Association were: J. Dreisbach, H. Niebel, Solomon Miller, John Kleinfelter, D. Thomas, and A. Ettinger.

The Discipline—re-arranged and improved by the brethren J. Dreisbach and H. Niebel—was examined and approved. Its publication was deferred until after the meeting of the Social Conference, with instructions that, if no union be effected by that body, fifteen hundred copies of the revised Discipline be published as soon as possible. The new hymn book "*Das Geistliche Saiten Spiel*" was examined and approved. Fifteen hundred copies were ordered to be published at once. The General Conference adjourned with the customary resolution of sanction to the proceedings, of reliance upon God and diligence in his service. Attached to the proceedings are the following names: J. Dreisbach, H. Niebel, J. Erb, J. Stambach, J. Kleinfelter, S. Miller, D. Thomas, J. Dehoff, J. Fruch, and A. Ettinger.

1817.

The Tenth Annual Conference.

President, Henry Niebel.

Secretary, John Kleinfelter.

The Conference met in our meeting-house at New Berlin, Pa., on Monday, June 2d, 1817, and continued in session five days. After the opening exercises, H. Niebel was elected chairman and John Kleinfelter, secretary. During the investigation of the conduct of the preachers, two were deposed and expelled from the Association on account of unchristian conduct, and three were deposed from the ministry for neglect of duty, the Conference declaring it to be improper to grant a preacher's license to men who preach but a few times during a year or perhaps not at all, and who neglect those duties which are for their own edification and for that of the church. D. Thomas and A. Henig located on account of bodily infirmities, and P. Schmidt on

account of family cares. John Kleinfelter, Jacob
Kleinfelter, and J. Stambach were ordained to the office
of Elder; J. Bruer and A. Ettinger, to the office of
Deacon. Five were received as preachers on trial,—
James Barber, Henry Wieand, Adam Kleinfelter, Benjamin Boesher, and Samuel Muck. The Conference
elected J. Dreisbach, H. Niebel, and John Kleinfelter
a committee to assign to the preachers their fields of
labor.

The Conference ordered that in the event the regular
salary contributions and the subsidiary collections do
not suffice for the support of the preachers, special
collections shall be taken to cover the deficiency. The
following persons were elected to act as agents for the
Book Commission: Joseph Kleinfelter on York Cir.,
J. Erb on Franklin Cir., Jacob Kerber on Berkley Cir.,
Peter Ridy on Columbia Cir., Chr. Wolf on Lake Cir.,
Nicholas Neith on Somerset Cir., and A. Henig on
Canton Cir. J. Dreisbach was instructed to visit Lake
Cir., and H. Niebel, Canton and Lancaster (Ohio) Cirs.
during the year. The preachers received their licenses
and gave each other the class books and desirable infor-
mation upon all grave and important subjects, after which
the Conference adjourned in the usual manner.

APPOINTMENTS.

CANAAN DISTRICT—J. Dreisbach, P. E.

Franklin Cir.—M. Walter.
Berkley Cir.—J. Bruer.
York Cir.—Jacob Kleinfelter and B. Boesher.
Lancaster Cir.—A. Ettinger and J. Barber.
Schuylkill Cir.—J. Frueh and S. Muck.
Lake Cir.—J. Shilling.

SALEM DISTRICT—H. Niebel, P. E.

Columbia Cir.—L. Zimmerman.
Union Cir.—B. Ettinger and F. Kallreiter.
Centre Cir.—M. Dehoff.
Bedford Cir.—J. Rickel.
Somerset Cir.—J. Stambach and H. Wicand.
Lancaster (Ohio) Cir.—John Kleinfelter and A. Kleinfelter.
Canton Cir.—J. Dehoff.

1818.

The Eleventh Annual Conference.

President, John Dreisbach.
Secretary, Henry Niebel.

The Annual Session of 1818 was held in our church at New Berlin, Pa., beginning on Monday, June 1st, and continuing until June 5th. The religious exercises at the opening were followed by organization. J. Dreisbach was elected president and H. Niebel, secretary. The following brethren located: J. Fruch and A. Ettinger on account of bodily infirmities; H. Wieand and J. Bruer on account of family concerns. J. Fruch, J. Rickel, M. Dehoff, B. Ettinger, F. Kaltreiter, J. Schilling, and J. Barber were ordained to the office of Deacon. The following received license as preachers on trial: Henry Hassler, John Breidenstein, Samuel Witt, and John Peters. J. Dreisbach and H. Niebel were re-elected to the office of Presiding Elder for a period of four years. They exchanged districts. The Conference elected J. Dreisbach, H. Niebel, and John Kleinfelter a committee to assign to the preachers their circuits for the coming year.

Inasmuch as there was not enough money to satisfy the needs of the preachers, the Conference gave to each a writing in the form of a petition addressed to the members of the Association asking them to bestow such gifts upon needy preachers as will secure for them that which, in the opinion of the Conference, is necessary to their support, and which was not in the power of the Conference to give; such contributions to be known as collections.

The following was established as a law to regulate the

reception of persons coming from the Methodist Episcopal Church. Only such members of that church shall
be received into our Association who come with the
consent of their preacher, who have removed from the
bounds of their church into the territory of ours, or
who for sufficient reasons, as for example, on account of
language, have withdrawn from their church in a regular manner. And whoever of our preachers receives
them in any other manner shall be dealt with as a gross
offender and transgressor. It was unanimously resolved
that none of our ministers be allowed to wear gloves
during Summer, nor to use silver-plated bridle bits or
stirrups, or loaded whips, and in no case to adorn their
person with large watch keys; this resolution to be posi-
tively observed by all of our ministers whether they be
connected with the Annual or with the Quarterly Conferences.

The advisability of publishing one or more books
during this year was left to the discretion of J. Dreisbach, H. Niebel, and S. Miller. J. Dreisbach and H.
Niebel were instructed to write to the trustees ordering
that the subsidiary collections be brought to the next
annual session. Each preacher received his license,
after which the Conference adjourned in the usual
manner.

APPOINTMENTS.

CANAAN DISTRICT—*H. Niebel, P. E.*

Schuylkill Cir. — M. Dehoff and A. Kleinfelter.

Lancaster Cir. — J. Schilling and B. Boesher.

York Cir. — John Kleinfelter and J. Breidenstein.

Franklin Cir.—H. Hassler.

Berkley Cir.—Jacob Kleinfelter.

Lake Cir.—F. Kaltreiter.

SALEM DISTRICT—*J. Dreisbach, P. E.*

Union Cir.—J. Stambach and J. Dehoff.

Centre Cir.—L. Zimmerman and J. Peters.

Bedford Cir.—J. Rickel.

Somerset Cir.—J. Barber and S. Witt.

Canton Cir.—M. Walter.

Lancaster (Ohio) Cir.—B. Ettinger and S. Muck.

1819.

The Twelfth Annual Conference.

President, J. Dreisbach.

Secretary, H. Niebel.

On Monday, June 7, 1819, the members of Conference assembled at New Berlin, Pa., and continued in session five days. After the opening exercises J. Dreisbach was elected president and H. Niebel secretary. During the investigation of the conduct of the preachers, two itinerants and one local preacher were expelled for unchristian behavior. H. Niebel and J. Rickel located on account of bodily infirmities. J. Walter died during the past year (December 3, 1818, aged 37 years, 3 months and 6 days.) A. Kleinfelter, S. Muck, and Jacob Frey were ordained to the office of Deacon. Jacob Peters, David Wolf, and Jacob Baumgartner were licensed as preachers on trial. The Conference elected J. Dreisbach, H. Niebel, and John Kleinfelter a committee to station the preachers.

The preachers in charge received written orders on the trustees of the subsidiary fund to send the subsidiary collections to the next Annual Conference with the preachers, in case they themselves cannot come. Each preacher received his license, after which the Conference adjourned.

APPOINTMENTS.

CANAAN DISTRICT—*J. Dreisbach, P. E.**

Schuylkill Cir. — J. Schilling and J. Baumgartner.

Lancaster Cir.—L. Zimmerman and S. Muck.

York Cir.—M. Walter and M. Dehoff.

Franklin Cir.—J. Frueh.

Berkley Cir.—B. Ettinger.

Lake Cir.—John Kleinfelter.

*Dreisbach was presiding elder of both districts this year.

Union Cir.—H. Hassler and J. Breidenstein.

Centre Cir.—J. Stambach and Jacob Peters.

Bedford Cir.—S. Witt.

Somerset Cir.—A. Kleinfelter and John Peters.

Canton Cir. — Jacob Kleinfelter and Jacob Frey.

Lancaster Cir. (Ohio)—J. Barber and D. Wolf.

1820.

The Second General Conference and the Thirteenth Annual Conference.—A Joint Session.

President, John Dreisbach.

Secretary, Henry Niebel.

A joint session of the regular Annual Conference and the Second General Conference was held at New Berlin, Pa., beginning on Monday, June 5th, 1820, and continuing five days. J. Dreisbach was elected president and H. Niebel secretary. J. Stambach located on account of bodily infirmities and John Peters, S. Witt, and Jacob Frey on account of family cares. J. Erb was elected Presiding Elder, and J. Dreisbach, General Book Agent. The following brethren were ordained to the office of Elder,—M. Walter, J. Barber, M. Dehoff, J. Frueh, B. Ettinger, and J. Shilling; and these to the office of Deacon,—H. Hassler, J. Breidenstein, D. Wolf, and G. Lanz. Daniel Middlekauf was received as preacher on trial. J. Stambach was elected a member of the General Book Commission. During the past year (1819) Solomon Miller, General Book Agent, died. J. Dreisbach, J. Erb, and L. Zimmerman were appointed a committee to station the preachers.

The collection of hymns, written and translated by J. Dreisbach and Dan'l Bertolet and arranged by the former, were ordered to be published. Such other hymns, sermons, and brief productions as were of a profitable character were also recommended for publication. J. Dreisbach, H. Niebel, and J. Stambach were appointed a standing committee for the year to superintend these publications. The preachers received their annual licenses after which the Conference adjourned.

APPOINTMENTS.

CANAAN DISTRICT—*J. Erb, P. E.*

Schuylkill Cir.—B. Ettinger and Jacob Peters.
Lancaster Cir.—John Kleinfelter and D. Wolf.

York Cir.—J. Barber and J. Dehoff.
Franklin Cir.—L. Zimmerman.
Berkley Cir.—J. Frueh.
Lake Cir.—S. Muck.

SALEM DISTRICT—*J. Dreisbach, P. E.*

Union Cir.—A. Kleinfelter and G. Lanz.
Centre Cir.—J. Shilling and J. Baumgartner.
Bedford Cir.—J. Rickel.
Somerset Cir.—M. Walter and M. Dehoff.

Canton Cir.—H. Hassler and D. Middlekauf.
Lancaster Cir. (Ohio)—Jacob Kleinfelter and J. Breidenstein.

1821.

The Fourteenth Annual Conference.

President, John Erb.
Secretary, Jacob Kleinfelter.

In the town of New Berlin, Pa., the Annual Conference of 1821 was held. The session was opened on June 4th, with prayer and supplication to God for His blessing, and continued in session five days. The Conference organized by electing John Erb president and Jacob Kleinfelter secretary. Two itinerant and two local preachers were deposed from the ministry and the latter expelled from the Association. J. Dreisbach, J. Rickel, J. Fruch, S. Muck, J. Shilling, L. Zimmerman, and G. Lanz located on account of bodily infirmities. John Kleinfelter was elected to the office of Presiding Elder. J. Dehoff and A. Kleinfelter were ordained to the office of Elder; J. Baumgartner, John Vandersal, and Chr. Wolf, to the office of Deacon. John Seybert, Fred. Glasser, Jacob Bixler, John Stoll, and John Eisenberger were received as preachers on trial. J. Erb, John Kleinfelter, and J. Dreisbach were appointed a committee to station the preachers. By unanimous consent John Dreisbach, General Book Agent, received $24.00 for his services in superintending the printing establishment and the book department and for keeping the books of the establishment. The standing book committee was authorized to lease the establishment for three years. Should this not prove practicable, they were to carry on the publishing interests or abandon the work altogether, as they might deem most profitable to the Association. Each preacher received his license after which the Conference adjourned.

APPOINTMENTS.

CANAAN DISTRICT—*J. Erb, P. E.*

Schuylkill Cir.—Jacob Kleinfelter and J. Bixler.

Lancaster Cir.—J. Breidenstein and J. Eisenberger.

York Cir.—B. Ettinger and J. Vandersal.

Franklin Cir.—J. Baumgartner.

Berkley Cir.—J. Dehoff.

Lake Cir.—M. Walter.

SALEM DISTRICT—*John Kleinfelter, P. E.*

Somerset and Bedford Cir.—J. Barber and D. Middlekauf.

Canton Cir. — H. Hassler and Jacob Peters.

Lancaster Cir. (Ohio)—A. Kleinfelter and J. Stoll.

Centre Cir.—D. Wolf and M. Dehoff.

Union Cir.—J. Seybert and F. Glasser.

President, John Kleinfelter.
Secretary, John Erb.

The Annual Conference session of 1822 was held on Union Circuit, in New Berlin, Pa. The session continued from June 3d to 6th. John Kleinfelter was elected president and J. Erb secretary. B. Ettinger and M. Walter located on account of bodily infirmities, and M. Dehoff on account of family affairs. The following were ordained: D. Wolf, H. Hassler, and J. Breidenstein to the office of Elder, and J. Seybert and D. Middlekauf to the office of Deacon. Wm. Scholty, John W. Miller, Joseph Long, Abraham Becker, Philip Wagner, and Fred. Borauf were newly received as preachers on trial. The committee elected to station the preachers consisted of J. Erb, John Kleinfelter, and Jacob Kleinfelter.

Inasmuch as the Chief Book Commission has had but few meetings on account of the absence of its lay members, the duties incident to the reckoning thus devolving upon the ministerial members, and inasmuch as the preachers attend Annual Conference at all events, it was deemed advisable to elect preachers only as members of the commission. In accordance with this, the following were elected:—J. Dreisbach, General Book Agent, J. Erb, John Kleinfelter, Jacob Kleinfelter, J. Dehoff, D. Wolf, and J. Seybert. After the preachers had received their licenses, the Conference adjourned.

APPOINTMENTS.

CANAAN DISTRICT—*J. Erb, P. E.* *

Union Cir.—Jacob Barber and J. Eisenberger.

Centre Cir. — D. Middlekauf and J.
Stoll.

York Cir. — A. Kleinfelter and W.
Sholty.

Lancaster Cir. — J. Vandersal and J.
W. Miller.

Schuylkill Cir.—J. Breidenstein and F.
Borauf.

Lake Cir.—J. Dehoff.

SALEM DISTRICT—*John Kleinfelter, P. E.*

Franklin Cir.—Jacob Kleinfelter and
A. Becker.

Berkley Cir.—F. Glasser.

Somerset Cir.—J. Baumgartner and J.
Long.

Canton Cir.—J. Seybert and P. Wagner.

Lancaster Cir. (Ohio)—D. Wolf and J.
Peters.

H. Hassler to seek and organize a new
Circuit.

1823.

The Sixteenth Annual Conference.

President, John Erb.

Secretary, John Kleinfelter.

The members of Conference assembled on York Circuit in the town of Strasburgh, York Co., Pa., on June
2d, 1823, and devoted three days to the transactions of
the annual session. After the usual devotional exercises the Conference organized by electing John Erb
president and John Kleinfelter secretary. J. Erb, D.
Wolf, J. Vandersal, J. Miller, and J. Eisenberg located
on account of bodily infirmities; H. Hassler and W.
Scholty, on account of family concerns. James Barber
and Adam Kleinfelter were newly elected to the office
of Presiding Elder. After the ordination sermon, J.
Stoll, F. Glasser, and W. Scholty were ordained to the
office of Deacon. The following were newly received

*On account of the sickness of both Vandersal and Miller, J. C. Reisner traveled
on Lancaster Circuit about one-half of the ensuing year.

as preachers on trial: J. Conrad Reisner (licensed and in active service the year previous), Conrad Kring, Jacob Foy, Thomas Buck, and Benjamin Bicksler. The committee to station the preachers consisted of John Kleinfelter, J. Erb, J. Barber, A. Kleinfelter, and Jac. Kleinfelter. It was decided that in case the Conference provide a preacher with a horse, the said horse shall be the property of the Conference. Furthermore if money is advanced to a preacher and he does not preach longer than two years he shall be required to refund the money. The Conference adjourned after each preacher had received his license.

APPOINTMENTS.

SALEM DISTRICT—*J. Barber, P. E.*

Union and Centre Cir —J. Breidenstein, A. Becker, and J. Foy.

Somerset Cir.—J. Dehoff and T. Buck.
Lake Cir.—F. Glasser.

CANAAN DISTRICT—*John Kleinfelter, P. E.*

Lancaster Cir.—Jac. Kleinfelter.
York Cir.—B. Bicksler and C. Kring.
Schuylkill Cir.—J. Seybert.

Franklin Cir.—J. Long and J. C. Reisner.

OHIO DISTRICT—*A. Kleinfelter, P. E.*

Lancaster Cir.—J. Stoll and P. Wagner.
Canton Cir.—J. Baumgartner.

J. Frey was instructed to seek and organize a new Circuit.

1824.
The Seventeenth Annual Conference.

President, John Kleinfelter.
Secretary, Jacob Kleinfelter.

The session of 1824 was held from the 7th of June to the 10th, in the town of Strasburgh, (Shrewsbury,) York Co., Pa. After the opening exercises which consisted of the usual religious services, the Conference

4

organized by electing John Kleinfelter president and
Jacob Kleinfelter secretary.   Jacob Peters died during
the past year.   J. Breidenstein located on account of
bodily infirmities; J. Frey and J. Baumgartner, on account of family cares.   John Kleinfelter located but
agreed to serve as presiding elder on Lancaster and
Schuylkill circuits.   J. Seybert was ordained to the
office of Elder, and J. Long, A. Becker, P. Wagner, and
J. C. Reisner, to the office of Deacon.   Henry Wissler
and Daniel Manwiller were newly received on trial.
Fred. Borauf was again received.   A committee was
elected to station the preachers.   After each preacher
had received his license the Conference adjourned.

APPOINTMENTS.

SALEM DISTRICT—*J. Barber*, *P. E.*

Union and Centre Cir.—P. Wagner, C. Kring, and T. Buck.

Somerset Cir.—J. Stoll and F. Borauf. Lake Cir.—F. Glasser.

CANAAN DISTRICT—*John Kleinfelter*, *P. E.*

Schuylkill Cir.—J. C. Reisner and J. W. Miller.

Lancaster Cir.—W. Scholty and A. Becker.

Without a Presiding Elder.

York Cir.—J. Seybert and J. Bicksler.* Franklin and Berkley Cir. — Jacob

Kleinfelter, B. Bicksler and H. Wissler.

OHIO DISTRICT—*A. Kleinfelter*, *P. E.*

Canton Cir.—J. Foy. Mansfield Cir.—J. Dehoff.

Lancaster Cir.—J. Long and D. Manwiller.

1825.

The Eighteenth Annual Conference.

President, Adam Kleinfelter.
Secretary, John Seybert.

*J. Bicksler located during the year, on account of ill health, whereupon J. Sey-
bert appointed J. M. Saylor to fill the vacancy until the next Annual Conference
session, a period of seven months.—S. C. B.

The members of Conference assembled in annual session, June 7th, 1825, at New Berlin, Union Co., Pa. After an exhortation by J. Dreisbach, the session was opened with the usual religious exercises. A. Kleinfelter was elected president. He appointed J. Seybert secretary. During the examination into the doctrines and conduct of the preachers two were deposed from the ministry, one of whom was expelled from the Association, because of unchristian conduct and gross offences. J. Stoll and J. Bicksler located on account of bodily infirmities; John Kleinfelter, Jacob Kleinfelter, B. Bicksler, and F. Glasser, on account of family concerns. J. Seybert was elected to the office of Presiding Elder. J. Stoll was ordained to the office of Elder; C. Kring, J. W. Miller, J. Foy, and T. Buck, to the office of Deacon. The following were newly received as preachers on trial: John Hamilton, Jacob Erly, Joseph M. Saylor, George Reich, George Schneider, and Benjamin Becker, M. D., A. Kleinfelter, J. Barber, and J. Seybert were elected a committee to assign to the preachers their fields of labor. It was resolved that an edition of one thousand copies of *Die Geistliche Viole*, with an appendix of eight additional hymns, be published during this year. The Conference leased the printing establishment to George Miller, the printer, for one year at a rent of $60, agreeing to furnish him with a sufficient quantity of pica type. Abraham Buchman presented $40 to the Conference to be applied to the purchase of a horse for an indigent itinerant preacher. To this amount $10 from the subsidiary collections were added and the entire sum given to an itinerant for the prescribed purpose, with the proviso that the horse shall be his as long as his conduct is in keeping with the word of God and our Discipline. Otherwise the horse becomes the property of the Conference.

After the sermon and exhortation on Friday forenoon, the Conference adjourned with the usual resolution of approval of the proceedings. J. Seybert adds that there existed peace and harmony among them and a new bond of love; also the determination to disseminate the word of God to the best of their ability, with prayer, exhortation, and preaching, and to live as a salt of the earth and a light of the world in self denial, faithfulness, and constancy until death, through Jesus Christ our Lord.

APPOINTMENTS.

CANAAN DISTRICT—*J. Seybert, P. E.*

*Schuylkill Cir.—C. Kring and J. Erly.
†Lancaster Cir. — T. Buck and B. Becker.

†York Cir.—J. C. Reisner and J. M. Saylor.
Franklin and Berkley Cir.—P. Wagner and F. Borauf.

SALEM DISTRICT—*J. Barber, P. E.*

Union Cir.—J. W. Miller and G. Reich.
Centre Cir.—J. Foy and D. Manwiller.

Somerset Cir.—A. Becker and J. Hamilton.
Lake Cir. — C. Wolf and F. Glasser, local preachers.

OHIO DISTRICT—*A. Kleinfelter, P. E.*

Lancaster Cir.—J. Long and G. Schnelder.

Mansfield Cir.—J. Dehoff.
Canton Cir.—H. Wissler.

1826.

The Third General Conference‡ and the Nineteenth Annual Conference.—A Joint Session.

President, John Seybert.

Secretary, J. C. Reisner.

---

*In the Fall of 1825 J. Erly was taken sick. Under the direction of the Presiding Elder, F. Hoffman took his place and served on this charge until the Annual Conference of 1826.

†During the year B. Becker left Lancaster Circuit; J. M. Saylor was appointed to take his place.

‡This is not designated in the official records as a General Conference, but there

The Conference met on the 5th day of June, 1826, in our meeting-house at New Berlin, Pa. The session was opened with devotional exercises. John Seybert was elected president; he appointed J. C. Reisner secretary. One preacher was deposed from the ministry because of immoral conduct. The following brethren located: J. Foy on account of bodily infirmities and B. Becker, F. Borauf, and J. Dehoff, on account of family cares. P. Wagner, J. C. Reisner, J. Long, and A. Becker were ordained to the office of Elder; H. Wissler, D. Manwiller, and Michael Hassler, to the office of Deacon. These solemn ordination services which consisted of an appropriate sermon, an exhortation, fervent prayers, and the laying on of hands, were crowned with blessings. Francis Hoffman and Samuel Tobias were newly received as preachers on trial. A stationing committee was appointed, consisting of J. Seybert, J. Barber, and J. Long. Five brethren were added to the Chief Book Commission, after which it consisted of J. Dreisbach, General Book Agent, J. Seybert, J. C. Reisner, J. Miller, T. Buck, J. Hamilton, and J. M. Saylor.

J. Dreisbach, the General Book Agent, gave the Book Commission a report of the book concern. The Commission audited his accounts and made an entry in the books of the Printing House, as has been done annually since the establishment is in existence. It was resolved that our books be sold at the following prices: the large Hymn Book (*Saitenspiel*) at $1.00; the *Viole* at 50 cents; the New Testament at $1.00;

is a marginal note in which J. Dreisbach declares it to have been a General Conference as well as the regular Annual Conference session.—S. C. B.

the Church Discipline at 40 cents; the tract *Menschen Furcht* at 37½ cents, and *Thætiges Christenthum* at 50 cents. The preachers received an average discount of ten per cent. on these prices. Several spiritual songs, recently composed, were ordered to be printed in pamphlet form, an edition of five hundred copies to be published for the use of this Conference.

At the Annual Conference session at Strasburgh, in 1824, the following resolution was adopted, but inasmuch as it was not entered upon the records, it was re-enacted and recorded at this session as follows: *Resolved*, That an annual Conference of Local Preachers shall be held by each presiding elder in his district shortly before the annual session of the conference of traveling preachers. The chief object of this conference is to be the investigation of the conduct and doctrines of the local preachers, a report of which is to be made to the regular conference of itinerants.

In answer to a petition from the brethren of the Ohio District, it was resolved that an annual conference of itinerant preachers be organized in that district under the name of "THE WESTERN CONFERENCE OF THE EVANGELICAL ASSOCIATION;" that this conference shall meet in annual session at least three weeks earlier than the EASTERN CONFERENCE in Pennsylvania, and have full right to transact annual conference business in accordance with the directions of our Discipline. It was furthermore enacted that the Western Conference shall send its proceedings to the presiding elders or president of the Eastern Conference; that an equality be observed between the two conferences in the division of the general salary and the subsidiary collections until such time when the Western Conference shall find itself able to support its traveling preachers, and that the proceedings of both conferences as well as the accounts with the preachers be recorded in the old conference record. The Western Conference was, however, instructed to keep a correct conference record for its own use.

The Conference adjourned in the usual manner. Love peace, and unity crowned this assembly of preachers. Blessed be God now and forever, Amen! Amen!

APPOINTMENTS.

CANAAN DISTRICT—*J. Seybert, P. E.*

Schuylkill Cir. — T. Buck and G. Schneider.
Lancaster Cir.—J. W. Miller.

York Cir.—A. Becker and J. Bruer.
Franklin and Berkley Cir —D. Manwiller and J. Hamilton.

SALEM DISTRICT—*J. Barber, P. E.*

Union Cir.—J. C. Reisner.
Centre Cir.—P. Wagner and S. Tobias.

Somerset Cir.—H. Wissler, G. Reich, and J. Frey.
Lake Cir.—J. Erly.

OHIO DISTRICT—*A. Kleinfelter, P. E.*

Lancaster Cir. — C. Kring and J. M. Saylor.

Mansfield and Canton Cirs.—J. Long and F. Hoffman.

"Who hath despised the day of small things?"—
Zech. iv : 10.

The Eastern and the Western Conferences.

1827-1839.

"And the Lord added to the church daily such as should be saved."—ACTS II : 47.

EXPLANATORY.

The Ohio District being so far removed from the rest of the work as to occasion great inconvenience and expense to the preachers to meet in one annual session, it was constituted a separate conference to be known as the "Western Conference." The old conference was called the "Eastern Conference." Their relation was peculiar, the Western being subordinate to and in some respects identical with the Eastern. The Eastern Conference frequently stationed the preachers of the Western, and the latter sent its proceedings to the former for approval. Although the annual sessions of the Western Conference were held prior to those of the Eastern, yet it has been considered most in keeping with the scope of this volume to let the proceedings of the Eastern appear first each year.

1827.

The General* and the Eastern Conferences.—A Joint Session.

President, James Barber.

Secretary, J. Conrad Reisner.

The first (20th) annual session of the Eastern Conference of the Evangelical Association convened in Orwigsburg, Pa., June 4th, 1827. At the same time and place the GENERAL CONFERENCE of the Association was held. The session was opened with religious exercises. J. Barber was elected president, whereupon he appointed J. C. Reisner secretary. During the investigation of the doctrines and conduct of the preachers a deacon was deposed from the ministry. A. Becker located on account of bodily infirmities. John Vandersal and John Schneider died during the past year. P. Wagner was elected to the office of Presiding Elder. T. Buck and J. W. Miller were ordained Elders, and G. Reich, J. Hamilton, and D. Focht, Deacons. George Mattinger, George Enders, and Wm. Stoll were newly received as preachers on trial. The following were

---

*Some assert that this session was not a General Conference; the official records, however, so denominate it.—S. C. B.

elected a stationing committee : J. Barber, J. Seybert, and P. Wagner.

The following statistics,* given in full, show the membership of this Conference after the *Western Conference* had been nominally detached :

	Newly Converted.	Newly Received.	Entire Membership.
Schuylkill Cir........	95	97	385
Lancaster Cir........	50	64	311
York Cir...........	30	60	342
Franklin Cir........	62	80	205
Berkley Cir.........	12	36	92
Union Cir..........	32	42	192
Centre Cir..........	9	8	213
Somerset Cir........	3	6	249
Lake Cir...........	..	..	55
	293	393	2,044

The amount contributed to the general salary fund was $704.59 ; for subsidiary purposes, $105.40 ; making a total of $809.99. This amount added to that contributed by the Western Conference aggregated $922.55, which was distributed among twenty preachers in both conferences. It was found that the entire number of itinerant and local preachers in the Association was seventy.

The following is a list of the preachers of this Conference according to their station and order :

Presiding Elders,—J. Seybert and P. Wagner ;

Elders,—J. Barber, J. C. Reisner, B. Ettinger, J. Dreisbach, J. Breidenstein, A. Becker, John Kleinfelter,

---

*Hereafter the statistics reported at each session will be found in the regular Statistical Tables at the end of this volume.

H. Niebel, L. Zimmerman, J. Stambach, M. Walter, J. Stoll, J. Fruch, T. Buck, and John Miller;

Deacons,—D. Thomas, A. Buchman, A. Ettinger, J. Rickel, C. Wolf, G. Lanz, J. Baumgartner, F. Glasser, Jacob Frey, D. Middlekauf, H. Wissler, D. Manwiller, G. Reich, J. Hamilton, and D. Focht;

On Trial,—G. Schneider, S. Tobias, G. Mattinger, G. Enders, and Wm. Stoll.

The Quarterly Conferences were instructed to co-operate with the presiding elders in the appointment of proper persons whose duty it shall be to collect funds throughout the entire Association for the support of the worn-out preachers and their families; with this under-standing, however, that the Eastern and Western Con-ferences shall each support the said families within their respective bounds, in accordance with the provi-sions of our Church Discipline. The Conference author-ized J. Dreisbach, J. Barber, and B. Ettinger to sell the personal property of the Printing Establishment and apply the proceeds to the management of the book trade, subject to the directions of the conferences. The Conference adjourned. Love, peace, and unity crowned this session, blessed be God now and for evermore, Amen!

APPOINTMENTS.

CANAAN DISTRICT—*J. Seybert, P. E.*

Schuylkill Cir.—J. C. Reisner and H. Wissler.

Lancaster Cir.—J. M. Saylor and W. Stoll.

York Cir.—T. Buck and J. Bruer.

Franklin and Berkley Cirs.—J. Hamil-ton and F. Hoffman.

SALEM DISTRICT—*P. Wagner, P. E.*

Union Cir.—B. Ettinger and G. Mat-tinger.

Centre Cir.—J. Barber and G. Schnei-der.

Somerset Cir.—D. Manwiller, S. To-bias, and J. Allen.

Lake Cir.—G. Reich.

President, Adam Kleinfelter.
Secretary, Joseph Long.

The first annual session of the Western Conference was held in Wayne Co., Ohio, and was opened with devotional exercises on May 7th, 1827. A. Kleinfelter was elected president; he appointed J. Long secretary. The investigation of the conduct of the preachers was held in accordance with established usage. C. Kring was ordained Elder, and J. M. Saylor, Deacon.

The following statistics, given in full, show the status of this Conference at its first annual session:

	Newly Converted.	Newly Received.	Entire Membership.
Wooster Cir..........	15	27	176
Canton Cir...........	4	7	158
New Lancaster Cir....	24	26	160
Sandusky Cir.........	10	25	29
	53	85	523

The total contributions to the general salary fund were $112.56. The following were the preachers, according to their station and order, who comprised this Conference at its origin:

Elders,—Adam Kleinfelter, John Erb, John Schilling, Jacob Kleinfelter, David Wolf, Joseph Long, Conrad Kring, John Dehoff, Henry Hassler, and Moses Dehoff;

Deacons,—John Rickel, Joseph M. Saylor, Adam Henig, and Jacob Frey;

Preachers on Trial,—Francis Hoffman, John Peters, Matthew Wunder, John Miller, Henry Dauny, Fred.

Borauf, John Thomas, Jacob Dissler, Peter Miller, Henry Stauffer*, and Samuel Seger.

APPOINTMENTS.*

Canton Cir.—J. Long.
Wooster Cir.—C. Kring.
Sandusky Cir.—A. Kleinfelter.

Lancaster Cir. —J. Miller and G. Enders.†

It was resolved that J. Long shall attend the general meetings in the Fall, and A. Kleinfelter in the Spring of the year. Each preacher received his license and the Conference adjourned. After the preachers present had signed the proceedings in token of approval and obedience, each went in peace to his work.

1828.

The Eastern Conference.—The Second (21st) Annual Session.

President, John Seybert.
Secretary, J. Conrad Reisner.

The members of the Eastern Conference assembled in annual session June 2d, 1828, in New Berlin, Union Co., Pa. The Conference was opened with the customary devotional exercises, after which J. Seybert was elected president. He appointed J. C. Reisner secretary. A local preacher and a preacher on trial were deposed from the ministry on account of immoral conduct. J. C. Reisner and J. M. Saylor located on account of bodily infirmities, and B. Ettinger on account of family concerns. Thomas Buck was elected

---

'The Western Conference was without a presiding elder during the year.
†These two brethren were " sent out " by the Eastern Conference.

Presiding Elder. J. Bruer and D. Manwiller were ordained Elders, F. Hoffman and J. G. Conser, Deacons. The brethren Wm. W. Orwig, Jacob Hoock, John H. Yambert, and Elias Stoever were newly received as preachers on trial. The committee chosen to assign to the preachers their fields of labor consisted of J. Barber, J. Seybert, T. Buck, P. Wagner, and A. Kleinfelter.

The total amount contributed by the two Conferences for the general salary fund and for subsidiary purposes was distributed among twenty-four preachers in both conferences. The total number of itinerant and local preachers in the Association was eighty.

It was resolved that a married preacher having spent five years in active service shall receive for salary an amount double that of an unmarried one, the salaries to be paid out of the general and subsidiary collections. Of the special support given to the families of itinerants an account is to be kept and rendered under the name of subsidiary contributions, whether it be received in the form of grain, meat, cloth, flax, or anything else. This action is to be announced to the friends on the circuits. The preachers in both conferences were instructed to make diligent efforts to increase the annual subsidiary collection. The Conference consented to the reception of F. Shaner by the Western Conference and approved the remainder of the proceedings of that body.

One of the preachers on trial having married before his probation had ended, he was excused by the Conference upon his plea that he had been betrothed before he entered the itinerancy, and because of the fact that in all other respects his conduct during his probation was unexceptionable. It was, however, resolved that hereafter no preachers are to be received until it has been ascertained that they are free from similar obligations.

H. Niebel and P. Wagner were elected members of the Chief Book Commission in the places of J. M. Saylor and J. Hamilton, who were not present. The Commission audited the accounts of J. Dreisbach, General Book Agent, and found them correct. J. Dreisbach was authorized to sell the Book Establishment upon terms subject to his discretion. George Miller, the printer, was appointed the agent of the Conference to attend to the book trade. The Conference adjourned in the usual manner.

APPOINTMENTS.

CANAAN DISTRICT—*J. Seybert, P. E.*

Schuylkill Cir.—A. Kleinfelter and J. W. Miller.

Lancaster Cir.—C Kring.

York Cir.—J. Hamilton and J. H. Yambert.

Franklin and Berkley Cir.—G. Reich and J. Hoock.

SALEM DISTRICT—*T. Buck, P. E.*

Union Cir.—F. Hoffman and G. Enders.

Centre Cir.—J. Barber and W. W. Orwig.

Somerset Cir.—J. Bruer and G. Mattinger.

Lake Cir.—P. Wagner.

OHIO DISTRICT, (Western Conference)—*J. Long, P. E.*

Canton Cir.—D. Manwiller and S. Tobias.

Lancaster Cir.—H. Wissler and E. Stoever.

Sandusky Cir.—G. Schneider.

The Western Conference.

President, Joseph Long.
Secretary, John W. Miller.

5

On the fifth day of May, the Western Conference session of 1828 was opened with religious exercises at Uniontown, Stark Co., Ohio. The Conference organized by electing J. Long president, who appointed J. W. Miller secretary. During the investigation into the doctrines and conduct of the preachers, a deacon was deposed from the ministry and expelled from the Association, because of immoral conduct. It was resolved that J. Long serve as Presiding Elder as much as his enfeebled health will allow. He had traveled only six or seven months during each of the two preceding years. F. Shaner was again received and ordained to the office of Deacon. J. W. Miller was delegated to take to the Eastern Conference the subsidiary collection and the accounts of the general salary contributions and traveling expenses of the preachers, in order that all the contributions might be included in one general account.

APPOINTMENTS.

It was decided that the Eastern Conference shall station the preachers in this Conference for the ensuing year, that at least three of them be ordained preachers and that A. Kleinfelter represent this Conference in the stationing committee of the Eastern Conference.

1829.

The Eastern Conference.—The Third (22d) Annual Session.

President, Thomas Buck.
Secretary, John Seybert.

The members of the Eastern Conference assembled in our Evangelical meeting-house at New Berlin, Union Co., Pa., on June 1st, 1829. At the opening of the session our Evangelical Conference Rules were read, after which those present engaged in devotional exercises. T. Buck was elected president. He appointed J. Seybert secretary. Two preachers were deposed from the ministry and one of them expelled from the Association. J. W. Miller located on account of family affairs. J. Stambach, an elder, died during the past year, and we entertain the hope that for him faith has changed to sight, labor has been rewarded with rest, and that having sown to the spirit he is reaping life everlasting.

J. Seybert was re-elected Presiding Elder for a period of four years. The following were newly received on trial: Geo. Brickley, Joseph Ebbert, Solomon G. Miller, Jacob Schnerr, and Wm. Ray. T. Buck, J. Seybert, and A. Kleinfelter were elected a committee to station the preachers in both conferences.

The total contributions of both conferences were distributed among twenty-two preachers. Salary for two months was deducted from the support of one itinerant because he was in good health and engaged in secular business during that time.

On account of age and failing health, Martin Dreisbach resigned his office as trustee of the subsidiary fund and bequests. His accounts were audited and found correct. J. Barber, H. Wissler, J. M. Saylor, and A. Kleinfelter were elected to fill vacancies in the Book Commission, the other members being J. Dreisbach, General Book Agent, H. Niebel, and T. Buck.

J. Dreisbach, General Book Agent, made a report which was audited and found correct. J. Seybert was elected chief trustee of the moneys and other property which have been and will be bequeathed for the use of our Evangelical ministry, with instructions to hold himself in readiness to give an account of his trust at any time it may be required of him. T. Buck was elected trustee of the book money, to appropriate it according to the directions of the Conference. The resolution of the Western Conference in the proceedings of 1829, with reference to re-baptizing persons, was considered and endorsed. It was resolved that our Church Discipline be translated into English and published as soon as possible.

APPOINTMENTS.

CANAAN DISTRICT—*T. Buck, P. E.*

Schuylkill Cir.—C. Kring and J. Ebbert.

Lebanon Cir.—H. Niebel and W. W. Orwig.

Lancaster Cir.—J. M. Saylor and G. Enders.

York Cir.—D. Manwiller and S. Tobias.

Franklin and Berkley Cir.—J. Hamilton, J. Bruer, and W. Ray.

SALEM DISTRICT—*J. Seybert, P. E.*

Union Cir.—J. Barber and J. G. Zinser.

Centre Cir.—F. Hoffman and S. G. Miller.

Somerset Cir. — H. Wissler and G. Brickley.

Lake Cir.—G. Reich.

WESTERN CONFERENCE, OHIO DISTRICT—*J. Long, P. E.*

Canton Cir.—A. Kleinfelter and E. Stoever.

New Lancaster Cir.—J. H. Yambert and G. Schneider.

Sandusky Cir.—G. Mattinger.

The Western Conference.

President, Joseph Long.

Secretary, Henry Wissler.

The Western Conference met in annual session on Canton Circuit, Tuscarawas Twp., Stark Co., Ohio, May 4th, 1829. The brethren elected J. Long president, who appointed H. Wissler secretary. Charges having been preferred against a preacher for baptizing a person who had already been baptized in infancy, the subject was taken under consideration. The deliberations resulted in a unanimous resolution expressly forbidding our preachers to re-baptize under any circumstances. For this action the following reasons were assigned: 1st, Our Church Discipline gives no such directions; 2d, We can find no authority in the Sacred Scriptures for re-baptism; 3d, It is our belief that its introduction would be followed by evil consequences.

A local preacher was deposed from the ministry and expelled from the Association for immoral conduct. During the past year Jacob Kl infelter "the second," a local preacher, died. He has gone from labor to rest and from seed time to harvest. G. Schneider, S. Tobias, and Elias Stoever were ordained to the office of Deacon. John G. Zinser was newly received on trial.

APPOINTMENTS.

J. Long was appointed to serve as Presiding Elder on the district as much as his strength would allow. Elias Stoever was appointed to Canton Circuit, and G. Schneider to Lancaster Circuit. It was agreed that the Eastern Conference station the remainder of the district. H. Wissler was delegated to take a correct copy of the proceedings to the Eastern Conference. The session adjourned in the usual manner.

President, Thomas Buck.

Secretary, John Seybert.

On Monday, June 1st, 1830, the Eastern Conference met in our meeting-house at Orwigsburg, Pa. After the customary opening exercises, which included the reading of a portion of our Church Discipline, the Conference was organized by the election of Thomas Buck as president who appointed J. Seybert secretary. Four preachers were deposed from the ministry: an itinerant deacon for neglect of duty and for leaving his circuit without a cause; a local preacher for distilling brandy; another local preacher on account of uncharitable expressions against our disciplinary management; and a local elder for unchristian conduct. J. Hamilton, H. Wissler, and J. M. Saylor located on account of bodily infirmities; F. Hoffman and J. Ebbert, on account of family concerns. Henry Meyer, a local preacher, died during the past year, of whom we entertain the hope that he has passed from faith to sight. Charles Hammer, Daniel Kehr, John S. Himmelreich, and Robert G. Hunter were newly received as preachers on trial. The committee elected to station the preachers consisted of T. Buck, J. Seybert, and H. Niebel.

A resolution was adopted to the effect that such preachers of the Eastern and Western conferences who, on account of neglect of duty, do not secure as much for the general salary and subsidiary funds as in the judgment of the Conference they could have gathered, shall have their salaries lessened at the discretion of the Conference. It was also resolved that married traveling preachers of the Western Conference shall be entitled to double salary with those of the Eastern, upon the condition that that conference labor diligently to secure funds for this purpose. It was agreed to call a session of the General Conference, to be held in Hains Twp., Centre Co., Pa., and to begin on the first Monday in November.

The transactions of the Western Conference were taken under consideration. It was resolved that henceforth no such ordination as that of M. Kibler shall take place, as long as our Church Discipline has not been changed. The Western Conference was denied the privilege of appointing a general book agent. George Miller, the printer, was ordered to print 2,000 copies of the *Viole*, in New Berlin, Pa., at $20 per hundred. The retail price of the Church Discipline was fixed at 31¼ cents per copy.

APPOINTMENTS.

CANAAN DISTRICT—*T. Buck, P. E.*

Schuylkill Cir.—E. Stoever and J. G. Zinser.
Lebanon Cir.—W. W. Orwig and C. Hammer.
Berkley Cir.—W. Ray.
Lancaster Cir. — H. Niebel and J. Schnerr.
York Cir —G. Brickley and J. Bruer.
Franklin Cir. — C. Kring and R. G. Hunter.

SALEM DISTRICT—*J. Seybert, P. E.*

Union Cir.—G. Schneider and S. Tobias.
Centre Cir.—J. Barber.
Lake Cir.—F. Glasser.
Somerset Cir. — S. G. Miller and W. Roehrig.

OHIO DISTRICT, WESTERN CONFERENCE—*J. Long, P. E.*

Canton Cir.—J. H. Yambert and D. Kehr.
Sandusky Cir.—G. Enders.
Lancaster Cir.—G. Mattinger and J. S. Himmelreich.

President, Joseph Long.

Secretary, Adam Kleinfelter.

The members of the Western Conference assembled in annual session on Canton Circuit, Plain Twp., Stark Co., Ohio, on May 3d, 1830. The Conference was opened with devotional exercises. J. Long was elected president. He appointed A. Kleinfelter secretary. A. Kleinfelter located on account of bodily infirmities. M. Kibler and L. Heucky were ordained to the office of Deacon. The following were newly received as preachers on trial: Wm. Roehrig, Absalom B. Schaefer, and Christopher Aubel. J. Long was presiding elder. Only one preacher, Geo. Mattinger, was stationed, the remainder of the stationing having been referred to the Eastern Conference.

1830.

The General Conference.

President, Joseph Long.

Secretary, John Seybert.

The General Conference of 1830 convened on Nov. 1st in the house of Adam Henig in Hains Twp., Centre Co., Pa. The session was opened with religious exercises. J. Long was elected president. He appointed J. Seybert secretary. The following representatives of the two annual conferences constituted the General Conference: T. Buck, J. Seybert, and J. Long presiding elders; H. Niebel, J. Barber, C. Kring, J. Bruer (not present), J. Dreisbach, and H. Hassler elders. These represented the two annual conferences.

The Church Discipline was examined and improved. J. Seybert and T. Buck were appointed to transcribe the improved portions and to arrange them properly for publication. Subsequently J. Dreisbach and II. Niebel were added to this committee with instructions to examine thoroughly the entire work prior to its publication. J. Dreisbach was appointed to read proof. It was also resolved that the new edition of the Discipline be translated into English as soon as possible. The following officers were elected: J. Dreisbach, General Book Agent; G. Miller, Assistant; and T. Buck, Steward of the book funds.

It was resolved that our itinerant preachers labor diligently among the German-speaking people of the country, and that it is the sense of the General Conference that no more preachers shall be received into the traveling connection who are not somewhat proficient in the German language. The Western Conference was instructed to submit its proceedings annually to the Eastern for approval, the records to be conveyed by a presiding elder.

1831.

The Eastern Conference.—The Fifth (24th) Annual Session.

President, Thomas Buck.
Secretary, John Seybert.

The members of the Eastern Conference assembled in annual session June 6th, 1831, in our meeting-house at Lebanon, Pa. After devotional exercises the Conference organized by electing T. Buck president, who appointed J. Seybert secretary. Two local preachers and one itinerant were deposed from the ministry on account of improper conduct. An elder was deposed for having promulgated doctrines contrary to the Word of God. S. Tobias located on account of bodily infirmities. D. Manwiller died during the past year. H. Niebel was elected Presiding Elder and J. Rank, General Book Agent. E. Stoever was ordained Elder and J. G. Zinser, S. G. Miller, J. Schnerr, and W. Ray, Deacons. The ordination of A. Riem was submitted to the Western Conference. The following were newly received on trial: Daniel Brickley, George Anstein, John P. Leib, Wm. Wagner, Charles Hesser, Jacob Borkert, John Campbell, and Henry Fisher. The committee appointed to assign to the preachers their circuits consisted of J. Seybert, H. Niebel, J. Long, and J. Barber.

The proceedings of the Western Conference were inspected and approved. Preachers were prohibited from publishing any manuscripts which have not met the approval of their annual conference. J. C. Reisner was appointed to prepare an abstract of the Biography of George Miller and to supplement it with an account of the last illness, the death, and burial of the deceased; the work to be submitted to T. Buck, H. Niebel, and A. Ettinger for inspection. The Conference territory was divided into three presiding elder districts.

APPOINTMENTS.

CANAAN DISTRICT—*H. Niebel, P. E.*

Schuylkill Cir. — J. Schnerr and J. Young.

Lebanon Cir.—J. G. Zinser and J. P. Leib.

Lancaster Cir.—E. Stoever and H. Fisher.

ZION DISTRICT—*T. Buck, P. E.*

York Cir.—W. W. Orwig, D. Brickley, and J. Roessner.

Franklin Cir. — G. Brickley and J. Borkert.

Berkley Cir.—G. Enders.*

Somerset Cir.—C. Kring, B. Bickslcr, and G. Anstein.

SALEM DISTRICT—*J. Seybert, P. E.*

Union Cir.—J. M. Saylor and W. Wagner.

White Deer Cir.—J. Barber and C. Hammer.

Lake Cir.—G. Schneider and J. Campbell.

Centre Cir.—P. Wagner and C. Hesser.

The Western Conference.

President, Joseph Long.

Secretary, J. H. Yambert.

The Western Conference met in annual session May 2d, 1831, on Canton Circuit, Green Twp., Stark Co., Ohio. The proceedings were opened with the usual devotional exercises. The Conference elected J. Long president who appointed J. H. Yambert secretary. A deacon was deposed from the ministry and expelled from the Association on account of immoral conduct. Geo. Mattinger and J. H. Yambert were ordained Elders. Michael Miller, Christian Leitner, and John Roessner were newly received as preachers on trial. It was resolved that when the Conference gives the use of a horse to an itinerant, it shall always be the property of the Conference, but if the preacher pay a part of the cost, he shall be held responsible for the balance only.

APPOINTMENTS.

OHIO DISTRICT—*J. Long, P. E.*

Canton and Wooster Cirs.—G. Mattinger, J. S. Himmelreich, and M. Miller.

Sandusky Cir.—J. H. Yambert and C. Leitner.

New Lancaster Cir.—S. G. Miller and D. Kehr.

*In the Fall of 1831 G. Enders left the circuit, and F. Hoffman was appointed by the presiding elder to fill the vacancy until the next annual conference session.—S. C. B.

President, Thomas Buck.

Secretary, John Seybert.

On Monday, June 4th, 1832, the members of the Eastern Conference met in the Evangelical meeting-house at New Berlin, Union Co., Pa. After the usual religious exercises the Conference proceeded to the transaction of business. T. Buck was elected president. He appointed J. Seybert secretary. An elder was deposed from the eldership and as deacon put on probation for one year. Three local preachers were deposed from the ministry for not preaching, three for unchristian conduct, one for opposition to the truth and for tolerating unchristian behavior in his family, one for unpeaceful conduct towards his relatives and one because of inefficiency; also one itinerant for dishonest transactions. H. Fisher, G. Enders, J. Bruer, and B. Bixler located on account of bodily infirmities. T. Buck was re-elected to the office of Presiding Elder. J. M. Saylor, W. W. Orwig, G. Brickley, and F. Hoffman were ordained Elders. The following were newly received on trial: Jacob Bell, Henry Bucks, Christian Thomas, Samuel Baumgartner, Daniel Fichtner, and Joseph Harlacher. T. Buck, H. Niebel, and J. Seybert were elected a committee to station the preachers.

The transactions of the Western Conference were inspected. The act of that conference granting a license to W. Ray was rejected. The reception of D. Poorman by that body was also rejected on the ground that it occurred not in accordance with the Discipline. It was resolved that in case an ordained preacher be found guilty of a transgression not sufficiently grave to exclude him from the kingdom of grace, and yet such as to require punishment, he shall be suspended from the exercise of all the functions of his office, except preaching, for a period not less than one year.

The members of the Book Commission were T. Buck, H. Niebel, J. Barber, J. G. Zinser, J. M. Saylor, C. Hammer, and J. P. Leib. The Conference ordered that 1,500 copies of George Miller's Biography be published, and that 1,000 copies of the Church Discipline be printed in the English language. It was made obligatory upon every local preacher to attend the Annual Local Preachers' Conference. An article on " The Evangelical Association" was prepared for insertion in Buck's Theological Dictionary. A. Ettinger and Jacob Hammer were appointed to obtain an act of incorporation from the Commonwealth of Pennsylvania for the Evangelical Association. The Conference resolved that a fund be established for the support of the superannuated preachers, and the widows and orphans of deceased preachers.* John Rank was elected trustee of this fund. The trustees of the Printing House were instructed to repair the building and to change it into a parsonage if possible, at the expense of the friends of the circuit; the house to remain the property of the Conference.

APPOINTMENTS.

CANAAN DISTRICT—*H. Niebel, P. E.*

Schuylkill Cir.—W. W. Orwig and D. Brickley.

Lebanon Cir. — J. Schnerr and J. P. Leib.

Lancaster Cir. — G. Brickley and F. Hoffman.

*This was the orig'n of the charitable funds of the Evangelical Association.

York Cir.—J. G. Ziuser, J. Roessuer, and H. Bucks.
Franklin Cir. — J. M. Saylor and J. Borkert.

Indiana Cir.—E. Stoever and A. Frey.
Shenandoah Cir.—G. Schneider and C. Thomas.
Somerset Cir.—D. Kehr and J. Harlacher.

SALEM DISTRICT—*J. Seybert*, *P. E.*

Union Cir.—S. G. Miller and C. Hesser.
Centre Cir.—P. Wagner and S. Baumgartner.
Lycoming Cir. — J. Barber and J. Young.

Lake Cir.—J. S. Himmelreich and J. Campbell.
Buffalo Cir.—C. Kring and J. Bell.
C. Hammer and G. Anstein were transferred to the Ohio District.

The Western Conference.

President, Joseph Long.
Secretary, J. H. Yambert.

This session of the Western Conference was held in Green Twp., Stark Co., Ohio. The proceedings were opened on May 7th, 1832, with religious exercises, after which J. Long was elected president. He appointed J. H. Yambert secretary. A preacher on trial was deposed for disobedience and frivolous conduct, and an elder, for disobedience and contumacy.

D. Kehr, J. S. Himmelreich, and A. Riehm were ordained to the office of Deacon. The following were newly received as preachers on trial: John Lutz, Elias Sichley, David Poorman, Aaron Yambert, and John J. Kopp. The Conference ordered the preparation of an article on "The Evangelical Association" for Buck's Theological Dictionary.

APPOINTMENTS.

OHIO DISTRICT—*J. Long*, *P. E.*

Canton Cir.—G. Anstein and J. J. Kopp.
Wooster Cir.—C. Hammer and C. Leitner.

Sandusky Cir.—G. Mattinger and E. Sichley.
New Lancaster Cir.—J. H. Yambert and M. Miller.

President, Thomas Buck.

Secretary, John Seybert.

The members of the Eastern Conference met in annual session at Orwigsburg, Schuylkill Co., Pa., on Monday, June 3d, 1833. The proceedings were opened with religious exercises. T. Buck was elected president. He appointed J. Seybert secretary. Two preachers were put on probation for improper conduct. Two others were deposed from the ministry and put on probation as members of the church for immoral conduct. J. S. Himmelreich and J. Borkert located on account of bodily infirmities. P. Wagner, W. W. Orwig, and J. M. Saylor were elected Presiding Elders. J. Schnerr and J. G. Zinser were ordained Elders ; J. Roessner, D. Brickley, Jacob Borkert, J. P. Leib, C. Hesser, J. Young, and J. Klein, Deacons. The following were newly received as preachers on trial : John Sensel, Isaac Deppen, Michael F. Maize, Solomon Altimos, Daniel Miesse, and Jacob Boas. The Conference elected the five presiding elders of both conferences a stationing committee. The transactions of the Western Conference were examined and approved.

T. Buck, W. W. Orwig, and J. C. Reisner were appointed a committee to publish a new edition of the *Geistliche Viole*. The committee was instructed to insert suitable morning and evening hymns and such as are appropriate to the burial service. It was resolved that an English hymn book be published and that J. M. Saylor and J. P. Leib be appointed to compile a collection of hymns for this purpose.

APPOINTMENTS.

CANAAN DISTRICT—*T. Buck, P. E.*

Schuylkill Cir.—J. P. Leib and 1. Deppen.

Lebanon Cir.—J. Schnerr and J. Sensel.

Lancaster Cir.—J. Roessner and J. Lutz.

ZION DISTRICT—*W. W. Orwig, P. E.*

York Cir.—J. G. Zinser and J. Harlacher.

Gettysburg Cir.—E. Stoever and H. Bucks.

Franklin Cir.—J. Barber and S. Baumgartner.

Shenandoah Cir.—J. Bell and M. F. Maize.

SALEM DISTRICT—*J. M. Saylor, P. E.*

Union Cir.—J. C. Reisner and F. Hoffman.

Lycoming Cir.—G. Schneider and G. Brickley.

Centre Cir.—C. Hesser and J. Young.

Somerset Cir.—D. Brickley and A. Frey.

Indiana Cir.—S. G. Miller and J. Boas.

CARMEL DISTRICT—*P. Wagner, P. E.*

Lake Cir.—D. Kehr and S. Altimos.

Mohawk Cir.—F. Glasser.

Buffalo Cir.—J. H. Yambert.

Erie Cir.—J. Seybert.

H. Niebel and C. Kring went to the Ohio District.

The Western Conference.

President, Joseph Long.

Secretary, J. H. Yambert.

On Monday, May 6th, 1833, the members of the Western Conference assembled in annual session in Pleasant Twp., Fairfield Co., Ohio. The Conference was opened in the usual manner. J. Long was elected president. He appointed J. H. Yambert secretary. A preacher on trial was deposed for neglect of duty. G. Anstein and C. Leitner located on account of bodily infirmities, and J. Long, on account of family concerns. Samuel Frey died during the year.

The Eastern Conference appointed H. Niebel Presiding Elder of this Conference. C. Hammer was ordained Elder, and M. Miller, S. Seger, and H. Danney, Deacons. The following were newly received as preachers on trial: Daniel Tobias, Peter Goetz, John Schrettler, and Henry McBride. It was unanimously resolved that the proceedings of the Conference be not published.

APPOINTMENTS.

OHIO DISTRICT—*H. Niebel, P. E.*

New Lancaster Cir.—C. Hammer and E. Sichley.

Sandusky Cir.—M. Miller and P. Goetz.

Canton Cir.—C. Kring and D. Tobias.

Wooster Cir.—J. J. Kopp and A. Yambert.

Miami Cir. — G. Mattinger and J. Schrettler.

1834.

The Eastern Conference.—The Eighth (27th) Annual Session.

President, W. W. Orwig.

Secretary, John Seybert.

On Monday, June 2d, 1834, the members of this Conference assembled in New Berlin, Union Co., Pa. Before proceeding to the transaction of business the brethren engaged in the customary devotional exercises. W. W. Orwig was elected president; he appointed J. Seybert secretary. A deacon was put on probation for improper conduct, and a presiding elder deposed from his office. Six preachers were deposed from the ministry, one for immoral conduct, two on account of inefficiency in the ministry, one because he resisted our Church Discipline, and two for neglect of duty and unchristian conduct. Several of these were expelled from the Association. T. Buck, J. H. Yambert, and

6

S. G. Miller located on account of family concerns; D. Miesse, J. Borkert, and J. Roessner, on account of bodily infirmities. Christian Wolf, John W. Miller, and Henry Young died during the past year. The following were newly received as preachers on trial: John Noecker, Jacob Saylor, Daniel Berger, Jacob Riegel, John Riegel, Peter Boetz, and John M. Sindlinger. The stationing committee consisted of the presiding elders. The transactions of the Western Conference were examined and approved.

Jacob Hammer was elected treasurer of the Charitable Funds of the Evangelical Association. A committee was appointed to inspect the English Hymn Book compiled by J. M. Saylor and J. P. Leib. A new edition of 1,500 copies of the *"Saitenspiel"* was ordered to be published; also 1,500 copies of the *"Lives of Jacob Albright and George Miller."* It was resolved that the next session of the General Conference be held at Orwigsburg, Schuylkill Co., Pa., to begin on the last Monday in May, 1835.

APPOINTMENTS.

CANAAN DISTRICT—*J. Seybert, P. E.*

Schuylkill Cir.—J. P. Leib and J. Sensel.

Lebanon Cir.—J. M. Saylor and John Riegel.

Lancaster Cir.—H. Fisher and Jacob Saylor.

ZION DISTRICT—*W. W. Orwig, P. E.*

York Cir. — J. Schnerr and M. F. Maize.

Gettysburg Cir.—D. Kehr and J. Noecker.

Cumberland Cir.—C. Hesser and A. Frey.

Shenandoah Cir.—S. Altimos and J. Schimp.

SALEM DISTRICT—*J. G. Zinser, P. E.*

Union Cir.—J. Young and D. Berger.

Lycoming Cir.—G. Brickley and S. Tobias.

Centre Cir.—F. Hoffman and J. M. Sindlinger.

Somerset Cir. — H. Bucks and G. Schneider.

Indiana Cir.—J. Lutz and P. Goetz.

CARMEL DISTRICT—*P. Wagner, P. E.*

Lake Cir.—J. Harlacher and J. Boas.

Mohawk Cir.—Jacob Riegel.

Buffalo Cir.—D. Brickley.

Erie Cir.—E. Stoever.

The Western Conference.

President, Henry Niebel.
Secretary, Charles Hammer.

This annual session was held in Lake Twp., Stark Co., Ohio, and was opened on Monday, May 5th, 1834. After the religious services, H. Niebel was elected president, who chose C. Hammer as secretary. A deacon was deposed for neglect of duty. Three others were deposed, one on account of disobedience, another for unchristian conduct, and the third on account of dishonest transactions for which he was also expelled from the Association.

M. Miller located on account of bodily infirmities. Fred. Borauf died during the past year. J. J. Kopp and E. Sichley were ordained to the office of Deacon. The following were newly received as preachers on trial: Peter Wiest, Samuel Van Gundy, and Jacob Frey.

APPOINTMENTS.

OHIO DISTRICT—*H. Niebel,* P. E.

Lancaster Cir.—S. Baumgartner and G. Mattinger.
Wooster Cir.—E. Sichley and D. Tobias.
Sandusky Cir.—J. J. Kopp and A. Yambert.
Canton Cir.—C. Hammer and S. Van Gundy.
Miami Cir.—C. Kring and P. Wiest.

1835.

The General Conference.

President, Henry Niebel.
Secretary, J. G. Zinser.

In accordance with a resolution adopted by the Eastern Conference, the General Conference convened on

May 25th, 1835, at Orwigsburg, Schuylkill Co., Pa. Singing, prayer, and the reading of the Sacred Scriptures constituted the opening exercises. H. Niebel was elected president. He appointed J. G. Zinser secretary. The following named elders constituted this General Conference: J. G. Zinser, J. Seybert, W. W. Orwig, P. Wagner, J. Barber, J. Breidenstein, J. C. Reisner, J. H. Yambert, J. Schnerr, D. Kehr, S. G. Miller, G. Brickley, F. Hoffman, E. Stoever, and J. M. Saylor of the Eastern Conference; H. Niebel, J. Long, C. Hammer, and C. Kring of the Western Conference. The preachers were investigated concerning their doctrines and conduct during the past year.

Some changes of boundaries were made in several presiding elder districts. Somerset, Indiana, and Erie circuits were detached from the Eastern Conference and annexed to the Western, and these three fields together with Canton Circuit, were formed into a district called Carmel District. In this new arrangement the Eastern Conference included three districts and the Western two. It was resolved that the Western Conference meet annually on the first Monday in March, and the Eastern, on the third Monday following. The presiding elders of both annual conferences were stationed.

The Conference ordered that 4,000 copies of the *Geistliche Viole* be published, and that a copyright of the work be secured in the name of J. Seybert of Pennsylvania and H. Niebel of Ohio. The preachers were instructed to gather data for the compilation of a book on the life and ministerial career of John Walter. It was resolved that hereafter the transactions of the

Quarterly Conferences be recorded in suitable minute-books to be kept for that purpose.

At this session the Association decided to publish a religious paper to be called *Der Christliche Botschafter*. J. Long, J. C. Reisner, and C. Hammer were appointed a committee to prepare a brief summary setting forth the character of the contemplated periodical. This committee reported the following outline of the design and contents of the *Christliche Botschafter:* 1st, To impart the divine truths of Holy Writ in their unadulterated purity and in such a manner as can be plainly understood by the common people; 2d, The dissemination of religious intelligence, and facts concerning the progress of true Christianity, with special reference to the work among the Germans of America; 3d, The interpretation and discussion of passages of Scripture; 4th, The biographies of pious, God-fearing persons; 5th, Useful and edifying natural history, etc.

P. Wagner, J. M. Saylor, and C. Hammer were appointed to prepare rules governing the issue of the periodical. They reported the following: 1st, The *Christliche Botschafter* shall be issued monthly at a subscription price of seventy-five cents a year, to be paid within the year, but in case the payment is not prompt the subscription charge to be one dollar; 2d, Subscriptions for a period of less than six months will not be received, and whoever desires to stop the paper must first pay all arrearages; 3d, Every preacher in charge in the Association is an agent to secure subscriptions and receive the money; 4th, All letters, communications, etc., not coming from the regular agents should be sent pre-paid.

It was resolved that the preachers in charge—the agents—shall solicit subscriptions, collect the money, and make an annual settlement with their respective presiding elders who are to constitute a general committee in each conference. The profits flowing from this project are to be applied in the same manner as the other book profits. It was furthermore resolved that each presiding elder shall receive for his trouble a royalty of one cent on every small book and two cents on every large book that is sold in his district and delivered through him to his preachers. The committee of the Eastern Conference was instructed to publish the *Christliche Botschafter* as soon as the number of subscribers has reached 700, this committee to take charge of the entire matter.

The Conference resolved that wherever practicable German Sabbath schools are to be organized and conducted in the congregations of our Evangelical Association, and that it be made the duty of every preacher in charge to strive earnestly to carry out this purpose.

The Conference ordered that a Local Preachers' Conference be held annually on each circuit, shortly before the session of the regular Annual Conference, and that all local preachers shall be under obligations to attend. W. W. Orwig, J. Long, and J. C. Reisner were appointed to formulate rules governing the transactions of Local Preachers' Conferences. They reported the following:

Local Preachers' Conferences and their Transactions.

Question. Who are the members of the Local Preachers' Conference? *Answer.* All local and traveling preachers who are found within the bounds of the circuit where each of these conferences is held. The presiding elder is also a member. *Ques.* Who is authorized to appoint the time and place of the meeting of these conferences? *Ans.* The presiding elder. In case he neglects it the preacher in charge shall do so. *Ques.* What are to be the transactions of the Local Preachers' Conference and who is to be the president? *Ans.* The presiding elder is to act as president and in his absence the preacher in charge. The records are to be sent to the Annual Conference for inspection. The Local Preachers' Conference is to inquire into the conduct of the local preachers, and when charges are preferred, to investigate them and decide upon them by a majority of votes, according to the directions of our Church Discipline; also to receive preachers on trial, if any such present themselves.

H. Niebel, J. Barber, and J. G. Zinser were appointed to formulate rules regulating the support of traveling preachers. They reported as follows: 1st. Newly married or single preachers received into the traveling connection shall be obliged to travel five years before they are permitted to draw any support for their families. 2d. After the five years, a married preacher without children shall receive half again as much support as a single preacher; with one or two children, three-fourths again as much, and with three or more children, twice as much. 3d. In case a preacher who was married two or more years previous to his entrance be received into the traveling connection he shall, after he has traveled two years, receive salary according to the second paragraph of this report.

The Conference resolved to incorporate an organization under the name of the " Charitable Society of the Evangelical Association," to be located in Orwigsburg, Schuylkill Co., Pa., and to consist of the following nine persons :   J. Seybert, J. P. Leib, Jacob Hammer, Joseph Hammer, Eli Hammer, S. Rickert, John Rickert, W. Wildermuth, and Andrew Swalm.   A committee, consisting of J. Long, W. W. Orwig, and J. C. Reisner, was appointed to construct a plan of organization. They reported the following: 1st, No person can become a member of this Society who is not 21 years of age, a member of the Evangelical Association for at least one year, and a citizen of Pennsylvania; 2d, In case of vacancies occurring through death, resignation, or expulsion from the church, the Society shall nominate double the number of those whose seats have become vacant, from which nominees the next General Conference shall elect the required member or members; 3d, This incorporated Society shall have charge of all charitable funds and bequests, loan the money at lawful interest and annually pay the income to the Eastern Conference of the Evangelical Association.

1835.

The Eastern Conference.—The Ninth (28th) Annual Session.

President, W. W. Orwig.
Secretary, John Seybert.

This Conference convened in Lebanon, Pa., June 1st, 1835.   After engaging in appropriate religious exercises the Conference organized by electing W. W. Orwig president, who appointed J. Seybert secretary. A preacher was deposed from the ministry for neglect of duty and immoral conduct. S. Tobias and D. Kehr located on account of bodily infirmities. C. Hesser, J. P. Leib, and D. Brickley were ordained to the office of Elder; J. Boas, H. Fisher, J. Sensel, J. Lutz, A. Frey, M. F. Maize, and S. Altimos, to the office of Deacon. The following were newly received as preachers on trial: Sebastian Mosser, Henry Thomas, John A. Jacobs, Fred. Miller, Daniel N. Long, John Poorman, Henry Kegel, Jacob Kehr, Samuel Friess, and George Seger. The presiding elders of both conferences were appointed to station the preachers. The transactions of the Western Conference were examined and approved.

APPOINTMENTS.

CANAAN DISTRICT—J. Seybert, P. E.

Schuylkill Cir.—C. Hammer and S. Mosser.

Lehigh Cir.—J. M. Saylor and Jacob Riegel.

Lebanon Cir.—C. Hesser and H. Thomas.

Lancaster Cir.—Jacob Saylor and John Riegel.

Philadelphia—J. Schnerr.

ZION DISTRICT—W. W. Orwig, P. E.

York Cir.—F. Hoffman and H. Fisher.

Gettysburg Cir.—S. G. Miller and J. A. Jacobs.

Cumberland Cir.—J. P. Leib, G. Schneider, and F. Miller.

Shenandoah Cir.—J. Schimp and D. N. Long.

SALEM DISTRICT—P. Wagner, P. E.

Union Cir.—J. Sensel and J. Poorman.

Columbia Cir.—D. Berger and J. M. Sindlinger.

Centre Cir.—J. Brickley and H. Kegel.

Lycoming Cir.—J. Young.

Lake Cir.—M. F. Maize and J. Kehr.

Buffalo Cir.—J. Harlacher and S. Friess.

CARMEL DISTRICT—J. G. Zinser, P. E.

Somerset Cir.—J. Lutz, A. Frey, and G. Seger.

Indiana Cir.—S. Altimos and J. Boas.

Erie Cir.—D. Brickley and J. Noecker.

Canton Cir.—E. Stoever and P. Goetz.

The Western Conference.

President, Henry Niebel.

Secretary, Charles Hammer.

The session of 1835 was held in Lake Twp., Stark Co., Ohio, and was opened on May 4th with the customary religious exercises. H. Niebel was elected president. He appointed C. Hammer secretary. Four preachers were deposed from the ministry, one for not preaching, another for unmerciful treatment of a poor widow, a third for improper business transactions, and a fourth on account of immoral conduct. The last was also expelled from the Association. J. Schilling withdrew from the church. J. Roessner located on account of bodily infirmities and G. Mattinger, on account of family concerns. Daniel Tobias and Abraham Riem died during the past year. Joseph Ebbert was ordained to the office of Deacon. H. Niebel, C. Kring, and C. Hammer were appointed to station the preachers.

APPOINTMENTS.

OHIO DISTRICT—*H. Niebel, P. E.*

Canton Cir.—J. Frey.
Wooster Cir.—H. Bucks and P. Wiest.
Mansfield Cir.—J. J. Kopp and S. Van Gundy.

Sandusky Cir.—S. Baumgartner and A. Yambert.
Lancaster Cir.—C. Kring and A. Eby.
Miami Cir.—E. Sichley.

1836.

The Eastern Conference.*—The Tenth (29th) Annual Session.

President, Philip Wagner.
Secretary, C. Hammer.

The members of the Eastern Conference assembled at Rebersburg, Centre Co., Pa., March 28th, 1836.

*From this time forth the proceedings of the Western Conference were no longer entered upon the record of the Eastern.

The session was opened with devotional exercises. P. Wagner was elected president. He appointed C. Hammer secretary. Two preachers were deposed for immoral conduct. J. M. Saylor located on account of bodily infirmities and S. G. Miller, on account of family concerns. J. P. Leib was elected to the office of Presiding Elder. The following were newly received on trial: Christian Holl, Martin Hartman, Henry Westhafer, Ludwig Schuppert, and Jacob Vogelbach. The presiding elders of both conferences were elected a committee to station the preachers. The proceedings of the Western Conference were examined and approved, after which the presiding elders were stationed by the Conference.

Committees were appointed to examine a manuscript by Samuel Miller, entitled "*Das Kernwesen von der Erlösung so durch Christum geschehen*," and Solomon Miller's "*Kette der Vernunft*," a translation from the English (Chain of Reason), with instructions to publish these works if they think proper. J. M. Saylor was elected trustee of the book funds. P. Wagner, A. Ettinger, and J. M. Saylor were appointed to compose and publish a Sunday school book. It was resolved that a General Conference shall be held, to begin November 14th, 1836, in Somerset Twp., Somerset Co., Pa. Salem District was divided and the part which was detached was called Moriah District. The Conference ordered that a committee be appointed annually whose duty it shall be to inquire into the accounts of the preachers stationed in cities, to estimate the excess of their expenses over those stationed on rural charges and to remunerate them accordingly.

CANAAN DISTRICT—*J. Seybert, P. E.*

Schuylkill Cir.—J. Barber and H. West-hafer.

Reading Cir.—Jacob Saylor.

Lebanon Cir.—J. Young and M. Hart-man.

Lancaster Cir.—John Riegel and L. Schuppert.

Philadelphia—J. Schnerr.

ZION DISTRICT—*J. P. Leib, P. E.*

York Cir.—G. Brickley.

Gettysburg Cir.—J. Jacobs and H. Thomas.

Cumberland Cir.—C. Hesser and F. Miller.

Shenandoah Cir.—M. F. Maize.

SALEM DISTRICT—*P. Wagner, P. E.*

Union Cir.—D. Berger and C. Holl.

Columbia Cir.—J. M. Sindlinger.

Centre Cir.—J. Sensel and H. Kegel.

Lycoming Cir.—F. Hoffman and S. Mosser.

MORIAH DISTRICT—*W. W. Orwig, P. E.*

Lake Cir.—Jacob Riegel and P. Henne-berger.

Buffalo Cir.—C. Hammer and J. Kehr.

Buffalo Sta.—J. Harlacher.

WESTERN CONFERENCE.

Indiana Cir.—D. Long.

Somerset Cir.—D. Kehr.

1836.

The General Conference.

President, Henry Niebel.

Secretary, Charles Hammer.

The General Conference of 1836 convened in Somerset Twp., Somerset Co., Pa., on the 14th of Nov., 1836. After the opening exercises which consisted of prayer, song, and exhortation, H. Niebel was elected president. He appointed C. Hammer secretary. The following elders were present: H. Niebel, C. Hammer, S. Baumgartner, S. G. Miller, J. G. Zinser, E. Stoever, H. Bucks, J. Young, J. Schnerr, C. Hesser, J. Seybert, W. W. Orwig, P. Wagner, D. Brickley, G. Brickley, F. Hoffman, J. J. Kopp, J. P. Leib, and D. Kehr.

It was resolved that a new printing house and book

bindery be established within the bounds of the Eastern Conference. Arrangements were accordingly made to purchase or build a house in New Berlin, Union Co., Pa., suitable at once for carrying on the printing business and as a dwelling house, with the understanding, however, that in case not enough money be forthcoming for this purpose a suitable building is to be rented. W. W. Orwig was elected editor of the *Christliche Botschafter*. He was instructed to assume the duties of general book agent also, in case Geo. Miller resigns the office.

The Conference resolved that the editor of the *Christliche Botschafter* shall always be elected by the General Conference and that no person can be elected more than twice in immediate succession; that the editor, the presiding elder of the district including the establishment, and John Rank shall be trustees to superintend the printing establishment of the Evangelical Association, the first two to be standing trustees. Provision was made that, in case either of these trustees should die, resign, or be deposed, the preacher in charge of the circuit whereon the establishment is located is to take his place until the next session of the General Conference. In case of a vacancy in the editorship, the remaining trustees, together with the preacher in charge of the circuit, are to elect a successor until the next annual session of the Eastern Conference. C. Hammer was elected Presiding Elder in the place of W. W. Orwig, and S. Witt was ordained Deacon. The salary of the editor of the *Christliche Botschafter* was fixed at a sum equal to that received by other traveling preachers, with an additional allowance

equal to that of an unmarried preacher. J. C. Reisner
was appointed to prepare a German A, B, C, and Spell-
ing Book to be published for the use of children.

The following form of a recommendation for members removing from one circuit to another was adopted :
This is to certify that A——— B——— is a member
of our Evangelical Association.

  E—— Cir. C——— D——— Preacher in Charge.
———A. D. 18—.

A new edition of 4,000 copies of the "*Viole*" was
ordered to be printed. The General Conference decided
that the two annual conferences shall henceforth be
independent of each other as regards all their transactions, with the exception of the contributions for the
support of the preachers. It was agreed that the
Western Conference annually send two delegates to the
Eastern, who shall serve in conjunction with a committee of three from the latter to inspect all manuscripts
intended for publication. The Conference adjourned
to meet on the fourth Monday in March, A. D. 1839,
on Centre Circuit.

1837.

The Eastern Conference.—The Eleventh (30th) Annual
Session.

President, Philip Wagner.
Secretary, Charles Hammer.

The session of 1837 was held at New Berlin, Pa.,
beginning March 27th, 1837. The religious exercises
at the opening were followed by organization. P.
Wagner was elected president. He appointed C. Ham-

mer secretary. The ordination of a preacher was withheld because of his improper conduct; another was deposed for unchristian conduct. J. Hartman located. P. Wagner was newly elected to the office of Presiding Elder. John Young and M. F. Maize were ordained Elders; II. Kegel, J. Kehr, J. Jacobs, II. Thomas, P. Henneberger, and S. Mosser, Deacons. The following were newly received on trial: Henry Stoetzel, Moses Bauer, Geo. Dellinger, Geo. Schaeffer, Benjamin Aepley, Geo. T. Haines, Charles Wagner, Jacob Miller, Jacob Rank, Michael Eiss, Christian Hummel, and Henry Miesse. The presiding elders were elected a committee to station the preachers. The preachers were instructed to collect money annually wherewith to defray the expenses incurred in feeding their horses during the annual session of Conference. In case more than a sufficient amount is secured during any one year, the surplus shall be kept in a fund until the ensuing year and then applied to the same purpose.

The following was resolved: 1st, That 1,500 copies of "*Die Nachfolge Jesu Christi*," by Thomas A. Kempis, be printed, subject to the approval of the committee of publication; 2d, That 1,000 copies of the German "*Sprachlehre*" written by J. Vogelbach, be printed, provided it be approved by the committee of publication; 3d, That 1,000 copies of Miller's "*Thætiges Christenthum*" be printed; 4th, That the committee on printing affairs be instructed to publish various editions of the Bible to be sold by the Association; 5th, That three or four thousand Sunday school tickets be issued; 6th, That 500 pamphlets containing the constitution of the Charitable Society be published.

APPOINTMENTS.

CANAAN DISTRICT—*J. Seybert, P. E.*

Schuylkill Cir.—T. Buck.

Lykens Cir. — J. Barber and P. Schwilly.

Reading Cir.—Jacob Saylor and M. Eis.

Lebanon Cir. — F. Hoffman and J. Vogelbach.

Lancaster Cir.—J. M. Sindlinger and J. Noecker.

Philadelphia Sta.—C. Hesser.

ZION DISTRICT—*J. P. Leib, P. E.*

York Cir.—J. Sensel and H. Westhafer.

Gettysburg Cir.—J. Schnerr and F. Miller.

Cumberland Cir.—M. F. Maize, Chr. Holl, and G. Schaffer.

Shenandoah Cir.—P. Henneberger and M. Bauer.

SALEM DISTRICT—*P. Wagner, P. E.*

Union Cir.—J. Jacobs and H. Thomas.

Columbia Cir.—G. Brickley and L. Shuppert.

Lycoming Cir.—S. Mosser and G. T. Haines.

Centre Cir.—D. Berger and W. Heim.

MORIAH DISTRICT—*C. Hammer, P. E.*

Dansville Cir.—J. Kehr.

Lake Cir.—H. Kegel and G. Dellinger.

Buffalo Cir.—Jacob Riegel and H. Stoetzel.

Buffalo Sta.—J. Harlacher.

WESTERN CONFERENCE.

Lancaster Cir.—John Riegel.

Somerset Cir.—John Young.

.   -

1838.

The Eastern Conference.—The Twelfth (31st) *Annual Session.*

President, Philip Wagner.

Secretary, Francis Hoffman.

The members of the Eastern Conference assembled at Orwigsburg, Schuylkill Co., Pa., on Mar. 28th, 1838. P. Wagner was elected president. He appointed F. Hoffman secretary. A local deacon was reproved for neglect of duties. A local preacher was deposed and put on probation six months for immoral conduct; another was deposed for unbecoming conduct toward the ministry. J. Harlacher and J. Kehr located on account of bodily infirmities; Jacob Saylor on account of family concerns. Philip Breidenstein and Andrew Yeakel died during the year. J. Seybert was re-elected, and T. Buck newly elected to the office of Presiding Elder. Daniel Berger, Jacob Saylor, Jacob Riegel, and J. M. Sindlinger were ordained Elders; J. Vogelbach, W. Heim, H. Westhafer, Fr. Miller, Chr. Holl, and Geo. Schaeffer, Deacons. The following were newly received on trial: Frederick Krecker, Wm. Mintz, John Rosenberger, Samuel Krall, and Alex. Longsdorf. The presiding elders and H. Bucks were elected a committee to station the preachers. Four hundred and ten dollars were sent to the Western Conference for the support of preachers.

It was resolved that no traveling preacher who practices medicine shall be allowed to take pay for his medical services.

The Conference adopted the following resolutions:

Resolved, That upon each charge a parsonage shall be erected, if practicable, and that the Quarterly Conference elect three men as trustees, who shall, by the advice of the presiding elder and preacher in charge, select a suitable locality on the circuit for the erection or purchase of such a house. *Resolved*, That in case any portion of the money collected for the feeding of the preachers' horses at conference remain, it be appropriated for the additional support of such preachers who make application, and in the event of a balance still remaining, it shall be retained in the book fund until the next annual session, when it is to be merged into the general salary fund.

Canaan District was divided and the new part called Philadelphia District. It was resolved that the Con-

7

ference be empowered to station the presiding elders. The following were ordered to be printed : 3,000 copies of the small English Hymn Book, 2,000 copies of Kempis's Imitation of Christ, 2,000 copies of Miller's "*Thœtiges Christenthum*," and 2,000 copies of Air's Sermons, if approved by the committee. The Conference decided that the new edition of the English Hymn Book should contain no more than six additional hymns. A Missionary Society was organized by the members of the Conference.

Resolved, That the universal use of tobacco in our day is a great evil, that we will unanimously protest against it, and that no preacher among us shall be allowed to engage in its traffic.

APPOINTMENTS.

CANAAN DISTRICT—*T. Buck*, P. E.

Lykens Cir.—D. Kehr and S. Mosser.
Schuylkill Cir.—M. F. Maize.
Womelsdorf Cir.—J. Schnerr.

Lebanon Cir.—J. Vogelbach and W. Mintz.
Lancaster Cir.—J. Sindlinger and J. Rosenberger.

PHILADELPHIA DISTRICT—*J. P. Leib*, P. E.

Philadelphia Sta.—C. Hesser.
Reading Cir.—H. Fisher and M. Els.

Lehigh Cir.—F. Hoffman and P. Himmelberger.

ZION DISTRICT—*P. Wagner*, P. E.

York Cir.—J. Sensel and W. Heim.
Gettysburg Cir.—G. Schaffer and H. Westhafer.

Cumberland Cir.—J. Young, J. Jacobs, and S. Krall.
Shenandoah Cir.—F. Miller and M. Bauer.

SALEM DISTRICT—*J. Seybert*, P. E.

Union Cir.—H. Thomas and H. Kegel.
Columbia Cir.—J. Barber, B. Aeply, and F. Krecker.

Centre Cir.—D. Berger and A. Longsdorf.
Lycoming Cir.—G. Brickley and P. Schwilly.

MORIAH DISTRICT—*C. Hammer*, P. E.

Lake Cir.—Jacob Riegel and C. Hummel.

Dansville Cir.—H. Stoetzel.
Buffalo Cir.—C. Holl and G. T. Haines.

WESTERN CONFERENCE.

Indiana Cir.—J. Noecker.

Somerset Cir.—G. Dellinger.

1839.

The General Conference.

President, Thomas Buck.
Secretary, George Brickley.

The General Conference of the Evangelical Association met in Haines Twp., Centre Co., Pa., on March 25th, 1839. After the devotional exercises, T. Buck was elected president, whereupon he appointed G. Brickley secretary. The following elders were present: From the *Eastern Conference,*—T. Buck, G. Brickley, F. Hoffman, C. Hammer, M. F. Maize, D. Berger, J. Barber, D. Kehr, J. M. Sindlinger, C. Hesser, S. G. Miller, P. Wagner, J. Sensel, J. Harlacher, J. Young, J. Seybert, J. P. Leib, and W. W. Orwig; from the *Western Conference,*—J. Long, H. Niebel, J. G. Zinser, H. Bucks, E. Stoever, J. Boas, A. B. Shaefer, S. Van Gundy, J. Lutz, P. Wiest, P. Goetz, A. Yambert, and J. J. Kopp.

It was resolved that the *Christliche Botschafter* be issued bi-monthly after the completion of its fifth year at a subscription price of $1.00 *per annum* if paid within the year, if after the close of the year, $1.25; that all traveling preachers and worn out preachers who have traveled shall receive the paper free; that such persons who secure six subscribers and make themselves responsible for the payment of the money, shall receive one copy free, the agents excepted.

The Conference decided that no preacher who travel without having been appointed by a conference shall receive support. Each annual conference was authorized to fix the salaries of the preachers stationed in cities. The following rule with reference to local preachers was adopted: In case a local preacher absents himself from conference sessions without well founded reasons he shall be punished; if he is a preacher on trial, his license shall be withheld for one year; if ordained, his ordination shall be withheld; for a second offence he is to be deposed from the ministry.

The two old conferences were divided into three, as follows: The *East Pa. Conference*, to include Canaan, Philadelphia, and Moriah districts; the *West Pa. Conference*, Salem, Zion, and Carmel districts; the *Ohio Conference*, Ohio, Tabor, and Sandusky districts.

The organization and constitution of a Missionary Society were submitted to the Conference and adopted, the society to be known as "The Missionary Society of the Evangelical Association of North America." The Conference ordered that a German pocket Bible be stereotyped. A sufficient number of advance subscribers paid $2.50 and $2.75 for the work. It was also resolved that "*A History of the Evangelical Association*" be prepared and published; the work to contain an account of the origin, progress and most important events of the Evangelical Association. C. Hammer was appointed to gather materials having reference to the origin and progress of the Association in the West Pa. Conference, J. Driesbach in the Ohio Conference, and T. Buck in the East Pa. Conference. W. W. Orwig was appointed to arrange the materials thus gathered and to prepare them for publication, the first edition of the history to be limited to 3,500 copies.

It having been proposed to change the rules in our Church Discipline which govern the temporal economy of the church, committees were appointed to inspect the various portions of the Discipline treating of these subjects.

John Seybert was elected Bishop, W. W. Orwig was re-elected editor of the *Christliche Botschafter*, and Charles Hammer, general book agent. T. Buck, W. W. Orwig, and C. Hammer were appointed to correct the grammatical and typographical errors in the Church Discipline. J. Seybert, J. Long, and G. Brickley were appointed to formulate rules empowering the General Conference to make changes in the laws of our church.

The manufacture of spirituous drinks for any purpose other than medicinal, was strictly prohibited among the members of our church.

[An anti-slavery resolution was adopted, the text of which does not appear upon the official records. From the current numbers of the *Christliche Botschafter* it apears that the resolution prohibited all members of the church from owning slaves or engaging in the slave trade.—S. C. B.]

Our preachers were authorized to administer, preach, and defend infant as well as adult baptism according to our form; also to re-baptize such persons who were baptized in their childhood if they make application and cannot otherwise satisfy their consciences, no preacher being allowed, however, to *advocate* re-baptism.

The Conference adjourned to meet on the first Monday in November 1843, on Tabor District, Ohio Conference.

1839.

The Eastern Conference.—The Thirteenth (32d) Annual Session.

President, Bishop John Seybert.
Secretary, Francis Hoffman.
Assistant Secretary, George Brickley.

The members of the Eastern Conference assembled in Lebanon, Pa., April 11th, 1839, Bishop J. Seybert presiding. After conducting the opening exercises the president appointed F. Hoffman secretary, who chose Geo. Brickley his assistant. Two preachers were deposed from the ministry, one for incompetency, and the other for engaging in certain political affairs. Several were put on probation. J. Schnerr, H. Kegel, and Jacob Riegel located on account of bodily infirmities; S. Krall and Fr. Miller, on account of family concerns. G. Brickley and J. M. Sindlinger were elected to the office of Presiding Elder. J. A. Jacobs and S. Mosser were ordained Elders; Chr. Hummel, B. Aepley, H. Stoetzel, G. T. Haines, and P. Schwilly, Deacons. The following were newly received on trial: John Kraemer, Joseph Rissman, Joseph Best, Henry Roland, Abraham Forry, David Mertz, George Ramige, John Kaufman, and George Dressler. The committee to station the preachers consisted of Bishop Seybert, T. Buck, C. Hammer, J. P. Leib, P. Wagner, G. Brickley, and J. M. Sindlinger. The salary of the preacher in Philadelphia was fixed at $250 for the year.

It was resolved that the East Pa. Conference shall convene on Wednesday, Mar. 25th, 1840, at Schuylkill Haven, Pa., and the West Pa. Conference on Wednesday, Apr. 8, 1840, at New Berlin, Pa.

APPOINTMENTS.

[The New East Pa. Conference.]

CANAAN DISTRICT— *T. Buck, P. E.*

Lykens Cir.—B. Aepley and M. Lehn.
Pottsville and Minersville Sta.—M. F. Maize.
Schuylkill Cir.—C. Hesser.

Lebanon Cir.—F. Hoffman, F. Krecker, and D. Mertz.
Lancaster Cir.—G. Schaffer and J. Kraemer.

PHILADELPHIA DISTRICT— *J. P. Leib, P. E.*

Lehigh Cir.—D. Berger and G. T. Haines.

Philadelphia Sta.—J. Vogelbach.
Reading Cir.—W. Heim and W. Mintz.

MORIAH DISTRICT— *J. M. Sindlinger, P. E.*

Dansville Cir.—D. Kehr.
Lake Cir.—J. Harlacher.

Buffalo Cir.—P. Schwilly and G. Ramige.

[The New West Pa. Conference.]

ZION DISTRICT— *P. Wagner, P. E.*

York Cir.—H. Fisher and J. Rosenberger.
Gettysburg Cir. — J. Sensel and P. Henneberger.

Cumberland Cir. — J. A. Jacobs, A. Forry, and H. Westhafer.

SALEM DISTRICT— *G. Brickley, P. E.*

Union Cir.—J. Barber and J. Best.
Centre Cir.—H. Thomas and H. Roland.

Columbia Cir.—S. Mosser and A. Longsdorf.
Lycoming Cir.—J. Young and J. Kissman.

MISSIONS.—*(Included in both Conferences.)*

New York City Mission—J. Burghart.
Waterloo (Upper Canada) Mission—C. Holl.

Mohawk Mission—C. Hummel.
Black Creek (Upper Canada) Mission— M. Eis.

"And daily in the temple, and in every house, they ceased not to teach and preach Jesus Christ."—ACTS V: 42.

The East Pennsylvania Conference.

1840-1887.

"And they divided the land."—JOSH. XIV: 5.

PREFACE.

The General Conference of 1839 re-districted the church into three annual conferences called respectively The East Pa. Conference, The West Pa. Conference, and The Ohio Conference. With the first of these, embracing the territory upon which the Evangelical Association first found footing, the remainder of these pages will be principally occupied. The official records of the East Pa. Conference will be interspersed, however, with extracts from the quadrennial proceedings of the General Conference. These extracts have either direct reference to the work and personnel of the East Pa. Conference or form important links in the chain of events.

The East Pennsylvania Conference.

— —

1840.

The First (33d) Annual Session.

President, Bishop John Seybert.
Secretary, Jacob Vogelbach.
Assistant Secretary, Francis Hoffman.

The East Pennsylvania Conference met at Schuylkill Haven, Pa., on March 25th, 1840, and continued in session seven days. The Conference was opened with religious exercises, consisting of a Scripture reading, singing, and prayer. An appropriate selection from the Church Discipline was also read.* Bishop Seybert presided. He appointed J. Vogelbach secretary, who chose F. Hoffman as his assistant.† J. P. Leib was re-elected Presiding Elder. J. Vogelbach, W. Heim, G. Schaffer, and C. Holl were ordained to the office of Elder; W. Mintz, F. Krecker, J. Rosenberger, M. Eis, and M. Lehn, to the office of Deacon. The following were newly received on trial: Frederick Danner, David Fisher, and Michael Sindlinger. The salary of an unmarried preacher was $48.60.

---

*Hereafter the devotional exercises at the opening of each annual session will not be mentioned.

†This method of organizing has prevailed until the present time. It will therefore not be necessary to allude to it in the record of each session.

PHILADELPHIA DISTRICT—*J. P. Leib*, P. E.

Philadelphia Sta.—J. Vogelbach.

Milford Cir. — J. Sensel and H. Stoetzel.*

Lehigh Cir.—M. F. Maize and G. T. Haines.

Reading Cir.—Jacob Saylor and Henry Fisher.

CANAAN DISTRICT—*T. Buck*, P. E.

Lykens Cir.—C. Holl and Wm. Mintz.

Schuylkill Cir. — F. Hoffman, Chas. Hesser, and D. Mertz.

Lebanon Cir.—D. Berger and F. Danner.

Lancaster Cir.—Wm. Heim and J. Kraemer.

MORIAH DISTRICT—*J. M. Sindlinger*, P. E.

Mohawk Cir. — C. Hummel and G. Ramige.

Lake Cir.—M. Lehn and D. Fisher.

Buffalo Cir.—P. Schwilly.

Buffalo Sta.—Fred. Krecker.

Black Creek Cir.—M. Eis and M. Sindlinger.

Waterloo Miss.—J. Harlacher.

New York Miss.—Jacob Burkhardt.

1841.

The Second (34th) Annual Session.

President, Bishop John Seybert.

Secretary, William Mintz.

Assistant Secretary, Francis Hoffman.

The Conference met in annual session on Wednesday, Mar. 17th, 1841, in Fayette Twp., Seneca Co., N. Y., Bishop Seybert presiding. T. Buck, H. Fisher, and F. Danner were appointed a finance committee. H. Stoetzel and D. Mertz located on account of bodily infirmities. Leonhard Zimmerman died during the year. G. T. Haines, C. Hummel, P. Schwilly, and M. Eis were ordained Elders; J. Kraemer, G. Ramige, and F. Danner, Deacons. Solomon Neitz, William Garret, David Fisher, and Michael Sindlinger were continued as preachers on trial. Jacob Dareich was newly received on trial. The Bishop and the presiding elders were constituted a stationing committee.

*H. Stoetzel served on Milford Circuit until September, 1840, when Solomon Neitz took his place and entered active work.

The following statistics show the total membership on each charge in the Conference at this time:

Philadelphia Sta.....	219	Lancaster Cir......	290
Milford Cir........	175	Mohawk Cir.......	166
Lehigh Cir........	218	Lake Cir..........	274
Reading Cir......	175	Buffalo Cir........	159
Lykens Cir........	213	Buffalo Sta.........	59
Schuylkill Cir......	318	Black Creek Cir.....	109
Lebanon Cir.......	261	Waterloo Miss......	87

Total membership of the Conference........ 2,723

These are the preachers of the Conference according to their station and order:

Bishop,—John Seybert.

Presiding Elders,—J. P. Leib, T. Buck, and J. M. Sindlinger.

Elders,—J. Breidenstein, F. Hoffman, C. Hesser, H. Fisher, J. Harlacher, M. F. Maize, J. M. Saylor, John Kleinfelter, J. Sensel, D. Berger, Jacob Riegel, J. Schnerr, Jacob Saylor, J. C. Reisner, C. Holl, W. Heim, P. Schwilly, G. T. Haines, C. Hummel, and M. Eis.

Deacons,—D. Thomas, J. Burkhart, S. Tobias, J. Klein, M. Lehn, F. Glasser, J. Kramer, G. Ramige, F. Danner, H. Stoetzel, D. Focht, W. Mintz, F. Krecker, S. Muck, and J. Kehr.

Continued on Trial,—D. Fisher, M. Sindlinger, S. Neitz, D. Mertz, and William Garret.

Newly Received on Trial,—Jacob Dareich.

APPOINTMENTS.

PHILADELPHIA DISTRICT—*J. P. Leib,* P. E.

Philadelphia Sta.—C. Hesser.   [ret.

Milford Cir.—G. T. Haines and W. Gar-

Reading Sta.—J. Burkhart.

Lehigh Cir. — M. F. Maize and J. Kraemer.

Womelsdorf Clr.—Jacob Saylor.

CANAAN DISTRICT—*T. Buck, P. E.*
Lancaster Cir.—H. Fisher and C. Holl.
Lebanon Sta.—D. Berger.
Dauphin Cir.—J. Sensel.
Orwigsburg Cir.—W. Mintz.
Schuylkill Cir.—F. Hoffman.
Pottsville Sta.—W. Heim.
Lykens Cir.—F. Danner and S. Neitz.
MORIAH DISTRICT—*J. M. Sindlinger*,
   P. E.

Mohawk Cir.—G. Ramige and D.
   Fisher.
Lake Cir.—M. Lehn and Michael Sind-
   linger.
Buffalo Cir.—C. Hummel.
Buffalo Sta.—F. Krecker.
Black Creek Cir.—P. Schwilly.
Waterloo Cir.—J. Harlacher and J.
   Dareich.
New York Miss.—M. Eis.*

1842.

The Third (35th) *Annual Session.*

President, Bishop John Seybert.
Secretary, Henry Fisher.
Assistant Secretary, William Mintz.

The members of the Conference assembled in Allentown, Pa., March 2d, 1842, Bishop Seybert presiding. J. Burkhart located on account of bodily infirmities, and J. Harlacher, on account of family concerns. T. Buck received permission to remain in the itinerancy and to travel according to his strength. H. Fisher was elected Presiding Elder. W. Mintz, F. Krecker, and M. Lehn were ordained Elders; S. Neitz, D. Fisher, M. Sindlinger, C. Meyers, S. Miesse, and D. Mertz, Deacons. The following were newly received on trial: Henry Sauer, Joseph Gross, Thomas Steck, and Wm. Schmidt. Thomas Buck was appointed to assist the Bishop and presiding elders in the work of stationing the preachers. The following were appointed a committee on finance to distribute the money contributed for salaries: T. Buck, H. Fisher, and F. Danner. T. Buck and J. M.

*M. Eis served this mission during a part of the year, after which Christian Meyers took his place.

Saylor were appointed a committee to examine manuscripts offered for publication. This committee was instructed to act in connection with similar committees from the other annual conferences. After the usual distribution of salaries as prescribed by the Discipline, a balance remained which was divided among those who needed it most.

APPOINTMENTS.

PHILADELPHIA DISTRICT — H. Fisher, P. E.
Philadelphia Sta.—M. F. Maize.
Milford Cir.—C. Hummel, J. Kramer, and Joseph Gross.
Lehigh Cir.—C. Hesser and W. Mintz.
New York Miss.—C. Meyers.
Womelsdorf Cir.—F. Hoffman and P. Schwilly.
Philadelphia, Germantown, and Manayunk Miss.—J. M. Saylor.

CANAAN DISTRICT—J. P. Leib, P. E.
Lancaster Cir.—J. C. Reisner, J. Dareich, and T. Steck.
Lebanon Cir —Jacob Saylor and F. Danner.

Schuylkill Cir.—D. Berger and S. Neitz.
Pinegrove Cir.—T. Buck.
Pottsville Sta.—W. Heim.
Lykens Cir.—J. Sensel and G. T. Haines.

MORIAH DISTRICT — J. M. Sindlinger, P. E.
Mohawk Cir.—M. Lehn and H. Sauer.
Jefferson Cir.—D. Fisher.
Lake Cir.—C. Holl and M. Sindlinger.
Buffalo Cir.—G. Ramige.
Buffalo Sta.—Jacob Riegel.
Black Creek Cir.—J. Kehr.
Waterloo Cir.—M. Eis and W. Schmidt.
Rochester Miss.—F. Krecker.

1843.

The Fourth (36th) Annual Session.

President, Bishop John Seybert.
Secretary, Henry Fisher.
Assistant Secretary, Christian Meyers.

The session of 1843 was held in the Evangelical meeting-house at Lebanon, Pa., beginning March 22d. W. Heim located on account of bodily infirmities. Four preachers were deposed for unchristian conduct, one of

whom was expelled from the Association. W. Mintz
and M. Lehn were elected to the office of Presiding
Elder. Elders' orders were granted to G. Ramige, F.
Danner, J. Kramer, and J. Kehr; Deacons' orders to J.
Dareich. The following were newly received on trial:
Jacob C. Farnsworth, Theobald Schneider, George C.
Schmidt, Wm. L. Reber, John Raus, and Fred. Scharfe.
The finance committee consisted of J. M. Saylor, Jacob
Saylor, and F. Danner. The Conference appointed C.
Hesser, M. F. Maize, and H. Fisher a committee to
audit the accounts of the missionaries. The following
were elected delegates to the next General Conference:
J. P. Leib, W. Mintz, J. C. Reisner, J. M. Saylor, H.
Fisher, M. Lehn, C. Hesser, F. Hoffman, M. F. Maize,
and H. Bucks; alternates, Jacob Saylor, D. Berger,
and Jacob Riegel. The Conference appointed J. P.
Leib a delegate to the West Pa. Conference to present
to that body the recommendations of changes in the
Discipline proposed by the East Pa. Conference.

BOUNDARIES.

Moriah District was divided and formed into Niagara
and Mohawk districts. Rochester Mission was discontinued. A mission was located in Lancaster City, Pa.

CHURCH AFFAIRS.

A committee, consisting of C. Hesser, M. F. Maize,
and H. Fisher, was appointed to inquire into the practicability of building a new church in New York City,
and if deemed advisable, to carry out the project; H.
Fisher was appointed treasurer.

APPOINTMENTS.

PHILADELPHIA DISTRICT—*H. Fisher,* P. E.
Philadelphia Sta.—M. F. Maize.
Milford Cir.—W. L. Reber, J. Kramer, and G. C. Schmidt.
Lehigh Cir—C. Hesser and J. C. Farnsworth.
Monroe Cir.—G. T. Haines.
Womelsdorf Cir.—D. Berger and F. Scharfe.
New York Miss.—C. Hummel.
Germantown Miss.—J. M. Saylor.

CANAAN DISTRICT—*J. P. Leib,* P. E.
Lancaster Cir.—Jacob Saylor, T. Steck, and S. Miesse.
Lebanon Cir.—F. Danner and S. Neitz.
Orwigsburg Sta.—J. Sensel.

Lykens Cir.—J. C. Reisner and C. Holl.
Pinegrove Sta.—F. Hoffman.
Schuylkill Haven Sta.—C. Meyers.
Pottsville Sta.—H. Bucks.

MOHAWK DISTRICT—*W. Mintz,* P. E.
Mohawk Cir. — D. Fisher and T. Schneider.
Jefferson Cir.—M. Sindlinger.
Lake Cir.—F. Krecker and H. Sauer.
Dansville Cir.—J. Dareich.

NIAGARA DISTRICT—*M. Lehn,* P. E.
Buffalo Cir.—G. Ramige.
Buffalo Sta.—Jacob Riegel.
Black Creek Cir.—J. Kehr.
Waterloo Cir.—M. Eis and J. Raus.

1843.

*The General Conference.**

Presidents, Bishops John Seybert and Joseph Long.
Secretary, A. B. Schaeffer.
Assistant Secretaries, H. Fisher and Chas. Hammer.

The General Conference met in Summit Co., Ohio, on October 23d, 1843, and continued in session eleven days. During the investigation of the members of the Conference no charges were preferred. All the delegates elected by the East Pa. Conference were present, with the exception of Charles Hesser whose death, caused by an accident, occurred on his way to this Conference session. Jacob Saylor, first alternate, took his place. It was unanimously resolved that a special service be held in memory of the deceased delegate. In accordance with this resolution the members of the Gen-

---

*See Preface on page 98.

8

eral Conference assembled at the house of Elias
Stoever, whence they proceeded in procession to the
meeting-house in which the sessions of the Conference
were held.   Here Bishop Seybert preached a sermon
from the words " For he was a good man and full of
the Holy Ghost and of faith."—Acts xi: 24.

The salary of an unmarried itinerant preacher was
fixed at $100.00 per annum ; a married itinerant to re-
ceive $100.00 additional for his wife and $25.00 additional for each of his children under 14 years of age.
Besides this a reasonable allowance was to be granted
for traveling expenses.   John Seybert was re-elected
and Joseph Long newly elected to the office of Bishop.
J. C. Reisner of the East Pa. Conference was elected
general book agent, and Adam Ettinger of the West
Pa. Conference, editor of the *Christliche Botschafter.*

The name of Canaan District in the East Pa. Conference was changed to Harrisburg District.   The last
Wednesday in February was fixed as the time to open
the annual sessions of the East Pa. Conference.

Bishops Seybert and Long, A. Ettinger, editor of the
Christliche Botschafter, J. C. Reisner, General Book
Agent, and W. W. Orwig were appointed a committee
to prepare a course of study for our junior preachers
and for candidates for the ministry.   It was made obligatory upon all such to give diligent study to this
course.

The Conference ordered that the interest accruing
from the Charitable Society funds and the profits arising from the printing establishment are to be divided
in equal shares among the different annual conferences
and that each conference be required to support its own

claimants. The Charitable Society was advised to loan
$1,200.00 to the congregation at Philadelphia and
$300.00 to the congregation at Rochester, provided
these congregations can give ample security and reliable
assurances of paying the interest annually.   J. P. Leib,
J. M. Saylor, and M. F. Maize were appointed to inquire into the affairs of the congregation at Rochester.

In view of the rapid spread of the English language
in the Association, authority was conferred upon each
annual conference to organize within its bounds whenever it may be deemed advisable, an English conference, to consist of ten or more English preachers. The
membership of the entire Evangelical Association at
this time was 13,070, distributed among the conferences
as follows: East Pa., 4,372 ; West Pa., 4,508 ; Ohio,
4,190. The old conference record thus far in the possession of the East Pa. Conference was set apart as a
record for the proceedings of the General Conference
only, to be kept in custody by the book establishment.

1844.

The Fifth (37th) Annual Session.

President, Bishop John Seybert.
Secretary, Fred. Danner.
Assistant Secretary, Wm. Mintz.

The Conference met in the Evangelical meeting-
house at Orwigsburg, Pa., Feb. 28th, 1844, and continued in session until March 8th. H. Sauer located
on account of bodily infirmities and C. Holl on account
of family concerns. C. Hesser had died during the

year. H. Bucks was elected Presiding Elder. C.
Meyers and S. Neitz were ordained Elders; J. C. Farns-
worth, T. Steck, and D. K. Miesse, Deacons. It was
resolved that for sufficient reasons Wm. Schmidt shall
be ordained Deacon in the interim of the sessions. The
following were newly received on trial: Martin Lauer,
Abraham Shultz, John Bush, John Eckert, Samuel
Spohn, Daniel Wieand, and John G. Marquardt. The
bishops and the presiding elders stationed the preachers.
The following committees were appointed: On Finance,
M. F. Maize, W. Mintz, and W. L. Reber; To Audit
Accounts of Missionaries,—M. F. Maize, H. Bucks, and
Jacob Saylor; To Examine Manuscripts for Publica-
tion,—J. P. Leib and J. M. Saylor.

F. Krecker was appointed to make abstracts of the
proceedings of former sessions of this Conference
recorded in the old conference book and to transcribe them into a new one. H. Buck was appointed to
report the proceedings of this session to the *Christliche
Botschafter*. The Conference paid a bill of $8.00 for
accidental damages to a team used by the brethren, H.
Fisher, C. Hesser, M. F. Maize, and J. M. Saylor, on
their way to the recent General Conference session.
[From this accident C. Hesser had sustained injuries
with fatal results.]

The brethren agreed that in the future, gifts received
are not to be charged as salary.

BOUNDARIES.

Reading, Pa., and Syracuse, N. Y., were taken up as
missions. Two new circuits were formed, called respectively Northampton and Dauphin; the former to

consist of parts of Milford and Lehigh circuits; the latter to comprise parts of Lebanon and Lancaster circuits. Pinegrove station was annexed to Lebanon Cir.

APPOINTMENTS.

PHILADELPHIA DISTRICT—*H. Fisher*, P. E.
Philadelphia Sta.—D. Berger.
Milford Cir.—J. C. Farnsworth and W. L. Reber.
Northampton Cir.—C. Hummel and G. C. Schmidt.
Lehigh Cir.—F. Hoffman.
Monroe Cir.—G. T. Haines.
Womelsdorf Cir.—F. Danner and F. Scharfe.
New York Miss.—M. F. Maize.
Germantown Miss.—F. Krecker.
Reading Miss.—J. M. Saylor.

HARRISBURG DISTRICT—*H. Bucks*, P. E.
Lancaster Cir.—John Sensel and Abr. Shultz.
Lebanon Cir.—S. Neitz and J. G. Bush.

Dauphin Cir.—Jacob Saylor and T. Steck.
Lykens Cir.—J. Kramer and E. Bast.
Pottsville Sta.—W. Heim.
Schuylkill Haven Sta.—C. Meyers.
Orwigsburg Cir.—J. P. Leib.

MOHAWK DISTRICT—*W. Mintz*, P. E.
Mohawk Cir.—S. Miesse and Mich. Sindlinger.
Jefferson Cir.—M. Eis.
Lake Cir.—G. Ramige and J. Raus.
Syracuse Miss.—Jacob Riegel.

NIAGARA DISTRICT—*M. Lehn*, P. E.
Dansville Cir.—J. Dareich.
Buffalo Cir.—D. Fisher.
Buffalo Sta.—J. Burkert.
Black Creek Cir.—T. Schneider.
Waterloo Cir.—J. Kehr and M. Lauer.

1845.

The Sixth (38th) Annual Session.

President, Bishop J. Long.
Secretary, William Mintz.
Assistant Secretaries, F. Danner and F. Krecker.

The members of Conference assembled in the Immanuel Church, Philadelphia, Pa., February 26th, 1845. M. Edel resigned his license as local preacher. Jacob Saylor located on account of family concerns. A preacher was deposed from the ministry for unchristian conduct. Daniel Focht, a local preacher, died during the year. The following committees were appointed: On Finance,—J. M. Saylor, M. F. Maize, and W. Mintz; On Books,—J. P. Leib and J. M. Saylor.

The following business rules were adopted: 1st, The members of the Conference shall retain the seats, chosen at the opening of the session, during the entire session. 2d, Any one wishing to speak shall rise. In case more than one should address the Chair at the same time, the Bishop shall decide who is entitled to speak. 3d, No one shall be interrupted while speaking, except in case of a misapprehension of the subject before Conference, or in case he presents anything out of order, and then only when so decided by the president or by a majority of the members of Conference. 4th, All remarks concerning others shall be made in the spirit of brotherly love.

Elders' orders were granted to Jacob Dareich and Samuel Miesse; Deacons' orders to W. L. Reber, G. C. Schmidt, F. Scharfe, Theobald Schneider, E. Bast, and D. W. Krissinger. Reuben Deisher and Christophel Yeakel were newly received on trial. The following were received into the itinerancy: J. G. Marquardt, J. Eckert, D. Wieand, and C. Holl. The Conference ordered the preachers in charge to procure suitable class-books in which the quarterly contributions for the preacher's salary are to be recorded, the money to be paid to the preacher at each Quarterly Conference. The book committee was instructed to print English and German marriage certificates, and to have the large and the small alphabet and the a, b, abs printed on card boards. The preachers were instructed to organize missionary auxiliaries at each appointment.

BOUNDARIES.

Pinegrove and the upper portion of Dauphin Cir.

were formed into Dauphin Cir. Germantown Miss. and the lower portions of Milford and Northampton circuits were organized into Germantown Cir. Orwigsburg Cir. and Schuylkill Haven Sta. were formed into Schuylkill Cir. Lykens Cir. was divided into two circuits, the one to retain the name of Lykens and the other to be called Mahantongo. Millerstown, Kutztown, and Hefners were added to Milford Cir. A mission was located in Albany, N. Y.

CHURCH AFFAIRS.

The brethren H. Fisher and J. M. Saylor were instructed to act according to their discretion with reference to the completion of the church building in the city of Reading, Pa.

APPOINTMENTS.

PHILADELPHIA DISTRICT — *Henry Fisher, P. E.*
Philadelphia Sta.—D. Berger.
Germantown Cir.—C. Meyers and J. Eckert.
Milford Cir.—J. Farnsworth and G. C. Smith.
Northampton Cir.—E. Bast and A. Shultz.
Lehigh Cir.—F. Hoffman.
Monroe Cir.—C. Hummel.
Womelsdorf Cir.—F. Danner, T. Steck.
New York Miss.—M. F. Maize.
Reading Miss.—J. M. Saylor.

HARRISBURG DISTRICT—*Henry Bucks, P. E.*
Lancaster Cir.—W. L. Reber and C. Holl.
Lebanon Cir. — J. P. Leib and D. Wieand.
Dauphin Cir.—F. Krecker.

Lykens Cir.—J. Kramer and M. Sindlinger.
Mahantongo Cir.—J. Sensel.
Pottsville Sta.—Wm. Heim.
Schuylkill Cir.—Geo. T. Haines and F. Scharfe.

MOHAWK DISTRICT—*Wm. Mintz, P. E.*
Mohawk Cir.—S. Miesse and M. Lauer.
Jefferson Cir.—M. Eis.
Lake Cir.—G. Ramige and Jac. Burkhart.
Syracuse Miss.—Jac. Riegel.
Albany Miss.—J. G. Marquardt.

NIAGARA DISTRICT—*M. Lehn, P. E.*
Dansville Cir.—T. Schneider.
Buffalo Cir.—D. Fisher.
Buffalo Sta.—S. Neitz.
Black Creek Cir.—J. Dareich.
Waterloo Cir. — J. Kehr and J. G. Bosch.

1846.

The Seventh (39th) Annual Session.

President, Bishop John Seybert.
Secretary, Frederick Danner.
Assistant Secretaries, F. Krecker and C. Hummel.

The session of 1846 was opened on February 25th, in the Evangelical meeting-house at Schuylkill Haven, Pa. The following additional business rules were adopted: 1st, During the daily sessions all private business and conversations are strictly prohibited. 2d, No person shall be allowed to speak more than twice upon the same subject without permission from the president.

A local preacher was relieved of his office on account of imbecility. G. C. Schmidt located on account of bodily infirmities. Jacob Burkhart withdrew from the Conference in order to connect himself with the Ohio Conference. H. Fisher was re-elected, and J. M. Saylor newly elected to the office of Presiding Elder. J. Burkhart, J. C. Farnsworth, and D. Fisher were ordained Elders; M. Lauer, A. Shultz, J. G. Bosch, J. Eckert, and J. G. Marquardt, Deacons. The following were newly received on trial: Franklin Dotterer, John Koehl, Jacob Gross, and Philip Miller. The brethren, F. Dotterer, R. Deisher, J. Koehl, Jacob Gross, and P. Miller were received into the itinerancy. The conference claimants were: J. Schnerr, W. Heim, and the family of C. Hesser.

The following committees were appointed: On Finance,—J. M. Saylor, M. F. Maize, and F. Danner; On Books,—H. Fisher and H. Bucks; Examiners,—W. Mintz, H. Fisher, and H. Bucks.

It was resolved that this Conference recognizes the work of the American Tract Society as universally useful. Each preacher in charge was instructed to report at the next session the number of Sunday-schools, teachers, scholars, and the volumes in the Sunday-school libraries, on his field of labor. The Conference granted the Sunday-school of the Albany (N. Y.) Mission a donation of twenty dollars for the purchase of books. It was resolved that in case charges be preferred against a preacher at Conference, it shall be done in his presence.

The Conference decided that the interest money accruing from the Custer bequest is to be distributed among the superannuated preachers and their families residing in Pennsylvania. It was also resolved that the conference collection taken on each charge at the close of the year is to be added to the general contributions for salary, and that the expense of feeding the preachers' horses during each annual session shall be added to the traveling expenses for the ensuing year.

The first Monday after Whitsuntide was appointed as a day of prayer and fasting throughout the bounds of the Conference.

BOUNDARIES.

Philadelphia and Harrisburg districts were divided into three, to be known as the Philadelphia, Lebanon, and Orwigsburg districts. A mission was located in the city of Lancaster. The name of Monroe Cir. was changed to Carbon. Pinegrove and vicinity were taken from Dauphin Cir. and formed into a separate field.

PHILADELPHIA DISTRICT—*J. M. Saylor*, *P. E.*
Philadelphia Sta.—F. Hoffman.
Germantown Cir.—J. C. Farnsworth and D. Wieand.
Northampton Cir.—E. Bast and F. Dotterer.
Milford Cir.—C. Holl and J. Koehl.
Lehigh Cir.—J. Kramer.
New York Miss.—C. Meyers.

LEBANON DISTRICT—*Henry Bucks*, *P. E.*
Lebanon Cir.—G. T. Haines and M. Lauer.
Lancaster Cir. — F. Danner and M. Sindlinger.
Dauphin Cir.—T. Steck.
Womelsdorf Cir.—A. Shultz.
Reading Miss.—D. Berger.
Lancaster Miss.—W. L. Reber.

ORWIGSBURG DISTRICT—*H. Fisher*, *P. E.*

Schuylkill Cir.—M. F. Maize and R. Deisher.
Lykens Cir —J. Sensel and F. Scharfe.
Mahantongo Cir.—J. G. Bosch.
Pottsville Sta.—J. P. Leib.
Pinegrove Cir.—F. Krecker.
Carbon Cir.—C. Hummel.

MOHAWK DISTRICT—*Wm. Mintz*, *P. E.*
Mohawk Cir.—M. Eis and J. Eckert.
Jefferson Cir.—J. Kehr.
Lake Cir.—Jacob Riegel and P. Miller.
Syracuse Miss.—Samuel Miesse.
Albany Miss.—J. G. Marquardt.

NIAGARA DISTRICT—*M. Lehn*, *P. E.*
Dansville Cir.—G. Ramige.
Buffalo Cir.—T. Schneider.
Buffalo Sta.—S. Neitz.
Black Creek Cir.—J. Dareich.
Waterloo Cir. — D. Fisher and Jacob Gross.

1847.

The Eighth (40th) Annual Session.

President, Bishop Joseph Long.
Secretary, Francis Hoffman.
Assistant Secretaries, F. Krecker and S. Neitz.

The eighth annual session of the East Pennsylvania Conference was opened in our Evangelical meeting-house in Fayette Twp., Seneca Co., N. Y., on Feb. 23d, 1847, and continued until Wednesday, Mar. 3d. The following committees were appointed: On Worship,—W. Mintz, J. Riegel, and H. Fisher; On Finance,—J. M. Saylor, F. Danner, and M. Lehn; On Conference Claimants,—H. Bucks, H. Fisher, and J. M. Saylor; On Books,—H. Fisher and H. Bucks.

A preacher on trial and a local preacher were deposed from the ministry and expelled from the Association for unchristian conduct. Philip Miller located on account of bodily infirmities. J. P. Leib took a superannuated relation. Wm. Mintz and M. Lehn were re-elected and Jacob Riegel, newly elected to the office of Presiding Elder. Elders' orders were granted to E. Bast, F. Scharfe, T. Schneider, and W. L. Reber; Deacons' orders, to D. Wieand and Joseph Gross. The following were newly received as preachers on trial: Cornelius Loos, Jacob Adams, Levi Jacoby, and Jacob Wagner. The brethren, L. Jacoby, J. Wagner, C. Loos, J. Adams, S. Gaumer, and Jos. Gross were received into the itinerancy. The superannuated preachers were J. Schnerr and J. P. Leib; widow and orphans, Sister Hesser and children.

Bishop Long, H. Fisher, and F. Hoffman were appointed to prepare a resolution with reference to secret societies. They reported the following, which was adopted:

Resolved, That we recommend to General Conference the enactment of a law forbidding any preacher or lay member to join a secret society. By secret societies we mean all sworn associations which bind themselves by an oath and have secret signs by which the members recognize each other. Futhermore, this Conference advises all our preachers and members not to unite with any society in which it becomes necessary to mingle with worldly associations and to take part in meaningless and senseless mummeries. Such associations are contrary to the Word of God, causing great offence and proving dangerous to a christian.

The following were elected delegates to the General Conference: W. Mintz, H. Bucks, Jacob Riegel, M. Lehn, H. Fisher, J. M. Saylor, F. Danner, F. Hoffman, J. Kehr, M. Eis, D. Fisher, and J. P. Leib. The alternates were: C. Hummel, J. Kramer, and F. Krecker. The second Friday in September was appointed as a day of fasting and prayer throughout the bounds of the Conference.

BOUNDARIES.

Mohawk and Niagara districts were divided into three districts to be known respectively as Canada, Buffalo, and Albany districts. A part of Northampton Cir. was added to Lehigh and a part of Carbon Cir. to Northampton. Dauphin Cir. was annexed to Lebanon Cir. Reading Miss. was discontinued; Berne and vicinity were annexed and the entire field called Reading Cir. Orwigsburg and Schuylkill Haven were formed into two separate circuits. Pottsville was made a station, and Pinegrove Cir. was annexed to Mahantongo Cir., the whole to be known as Pinegrove Cir. A part of Waterloo Cir. was organized into Home Cir.

APPOINTMENTS.

PHILADELPHIA DISTRICT—*J. M. Saylor*, P. E.
Philadelphia Sta.—F. Hoffman.
Germantown Cir. — E. Bast and S. Gaumer.
Northampton Cir. — J. C. Farnsworth and Joseph Gross.
Lehigh Cir. —J. Kramer and D. Wieand.
Milford Cir.—C. Holl and C. Loos.
New York Miss.—C. Meyers.

LEBANON DISTRICT—*Henry Bucks*, P. E.
Lebanon Cir. — C. Hummel and R. Deisher.

Lancaster Cir. — F. Danner and J. Koehl.
Womelsdorf Cir. — A. Shultz and M. Sindlinger.
Reading Cir.—D. Berger.
Lancaster Miss.—J. Eckert.

ORWIGSBURG DISTRICT—*H. Fisher*, P.E.
Orwigsburg Cir.—W. L. Reber.
Schuylkill Cir.—M. F. Maize.
Pottsville Sta.—S. Neitz.
Lykens Cir.—J. Sensel and Wm. Helm.
Pinegrove Cir.—G. T. Haines and J. Adams.
Carbon Cir.—F. Krecker.

CANADA DISTRICT—*Mich. Lehn, P. E.*
Black Creek Cir.—J. G. Bosch.
Waterloo Cir.—D. Fisher.
Home Cir.—T. Schneider.

BUFFALO DISTRICT—*Wm. Mintz, P. E.*
Buffalo Sta.—M. Eis.
Buffalo Cir.—F. Scharfe and J. Wagner.
Dansville Cir.—J. Dareich.

Lake Cir.—S. Miesse and L. Jacoby.

ALBANY DISTRICT—*Jacob Riegel, P. E.*
Mohawk Cir.—G. Ramige and Jacob Gross.
Jefferson Cir.—J. Kehr.
Syracuse Sta.—J. G. Marquardt.
Albany Miss.—M. Lauer.

1847.

The General Conference.

Presidents, Bishops J. Seybert and J. Long.
Secretary, W. W. Orwig.
Assistant Secretaries, F. Hoffman, J. G. Zinser, and A. B. Shaeffer.

The regular quadrennial session of the General Conference* was held in our Evangelical meeting-house at New Berlin, Union Co., Pa. The session began on Wednesday, the twenty-ninth day of September, 1847. Both bishops and forty-five delegates were present. These delegates represented the East Pa., the West Pa., the Ohio, and the Illinois conferences. Charges were preferred against two delegates for living at variance with each other, and for misconduct in office. After spending nearly five days in an investigation, the Conference reproved them for their unpeaceful conduct, deprived them of their rights as delegates, and disqualified them for re-election to office at this session. The Conference also required of them that they become reconciled, amend their conduct and live peaceably hereafter. The vacant seats were then filled by the appoint-

---

*See Preface on page 98.

ment of two other brethren as delegates. It was
resolved that hereafter the vote be taken *viva voce*—aye
and no—instead of by a rising vote as has been the
general custom in our conferences in the past.

Inasmuch as the recommendation with reference to
secret societies was not presented to the General Conference in accordance with the directions of the Church
Discipline, it was not received. It was resolved that
the bishops shall be chosen from among the delegates
elected to the General Conference, and that they shall
always be eligible for re-election. Upon the recommendation of the West Penna. Conference it was
resolved that an English religious periodical be published as soon as possible. P. Wagner, J. Dreisbach,
J. Seybert, J. Long, C. Hammer, and J. M. Saylor
having been appointed a committee to designate the
name and conditions of this periodical, they recommended among other things that it be called *The Evangelical Messenger*.

The committee on statistics reported the total number
of preachers in the Evangelical Association as 319, the
total membership, 14,871. All that part of the East
Pa. Conference contained in the State of New York,
with the exception of New York City, and in Canada
was organized into a new conference district, to be called
"*The New York Conference.*" The Susquehanna
River with its northern branch as far as the boundary
line of the State of New York was adopted as the western and northern boundary of the East Pa. Conference.
In accordance with this, Luzerne Mission of the West
Pa. Conference, but lying east of the north branch, was
transferred to the East Pa. Conference.

Joseph Long and John Seybert were re-elected bishops of the Evangelical Association. N. Gehr was elected editor of the book establishment and H. Fisher general book agent. W. Bersch was appointed assistant editor. J. P. Leib was appointed to serve as presiding elder in the place of H. Fisher until the next annual session of the East Pa. Conference. The Conference adopted a resolution urging every preacher in charge to make diligent efforts to establish Sunday-schools wherever practicable.

1848.

The Ninth (41st) *Annual Session.*

President, Bishop John Seybert.
Secretary, Frederick Danner.
Assistant Secretaries, F. Krecker and S. Neitz.

The annual session of 1848 was held in the Evangelical meeting-house at Allentown, Pa., beginning Feb. 23d and closing March 1st. The following committees were appointed: Worship,—Bishop Seybert, J. M. Saylor, J. Kramer, J. P. Leib, and W. Mintz; Examiners,—W. Mintz, H. Fisher, H. Bucks, J. M. Saylor, and J. Riegel.

The action of the Quarterly Conference on a certain circuit in deposing a local preacher from the office of the ministry was approved. J. Kramer, Chr. Holl, Sam'l Miesse, G. Ramige, and J. C. Reisner located on account of temporal circumstances. Jacob Riegel located on account of bodily infirmities. Emanuel Dieder and Charles Bisse died. F. Hoffman and J. P. Leib were newly elected to the office of Presiding

Elder, after which the presiding elders were stationed. J. G. Bosch, J. Eckert, A. Shultz, J. G. Marquardt, and M. Lauer were ordained Elders; J. Koehl, S. Gaumer, Jacob Gross, and J. Adams, Deacons. John Schell, Isaac Hess, Noah McLehn, and Davis Hambright were newly received on trial. The following were received into the itinerancy: N. McLehn, D. Hambright, J. Schell, and I. Hess. The superannuated preachers were J. Schnerr and Jacob Riegel. The family of Charles Hesser also received support from the Conference.

S. Butz was appointed trustee of the Custer legacy. The New York Conference was released from the missionary debt, and it was ordered that the first meeting of that conference be held on the last Wednesday in April, 1849, in Buffalo, N. Y. Inasmuch as the members of the West Pa. Conference have indicated a desire to have Luzerne Mission remain within their conference bounds therefore resolved that it be left to that conference to supply the mission for the ensuing year.

On Monday forenoon the Conference celebrated the Lord's Supper.

D. Berger, J. C. Farnsworth, and C. Hummel were appointed a committee to prepare laws making the salaries paid by the various charges independent of each other. The committee made the following report, which was adopted:

1st, A committee shall be appointed annually to inquire into the circumstances of the superannuated preachers, and the widows and orphans of deceased ministers, and to determine the amounts which they are to receive. The support is to be derived from that portion of the interest accruing from the Custer legacy to which this Conference is entitled and from the interest of the Charitable Society funds. Should this not be sufficient, the balance is to be taken from the profits of the book establishment. 2d, In case two preachers serve on the same charge, they are to divide the salary according to their disciplinary claims. Should they receive more than such claims, they are to pay the surplus to the presiding elders. 3d, The presiding elders are entitled to the collections taken at the quarterly meetings and to one-half of the collections taken at the campmeetings and at the extra (revival) meetings, appointed by them. 4th, In case a presiding elder receives more than the average amount received by those preachers on his district who are entitled to the highest salaries, he shall pay the surplus into the conference fund. 5th, The bishop was authorized to lift collections at all his appointments, and in case he receives more than his allowance in this Conference to pay the surplus into the conference fund. In the event that he does not receive his allowance in this manner he shall receive the deficit in the same way as the presiding elders. 6th, The balance remaining in the treasury is to be distributed among those who are deficient in salary.

BOUNDARIES.

A part of Lykens Cir. and a part of Lebanon Cir. were formed into a new field, to be called Dauphin Circuit.

CHURCH AFFAIRS.

The presiding elder of Lebanon District and the

9

preacher in charge of Lebanon Circuit were authorized
to deal with the Stumpstown (Fredericksburg) Church
according to their discretion, with this proviso, however, that they shall not be allowed to sell a part of the
church to any other denomination.

Nine charges reported the following Sunday-school
statistics:

	Schools.	Teachers.	Scholars.
Philadelphia Sta.......	1	24	200
Germantown Cir........	2	10	70
Lehigh Cir.............	6	62	263
New York Sta.........	1	19	50
Lancaster Cir..........	1	10	50
Reading Sta...........	1	31	150
Schuylkill Haven Cir....	3	25	200
Pottsville Sta..........	1	10	45
Carbon Cir............	3	20	85
Total...............	19	211	1,113

APPOINTMENTS.

PHILADELPHIA DISTRICT—*F. Hoffman,*
P. E.
Philadelphia Sta.—S. Neitz.
Germantown Cir.—D. Wieand and J.
Schell.
Northampton Cir.—M. Sindlinger and
I. Hess.
Lehigh Cir.—H. Bucks and N. McLehn.
Milford Cir.—J. C. Reisner and C. Loos.
New York Sta.—D. Berger.

LEBANON DISTRICT—*J. P. Leib, P. E.*
Lebanon Cir. — C. Hummel and R.
Deisher.
Lancaster Cir.—A. Shultz and D. Ham-
bright.

Womelsdorf Cir.—C. Meyers and Jos.
Gross.
Reading Sta.—W. Heim.
Dauphin Cir.—J. Sensel.
Lancaster Miss.—F. Danner.

ORWIGSBURG DISTRICT—*J. M. Saylor,*
P. E.
Orwigsburg Cir.—G. T. Haines.
Schuylkill Cir.—E. Bast.
Pottsville Sta.—M. F. Maize.
Pinegrove Cir.—J Farnsworth and J.
Adams.
Lykens Cir. — W. L. Reber and J.
Koehl.
Carbon Cir.—F. Krecker.

THE NEW YORK CONFERENCE.

(Organized at the recent session of the General Conference.)

CANADA DISTRICT—*M. Lehn, P. E.*
Black Creek Cir.—Jacob Gross.
Waterloo Cir. — T. Schneider and J. Wagner.
Home Cir.—To be supplied.
BUFFALO DISTRICT— *W. Mintz, P. E.*
Buffalo Sta.—Mich. Els.
Buffalo Cir.—F. Scharfe and Levi Jacoby.

Lake Cir.—D. Fisher and S. Ganmer.
Dansville Cir.—[Not supplied].

MOHAWK DISTRICT—*Jac. Kehr, P. E.*
Mohawk Cir.—J. G. Bosch.
Jefferson Cir.—J. Darcich.
Syracuse Sta.—J. G. Marquardt.
Albany Miss.—M. Lauer.

1849.

The Tenth (42d) Annual Session.

President, Bishop Joseph Long.

Secretary, Frederick Danner.

Assistant Secretaries, F. Krecker and S. Neitz.

On the seventh of March, 1849, the members of the East Pa. Conference assembled in our Evangelical meeting house at Reading, Pa., and continued in session until March 12th. The following committees were appointed: On Worship,—J. P. Leib, J. M. Saylor, F. Hoffman, and W. Heim; On Finance,—M. F. Maize, W. L. Reber, and J. C. Farnsworth; Examiners,—not named.

An elder was deposed from the ministry for immoral conduct, but was retained as a member of the church for six months on probation. S. Neitz rested one year on account of bodily infirmities. J. Schnerr died during the time of the session. M. Sindlinger and D. Wieand were ordained to the office of Elder; C. Loos to the office of Deacon. F. L. Stoever and D. Shultz were received into the itinerancy. The following received license as local preachers: Lewis Snyder, Fred. L.

Stoever, Henry Kletzinger, and George Knerr. F. L.
Stoever was newly received on trial. The widows and
orphans of deceased preachers are the families of C.
Hesser and J. Schnerr. It was resolved that the presiding elders shall have their full support. In case,
however, they do not obtain their full salary, they are
to receive an equal share with the other preachers.

The General Conference of 1847 having ordered that
the founding of an educational institution in the church
shall be decided by the votes of the people throughout
the Evangelical Association, the vote taken in the East
Pa. Conference resulted in 501 for, and 852 against
such an educational project.

BOUNDARIES.

Harrisburg and a part of Dauphin Cir. were constituted a mission. Tamaqua was made a mission. All
the appointments of Pinegrove Cir. north of the Broad
Mountain were annexed to Mahantongo Cir.

CHURCH AFFAIRS.

It was resolved that contributions be solicited through
the *Chr. Botschafter* for the erection of a church in
Lancaster, Pa. J. P. Leib, D. Berger, Dr. Mellinger,
F. Danner, and Joseph Gross were appointed a committee to superintend the erection of said church.

MEMORIAL.

Jacob Schnerr fell asleep, happy in the Lord, on
Mar. 10th, 1849. For a number of years he labored in
the Master's vineyard with great blessing, and through
his instrumentality many were saved. May his body
rest in peace until the great day of the resurrection!

APPOINTMENTS.

PHILADELPHIA DISTRICT—*F. Hoffman*, P. E.
Philadelphia Sta.—C. Hummel.
Germantown Cir.—F. Krecker and F. L. Stoever.
Milford Cir.—W. L. Reber and N. McLehn.
Lehigh Cir.—H. Bucks and J. Eckert.
Northampton Cir.—D. Wieand and I. Hess.
New York Sta.—C. Loos.

LEBANON DISTRICT—*J. P. Leib*, P. E.
Lebanon Cir.—W. Heim and J. Adams.
Lancaster Cir. -- Jos. Gross and J. Schell.
Chester Cir.—D. Hambright.

Womelsdorf Cir. — J. Sensel and F. Danner.
Reading Sta.—Chas. Meyers.
Lancaster Miss.—D. Berger.
Harrisburg Miss.—Jacob Farnsworth.

ORWIGSBURG DISTRICT—*J. M. Saylor*, P. E.
Orwigsburg Cir.—G. T. Haines.
Schuylkill Cir.—E. Bast.
Pottsville Sta.—M. F. Maize.
*Pinegrove Cir.—To be supplied.
Lykens Cir.—J. Koehl and S. Gaumer.
Carbon Cir.—M. Sindlinger.
Mahautongo Cir.—A. Shultz and Jacob Gross.
Tamaqua Miss.—D. Shultz.

1850.

The Eleventh (43d) Annual Session.

President, Bishop John Seybert.

Secretary, Fred. Danner.

Assistant Secretaries, Henry Bucks and Christian Meyers.

The East Pa. Conference convened in annual session in the Emanuel Church, Philadelphia, Pa., February 27th, 1850. F. Krecker was appointed to record the proceedings in the English language. The business rules of 1845 were adopted.

The following committees were appointed: On Worship,—J. P. Leib J. M. Saylor, F. Hoffman, and

---

*H. Fisher had resigned as general book agent and was appointed to Pinegrove Cir. Inasmuch, however, as the West Penna. Conference found it difficult to supply his place, at the request of the bishop and of that conference he consented to resume the position of book agent.

C. Hummel; On Finance,—M. F. Maize, W. L. Reber,
and E. Bast; To Audit Accounts,—F. Hoffman and M.
Sindlinger.

M. F. Maize and John Eckert received permission to
rest for a period in order to regain their health.   D.
Berger and C. Loos located.   Fred. L. Stoever died
during the past year.   Joseph Gross, S. Gaumer,
Jacob Gross, J. Adams, and J. Koehl were ordained to
the office of Elder.   N. McLehn, D. Hambright, J.
Schell, and Isaac Hess, to the office of Deacon.
A. Ziegenfus received license.   The following were
received into the itinerancy: Henry Bisse, Andrew Ziegenfus, George Knerr, and Reuben Deisher.
The Conference elected F. Danner Presiding Elder.
F. Hoffman was appointed to preach the conference sermon at the opening of the next annual
session.   M. F. Maize, J. P. Leib, D. Saylor, Jacob
Hammer, and John Hammer were appointed a committee to ascertain whether the public buildings at
Orwigsburg, Pa., made vacant by the removal of the
county seat to Pottsville, can be procured for our contemplated institution of learning.   The committee was
instructed to report at the next annual session.

The Conference passed a resolution recommending to
the General Conference the adoption of a law requiring
a six months' probation in the reception of persons into
the church.   Another recommendation to introduce a
law permitting a preacher to locate on account of temporal circumstances was adopted.   The Conference appointed J. M. Saylor, S. Neitz, and C. Hummel to
examine junior preachers in their studies at the next
annual session, the examination to take place on the

Tuesday afternoon previous to the opening of the Conference.

II. Bucks, C. Hummel, and F. Krecker were appointed a committee to prepare resolutions with reference to the establishment of a mission in Germany. They made the following report, which was adopted: *Dear Brethren:*—Inasmuch as we have been permitted, through the gracious Providence of God, to see the middle of the first century of our existence as a Church, and inasmuch as many of our preachers, as well as members, consider themselves debtors to their brethren according to the flesh in the old Fatherland, and have therefore expressed the wish that a mission might be established in Germany, and have also declared a willingness to support such a mission; we believe that God has given us indications that the time has come for us to begin to labor there, especially in view of the fact that the day is probably not far distant when the followers of Rationalism and those holding Orthodox views will hold separate assemblies for worship, and because many of our friends and relatives living in Germany are still found in the path of error. We also have reason to believe that by the establishing of a mission in Germany, and by a more intimate acquaintance with those of Orthodox views, we as a church will become more active and useful in the kingdom of God; therefore be it

Resolved, That we recommend to Conference the following: 1st, That in case the necessary support be forthcoming, and suitable men be found, we as a Conference favor the establishing of a mission in Germany; 2d, That we request our sister conferences to co-operate with us in carrying out this undertaking, in the following manner: (*a*), That each of the Annual Conferences choose one man, and these men chosen by the different conferences, together with the bishops, shall constitute a board which shall make all necessary arrangements for the establishment of a mission in case it be found practicable; (*b*,) That as soon as the bishops consider the carrying out of the project feasible, subscriptions shall be opened in our church periodicals, and money received for said object; (*c*,) That each preacher in charge is hereby authorized to receive money for this purpose and forward the same to the Treasurer of our Parent Missionary Society. Upon the adoption of the above report J. P. Leib was elected to represent this Conference in the afore-mentioned board. The Conference ordered that the present year be observed as a year of jubilee in the churches, and appointed M. F. Maize, F. Krecker, and W. L. Reber a committee to draft a plan. The committee reported the following which was adopted:

Beloved Brethren! Inasmuch as the present year closes the first half of the first century of the Evangelical Association, and inasmuch as the Lord has so richly blessed the church throughout and has, in spite of all opposition, enlarged her borders and multiplied her numbers, therefore, this Conference recommends to all the preachers and members within its jurisdiction, that the present year be celebrated as a Year of Jubilee and that we render unto the Highest a special praise and thank offering by the general observance of a day of thanksgiving and by voluntary contributions for religious and charitable purposes. We also entertain the hope that our sister conferences will arrange for a similar observance. For the accomplishment of this purpose the committee recommends the following resolutions: 1. That our bishops appoint a day near the middle of October for the contemplated Thanksgiving Day, more especially because JACOB ALBRIGHT, the founder of our Church, entered upon his work as an itinerant preacher in that month of the year 1796. 2. That public worship be held in all the congregations embraced within our conference territory, on the forenoon and evening of said day. To this end the Conference recommends that all itinerant and local preachers officiate at the usual hour in the forenoon, and that in such congregations and classes where there is no preaching, a prayer meeting be held; the same plan to be observed in the evening. 3. That a collection be lifted at each service for the support of our home missions. 4. That each preacher in charge shall on this day open a subscription list—which is to remain open until the end of the year—for the support of the following objects: (a) For the erection and support of three mission churches; one on Harrisburg Mission, one on Philadelphia Mission, and for the payment of the debt on the Lancaster church. (b) For the establishment of an academy or institution of learning for the young within the bounds of this Conference.

BOUNDARIES.

Tamaqua Mission was discontinued. A new mission was located in southern Philadelphia, to be known as Southwark Mission. Bethlehem was taken from Lehigh Cir. and annexed to Northampton Cir.

It was resolved to erect a church at the grave of Jacob Albright, the sainted founder of the Evangelical Association, the building to be 40 ft. by 60 ft. in size and to consist of two stories. The Conference ordered that the church be known as *The Albright Church, erected in the fiftieth year of the Evangelical Association in memory of the sainted Jacob Albright, founder of the Evangelical Association of North America.* J. P. Leib, J. M. Saylor, and F. Danner were appointed to superintend the erection of the building.

The preacher in charge of Lancaster Mission was instructed to endeavor to carry out the plan adopted at the last annual session for the liquidation of the church debt there.

APPOINTMENTS.

PHILADELPHIA DISTRICT—*F. Hoffman,* P. E.
Philadelphia Sta.—C. Hummel.
Philadelphia Miss.—Wm. Heim.
Germantown Cir.—F. Krecker and A. Ziegenfus.
Milford Cir.—I. Hess and N. McLean.
Lehigh Cir.—M. Sindlinger.
Northampton Cir.—H. Bucks.
New York Sta.—J. Koehl.

LEBANON DISTRICT—*F. Danner,* P. E.
Lebanon Cir. — A. Schultz and J. Adams.
Lancaster Cir.—S. Gaumer and G. Knerr.
Chester Cir.—D. Hambright.

Womelsdorf Cir.—D. Wieand and J. Sensel.
Reading Sta.—J. M. Saylor.
Lancaster Miss.—W. L. Reber.
Harrisburg Miss.—J. C. Farnsworth.

ORWIGSBURG DISTRICT — *J. P. Leib,* P. E.
Orwigsburg Cir.—E. Bast.
Schuylkill Haven Cir.—C. Meyers.
Pottsville Sta.—S. Neitz.
Pinegrove Cir.—J. Schell.
Lykens Cir.—Joseph Gross and R. Deisher.
Mahantongo Cir.—Jacob Gross and H. Bisse.
Carbon Cir.—G. T. Halnes.

— — — — —

1851.

The Twelfth (44th) Annual Session.

President, Bishop J. Long.

Secretary, Fred. Krecker.

Assistant Secretaries, Henry Bucks and Chr. Hummel.

The annual session of 1851 was held in the Evangelical church at Schuylkill Haven, Pa., February 26th, and continued until Wednesday, March 5th, Bishop J. Long presiding. In accordance with a resolution passed at the last session, F. Hoffman preached the conference sermon in the forenoon of the first day, taking for his text I Pet. v: 1-4. W. L. Reber was appointed to record and read the proceedings in the English language. The following committees were appointed: On Worship,—J. P. Leib, F. Hoffman, F. Danner, and C. Meyers; On Finance,—M. F. Maize, G. T. Haines, and E. Bast; On Letters,—J. P. Leib, F. Hoffman, and F. Danner. A local preacher was deposed from the ministry and expelled from the church. John Sensel located on account of bodily infirmities. David Shultz died during the past year. M. F. Maize was retained in the itinerancy with permission to rest. J. G. Marquardt was received into the Conference with the proviso that if the Board of Foreign Missions should send him to Germany he be released from his Conference relation. Jesse Young and G. J. Miller received license as preachers on trial. The following were received into the itinerancy: Samuel G. Rhoads, Christian Gingrich, Lewis Snyder, Jesse Young, and Nicholas Goebel. The brethren W. Garret and H. Bisse were ordained Deacons. The contributions during the Year of Jubilee were as follows: For the Philadelphia Mission church, $187.21; Lancaster church, $117.99; Harrisburg Mission church, $15.79; Home Missions, $100.

The Conference resolved that when an unmarried

preacher, who has traveled four or more years, receives an appointment without giving the brethren under whose supervision he travels due notice of his intention to get married, he shall not receive support for his wife during that year. The presiding elders were re-appointed to their former districts. Brother Daniel Griebel having donated one hundred dollars to the Conference for the missionary cause a resolution of hearty appreciation was tendered him. The Conference agreed to give to the bishops a reasonable allowance for traveling expenses in addition to their salaries. J. M. Saylor and J. P. Leib were appointed a committee to examine all manuscripts offered for publication. The Bishop was instructed to appoint a committee of examiners and to assign to each the particular department of knowledge in which he is to examine junior preachers. He appointed the following: J. M. Saylor for theology and Bible reading; J. P. Leib, church discipline; F. Krecker, grammar and rhetoric; and S. Neitz, church history, secular history, and geography. It was resolved that no preacher who does not reside upon his field of labor shall be allowed to receive house rent from his circuit or district except by special permission from the Conference. The Conference requested of F. Hoffman the manuscript of his conference sermon for publication. S. Neitz was appointed to preach the conference sermon at the next session.

The following recommendations to General Conference were considered and acted upon: 1. To give the bishops authority to transfer a preacher from one conference to another provided the preacher himself, his presiding elder, and the presiding elders of the conference to which he is to be transferred are all agreed ; 17 yeas, 16 noes.   2. That class leaders be elected only once in two years; 27 yeas, 2 noes.   3. To introduce a system of six months' probation in the reception of members into the church, except in such cases where preachers and congregations deem it more advisable to receive persons as members in full; 26 yeas, 3 noes. 4. That such persons who have never been baptized in the name of the Triune God, shall be baptized at the time when they are received into full membership; 22 yeas, 7 noes.   5. A paragraph concerning secret societies ; 2 yeas, 27 noes.   6. To grant to a preacher the privilege of locating on account of temporal circumstances; Unanimously no.   7. That our first Article of Faith, with reference to the Trinity shall reappear in its first form as in A. D. 1809; 28 yeas, 1 no.   8. To appoint three stewards on each circuit and station, whose duty it shall be to administer the temporal affairs of the charge with reference to the salary of the preacher ; 7 yeas, 26 noes.

The following were elected delegates to the General Conference : J. P. Leib, F. Hoffman, S. Neitz, F. Danner, J. M. Saylor, C. Hummel, F. Krecker, M. F. Maize, H. Bucks, and C. Meyers ; alternates, W. L. Reber, G. T. Haines, and J. C. Farnsworth. The preachers were instructed to lift collections on all fields of labor to defray the traveling expenses of the delegates.

BOUNDARIES.

Germantown was taken from Germantown Cir. provided the stationing committee can find a man willing to serve for the salary he will receive there. A new mis-

sion was located in the State of Maryland, to be called
Cecil Mission. A mission was located in the State of
New Jersey, to be known as New Jersey Mission.

CHURCH AFFAIRS.

E. Bast was appointed treasurer of the moneys collected for the erection of churches upon Philadelphia
and Harrisburg districts and also of the money received
for an institution of learning. Thomas Scip presented a
claim of $2,500.00 against the Albright church, where-
upon the Conference appointed a committee consisting
of J. M. Saylor, M. F. Maize and A. Shultz with instructions to borrow the sum of $800.00 toward the
payment of this claim; J. M. Saylor to act as treasurer of the money collected for the church. It was
resolved that during the month of May next every
member of the church within the bounds of this Conference shall be asked to contribute toward the liquidation of this debt. Thomas Scip having sustained a
serious financial misfortune during the building of the
church on account of a heavy rain storm, the Conference allowed him an extra compensation of $300.00.

APPOINTMENTS.

PHILADELPHIA DISTRICT—*F. Hoffman*,
  P. E.
Philadelphia Sta.—S. Neitz.
Philadelphia Miss.—J. G. Marquardt
Germantown Sta.—J. Eckhart.
Germantown Cir.—M. Sindlinger and
  C. Gingrich.
Milford Cir.—A. Schultz and I. Hess.
Lehigh Cir.—C Hummel and N. Goebel.
Northampton Cir.—H. Bucks and A.
  Ziegenfus.
New York Sta.—J. Koehl.
New Jersey Miss.—F. Krecker.

LEBANON DISTRICT—*F. Danner*, P. E.
Lebanon Cir. — C. Meyers and S. G.
  Rhoads.
Lancaster Cir. — N. McLean and G
  Knerr.
Womelsdorf Cir.—D. Wieand and J.
  Adams.
Chester Cir.—L. Schneider.
Reading Sta.—J. M. Saylor.
Lancaster Miss.—W. L. Reber.
Harrisburg Miss.—Jacob Gross.
Cecil Miss.—D. Hambright.

ORWIGSBURG DISTRICT—*J. P. Leib, P.E.*
Orwigsburg Cir. — E. Bast and R.
  Deisher.
Schuylkill Haven Cir.—U. Bisse.
Pottsville Sta.—Jos. Gross.
Pinegrove Sta.—J. Schell.

Lykens Cir. — J. C. Farnsworth and
  Jesse Young.
Mahantongo Cir. — W. Heim and S.
  Gaumer.
Carbon Cir.—G. T. Haines,

1851.

The General Conference.

Presidents, Bishops J. Seybert and J. Long.
Secretary, Henry Bucks.
Assistant Secretaries, J. Boas, C. G. Koch, W. Mintz,
and J. J. Esher.

The members of General Conference assembled in
our Evangelical meeting-house near Flat Rock, Ohio,
on Wednesday, Sept. 17th, 1851. Both bishops and
fifty-five delegates were in attendance. The conduct
of the delegates was investigated; no charges were preferred.

Permission was given to preachers and congregations
to introduce a system of six months' probation in the
reception of members wherever such a course is considered more beneficial. The removal of our book
establishment from New Berlin to a more suitable place
became a subject of considerable discussion at this session. It was finally decided that the removal shall take
place, provided the cost of the new property does not
exceed $12,000.00 and that three-fourths of this amount
is secured by reliable subscriptions prior to the change.
Cleveland, Philadelphia, Harrisburg, Pittsburg, and
New Berlin were nominated as suitable places. The
result of the ballot was the selection of Cleveland, O.,

by a majority of five votes. The Conference ordered that subscription lists be opened in the church periodicals and that the presiding elders and preachers in charge throughout the church be authorized to solicit contributions in order to secure the stipulated amount.

The Association numbered 195 traveling preachers, 185 local preachers, and 21,179 members. The following officers were elected: Bishops, John Seybert and Joseph Long; editor of the *Christliche Botschafter*, and general book agent, W. W. Orwig; assistant editor, J. G. Zinser; editor of the *Evangelical Messenger*, H. Fisher. John Nicolai was appointed missionary to Germany. A new conference was formed and called *The Pittsburg Conference*.

1852.

The Thirteenth (45th) Annual Session.

President, Bishop John Seybert.
Secretary, Abraham Schultz.
Assistant Secretary, Christian Meyers.

The East Pa. Conference met in annual session at Pinegrove, Schuylkill Co., Pa., February 25th, 1852. On the forenoon of the first day S. Neitz preached the conference sermon from Matt. IV: 17. In the afternoon the Bishop opened the Conference in the usual manner. The following committees were appointed: On Worship,—The Bishop, the presiding elders, and the preacher in charge of the circuit; On Finance,—M. F. Maize, J. C. Farnsworth, and F. Danner; On

Letters,—J. M. Saylor, C. Hummel, J. P. Leib, J. Gross, and F. Hoffman. On account of the serious illness of his wife, F. Danner resigned the office of Presiding Elder and took no appointment, the Conference granting him the necessary time to take care of his household. M. F. Maize was permitted to rest. Jesse Young received permission to attend school one year. N. McLean located in order to go West. John Rippley, a local preacher, died during the past year. F. Hoffman and J. P. Leib were re-elected, and G. T. Haines was newly elected to the office of Presiding Elder. N. McLean, I. Hess and J. Schell were ordained Elders; A. Ziegenfus, L. Snyder, George Knerr, S. G. Rhoads, and C. Gingrich, Deacons. The following were newly received on trial: Jesse L. Fritz, Ephraim Ely, Wm. Rogers, Adam Hinkel, and Abraham Saylor. C. Loos, H. C. Major, and E. Ely were received into the itinerancy. F. Danner was made an advisory member of the stationing committee.

The preachers were ordered to give catechetical instructions wherever practicable. A committee of five was appointed to inquire whether those preachers who make application for support from the Conference have done their duty in gathering funds for this purpose, and in case any are found guilty of neglect to report them. W. L. Reber was appointed agent to collect for the liquidation of the debt resting upon the Albright church, and I. Hess, treasurer.

BOUNDARIES.

A committee, consisting of the three presiding elders, the treasurer, and the secretary of the Missionary So-

10

ciety, was appointed to locate an English mission in the
city of Philadelphia, if practicable. Cecil Mission was
discontinued and incorporated in Chester Cir. New
Jersey Miss. was changed to a circuit, but not being
able to support its preacher it received an allowance of
$60.00 from the missionary treasury. Chester Circuit
also received $125.00 out of the missionary funds. The
congregation at Stumpstown (Fredericksburgh), Lebanon
Co., Pa., was advised not to sell any part of their
church property to another denomination, but to conduct affairs under the present management until our
next annual session.

TEMPERANCE.

Whereas, We as a Conference believe the abuse of
spirituous drinks to be a great evil in our nation; therefore *Resolved*, That J. C. Farnsworth, M. F. Maize,
and W. L. Reber be a committee to prepare a suitable
petition, to be signed by the members of this Conference,
and addressed to the present session of the legislature,
praying for a reconsideration of our present license
system and for the introduction of the Maine law in its
stead. The committee made the following report,
which was adopted: *Inasmuch* as efforts are being
made in our legislature to enact a law prohibiting throughout the entire State the sale of intoxicating liquors as a
beverage; therefore *Resolved*, 1st, That we consider
it to be the duty of all Christian ministers and citizens
to testify against the great evil of intemperance and to
combine for its utter extermination; 2d, That in the
judgment of this Conference the only effectual method
for its extermination is the adoption and execution in our

State of the Maine law, and that we will recommend it to our congregations and encourage them to petition our legislature for this purpose as soon as possible.

APPOINTMENTS.

PHILADELPHIA DISTRICT—*G. T. Haines, P. E.*
Philadelphia Sta.—S. Neitz.
Philadelphia Miss.—J. Koehl.
Germantown Sta.—J. Eckert.
Germantown Cir.—Jos. Gross and M. Sindlinger.
Milford Cir.—H. Bucks and A. Schultz.
Lehigh Cir.—C. Hummel and Jacob Gross.
Northampton Cir.—F. Krecker and E. Ely.
New York Sta.—J. G. Marquardt.
New Jersey Cir.—C. Gingrich and H. Major.

LEBANON DISTRICT—*F. Hoffman, P. E.*
Lebanon Cir.—C. Meyers and A. Ziegenfus.

Lancaster Cir.—F. Danner and D Wieand.
Womelsdorf Cir.—J. Adams and I. Hess.
Chester Cir.—L. Schneider and D. Hambright.
Reading Sta.—J. C. Farnsworth.
Lancaster Miss.—R. Deisher.
Harrisburg Cir.—H. Bisse.

ORWIGSBURG DISTRICT—*J. P. Leib, P. E.*
Orwigsburg Cir.—S. G. Rhoads.
Schuylkill Haven Cir.—J. Schell.
Pottsville Sta.—E. Bast.
Pinegrove Cir.—J. M. Saylor.
Lykens Cir.—W. Heim and N. Goebel.
Mahantongo Cir.—C. Loos and S. Gaumer.
Carbon Cir.—G. Knerr.

1853.

The Fourteenth (46th) Annual Session.

President, Bishop J. Long.
German Secretary, Henry Bucks.
English Secretary, Frederick Krecker.
Assistant Secretaries, Chr. Hummel, John Schell, and W. L. Reber.

The Conference of 1853 convened in Salem church, Reading, Pa., on Wednesday, February 23d. The following committees were appointed: On Worship,— The Bishop, the presiding elders, and the preacher in charge of Reading Sta.; On Letters,—F. Hoffman, J.

P. Leib, G. T. Haines, S. Neitz, and A. Schultz; On
Finance,—A. Schultz, 1. Hess, and M. F. Maize; To
Audit Accounts,—A. Schultz, W. Heim, and E. Bast.
The following were retained in the itinerancy without
an appointment: M. F. Maize for one year in order to
rest; F. Danner one year on account of family affairs;
and J. Adams six months on account of temporal con-
cerns. Credentials were granted to Jesse Young. John
Sensel died during the past year. C. Loos and R. Deisher
were ordained Elders; H. C. Major and N. Goebel,
Deacons. The following received license as preachers
on trial: Peter V. Platz, Theophilus G. Clewell, Wm.
Yost, Zachariah Hornberger, Simon P. Reinoehl, Levi
Kelly, and Henry Koester. The following were received into the itinerancy: D. Berger, Jesse Yeakel,
T. G. Clewell, W. Yost, S. P. Reinoehl, L. Kelly, and
F. P. Lehr. The Conference organized itself into a
Missionary Society. S. Neitz, F. Krecker, and C.
Hummel were appointed a committee to draft appropriate resolutions. Their report, which is as follows,
was adopted: WHEREAS, This Conference feels assured
that speedy measures will be adopted by the Evangelical
Association for the establishment of a heathen mission;
therefore; *Resolved*, That all the preachers in charge in
the Conference are authorized to gather funds for such
a mission and to transmit them to the treasurer of our
conference missionary auxiliary, who shall forward
them to the treasurer of the Missionary Society of the
Evangelical Association. On Monday forenoon the
Bishop asked to be excused from further attendance in
order to reach the session of the West Pa. Conference
in proper time. The Conference excused him and

elected J. P. Leib chairman. The examiners appointed at the session of 1851 were continued in office.

BOUNDARIES.

Easton and New Jersey were taken up as a mission, and New Jersey Cir. was called Warren. That part of Northampton Cir. lying north of the Blue Mountain was constituted a separate field of labor and called Monroe Cir. Williams Township was taken from Lehigh Cir. and annexed to Northampton. The northwestern part of Milford Cir. and the northern part of Womelsdorf Cir. were detached and formed into a new field called Kutztown. Lebanon was made a station. A part of Orwigsburg Cir. and an appointment from Carbon Cir. were united into a new field called Schuylkill.

CHURCH AFFAIRS.

W. L. Reber reported having collected $1,094.38 in subscriptions for the Albright church. J. Eckert was appointed agent for the church for the current year, and I. Hess was re-elected treasurer.

H. C. Major, with the assistance of L. Snyder, was authorized to collect money for a meeting house in Hunterdon Co., N. J. The presiding elder of Orwigsburg Dist. and the preacher in charge of Carbon Cir. were authorized to sell the meeting house in Upper Tomensing Twp., Carbon Co., and to apply the proceeds to the erection of another in Roehrig's class.

APPOINTMENTS.

PHILADELPHIA DISTRICT—*G. T. Haines*, P. E.
Philadelphia Sta.—J. M. Saylor.
Philadelphia Miss.—J. Koehl.

Germantown Sta.—M. Sindlinger.
Germantown Cir.—Jos. Gross and J. Yeakel.
Milford Cir.—H. Bucks and S. Gaumer.

Lehigh Cir.—C. Meyers and Jac. Gross.

Northampton Cir.—F. Krecker and Wm. Yost.

Monroe Cir.—C. Gingrich.

Easton Miss.—[To be supplied].

Warren Cir.—Lewis Snyder.

New Jersey Miss.—H. C. Major.

New York Sta.—J. G. Marquardt.

LEBANON DISTRICT—F. Hoffman, P. E.

Lebanon Sta.—D. Berger.

Lebanon Cir.—W. L. Reber and T. G. Clewell.

Harrisburg Cir.—H. Bisse.

Womelsdorf Cir.—C. Hummel and E. Ely.

Lancaster Cir.—D. Wieand and D. Hambright.

Lancaster Miss.—R. Deisher.

Reading Sta.—J. C. Farnsworth.

Kutztown Cir.—I. Hess and S. P. Reinoehl.

Chester Cir.—L. Kelly and F. P. Lehr.

ORWIGSBURG DISTRICT—J. P. Leib, P. E.

Orwigsburg Cir.—S. G. Rhoads.

Schuylkill Haven Cir.—J. Schell.

Pottsville Sta.—E. Bast.

Pinegrove Cir.—S. Neitz.

Lykens Cir.—W. Heim and A. Schultz.

Mahantongo Cir. — C. Loos and N. Goebel.

Carbon Cir.—G. Knerr.

Schuylkill Cir.—A. Ziegenfus.

1854.

The Fifteenth (47th) Annual Session.

President, Bishop J. Seybert.

German Secretary, Henry Bucks.

English Secretary, Frederick Krecker.

Assistant Secretaries, C. Hummel and C. Meyers.

The East Pa. Conference held its regular annual session at Pottsville, Pa., beginning Feb. 22d, 1854. The following committees were appointed : On Worship,— The presiding elders and the preacher in charge of Pottsville ; On Finance,—J. M. Saylor, W. L. Reber, and M. F. Maize ; On Letters,—J. P. Leib, F. Hoffman, and G. T. Haines ; To Audit Accounts,—C. Hummel, A. Schultz, and I. Hess.

G. T. Haines resigned the presiding eldership on account of bodily infirmities. J. G. Marquardt received permission to rest in order to recuperate his health. A.

Schultz rested on account of bodily infirmities but was retained in the itinerancy. H. Bucks and C. Hummel located on account of family concerns. M. F. Maize and F. Danner were retained in the itinerancy without an appointment. H. A. Bisse died during the year. F. Krecker was elected Presiding Elder. G. Knerr, A. Ziegenfus, C. Gingrich, D. Hambright, and S. G. Rhoads were ordained Elders: E. Ely, J. Yeakel, and J. Rhoads, Deacons. J. O. Lehr was licensed as preacher on trial. The following were newly received as preachers on trial: Theodore Plattenberger, Reuben Yeakel, Henry Koester, Elias Miller, Moses Dissinger, and James O. Lehr.

C. M. Long made an appropriate address on the usefulness of the American Tract Society and more especially of the colporteur system, expressing the wish that the Conference formulate a resolution upon the subject. S. Neitz and another brother were appointed to prepare suitable resolutions. They reported the following which was adopted:

Resolved, That we continue to regard the operations of the American Tract Society with pleasure, and consider it a chosen vessel in God's hand for the advancement of his kingdom and the dissemination of the simple yet mysterious, momentous, and imperishable gospel of his Son. Regarding this Society as the voice of a preacher in the wilderness preparing the way of the Lord, we sincerely wish it the blessing of God and the favor of all men, the united co-operation of christendom and the guidance of the Holy Spirit, in order that the feet of his ambassadors of peace may speedily stand upon the mountains and hills of the earth, in all the kingdoms, republics, and dominions of the world and upon the shores of all the seas with the isles thereof, in the name of the Great Shepherd of the sheep. Amen!

It was resolved that between the time of this session and August next, collections shall be taken on all the fields of labor for the purpose of assisting such preachers whose income is inadequate. The late Father Frederick Miller, of Washington Twp.. Lehigh Co., Pa., having bequeathed $14,000.00 to the Evangelical Association, the Conference advised the Charitable Society to inquire into the matter. The following was adopted: Inasmuch as the book establishment of our Association has been very prosperous; therefore, *Resolved*, That its officers deserve praise for their fidelity in the management of its affairs, and that we desire the continued patronage of our members and of the friends of religion in general. The Conference requested the book establishment to organize a branch department in the city of Reading. The examiners of junior preachers who served last year were re-appointed. On Sunday forenoon Bishop Seybert preached an instructive and impressive ordination sermon to a large and attentive gathering, from Luke XII: 42.

BOUNDARIES.

The name of Germantown Cir. was changed to Montgomery Cir. Warren Cir. was annexed to New Jersey Miss. Harrisburg was again taken up as a mission to be supplied with a preacher if practicable. Eby's class was detached from Lebanon Sta. and annexed to Lebanon Cir. Conewaga class was taken from Lebanon Cir. and attached to Lancaster Cir. It was resolved that the Philadelphia English Miss. be supplied with a preacher; and in case this cannot be done, it shall continue under the arrangement made at the session of 1852. Conference decided that Tamaqua and Hamburg be supplied with missionaries during the current year, if possible.

CHURCH AFFAIRS.

The auditing committee reported that if all the subscriptions are paid, the debt on the Albright church will be reduced to $300.00. The Conference tendered a resolution of thanks to J. Eckert, the agent, for his labors and to the friends for their contributions. Brother Eckert was instructed to secure the outstanding subscriptions. Brother J. B. Dingeldein having made the congregation at New York the noble and very liberal offer to pay off the debt of $3,600.00 still resting upon our church there, provided the congregation agree to pay $100.00 annually into our missionaay treasury, it was resolved to accept the proposal, the Conference expressing its gratitude to the donor.

MEMORIALS.

Suitable resolutions were adopted relative to the decease of two brethren in the ministry, H. Fisher, editor of the *Evangelical Messenger*, and H. A. Bisse, a member of this Conference. F. Hoffman and the preacher in charge of Lykens Cir. were instructed to prepare suitable resolutions upon the decease of our beloved co-worker in the vineyard of the Lord, John Sensel, and to publish them in the *Christliche Botschafter*. No further action was taken at Conference because of a lack of necessary information.

PHILADELPHIA DISTRICT—*J. P. Leib,* P. E.
Philadelphia Sta.—J. M. Saylor.
Philadelphia Miss.—R. Deisher.
Philadelphia Eng. Miss.—[To be supplied].
Germantown Sta.—M. Sindlinger.
Montgomery Cir.—J. Koehl and R. Yeakel.
Milford Cir. — D. Wieand and H. Koester.
Lehigh Cir.—Chr. Meyer and Elias Miller.
Northampton Cir.—Geo. Knerr and S. P. Reinoehl.
Monroe Cir.—C. Gingrich.
Easton Miss.—J. Yeakel.
New Jersey Miss.—H. C. Major and L. Kelly.
New York Sta.—W. Heim.

LEBANON DISTRICT—*F. Krecker,* P. E.
Lebanon Cir.—N. Goebel and T. G. Clewell.

Lebanon Sta.—S. G. Rhoads.
Womelsdorf Cir.—C. Loos and E. Ely.
Chester Cir.—Jos. Gross and F. P. Lehr.
Lancaster Cir.—Jacob Adams and D. Hambright.
Lancaster Miss.—D. Berger.
Reading Sta.—E. Bast.
Kutztown Cir.—W. L. Reber and T. Plattenberger.
Dauphin Cir.—J. C. Farnsworth.
Harrisburg Miss.—J. Eckert.

ORWIGSBURG DISTRICT—*F. Hoffman,* P. E.
Orwigsburg Cir.—Isaac Hess.
Schuylkill Haven Cir.—Lewis Snyder.
Schuylkill Cir.—S. Gaumer.
Pottsville Sta.—J. Schell.
Pinegrove Cir.—S. Neitz.
Lykens Cir.—Jac. Gross and Moses Dissinger.
Mahantongo Cir.—A. Ziegenfus and J. O. Lehr.
Carbon Cir.—G. T. Haines and W. Yost.

1855.

The Sixteenth (48*th*) *Annual Session.*

President, Bishop J. Long.
Secretary, Solomon Neitz.
Assistant Secretary, Jesse Yeakel.

On the twenty-eighth day of February, 1855, the members of the East Pa. Conference assembled in the Immanuel Church, Philadelphia, to hold their sixteenth annual session. F. Krecker was appointed to prepare an abstract of the proceedings for the *Evangelical Messenger.* The following committees were appointed: On Worship,—The Bishop, the presiding elders, and the

preacher in charge of the congregation; On Finance,—
W. L. Reber, F. Danner, and J. C. Farnsworth; On
Letters,—J. P. Leib, F. Hoffman, F. Krecker, F. Dan-
ner, and G. T. Haines; On Boundaries,—J. P. Leib,
F. Hoffman, F. Krecker, S. Neitz, and E. Bast.

A member of the Conference was reproved by his
presiding elder for neglect of duty and for engaging in
so-called spirit-rappings. A preacher was continued
on probation for marrying before the expiration
of his time as preacher on trial. J. M. Saylor,
I. Hess, and C. Loos located on account of
family concerns; M. F. Maize and A. Schultz on
account of ill health. W. Heim took no appointment
on account of enfeebled health. The following were
ordained to the office of Deacon: T. G. Clewell, S. P.
Reinoehl, W. Yost, F. P. Lehr, P. H. Lehr, Joshua
Fry, Reuben Yeakel, and Adam Hinkel. The brethren,
J. Werner, F. Walker, C. S. Haman, Thos. Sebold,
and W. Bachman were newly received as preachers on
trial. J. C. Reisner was again licensed as preacher on
trial. The following were received into the itinerancy:
J. Frey, Joseph Werner, F. Walker, C. S. Haman, and
T. Sebold. The claimants for support are the widows
of C. Hesser, J. Schnerr, H. Bisse, and Jacob Gross.
The following was adopted:

Whereas, W. W. Orwig is engaged in the work of
compiling a history of the Evangelical Association;
therefore *Resolved*, That we will heartily co-operate
with our sister conferences in aiding the compiler, that
we will diligently gather correct and reliable data, and
that the presiding elders shall constitute a committee to
obtain from the brethren upon their districts and from

other sources such information as will prove helpful and valuable.

The preacher in charge of the Philadelphia Station was appointed to superintend a small book room until the next session of the General Conference. The following were elected delegates to General Conference: F. Hoffman, F. Kreeker, S. Neitz, G. T. Haines, J. P. Leib, F. Danner, W. L. Reber, J. M. Saylor, J. C. Farnsworth, C. Meyers, E. Bast, J. Schell, D. Berger, and M. F. Maize; Alternates,—Joseph Gross, I. Hess, and J. Adams. W. L. Reber was elected conference treasurer. F. Hoffman, J. P. Leib, S. Neitz, and F. Kreeker were appointed a committee to examine junior preachers.

BOUNDARIES.

New Jersey Mission was changed into a circuit. The Strohl appointment was taken from Northampton, and annexed to Lehigh Circuit. Palmyra and Conewaga classes were annexed to Dauphin Cir. The Conference resolved that the Philadelphia English Mission and Tamaqua Mission be supplied at this session; that Harrisburg Mission be served by a preacher who can labor in both languages; and that the Allentown congregation shall not become a station until the difficulties concerning the church property there are adjusted with the members of Lehigh Circuit.

EDUCATION.

Inasmuch as the West Pa. Conference has undertaken the institution of a seminary in New Berlin, Union Co., Pa., for the instruction of the youth of our church, and inasmuch as a delegation from the board of trustees of said seminary has made advances to this Conference praying us to co-operate with them; therefore

Resolved, That we will unite in the project according to the constitution and offer presented, the seminary to be named "Union Seminary of the East and West Pa. Conferences of the Evangelical Association of North America." For this resolution the following voted: F. Hoffman, J. P. Leib, J. M. Saylor, D. Berger, F. Krecker, E. Bast, C. Meyers, F. Danner, Jos. Gross, G. T. Haines, C. Loos, J. Schell, J. Koehl, J. G. Marquardt, D. Wieand, J. C. Farnsworth, M. Sindlinger, S. Gaumer, D. Hambright, J. Frey, J. P. Lehr, ——Eberhart, A. Ziegenfuss, L. Schneider, Chr. Gingrich, R. Deisher, H. C. Major, S. G. Rhoads, T. G. Clewell, S. P. Reinoehl, R. Yeakel, S. Neitz, I. Hess, W. Yost, and J. Yeakel. It was adopted. The following were elected trustees of the seminary: S. Neitz, M. F. Maize, J. M. Saylor, and F. Hoffman, ministers; E. Hammer of Pottsville, Levi Miller of Pinegrove, and Abr. Saylor of Schuylkill Haven, laymen. S. Neitz was appointed agent for the seminary for one year to solicit contributions, with the understanding that he receive his salary, rent, and traveling expenses out of the collections and subscriptions. It was agreed that those preachers who subscribe $100 or more for the seminary shall have the privilege of paying their subscriptions in three annual installments. S. Neitz and F. Hoffman were sent as delegates to the West Pa. Conference in the interests of the new institution.

FINANCE.

Receipts:

Regular contributions for salary........... $6,665.07
Conference collections.................... 547.78
Book establishment....................... 200.00
Charitable Society....................... 75.00
Interest from Custer legacy.............. 63.34

                                          7,551.19

Expenditures:

To preachers and claimants............... 7,476.19

Balance on hand.................... 75.00
Every preacher was paid in full for the first time.

APPOINTMENTS.

PHILADELPHIA DISTRICT—*J. P. Leib,* P. E.
Philadelphia Sta.—E. Bast.
Philadelphia Miss.—R. Deisher.
Philadelphia Eng. Miss.—T. G. Clewell.
Germantown Sta.—D. Wieand.
Montgomery Cir.—J. Koehl and C. S. Haman.
Milford Cir.—M. Sindlinger and T. Plattenberger.
Lehigh Cir.—Geo. Knerr and T. Sebold.
Northampton Cir.—G. T. Haines and L. Kelly.
Monroe Cir.—J. Frey and J. Miller.
Easton Miss.—J. Yeakel.
New Jersey Miss.—H. C. Major.
New York Sta.—J. G. Marquardt.

LEBANON DISTRICT—*F. Krecker,* P. E.
Lebanon Sta.—S. G. Rhoads.
Lebanon Cir.—N. Goebel and F. P. Lehr.
Womelsdorf Cir.—J. C. Farnsworth and J. O. Lehr.

Chester Cir.—Joseph Gross.
Lancaster Cir.—C. Gingrich and Eph. Ely.
Lancaster Miss.—D. Berger.
Reading Sta.—Jacob Adams.
Kutztown Cir.—W. L. Reber and H. Koester.
Dauphin Cir.—F. Danner.
Harrisburg Miss.—S. P. Reinoehl.

ORWIGSBURG DISTRICT—*F. Hoffman* P. E.
Orwigsburg Cir.—R. Yeakel.
Schuylkill Haven Cir.—L. Snyder.
Schuylkill Cir.—S. Gaumer.
Pottsville Sta.—J. Schell.
Pinegrove Cir.—W. Yost.
Lykens Cir.—D. Hambright, Moses Dissinger, and F. Walker.
Mahantongo Cir.—A. Ziegenfus and J. Werner.
Carbon Cir.—Chr. Meyers.
Tamaqua Miss.—J. Eckert.
Agent for *Union Seminary*—S. Neitz.

President, Bishops J. Seybert and J. Long.
Secretary, J. J. Esher.
Assistant Secretaries, J. G. Wolpert and B. Hengst.

The delegates representing their respective annual conferences assembled in Lebanon, Pa., Sept. 19th, 1855, to hold the regular quadrennial session of the General Conference.* The moral and official conduct of the delegates was investigated. No charges were preferred.

The Conference expressed approval and strong endorsement of the efforts made by the East Pa. and the West Pa. Conferences to establish an institution of learning. A new conference was formed and called *The Wisconsin Conference.* The general book agent was instructed to publish an English edition of the History of the Evangelical Association, and to issue a German Sunday-school monthly to be called *Der Christliche Kinderfreund.* It was resolved that Luzerne Circuit and Wilkesbarre Mission shall belong to the West Pa. Conference.

Bishops J. Seybert and J. Long were re-elected. C. G. Koch was re-elected editor of the *Christliche Botschafter* and J. Driesbach, of the *Evangelical Messenger.* C. Hammer was elected general book agent. The following statistics of the Association were reported at this session :

---

*See Preface on Page 98.

Itinerant preachers..	247	Stations..........	15
Local preachers....	227	Missions..........	42
Districts..........	22	Churches..........	343
Circuits..........	100	Total membership,	27,670

1856.

The Seventeenth (49th) Annual Session.

President, Bishop J. Seybert.
Secretary, Solomon Neitz.

The seventeenth annual session of the East Pa. Conference was held in Allentown, Pa., beginning Feb. 27th, 1856, Bishop J. Seybert presiding. Committees on worship, finance, letters, and boundaries were appointed.* E. Bast located on account of bodily infirmities. J. C. Farnsworth took no appointment. G. T. Haines took a superannuated relation. Levi Kelly received credentials. Frederick Danner died during the past year. S. Neitz and C. Meyers were elected to the office of Presiding Elder. E. Ely, J. Yeakel, N. Goebel, and L. Snyder were ordained Elders; H. Koester, J. O. Lehr, M. Dissinger, E. B. Miller, L. Kelly, T. Plattenberger, T. Sebold, I. Oberholzer, and W. Egge, Deacons. Samuel Werner was received as preacher on trial. The conference claimants are Sister Hesser, Sister Danner, Sister Schnerr and three children, Sister Gross and two children, and Sister Bisse and two children. It was resolved that during the month of July collections be lifted for the support

*The names of the members of these committees were not recorded by the secretary.

of the superannuated preachers and the widows and orphans of deceased ministers. The book rooms of the Conference were removed to the city of Reading and placed under the charge of Brother Wm. Gery. The following examiners of junior preachers were appointed: F. Hoffman in theology, F. Krecker in languages, J. P. Leib in church discipline, and S. Neitz in history. On Sunday, Bishop J. Seybert preached the ordination sermon choosing 2 Tim. II : 15, for his text.

BOUNDARIES.

Wiconisco was taken from Lykens Cir. and named Wiconisco Sta. Lancaster City Mission was changed into a station. Bernville was detached from Kutztown Cir. and annexed to Womelsdorf. Riegelsville was taken from Northampton Cir. and annexed to Lehigh.

CHURCH AFFAIRS.

The difficulties connected with our church property in Allentown were adjusted in the following manner: 1st, The congregation at Allentown has agreed to give to Lehigh Cir. for its perpetual use thirty feet of ground, including a stable, at the western end of the church lot, reserving, however, a ten-foot entrance from the northern end of said thirty feet for its own perpetual use. 2d, The congregation at Allentown and the circuit have agreed to assume equal shares of the debt still remaining on the property and in case any lawful claim should ever be made upon it from Springtown and vicinity, it shall be satisfied by a similar arrangement. 3d, It was furthermore agreed that either party shall assist the other in securing a lawful title to the divided portions of the property.

11

EDUCATION.

Resolved, That we will continue our support of Union Seminary in accordance with the conditions of our union with the West Pa. Conference as agreed at our session held in Philadelphia, and in case that conference appoint an agent we will receive him in a friendly spirit.   J. P. Leib, F. Hoffman, L. Snyder, J. C. Farnsworth, ministers, and E. Hammer, Abraham Saylor, and L. Miller, laymen, were elected trustees of the seminary.

FINANCE.

Receipts:

Balance on hand	$ 65.38
Conference collections	324.67
Charitable Society	75.00
Book establishment	350.00
Interest on Custer legacy	75.93
	890.98
Expenditures	890.50
Balance	.48

APPOINTMENTS.

PHILADELPHIA DISTRICT — *C. Meyers,* P. E.

Philadelphia Sta.—Jesse Yeakel.

Philadelphia Miss.—A. Ziegenfus.

Philadelphia Eng. Miss.—Not supplied.

Germantown Sta.—D. Wieand.

Montgomery Cir.—W. L. Reber and Jacob Zern.

Milford Cir.—N. Goebel and T. Plattenberger.

Lehigh Cir.—Geo. Knerr and W. Bachman.

Allentown Sta.—J. Schell.

Northampton Cir.—Joseph Gross and T. Sebold.

Monroe Cir.—S. Gaumer and E. B. Miller.

Easton Miss.—R. Yeakel.

New Jersey Cir.—R. Wright.

New York Sta.—J. G. Marquardt.

LEBANON DISTRICT—*F. Krecker,* P. E.

Lebanon Sta.—C. S. Haman.

Lebanon Cir.—Jacob Adams and F. P. Lehr.

Womelsdorf Cir.—Isaac Hess and H. Koester.

Reading Sta.—F. Hoffman.
Kutztown Cir.—J. Frey.
Lancaster Cir.—C. Gingrich and Moses Dissinger.
Lancaster Sta.—M. Sindlinger.
Chester Cir.—S. G. Rhoads.
Dauphin Cir.—J. O. Lehr.
Harrisburg Miss.—S. P. Reinoehl.

ORWIGSBURG DISTRICT—*S. Neitz, P. E.*
Orwigsburg Cir.—D. Berger.
Schuylkill Cir.—E. Ely.

Schuylkill Haven Cir.—T. G. Clewell.
Pottsville Sta.—J. P. Leib.
Pinegrove Cir.—Wm. Yost.
Lykens Cir.—W. Helm, D. Hambright, and F. Walker.
Mahantongo Cir.—L. Snyder and J. Werner.
Wiconisco Sta.—Not supplied.
Carbon Cir.—J. Koehl and R. Litzenberger.
Tamaqua Miss.—R. Deisher.

1857.

The Eighteenth (50th) Annual Session.

President, Bishop J. Long.
Secretary, Solomon Neitz.
Assistant Secretary, John Koehl.

On Wednesday, February 25th, 1857, the members of the East Pennsylvania Conference assembled in the First Evangelical Church in New York City, Bishop J. Long presiding. S. G. Rhoads was appointed to report the proceedings for the *Evangelical Messenger.* The following committees were appointed: On Worship,—The Bishop, the presiding elders, and the preacher in charge; On Finance,—W. L. Reber, I. Hess, and J. Eckert; On Letters,—The Bishop and the presiding elders; On Boundaries,—F. Krecker, S. Neitz, C. Meyers, J. P. Leib, and F. Hoffman; To Audit Church Accounts,—J. Yeakel, J. Gross, and W. Yost. J. C. Farnsworth located with the intention of entering the West Pa. Conference, where he had already been engaged in active service for several months. M. Sindlinger located on account of family concerns. T.

G. Clewell having been elected editor of the *Evangel-ical Messenger*, received credentials to enter the Ohio Conference. J. Frey, S. P. Reinoehl, W. Yost, R. Yeakel, and T. G. Clewell were ordained to the office of Elder; R. Litzenberger, F. Walker, Joseph Werner, C. S. Haman, and R. Wright, to the office of Deacon. Anastasius Boetzel received license as preacher on trial. H. Stoetzel was again received into the itinerancy. The conference claimants are Sister Schnerr and two children, Sister Hesser, Sister Bisse and three children, Sister Gross and two children, G. T. Haines and family, and one orphan of F. Danner. The general book agent was instructed to pay our book agent, Wm. Gery, ten dollars for his services up to this time. F. Hoffman, J. P. Leib, and S. Neitz were appointed to examine the junior preachers in their studies at the next session. S. Neitz was instructed to secure for the Conference the records of its transactions from the beginning, and in case he cannot obtain possession of the old book to make a transcription of it and present his charges at the next annual session. Henry Miesse having made a bequest of books to the Association, F. Krecker and C. S. Haman were appointed to inquire into the matter.

BOUNDARIES.

Heidelberg and vicinity in Lehigh Co., were taken up as a mission. Tamaqua Mission was placed under the supervision of the preacher in charge of Schuylkill Cir.

CHURCH AFFAIRS.

The stationing committee was instructed to appoint a collector for our church in Reading, Pa., with the understanding that his salary be paid out of the collections. The congregation at Bethlehem received permission to borrow money for the purpose of paying their church debt. A debt of $400.00 still remaining upon the Albright church, J. Eckert was appointed to gather, upon the most feasible plan, the subscriptions still outstanding.

EDUCATION.

Resolved, That we do not consider it expedient that another effort be made to collect funds within the bounds of this Conference for Union Seminary, and therefore pray the trustees of that institution to spare us in this respect, advising them, however, to appoint our three presiding elders agents upon their respective districts to collect the outstanding subscriptions and to give to the subscribers their certificates. S. Neitz, F. Krecker, and Elijah Hammer were elected trustees of the seminary.

APPOINTMENTS.

PHILADELPHIA DISTRICT—*C. Meyers*, P. E.
Philadelphia Sta.—Jesse Yeakel.
Philadelphia Miss.—A. Ziegenfus.
Germantown Sta.—Joseph Werner.
Montgomery Cir.—J. Frey and D. Hambright.
Milford Cir.—N. Goebel and S. Gaumer.
Lehigh Cir.—W. L. Reber and Moses Dissinger.
Allentown Sta.—J. Schell.
Northampton Cir.—J. Gross and R. Litzenberger.
Monroe Cir.—F. P. Lehr.
Easton Miss.—Reuben Yeakel.
New Jersey Cir.—Robt. Wright.
New York Sta.—F. Hoffman.

LEBANON DISTRICT— *F. Krecker*, P. E.

Lebanon Sta.—C. S. Haman.
Lebanon Cir.—H. Stoetzel and F Walker.
Womelsdorf Cir.—Isaac Hess and J. Zern.
Reading Sta.—W. Heim.
Kutztown Cir.—D. Wieand.
Lancaster Cir.—Jacob Adams and T. Sebold.
Lancaster Sta.—J. O. Lehr.
Dauphin Cir.—C. Gingrich.
Chester Cir.—S. G. Rhoads.
Harrisburg Miss.—J. G. Marquardt.

ORWIGSBURG DISTRICT—*S. Neitz*, P. E.
Orwigsburg Cir.—D. Berger.
Schuylkill Cir.—Eph. Ely.
Schuylkill Haven Cir.—J. P. Leib.
Pottsville Sta.—S. P. Remoehl.

Pinegrove Cir.—Lewis Snyder.
Lykens Cir.—T. Plattenberger and H. Koester.
Mahantongo Cir.—R. Deisher and E. B. Miller.

Wiconisco Sta.—Wm. Yost.
Carbon Cir.—J. Koehl and W. Bachman.
Heidelberg Miss.—Geo Knerr.

1858.

The Nineteenth (51st) *Annual Session.*

President, Bishop J. Seybert.
Secretary, Solomon Neitz.
Assistant Secretary, John Koehl.

The East Pa. Conference met in annual session at Weissport, Carbon Co., Pa., on Wednesday, Feb. 24th, 1858. S. P. Reinoehl was appointed to report the proceedings for the *Evangelical Messenger.* The following committees were appointed : On Worship, — The Bishop, the presiding elders, and the preacher in charge; On Letters,—The Bishop, S. Neitz, and C. Meyers; On Finance,—W. L. Reber, I. Hess, and S. G. Rhoads ; On Boundaries,—(not named.)

A traveling preacher on trial was deposed from the ministry. The license of a local preacher was withheld because he failed to perform the duties of his office. A. Hinkel withdrew from the church. M. Sindlinger located on account of bodily infirmities. D. Berger was retained in the itinerancy without an appointment. F. Hoffman was elected Presiding Elder. H. Stoetzel, H. Koester, T. Sebold, Elias B. Miller, T. Plattenberger, F. P. Lehr, and J. O. Lehr were ordained to the office of Elder ; W. Bachman, J. Zern, John H. Miller, Jesse Young, and H. Kempfer, to the office of Deacon. The following were received into the itineraney : Joseph Specht, Matthew Guhl, Jesse Young, Edmund Butz, Isaac Oberholser, Joseph Kutz, and A. Boetzel. The conference claimants were : Sister Schnerr and two children, Sister Hesser, Sister Bisse and three children, Sister Gross and two children, Brother N. Goebel, and one orphan of F. Danner.

At this session the Conference was profoundly agitated by a discussion of the doctrine of Christian holiness. It was agreed that the book department at Reading be recalled in case the management is not willing to pay Brother Gery $50.00 per annum for his services as agent. The preachers were instructed to use their influence among the members to have the parsonages furnished.

BOUNDARIES.

Philadelphia Mission was changed to a station to be known as South Phila. Station. Easton Mission was changed to a station and two classes from Northampton Cir. were annexed. Heidelberg Mission was discontinued, one part being annexed to Kutztown Cir. and the other part to Carbon Cir. Catawissa class was detached from Schuylkill Cir., and annexed to Tamaqua Mission. A mission was located in the city of New York. New Rochelle was constituted a mission. A new mission was located in the city of Philadelphia and named North Phila. Mission.

CHURCH AFFAIRS.

The agent for the church at Reading made a report which was approved. It was agreed that an agent for that church be again appointed for the ensuing year.

F. Hoffman, R. Yeakel, and J. Gross were appointed
to inquire into the practicability of building a church
in Harrisburg, Pa., during the coming year. H. C.
Major, a local preacher, was authorized to have charge
of the New Jersey Cir., his salary to consist of the voluntary contributions of the people.

EDUCATION.

WHEREAS, We perceive that Union Seminary is exerting a very wholesome influence and promises great
usefulness in the cause of education and religion; therefore be it *Resolved*, That we will use our influence to
further the best interests of that institution and will
welcome and encourage any agent appointed for the
purpose of collecting funds and securing students. We
recommend to the stationing committee the advisability
of appointing a suitable brother as agent for the seminary. W. Yost and B. Strickler were elected trustees
of Union Seminary. The committee to examine junior
preachers at the next session consisted of F. Hoffman,
W. L. Reber, S. G. Rhoads, and S. Neitz.

APPOINTMENTS.

PHILADELPHIA DISTRICT—*C. Meyers, P. E.*
Philadelphia Sta.—F. Krecker.
South Phila. Sta.—T. Plattenberger.
N'th Philadelphia Miss.—Jesse Yeakel.
Germantown Sta.—W. Bachman.
Montgomery Cir.—S. Gaumer and D. Hambright.
Milford Cir.—Isaac Hess and Jesse Young.
Lehigh Cir.—G. T. Haines and A. Boetzel.
Allentown Sta.—W. Heim.
Northampton Cir.—S. G. Rhoads and R. Litzenberger.

Monroe Cir.—F. P. Lehr and Joseph Werner.
Easton Sta.—W. L. Reber.
New York Sta.—H. Stoetzel.
New York Miss.—H. Koester.
Newark Miss.—M. Guhl.
New Rochelle Miss.—F. Walker.

LEBANON DISTRICT—*F. Hoffman, P. E.*
Lebanon Sta.—Reuben Yeakel.
Lebanon Cir.—A. Ziegenfus and I. Oberholzer.
Womelsdorf Cir.—Geo. Knerr and Jos. Kutz.
Reading Sta.—J. Koehl.

Kutztown Cir.—D. Wieand.
Lancaster Cir.—Th. Sebold and J. Zern.
Lancaster Sta.—J. O. Lehr.
Dauphin Cir.—J. Gross.
Chester Cir.—C. Gingrich.
Harrisburg Miss.—J. G. Marquardt.
Agt. for Reading Church.—Jac. Adams.

ORWIGSBURG DISTRICT—*S. Neitz, P. E.*
Orwigsburg Cir.—C. S. Haman.

Schuylkill Haven Cir.—J. P. Leib.
Schuylkill Cir.—Moses Dissinger.
Carbon Cir.—J. Schell and E. Butz.
Pinegrove Cir.—Lewis Snyder.
Lykens Cir.—R. Deisher and J. Specht.
Mahantongo Cir.—J. Frey and E. B. Miller.
Wiconisco Sta.—Wm. Yost.
Pottsville Sta.—S. P. Reinoehl.
Tamaqua Miss.—E. Ely.

1859.

The Twentieth (52d) Annual Session.

President, Bishop J. Long.
Secretary, Frederick Krecker.
Assistant Secretaries, John Koehl and Reuben Yeakel.
The twentieth annual session of the East Pa. Conference was held in Lancaster, Pa., beginning on February 23d, 1859. The standing committees were constituted as follows: On Worship,—The Bishop, the presiding elders, and the preacher in charge; On Letters,—The Bishop, C. Meyers, S. Neitz, and F. Hoffman; On Finance,—I. Hess, W. L. Reber, and J. Yeakel; On Boundaries,—C. Meyers, S. Neitz, F. Hoffman, G. T. Haines, and W. Heim; On Auditing Accounts,—W. Yost, L. Snyder, and W. L. Reber.

D. Berger was retained in the itinerancy without an appointment. J. Young located with the intention of going West, and I. Oberholzer, on account of family concerns. S. P. Reinoehl received permission to rest one year in order to recuperate his health. J. Eckert received credentials. Joseph Werner, F. Walker, R. Litzenberger, C. S. Haman, and Moses Dissinger were ordained to the office of Elder; M. Guhl, Jacob Schneider, B. Kreisley, D. Witmer, and C. H. Baker to the office of Deacon. Jonathan Miller and John Kurtz received license as preachers on trial. M. Sindlinger was again received, and J. A. Apgar, Jacob Schneider, and Thomas Bowman were newly received into the itinerancy. The conference claimants were Sister Schnerr and one child, Sister Hesser, Sister Bisse and two children, and Sister Gross and two children.

The Conference ordered that the preachers exchange boarding places every other day during the session. It was resolved that in case the publishing house continues a book department in the city of Reading the Conference will be satisfied with a discount of 25 per cent. on the books sold there. The following were elected delegates to the General Conference: F. Hoffman, J. P. Leib, S. Neitz, C. Meyers, F. Krecker, W. L. Reber, H. Stoetzel, J. Yeakel, and J. Breidenstein; alternates,— G. T. Haines, S. G. Rhoads, and J. Koehl. The preachers were instructed to lift collections during the month of June wherewith to defray the traveling expenses of the delegates. On Sunday forenoon Bishop Long preached an appropriate and powerful sermon from the text 1 Pet. v: 2-4, after which the candidates for orders were ordained.

BOUNDARIES.

New Rochelle Mission was abandoned. Camden, Glassborough, and vicinity, N. J., were taken up as a mission. Harrisburg was constituted a mission upon condition that not more than one hundred and twenty dollars need be appropriated from the missionary treasury. Berne was taken from Kutztown Cir. and attached to Womelsdorf Cir. Muehlbach and Schaeferstown classes were taken from Womelsdorf Cir. and annexed to Lebanon Sta.

CHURCH AFFAIRS.

Inasmuch as a debt still encumbered the Albright church, a committee was appointed to prepare lists of the unpaid subscriptions and to forward them to the preachers in charge who were instructed to do all in their power to gather the money during the coming year. It was furthermore agreed that should the required amount not be forthcoming by the next session, the preachers will unite and pay the remaining debt. C. Meyers, H. Stoezel, and N. Goebel were appointed to superintend the erection of a church in Newark, N. J.

EDUCATION.

Union Seminary being seriously crippled in its operations and influence on account of the numerous unpaid subscriptions among the people, the Conference entreated such debtors to pay their subscriptions as soon as possible, for the sake of their own honor and for the sake of the prosperity of that institution. Reuben Deisher was elected agent for the seminary and the brethren resolved to assist him to the extent of their ability. A subscription list was circulated in the Conference and the sum of $375.00 was secured. J. P. Leib, F. Hoffman, and Levi Miller were elected trustees of the seminary. The preachers were instructed to secure donations of books for the school. F. Hoffman, S. Neitz, J. Yeakel, and W. L. Reber were appointed to examine the junior preachers in their studies at the next annual session.

APPOINTMENTS.

PHILADELPHIA DISTRICT—C. Meyers, P. E.
Philadelphia Sta.—F. Krecker.
South Philadelphia Sta.—T. Plattenberger.
North Philadelphia Miss.—J. Yeakel.
Germantown Sta.—W. H. Bachman.
Montgomery Cir.—F. P. Lehr and Jos. Werner.
Milford Cir.—I. Hess and D. Wieand.
Lehigh Cir.—G. T. Haines and T. Bowman.
Allentown Sta.—W. Heim.
Northampton Cir.—S. G. Rhoads and E. Butz.
Monroe Cir.—S. Gaumer and D. Hambright.
Easton Sta.—W. L. Reber.
New Jersey Cir.—J. A. Apgar.
New York Sta.—H. Stoetzel.
New York Miss.—H. Koester.
Newark Miss.—N. Goebel.
Camden Miss.—J. Frey.
Norristown Miss.—J. Schneider.

LEBANON DISTRICT—F. Hoffman, P. E.

Lebanon Sta.—Reuben Yeakel.
Lebanon Cir.—J. Gross and F. Walker.
Womelsdorf Cir.—Jacob Adams and A. Boetzel.
Reading Sta.—J. Koehl.
Kutztown Cir.—A. Ziegenfus.
Lancaster Cir.—J. O. Lehr and J. Zern.
Lancaster Sta.—J. G. Marquardt.
Chester Cir.—C. Gingrich.
Dauphin Cir.—E. B. Miller.
Harrisburg Miss.—M. Guhl.

ORWIGSBURG DISTRICT—S. Neitz, P. E.
Orwigsburg Cir.—J. P. Leib.
Schuylkill Haven Cir.—C. S. Haman.
Schuylkill Cir.—Moses Dissinger.
Carbon Cir.—J. Schell and J. Specht.
Pinegrove Cir.—R. Litzenberger.
Lykens Cir.—Wm. Yost and M. Sindlinger.
Mahantongo Cir.—Geo. Knerr and Jos. Kutz.
Wiconisco Sta.—T. Sebold.
Pottsville Sta.—L Snyder.
Tamaqua Miss.—E. Ely.

1859.

The General Conference.

Presidents, Bishops J. Seybert and J. Long.
Secretary, C. G. Koch.
Assistant Secretaries, B. Hengst, J. J. Esher, and C. A. Schnake.

The delegates representing the eight annual conferences of the Evangelical Association assembled in the Zion Evangelical Church at Naperville, Ill., October 5th, 1859, to hold the regular quadrennial session of the General Conference.* The two bishops and fifty-two

*See Preface on page 98.

delegates were in attendance. Charges were preferred against a delegate for advocating theories contrary to our doctrines as defined in the Articles of Faith. The charge was declared sustained. The Conference resolved that an English Sunday-school periodical be published as soon as 5,000 subscribers have been secured. The new periodical was named *The Sunday-School Messenger*. At this session the board of publication was created. The name of the West Pa. Conference was changed to *The Central Pa. Conference.*

The number of bishops was increased to three. J. Seybert and J. Long were re-elected, and W. W. Orwig was newly elected to the office of Bishop. The other officers were elected as follows: General book agent, C. Hammer; editor of the *Christliche Botschafter*, C. G. Koch; editor of the *Evangelical Messenger*, T. G. Clewell; corresponding secretary of the Missionary Society, R. Yenkel. S. Neitz was elected to represent the East Pa. Conference in the board of publication. W. Garret and Daniel Saylor were elected trustees of the Charitable Society. *The Iowa Conference* was formed, and The Sunday-school and Tract Union organized. The delegates celebrated the Lord's Supper.

The following statistics of the Evangelical Association were reported:

Traveling Preachers.......................... 317
Local Preachers.............................. 268
Entire Membership...................... 38,310
Churches.................................... 434
Parsonages.................................. 81
Sunday-schools.............................. 423
Officers and Teachers....................... 4,452

Scholars.............................. 18,473
Catechetical Classes.......................   102
Catechumens... 1,291

1860.

The Twenty-First (53d) Annual Session.

President, Bishop W. W. Orwig.

Secretary, Jesse Yeakel.

Assistant Secretaries, J. Koehl and F. Krecker.

On Wednesday, Feb. 29th, 1860, the members of the East Pa. Conference met at Annville, Lebanon Co., Pa., to transact the business of their annual session. W. H. Bachman was appointed to report the proceedings for the *Evangelical Messenger.* The following committees were appointed: On Worship,—The Bishop, F. Hoffman, S. Neitz, J. Gross, and R. Yeakel; On Letters,—G. T. Haines, S. Neitz, C. Meyers, F. Hoffman, and C. S. Haman; On Finance,—I. Hess, S. G. Rhoads, and W. Yost; On Boundaries,—The presiding elders, G. T. Haines, and J. P. Leib.

It was announced that a local preacher had been deposed from the ministry and expelled from the church during the past year. E. Bast withdrew from the church. R. Deisher, S. Gaumer, W. Heim, and Joseph Werner located; the last two on account of bodily infirmities. W. L. Reber took a superannuated relation. Bishop John Seybert and Abraham Frey, a local preacher, died during the past year. S. Neitz was re-elected, and G. T. Haines and S. G. Rhoads were newly elected to the office of Presiding Elder, but S. G.

Rhoads declining to accept the office for reasons which were satisfactory to the Conference, L. Snyder was elected in his place. The presiding elders were stationed. Elders' orders were granted to W. H. Bachman and J. Zern, and Deacons' orders, to E. Butz, J. Specht, A. Boetzel, T. Harper, and J. Bertolet. George Harm received license as preacher on trial. A. Schultz was again received, and T. Harper, H. Kempfer, J. Steltzer, D. Yingst, L. Schmidt, G. B. Fisher, and S. S. Chubb were newly received into the itinerancy. S. Neitz was elected delegate to the board of missions. The claimants were Sister Schnerr and one child, Sister Hesser, and Sister Bisse and two children.

The custom of retaining in the itinerancy such preachers who had located was abolished. It was resolved that when a preacher becomes a widower and is obliged to continue housekeeping, his support shall be the same as though his wife were living. On Sunday forenoon Bishop Long preached the ordination sermon. In the afternoon Bishop Orwig ordained the candidates for orders, after which the Lord's Supper was solemnly observed. Bishop Orwig being necessitated to leave in order to preside over the Central Pa. Conference he was respectfully excused. Bishop Long presided during the remainder of the session. A committee was appointed to look after the affairs of the missions of this Conference during the year and to report at the next annual session. The Conference resolved to organize a Sunday-school and Tract Society, auxiliary to the parent society of the Evangelical Association. S. Neitz, J. Yeakel, and S. G. Rhoads were appointed to draft a suitable constitution and to report at the next annual session.

BOUNDARIES.

Williams Township was detached from Easton, and the latter constituted a mission. New York Mission was called Jersey City Mission. All the appointments on Lehigh Circuit south of Lehigh Mountain, together with Bethlehem, Freemansburg, and Williams Township were formed into a new field called Bethlehem Circuit; Cedar Creek, Catasauqua, Bliem's class, Emaus, and Macungie to remain as Lehigh Circuit. Pricetown, Oley, Friedensburgh, and Ccxtown (Fleetwood) were taken from Milford and annexed to Kutztown Cir., with the understanding that Hamburg and Leesport be taken into consideration by the preachers. Fisher's class was restored to Lebanon Circuit. Wiconisco Sta. was annexed to Lykens Cir., and Zion, Deepcreek, and Mahanoy were detached from the circuit and formed into a new field to be known as Ashland Cir. The Conference was divided into four presiding elder districts.

CHURCH AFFAIRS.

Permission was granted to the stationing committee to re-appoint the missionary of the North Philadelphia Miss. for one year additional, on account of the existing circumstances incident to the church building project.*

It was resolved that hereafter the New Jersey Cir. should receive no support from the Conference. Inasmuch as there still remained a debt upon the Albright Memorial Church, the preachers present paid it and resolved that henceforth the Conference will assume no responsibility for the financial management of this church and that all its affairs are herewith referred to

---

*This action was declared irregular by the General Conference of 1863.

the congregation worshipping there.   Permission was
given to the missionaries and collectors of mission
churches to gather contributions within the bounds of
the Conference.

EDUCATION.

L. Snyder and J. Swab were elected trustees of Union
Seminary.   L. Snyder, G. Knerr, and W. Yost were
appointed a visiting committee to attend the commencement exercises.   The last Thursday in February of each
year was appointed as a day of prayer for our several
institutions of learning.   The following were elected
to examine the junior preachers in their studies at the
next session: F. Hoffman in theology, W. L. Reber in
discipline, J. Yeakel in German grammar, S. G. Rhoads
in English grammar, and S. Neitz in secular and ecclesiastical history.

MEMORIAL.

WHEREAS, It pleased the Great Head of the Church
on the fourth day of January, 1859, to call our highly
esteemed and universally beloved first bishop, John Seybert, from the post of duty which he so faithfully
guarded, and to conduct his spirit into the world of the
blessed, therefore be it

Resolved, That in his decease our church has lost an
energetic and devoted shepherd and teacher, plain and
unassuming, but true.   Though deeply sensible of our
loss, we yet seek to be submissive to the will of God in
the mysterious ways of his Providence, and rejoice that
after having endured many labors and outstood many
conflicts, our sainted bishop has entered into rest.   We
pray that a double portion of his spirit may abide upon
our ministry now and at all times.   Amen!

12

APPOINTMENTS.

PHILADELPHIA DISTRICT—*G. T. Haines*, P. E.
Philadelphia Sta.—J. P. Leib.
South Philadelphia Sta.—F. Walker.
N'th Philadelphia Miss.—S. P. Reinoehl.
Germantown Sta.—C. Meyers.
Montgomery Cir.—T. Sebold and J. Kutz.
Milford Cir.—D. Wieand and T. Plattenberger.
Kutztown Cir.—A. Ziegenfus and R. Litzenberger.
Bethlehem Cir.—F. Krecker and H. Kempfer.
Camden Miss.—L. Schmidt.
Norristown Miss.—J. Schneider.

LEHIGH DISTRICT—*S. Neitz*, P. E.
Allentown Sta.—S. G. Rhoads.
Lehigh Cir.—Moses Dissinger.
Monroe Cir.—J. Frey and G. B. Fisher.
Carbon Cir.—A. Schultz and J. Specht.
Northampton Cir.—E. Butz and T. Bowman.
Easton Miss.—J. Yeakel.
New York Sta.—E. Ely.
Newark Miss.—N. Goebel.
Jersey City Miss.—H. Koester.

New Jersey Cir —D. Hambright.

LEBANON DISTRICT—*F. Hoffman*, P. E.
Reading Sta.—I. Hess.
Womelsdorf Cir.—C. Gingrich and T. Harper.
Lebanon Sta.—J. Koehl.
Lebanon Cir.—J. O. Lehr and M. Guhl.
Lancaster Sta.—J. G. Marquardt.
Lancaster Cir.—F. P. Lehr and J. Steitzer.
Chester Cir.—J. A. Apgar.
Harrisburg Miss.—A. Boetzel.
Dauphin Cir.—E. B. Miller.

ORWIGSBURG DISTRICT — *L. Snyder*, P. E.
Orwigsburg Cir.—H Stoetzel.
Schuylkill Cir. — J. Schell and D. Yingst.
Schuylkill Haven Cir.—C. S. Haman.
Pinegrove Cir.—Jacob Adams.
Tamaqua Miss.—W. H. Bachman.
Lykens Cir.—W. Yost and J Zern.
Mahantongo Cir.—G. Knerr and S. S. Chubb.
Ashland Cir.—M. Sindlinger.
Pottsville Sta.—J. Gross.

1861.

The Twenty-Second (54th) Annual Session.

President, Bishop J. Long.
Secretary, Jesse Yeakel.
Assistant Secretaries, John Koehl and S. G. Rhoads.

The members of the East Pa. Conference assembled in annual session at Schuylkill Haven, Pa., on Wednesday, February 27th, 1861, Bishop Long presiding. The secretary was instructed to report the proceedings to the *Evangelical Messenger.* The following standing committees were appointed: On Worship, — The Bishop, the presiding elders, and the preacher in charge; On Letters,—G. T. Haines, S. Neitz, C. Meyers, F. Hoffman, and L. Snyder; On Finance,—I. Hess, S. P. Reinoehl, and J. Schell; On Boundaries,—The Bishop and the presiding elders; On Statistics,—J. Gross, J. P. Leib, and A. Schultz; On Education,—F. Hoffman, W. Yost, R. Deisher, S. P. Reinoehl, and J. Yeakel; On Missions,—G. T. Haines, F. Hoffman, and W. L. Reber.

A. H. Theobold resigned his license as local preacher. This Conference was informed that a local preacher had been deposed from the ministry and expelled from the church during the year. Jacob Schneider located on account of ill health. D. Berger took a superannuated relation. C. B. Fliehr desiring to enter a western conference received credentials. M. Guhl was ordained to the office of Elder. The following were ordained to the office of Deacon: J. Kutz, D. Yuengst, T. Bowman, J. A. Apgar, J. Steltzer, Abr. Saylor, and H. Kletzing. J. K. Knerr received license as preacher on trial. W. Heim and R. Deisher were again received, and J. Kurtz and I. E. Knerr were newly received into the itinerancy. S. Neitz was elected delegate to the board of missions. The conference claimants were Sister Schnerr and one child, Sister Bisse and two children, and Sister Hesser.

It was resolved that hereafter the presiding bishop shall appoint the various committees, unless the Conference orders otherwise in special cases. The action of the board of publication of our church in appointing S. Neitz to write the biography of Bishop Seybert was endorsed, and he was advised to begin the work at once. In accordance with this action S. Neitz resigned his presiding eldership and W. L. Reber was elected in his place. The secretary was instructed to procure a suitable record in which to enter the statistics of the Conference. It was agreed that if the presiding elders can not collect their house rent in the ordinary way that they be permitted to draw the deficiency out of the general salary fund. The Conference resolved not to recognize the probation system and therefore not to take it into account in the statistics; nevertheless it was left optional with the various congregations to proceed according to their judgment in the reception of members. Pursuant to this, the question, "How many newly received members?" was substituted for "How many members on probation?" in the statistical blank.

The committee appointed for the purpose reported a constitution for a Sunday-school and Tract Society of this Conference. The report was adopted and the society organized by the election of the following officers: President, S. G. Rhoads; Vice President, J. Yeakel; Secretary, J. Koehl; Treasurer, F. Krecker. The members then paid in the sum of $26.45. A resolution strongly denouncing so-called gift-book enterprises and similar humbugs, and earnestly counselling preachers and people to use their influence against them was adopted. On Sunday forenoon Bishop Orwig preached the ordination sermon. The ordination services were held in the afternoon, after which preachers and people celebrated the Lord's Supper. Bishop Long preached in the evening.

Norristown and Phœnixville were constituted a mission. Annville, Steelston, Campelstown, Elmira, and Meyers class were called Annville Circuit. Jonestown, Mt. Nebo, Mountville, Fisher's class, Fredericksburgh, Union Church, and Boltz's class were called Jonestown Circuit. Tamaqua was made a station. Meyerstown, Eby's class, Schaeferstown, Albright church, Livingood class, Stricklerstown, and Richland were formed into Myerstown Circuit. Hasenberg, Brownstown, Fairville, Flickinger church, Reamstown, Adamstown, Mohn's church, Mohnsville, and Brendels were organized into Fairville Circuit. Bernville, Berne Twp., Klein's, Stranstown, Dundore's, Forge, Womelsdorf, and Newmanstown were called Womelsdorf Circuit. Catawissa Valley and Shamokin were annexed to Ashland Circuit. Cressona and Friedensburg were called Cressona Circuit. Zion class was taken from Ashland Cir. and annexed to Lykens Cir. Port Carbon and St. Clair was called Port Carbon Cir. Millerstown class was taken from Milford Cir. and annexed to Lehigh Cir. Hanover church was taken from Dauphin Cir. and attached to Annville Cir. An English mission was located in the city of Reading. New York Miss. was connected with Union Hill. The trustees of Mt. Bethel congregation, Cecil Co., Md, received permission to sell their church, pay the debts and report at the next session of the Conference.

EDUCATION.

The trustees representing this Conference were instructed to adopt measures for the endowment of Union

Seminary as soon as the financial condition of the country will warrant it, and to gather in all outstanding subscriptions and the scholarships of such persons who are sufficiently interested in the welfare of the school to surrender them. L. Snyder resigned the trusteeship of the seminary and J. Yeakel was elected in his place. H. Stoetzel and H. Eberly were newly elected trustees. W. H. Bachman, W. Heim, and A. Boetzel were appointed a visiting committee to attend the closing exercises of Union Seminary.

Recognizing the weighty responsibility resting upon us, with reference to the coming generation, and convinced of the usefulness of catechetical instruction, be it herewith *Resolved*, That in the coming year we will faithfully and diligently observe the duties imposed upon us by our Church Discipline in this respect.

APPOINTMENTS.

PHILADELPHIA DISTRICT—*G. T. Haines, P. E.*
Philadelphia Sta.—G. Knerr.
Sth. Philadelphia Sta.—F. Walker.
Nth. Philadelphia Miss.—J. G. Marquardt.
Germantown Sta.—C. Meyers.
Montgomery Cir.—T. Sebold and J. Kutz.
Milford Cir.—A. Ziegenfus and I. E. Knerr.
Kutztown Cir.—E. Butz and J. Kurtz.
Bethlehem Cir.—F. Krecker and H. Kempfer.
Glassborough Miss.—L. Schmidt.
Norristown Miss.—D. Wieand.

LEHIGH DISTRICT—*W. L. Reber, P. E.*
Allentown Sta.—S. G. Rhoads.
Lehigh Cir.—Moses Dissinger.
Monroe Cir.—T. Plattenberger and S. S. Chubb.
Carbon Cir.—A. Shultz and H. Koester.

Northampton Cir.—T. Bowman.
New Jersey Cir.—D. Hambright.
New York Sta.—E. Ely.
New York Miss.—J. Specht.
Newark Miss.—J. Steltzer.
Easton Miss.—J. Yeakel.

LEBANON DISTRICT—*F. Hoffman, P. E.*
Reading Sta.—I. Hess.
Reading Miss.—G. B. Fisher.
Lebanon Sta.—J. Koehl.
Lancaster Sta.—F. P. Lehr.
Dauphin Cir.—W. H. Bachman.
Annville Cir.—M. Guhl.
Jonestown Cir.—D. Yingst.
Meyerstown Cir.—J. O. Lehr.
Womelsdorf Cir.—N. Goebel.
Fairville Cir.—R. Deisher and E. B. Miller.
Lancaster Cir.—R. Litzenberger and T. Harper.
Chester Cir.—J. A. Apgar.
Harrisburg Miss.—H. Stoetzel.

ORWIGSBURG DISTRICT — *L. Snyder*, P. E.
Pottsville Sta.—C. S. Haman.
Orwigsburg Cir.—J. Schell.
Schuylkill Cir.—J. Zern.
Schuylkill Haven Cir.—W. Yost.
Pinegrove Cir.—J. Adams.

Lykens Cir. — C. Gingrich and A. Boetzel.
Mahantongo Cir. — W. Helm and M. Sindlinger.
Ashland Cir.—J. Gross.
Tamaqua Sta.—S. P. Reinoehl.
Cressona Cir.—J. P. Leib.
Port Carbon Cir.—J. Frey.

1862.

The Twenty-Third (55th) Annual Session

President, Bishop W. W. Orwig.
Secretary, John Koehl.
Assistant Secretary, C. S. Haman.

The twenty third session of the East Pa. Conference was held in the city of Reading, Pa., beginning on Wednesday, February 26th, 1862. S. G. Rhoads was appointed to report the proceedings of the Conference for the *Evangelical Messenger*. The Bishop appointed the following standing committees: On Worship,— The presiding elders and the preachers in charge of the Reading churches; On Letters,—J. Yeakel and J. P. Leib; On Finance,—S. P. Reinoehl, W. Yost, and F. Krecker; On Statistics,—C. Meyers, A. Shultz, and R. Deisher; On Education,—H. Stoetzel, J. Yeakel, and W. Yost; On Publication of Manuscripts,—S. Neitz and F. Krecker.

H. Kempfer, D. Hambright, and H. Koester located on account of family affairs, and T. Sebold on account of ill health. P. H. Lehr withdrew from the church. Credentials were granted to F. W. Walker who desired to unite with the Illinois Conference. S. Neitz was elected Presiding Elder. A. Boetzel, J. Specht, and E.

Butz were ordained to the office of Elder ; S. S. Chubb, L. Schmidt, G. B. Fisher, C. Wolf, and W. Rogers, to the office of Deacon.   The following were received as preachers on trial :   Wm. Alspach, Benjamin F. Bohner, Levi Miller, Augustus Scharf, Simon Frankenfield, Samuel Brown, Adam Goetschel, and David Lentz.   R. M. Lichtenwalner, C. K. Fehr, C. H. Baker, and Seneca Breyfogel were received into the itinerancy.   The Conference beneficiaries were Sister Schnerr and one child, Sister Bisse and one child, and Sister Hesser.   S. Neitz was elected delegate to the board of missions, and G. T. Haines alternate.

The Charitable Society of the Evangelical Association having requested the appointment of J. P. Leib as its agent during the year, the Conference granted the request and retained him in the itinerancy.   It was resolved that hereafter the roll of the Conference be called at the opening of each daily session, and the absentees held accountable.   The stationing committee was instructed to have a meeting for consultation at each annual session of the Conference, prior to the investigation of the moral and official conduct of the preachers.   The object of the meeting shall be to consider such brethren who, on account of incompetency or for other reasons, cause great difficulty in the stationing, and if there be such cases to report them to the Conference during the investigation.   S. Neitz, W. L. Reber, and G. T. Haines were appointed a standing committee on missions for the ensuing year.   The conference appointed J. P. Leib trustee of the Custer bequest, with instructions to gather in the money and to obtain good security for it.

On Sunday forenoon Bishop Orwig preached an unctious and instructive ordination sermon on 2 Tim. 4:5. In the afternoon the candidates for orders were ordained, after which preachers and people celebrated the Lord's Supper. C. Meyers delivered the communion address. In the evening, on account of the great throng of people, sermons were preached in the upper and lower audience rooms of the church. On Monday morning Bishop Orwig left the Conference in order to preside at the session of the Central Pa. Conference. He appointed S. Neitz chairman in his place.

BOUNDARIES.

Millersburg, Weber's class, Pauls Valley, and Fisher's class were taken from Lykens Circuit and organized into a new field, called Millersburg Cir. Schuylkill Haven was made a station. The Flat, Cressona, and St. Clair were formed into Cressona Cir. Ashland Cir. was extended to include Hazleton and the territory between Hazleton and Mahanoy City. Albany was taken from Schuylkill Cir. and annexed to Kutztown. Port Carbon was annexed to Pottsville Station. Rising Sun was transferred from the North Philadelphia Mission to Germantown Station. Reading Mission was taken from Lebanon District and added to Philadelphia District. Chester Cir. was taken from Lebanon District and annexed to Lehigh District.

CHURCH AFFAIRS.

It was resolved that in case application is made The Flat shall receive its rightful share of the parsonage at Schuylkill Haven. Inasmuch as the trustees of the

English Mission in the city of Reading have sent in a petition in which they obligate themselves to purchase and pay for the Mount Zion church of the Protestant Methodist congregation in that city, in case we send them a missionary for three years and support him; therefore, be it *Resolved*, That we regard this offer on the part of the mission a noble one and suggest to them not to be concerned about the continuation of their missionary appropriation in case they keep the promise made by the trustees, in the purchase of said building. It was decided that Dauphin Circuit is entitled to the entire amount of money collected for a parsonage and now in the possession of J. Ely, upon the ground that since their separation from Lebanon Cir. they have received none of the interest from their portion of the contributions; that J. Ely be authorized to pay the money to W. H. Bachman, preacher in charge of Dauphin Cir.; that this Conference approves of the action of the quarterly conference of Dauphin Cir. of February 12, 1862, viz: That W. H. Bachman shall pay the half of this money to H. Stoetzel (missionary at Harrisburg) for the church building at Harrisburg and that the balance of the money be applied to the erection of a church on Dauphin Cir. S. Neitz, H. Stoetzel and C. H. Baker were appointed a committee to superintend the erection of a church building at Harrisburg. S. Neitz, W. L. Reber and E. Ely were appointed a committee to act with reference to the affairs of our English Mission in Reading.

EDUCATION.

The trustees representing this Conference were instructed to continue Union Seminary upon condition that the aggregate salary of the teachers does not exceed sixteen hundred dollars. S. Neitz and J. P. Leib were elected ministerial trustees, and Henry Saylor lay trustee of the seminary. The Conference agreed to assist the newly elected agent in securing one hundred persons who are willing to pay $50 each, and in gathering smaller sums for the benefit of the seminary. J. Yeakel, H. Stoetzel, and W. Heim were appointed a visiting committee to attend the commencement exercises. The committee appointed at the last session to examine junior preachers in their studies was continued, with instructions to make suitable reports to Conference.

APPOINTMENTS.

PHILADELPHIA DISTRICT—*G. T. Haines*, P. E.
Philadelphia Sta.—G. Knerr.
Sth. Philadelphia Sta.—C. Meyers.
Nth. Philadelphia Miss.—J. G. Marquardt.
Germantown Sta.—M. Guhl.
Montgomery Cir.—F. Krecker (and one to be supplied.)
Milford Cir.—J. Adams and Seneca Breyfogel.
Kutztown Cir.—F. Butz and J. Kurtz.
Bethlehem Cir.—A. Ziegenfus and R. M. Lichtenwalner.
Glassborough Miss.—N. Goebel.
Norristown Miss.—D. Wieand.
Reading Miss.—J. A. Apgar.

LEHIGH DISTRICT—*W. L. Reber*, P. E.
Lehigh Cir.—1. Hess and C. K. Fehr.
Carbon Cir.—S. G. Rhoads (and one to be supplied.)
Allentown Sta.—T. Bowman.
Monroe Cir.—J. Gross.
Northampton Cir.—T. Harper and T. Plattenberger.
New Jersey Cir.—(To be supplied.)
New York Sta.—A. Schultz.
New York Miss.—J. Specht.

Newark Miss.—J. Steltzer.
Easton Miss.—J. Koehl.
Chester Cir.—G. B. Fisher.

LEBANON DISTRICT—*S. Neitz*, P. E.
Reading Sta.—E. Ely.
Womelsdorf Cir.—M. Dissinger.
Fairville Cir. — R. Deisher and S. S. Chubb.
Meyerstown Cir.—D. Yingst.
Lebanon Sta.—J. Schell.
Jonestown Cir.—J. Kutz.
Annville Cir.—L. Schmidt.
Lancaster Cir.—R. Litzenberger and C. H. Baker.
Lancaster Sta.—F. P. Lehr.
Dauphin Cir.—W. H. Bachman.
Harrisburg Miss.—H. Stoetzel.

ORWIGSBURG DISTRICT — *L. Snyder*, P. E.
Orwigsburg Cir.—J. O. Lehr.
Schuylkill Cir.—J. Zern.
Tamaqua Sta.—S. P. Reinoehl.
Schuylkill Haven Sta.—W. Yost.
Cressona Cir.—E. B. Miller.
Pinegrove Cir.—F. Hoffman.
Pottsville Sta.—C. S. Haman.
Ashland Cir.—J. Frey and I. E. Knerr.

Mahantongo Cir.—A. Boetzel and M. Sindlinger.

Lykens Cir.—C. Gingrich.

Millersburg Cir.—W. Heim.

J. P. Leib, agent for the Charitable Society.

J. Yeakel, collector for Union Seminary.

1863.

The Twenty-Fourth (56th) Annual Session.

President, Bishop W. W. Orwig.

Secretary, John Koehl.

Assistant Secretary, C. S. Haman.

The members of the East Pa. Conference assembled at Millersburg, Dauphin Co., Pa., on Wednesday, February 25th, 1863. In the absence of Bishop Long the Conference was opened by Bishop Orwig. F. Krecker was appointed to report the proceedings for the *Evangelical Messenger.* The following committees were appointed: On Letters,—C. Meyers, F. Hoffman, and J. P. Leib; On Worship,—W. Heim and the presiding elders; On Boundaries,—S. Neitz, G. T. Haines, W. L. Reber, and L. Snyder; On Finance,—I. Hess, S. P. Reinoehl, and R. Deisher; On Statistics,—A. Schultz, T. Bowman, and J. Schell; On Education,—J. P. Leib, H. Stoetzel, and S. G. Rhoads.

J. Frey located on account of ill health. Joseph Gross was placed in a local relation. D. Hechler, a local preacher, withdrew from the church. W. L. Reber resigned his office as presiding elder and J. Yeakel was elected to fill his place. T. Bowman, J. Steltzer, and D. Yingst were ordained Elders; J. Kurtz, C. K. Fehr, R. M. Lichtenwalner, C. B. Fliehr, I. E. Knerr, Seneca Breyfogel, and J. C. Bliem Deacons. C. Loose was again received, and C. B. Fliehr and D. Lentz were newly received into the itinerancy. The conference beneficiaries were Sister Hesser, Sister Schnerr, and Sister Bisse and one child.

The Conference resolved that the preachers shall not exchange boarding places during the session. Those present were forbidden to divulge any of the transactions occurring during secret session on penalty of being excluded from the investigations at the next annual session. Because of Bishop Orwig's delicate health, J. P. Leib was appointed to preach the ordination sermon in the event that Bishop Long should not arrive in time. But the latter having arrived he took the chair and presided during the remainder of the session. On Sabbath morning he preached the ordination sermon in his usually clear and powerful style, taking for his text, 2 Tim. 4:5, and producing a profound impression upon the entire congregation. In the afternoon after the ordination services the Conference and the assembled congregation participated in the Lord's Supper, during which the Holy Spirit was poured into the hearts of all present. S. Smith, of the Central Pa. Conference, preached in the evening.

The following were elected delegates to the General Conference: S. Neitz, G. T. Haines, J. Yeakel, L. Snyder, J. P. Leib, F. Hoffman, S. G. Rhoads, F. Krecker, C. Meyers, H. Stoetzel, and J. Koehl. The alternates were J. Schell, C. S. Haman, and I. Hess. It was ordered that collections to defray the traveling expenses of delegates to the General Conference be taken at all the appointments during the month of July, and that collections for the support of the superan-

nuated preachers be taken at all the appointments during the month of October. The preachers were instructed to organize missionary auxiliaries wherever it
is possible, and to gather contributions by other means.
Neglect of this important duty on the part of any was
to be rebuked by the presiding elder and reported to
the annual Conference. The Conference instructed the
presiding elders to see to it that a missionary sermon is
preached and contributions solicited at every campmeeting.

S. Neitz, S. G. Rhoads, and H. Stoetzel having been
appointed to prepare resolutions upon the affairs of the
country made the following report :

WHEREAS, We are in harmony with the Word of God,
as well as with our nineteenth article of faith which declares the Union, the Constitution and the Government of
the United States to have a rightful existence and to be a
great blessing to the church and to mankind ; and
whereas we consider the present fratricidal and satanic
rebellion in the South as groundless and without
righteous cause, and as high treason against our glorious
Union, which is the best government to be found in the
earth ; and whereas we consider African slavery a political, social and moral evil, the product of hell, "the sum
of all baseness," a remnant of heathenism, and according to the testimony of southern statesmen and patriots,
such as Johnson, Holt, Brownlow, and others, the only
true original cause of the present ungodly and hellish
rebellion ; therefore be it unanimously

Resolved, 1st, That we declare ourselves to be un-
conditionally in favor of the preservation of the Union
and the suppressing of the rebellion. 2d, That we

heartily approve of the honest and patriotic efforts of the President of the United States to extirpate the rebellion root and branch, and to place an undivided Union upon the broad foundation of civil and religious freedom as laid in the Constitution; that we welcome the "Emancipation Proclamation" as timely and as conformable to the spirit of the Constitution and the beck of divine Providence; that we unanimously unite in supporting with our influence and assistance our government in the stress of its conflict with high treason, tyranny, and slavery, in its heroic struggle for order, freedom, right, and the security of its citizens; and that above all we will remember the same in our prayers before God, for this is acceptable before the Lord our Saviour. 3d, That we observe with deep interest and with high regard the self-denying, sacrificing, and heroic spirit which our soldiers exhibit on every battlefield, and that we will remember them in our prayers and with our practical support. 4th, That we agree with the immortal Washington, the father of our precious freedom, in his farewell address, that party animosity—without regard to any party or section—is a menace to the preservation of the Union and of liberty, especially at the present time when the question is not one of party ascendancy, but of the maintenance and perpetuation of the Union and the life of the nation. We therefore earnestly and fraternally call upon all loyal and patriotic citizens, especially all members of the Evangelical Association, to keep themselves free from this destructive spirit and to refrain from supporting those political papers which cultivate such an influence. 5th, That we heartily approve of the attitude taken by our periodicals, the *Christliche Botschafter* and the *Evangelical Messenger*, with reference to the affairs of our country and upon the question of slavery, because we believe it to be the only truly loyal one in these times of high treason and secession, and that we therefore call to our editors, *Assert your convictions fearlessly, you shall and must be sustained!*

These resolutions were adopted amid great enthusiasm. T. G. Clewell, editor of the *Messenger*, was requested to send a copy of them to the President of the United States.

BOUNDARIES.

Norristown Mission was annexed to Montgomery Circuit. Camden class was added to South Philadelphia Station. "The Beach" was taken from Monroe Circuit and joined to a new mission called Wayne Mission. New York Mission was annexed to New York Station. Hazleton and vicinity was taken up as a mission. Port Carbon and St. Clair were taken from Pottsville Station and called Port Carbon Circuit.

CHURCH AFFAIRS.

The request of the members of the North Philadelphia Mission to sell their present church in order to build a new one was granted, Conference, however, not making itself in any way responsible for the new building. The congregation of our New York Station received permission to send out a collector to liquidate an oppressive debt. The preacher in charge of Annville Cir. was authorized to collect for a church (not named) on that circuit. R. Deisher was instructed to collect for our church at Harrisburg.

EDUCATION.

The Six Year Endowment Plan.

The financial condition of Union Seminary and the new plan of the trustees for the endowment of that institution were submitted by Bishop Orwig. The plan was adopted. It is as follows:

The endowment shall be $15,600; to be raised in six years, by subscriptions. These subscriptions shall be in sums of ten, five, and three dollars per annum for a period of six years. Subscribers of ten dollars per annum shall be entitled to six years' tuition for their contribution; those subscribing five dollars, to two and a half years' tuition; and those subscribing three dollars, to tuition for a half session each year of the six. As soon as the sum of $15,600.00 has been secured the endowment shall be valid. Each subscriber is requested to give a note for the amount of his subscription, to be paid in six annual installments without interest. In order to execute this plan effectively each of the two conferences interested is to appoint an agent whose duty it shall be to preach and solicit subscriptions. The financial statement of J. Yeakel, agent for the seminary during the past year, was as follows: Subscriptions secured, $6,059.00; cash receipts, $1,087.50; salary, house rent, and expenses, $509.82. H. Stoetzel was elected the agent for this Conference. Rev. R. Deisher and Messrs. J. Schwab and H. Wiest were elected trustees. W. Yost, C. S. Haman, and A. Schultz were appointed to visit the closing exercises of the seminary. The committee to examine junior preachers was re-appointed for next year.

13

APPOINTMENTS.

PHILADELPHIA DISTRICT—*G. T. Haines,* P. E.
Philadelphia Sta.—C. Loos.
South Philadelphia Sta.—C. Meyers.
North Philadelphia Miss.—J. Specht.
Germantown Sta.—M. Guhl.
Montgomery Cir.—F. Krecker (and one to be supplied.)
Milford Cir.—E. Butz and Seneca Breyfogel.
Kutztown Cir.—J. P. Leib and R. M Lichtenwalner.
Bethlehem Cir.—A. Ziegenfus and J. Kurtz.
Glassborough Miss.—N. Goebel.

LEHIGH DISTRICT—*J. Yeakel, P. E.*
Lehigh Cir.—Isaac Hess and R. Litzenberger.
Carbon Cir.—S. G. Rhoads and J. Zern.
Allentown Sta.—T. Bowman.
Monroe Cir.—T. Harper.
Northampton Cir.—W. H. Bachman and C. B. Fliehr.
New York Sta.—G. Knerr.
Newark Miss.—L. Schmidt.
Easton Miss.—J. Koehl.
Wayne Miss.—T. Plattenberger.

LEBANON DISTRICT—*S. Neitz, P. E.*
Reading Sta.—D. Wieand.
Womelsdorf Cir.—C. K. Fehr.

Fairville Cir.—E. Ely and C. H. Baker·
Myerstown Cir.—D. Yingst.
Lebanon Sta.—J. Schell.
Jonestown Cir.—J. H. Kutz.
Annville Cir.—M. Sindlinger.
Lancaster Cir.—M. Dissinger and S. S. Chubb.
Lancaster Sta.—W. L. Reber.
Dauphin Cir.—F. P. Lehr.
Harrisburg Miss.—R. Deisher.
Chester Cir.—G. B. Fisher (and one to be supplied.)
Reading (Eng.) Miss.—J. A. Apgar.

**ORWIGSBURG DISTRICT — ***L. Snyder,* P. E.
Orwigsburg Cir.—J. O. Lehr.
Schuylkill Cir.—J. Adams.
Tamaqua Sta.—A. Boetzel.
Schuylkill Haven Sta.—S. P. Reinoehl.
Cressona Cir.—E. B. Miller.
Pinegrove Cir.—F. Hoffman.
Pottsville Sta.—W. Yost.
Ashland Cir. — C. Gingrich and D. Lentz.
Mahantongo Cir.—A. Schultz and J. Steltzer.
Lykens Cir.—C. S. Haman.
Millersburg Cir.—W. Heim.
Hazleton Miss.—I. E. Knerr.
Port Carbon Cir.—J. G. Marquardt.
Agent for Union Seminary—H. Stoetzel.

1863.

The General Conference.

Presidents, Bishops J. Long and W. W. Orwig.
Secretary, Jesse Yeakel.
Assistant Secretaries, R. Dubs, J. G. Zinser, and C. A. Schnake.

The General Conference session of 1863 was held in Buffalo, N. Y., beginning October 1st and continuing until October 20th.* The delegates present represented nine annual conferences. The examination of the conduct of the delegates occurred with closed doors. The official conduct of the editors, the general book agent, and the corresponding secretary of the Missionary Society was investigated and no charges preferred. At this session *The Canada*, *The Michigan*, and *The Kansas* conferences were formed. It was resolved that an English Sunday-school periodical, called *The Sunday-School Messenger*, be published.

The elections resulted as follows: Bishops, J. Long and J. J. Esher; editor of the *Christliche Botschafter*, W. W. Orwig; editor of the *Evangelical Messenger*, T. G. Clewell; editor of the S. S. and Tract Literature, R. Yeakel; general book agent, C. Hammer; corresponding secretary of the Missionary Society, C. F. Deininger, who resigned, whereupon Wm. Yost was elected. S. Neitz was elected Presiding Elder of our Missions in Germany, but respectfully resigned, after which J. G. Wollpert was elected. S. Neitz was chosen to represent the East Pa. Conference in the board of publication. The Conference elected M. F. Maize, W. E. Boyer, Charles Wiltrout, and Thos. Clouse, trustees of the Charitable Society.

The following statistics were reported: Traveling Preachers, 386; Local Preachers, 358; Entire Membership, 47,674; Churches, 632; Parsonages, 129; Sunday-schools, 584; Officers and Teachers, 6,026; Scholars, 26,483; Catechetical Classes, 187; Catechumens, 1,687.

*See Preface on page 98.

1864.

The Twenty-Fifth (57th) Annual Session.

President, Bishop J. Long.
Secretary, Frederick Krecker.
Assistant Secretaries, Reuben Deisher and C. S. Haman.

The Conference was opened on Thursday, February 25th, 1864, in the Immanuel Evangelical Church at Phildelphia, Pa. The following committees were announced by the chairman: On Worship,—The preacher in charge and the presiding elders; On Letters,—J. P. Leib, F. Hoffman, and H. Stoetzel; On Statistics,—W. Heim, A. Schultz, and C. K. Fehr; On Finance,—J. Schell, S. P. Reinoehl, and G. B. Fisher; On Boundaries,—The Bishop and the presiding elders; On Education,—F. Hoffman, W. Yost, S. G. Rhoads, L. Snyder, and C. Meyers.

P. Schwerer, Levi Wentz, and H. Schwarz resigned their licenses as local preachers. John Kleinfelter, local elder, died during the past year. W. L. Reber, L. Schmidt, and R. Litzenberger located on account of ill health; W. H. Bachman, on account of family concerns. G. T. Haines and L. Snyder were re-elected to the office of Presiding Elder. S. S. Chubb, T. Harper, G. B. Fisher, C. H. Baker, and J. A. Apgar were ordained Elders and David Lentz, Deacon. John Eckert was again received as local elder. J. M. Saylor was again received into the itinerancy; B. F. Bohner, S. B. Brown, Adam Goetschel, and D. Z. Kemble were newly received. The following received license as preachers on trial: Jonas F. Yerger, Aaron H. Overholt, and Henry

Guelich.   The widows and orphans having claims upon the Conference for support are Sister Hesser, Sister Schnerr, and Sister Bisse and one child.   S. Neitz was elected delegate to the board of missions.   It was announced that W. Yost had been elected corresponding secretary of the Missionary Society by the General Conference and that M. Guhl had been called as missionary to California by the board of missions.   Bishop J. J. Esher was introduced to the Conference by S. Neitz and was cordially received.

The Conference resolved that the presiding elders shall always be present at the ordination of preachers and that the presiding bishop be required to give due notice to such who are to take part in the services.   On Sunday forenoon Bishop Long preached the ordination sermon from 1 Cor. iv :1-2.   After the sermon the newly elected deacon was ordained.   In the afternoon the elders were ordained after which the Lord's Supper was celebrated.

BOUNDARIES.

Catasauqua was taken from Lehigh Cir. and constituted a station.   New York Miss. was again taken up and supplied.   Norristown and Phoenixville were taken from Montgomery Cir. and formed into a station.   Tremont was taken from Pinegrove Cir. and called Tremont Cir.   An English Mission was located in Philadelphia.   Jonestown Cir. (with the exception of Zion class which was annexed to Meyerstown Cir.) was added to Annville Cir.   Bridesburg and vicinity were taken up as a mission.   Deibert class was taken from Schuylkill Haven and annexed to Cressona Cir.

CHURCH AFFAIRS.

The Conference urged the congregation at Hatfield to build a new church at Hatfield Way. C. Loos, H. Stoetzel, and J. Specht were appointed to inquire into the title of the ground held by the North Phila. Mission and to superintend the erection of a new church. Permission to collect was granted to all debt-burdened churches, with the proviso that only missionaries be allowed to go beyond their respective districts.

EDUCATION.

J. Yeakel, S. Neitz, and J. P. Leib were appointed delegates, and J. M. Saylor alternate, to the Central Pa. Conference to act with reference to the affairs of Union Seminary according to their best judgment. Trustees for Union Seminary were elected as follows: J. M. Saylor and C. S. Haman for three years; A. Schultz and S. P. Reinoehl for two years; and Henry Maize—lay member—for three years. The following is a statement of the finances of the seminary:

Receipts of the seminary from its origin to
    February 10, 1864................ $38,492.02¾
Expenditures of the seminary from its or-
    igin to February 10, 1864........... 38,492.02¾

Present financial status of the seminary:

Liabilities:

Outstanding scholarships...... $11,000.00
Borrowed money and interest.. 2,800.00
                ————— $13,800.00

Assets :

Scholarships...............$11,000.00
Unpaid subscriptions in East
   Pa. Conference...........   789.00
Unpaid subscriptions in Cent.
   Pa. Conference...........   812.00
Furniture.................   200.00
Cash on hand..............   28.14
                                     12,829.14

Present indebtedness........ $ 970.86

FINANCE.

Received from conference collections........ $218.27
   "   "   the Charitable Society........ 95.16
   "   "   " Book Establishment....... 150.00

Total...................................$463.43
Paid to conference claimants.............. 463.43

APPOINTMENTS.

PHILADELPHIA DISTRICT—*L. Snyder*, P. E.
Philadelphia Sta.—C. Loos.
Sth. Philadelphia Sta.—H. Stoetzel.
Nth. Philadelphia Miss.—J. Specht.
Philadelphia Eng. Miss.—J. A. Apgar.
Germantown Sta.—W. Heim.
Montgomery Cir.—Seneca Breyfogel and G. B. Fisher.
Norristown and Phœnixville. ——
Milford Cir.—E. Butz and J. Fry.
Kutztown Cir.—R. M. Lichtenwalner.
Bethlehem Cir.—N. Goebel and J. Kurtz.
Glassborough Miss.—M Sindlinger.
Bridesburg Miss.—W. H. Weidner.

LEHIGH DISTRICT—*J. Yeakel*, P. E.
Lehigh Cir.—F. Hoffman.
Carbon Cir.—J. Zern and A. Goetschel.

Allentown Sta.—J. Koehl.
Catasauqua Sta.—J. Schell.
Monroe Cir.—T Harper.
Wayne Miss.—T. Plattenberger.
Northampton Cir.—C. B. Fliehr and S. B. Brown.
New York Sta.—G. Knerr.
New York Miss.—C. Myers.
Newark Miss.—A. Ziegenfus.
Easton Miss.—I. Hess.
Hazleton Miss.—I. E. Knerr.

LEBANON DISTRICT—*S. Neitz*, P. E.
Reading Sta.—D. Wieand.
Reading Eng. Miss.—T. Bowman.
Womelsdorf Cir.—C. K. Fehr.
Fairville Cir.—C. H. Baker and B. F. Bohner.
Myerstown Cir.—J. Kutz.
Lebanon Sta.—S. S. Chubb.

Annville Cir.—D. Yingst.
Lancaster Cir.—M. Dissinger and G. Focht.
Lancaster Sta.—E. Ely.
Dauphin Cir.—F. P. Lehr.
Harrisburg Miss.—R. Deisher.
Chester Cir.—E. B. Miller.

ORWIGSBURG DISTRICT—G. T. Haines, P. E.
Orwigsburg Cir.—D. Z. Kembel.
Schuylkill Cir.—J. Adams.
Tamaqua Sta.—A. Boetzel.
Schuylkill Haven Sta.—S. P. Reinoehl.

Cressona Cir.—F. Krecker.
Pinegrove Cir.—J. O. Lehr.
Tremont Cir.—J. P. Leib
Pottsville Sta.—S. G. Rhoads.
Ashland Cir.—C. Gingrich and D. Lentz.
Mahantongo Cir.—A. Schultz and J. Steltzer.
Lykens Cir.—C. S. Haman.
Millersburg Sta.—J. M. Saylor.
Port Carbon—J. G. Marquardt.
W. Yost, Cor. Secy. of the Miss. Soc'y.
M. Guhl, missionary to California.

1865.

The Twenty-Sixth (58th) Annual Session.

President, Bishop J. Long.
Secretary, S. G. Rhoads.
Assistant Secretaries, Henry Stoetzel and C. B. Fliehr.

The Conference session of 1865 was opened on Wednesday, February 22d, 1865, in Salem Church, Allentown, Pa. The chairman appointed the following committees: On Worship,—The presiding elders and the preacher in charge; On Letters,—F. Hoffman, F. Krecker, and J. Schell; On Statistics,—A. Schultz, W. Heim, and R. Deisher; On Finance,—F. Krecker, R. M. Lichtenwalner, and C. Myers; On Boundaries, —The Bishop and the presiding elders; On Education, —J. Yeakel, F. Hoffman, L. Snyder, T. Bowman, and G. B. Fisher; On Church Affairs,—J. P. Leib, C. Loos, and C. S. Haman.

It was reported that a local preacher had been expelled from the church during the year. A. Boetzel, elder, withdrew from the church.   Immanuel Schugar, local preacher, died during the past year.   Geo. Focht, desiring to unite with a western conference, received his credentials.   Elders' orders were granted to C. K. Fehr, R. M. Lichtenwalner, I. E. Knerr, C. B. Fliehr, J. Kurtz, and Seneca Breyfogel.   Deacons' orders were granted to D. Z. Kembel, W. H. Weidner, B. F. Bohner, A. Goetschel, G. Harm, and G. Focht.   O. L. Saylor, L. N. Worman, W. W. Rhoads, J. C. Hornberger, J. N. Metzgar, J. Laros, L. Kolb, A. Leopold, and D. Yeakel received license as preachers on trial. W. H. Weidner, L. N. Worman, J. N. Metzgar, A. H. Overholt, J. C. Hornberger, A. Leopold, and B. Moyer were newly received into the itinerancy ; J. Fry and D. Hambright were again received.   A. Hinckel who had withdrawn in 1858 was again received into his former relation of deacon.   The widows and orphans who receive support from the Conference are Sister Hesser, Sister Schnerr, and Sister Bisse and one child.   Each of these widows received $100 for the year.

Permission was given to the Sons of Temperance of Allentown to hold their anniversary service in this church on Tuesday evening, February 28th.   It was resolved that a committee be appointed to distribute the appropriations to the missionaries for the past year and to fix the appropriations for the coming year.

The committee appointed to prepare resolutions relative to the civil affairs of this country consisted of J. Yeakel, J. M. Saylor, and J. Koehl.   They made the following report: WHEREAS We are still decidedly of the loyal opinion expressed upon former occasions, as becomes Christian citizens; and whereas, since the last session of this Conference, certain occurrences in the affairs of our country have taken place which deeply affect our national life and its future preservation; therefore be it *Resolved*, 1st, That we most heartily participate in the spirit of thanksgiving to God, which at present animates all true lovers of our glorious Union, because the Great Director of all things has of late given our armies such decided victories and consequently secured to the cause of right the ultimate triumph. 2d, That we herewith express our gratitude to God that the hour of *freedom for all*, by virtue of law, has finally come in this land, and that as a consequence we may entertain the hope that the glorious gospel will have free course throughout the entire land and find access to all. 3d, That the recommendation to Congress to change the constitution of the U. S. so as to acknowledge the Most High Being by name, meets with our approval, and that we heartily desire its accomplishment. 4th, That at the same time we give expression to our profound sympathy for the surviving families of our brave soldiers who gave their lives as an offering upon the field of battle, in captivity, and in the hospitals of the war; and that we implore the blessings of heaven upon all their sorrowing ones.

Notwithstanding the fact that the General Conference at its recent session ordered an English Sunday-school paper and fixed the price of that periodical, at the same time lowering the price of the *Kinderfreund*, the board of publication has at its last session very materially increased the price of both of these papers; therefore be it *Resolved*, That as a Conference we protest against the action of the board of publication as injurious to the spread of our Sunday-school periodicals, and earnestly request the board to recall their action upon this subject and to abide by the resolutions of the General Conference.

Bishop Long preached an appropriate and powerful ordination sermon on Sunday forenoon from Matt. xxiv: 45–51. After the sermon the ordination of deacons took place. A. Goetschel, who could not be present, was ordained deacon on the following Tuesday evening. In the afternoon, after the ordination of the elders, the Lord's Supper was celebrated. This service will never be forgotten by those who participated. To God be all the glory. In the evening E. Kohr, of the Central Pa. Conference, preached.

BOUNDARIES.

Mahanoy City and Westhaus were taken up as a mission. Deibert class was taken from Cressona Cir. and restored to Schuylkill Haven Sta.

CHURCH AFFAIRS.

A committee was appointed to inquire into the advisability of purchasing Mr. M. Costner's church in New Jersey. J. Specht reported that the congregation of North Philadelphia Miss. was necessitated to purchase their church lot in order to secure a legal title. The cost of the lot was $1,333.34. Of this he collected and paid $333.34, leaving a debt of $1,000.00. R. Deisher of the Harrisburg church reported that the amount collected for that church was $1,632.50, a few dollars more than the amount required. It was decided that all collectors for churches be limited to their respective presiding elder districts.

It was resolved that the Central Pa., the Pittsburg, the New York, and the Canada conferences be invited to unite with this Conference in establishing a college in the eastern part of our church. That an endowment of $150,000.00 be raised, and that as soon as $100,000.00 of this has been secured the subscriptions shall be binding. Each conference taking part in this project shall be required to assume such a share of the endowment as is proportionate to its membership. The following shall receive tuition free of charge, provided they reside within the bounds of any of the participating conferences: 1st, The orphans of soldiers who have fallen or will yet fall in the present civil war; 2d, The children of such soldiers who in consequence of their services are entitled to draw pension from the U. S. Government, the number of such children in attendance not to exceed fifty at any one time; 3d, The children of our deceased preachers and also those of our poor superannuated preachers, until said children reach the age of twenty-one years. That as soon as possible a missionary department be connected with the college. That as soon as two of the aforementioned conferences join with us, the project shall proceed. That in case Union Seminary be not re-opened those who hold scholarships against that institution shall be entitled to an equal amount of instruction in the preparatory department of the college. J. Yeakel was unanimously elected a delegate to confer with delegates appointed by such other conferences as will take part in the college enterprise and to adopt such further measures as will forward the movement;

and that Brother Yeakel shall also be collector to secure our share of the endowment by means of scholarships, upon condition that such a course is warranted by the action of the other conferences.   J. Adams was elected trustee of Union Seminary.   G. B. Fisher was appointed an examiner of junior preachers in the place of S. G. Rhoads for the next year, the other examiners remaining as in former years.

FINANCE.

Received from conference collections	$328.20
Received from the Charitable Society	78.91
Received from the Book Establishment	100.00
Total	$507.11
Paid to conference claimants	507.11

MISSIONARY APPROPRIATIONS.

Nth. Phila. Miss.	$225	Hazleton Miss.	$250
Phila. Eng. Miss.	325	Reading (Eng.) Miss.	325
Glassborough Miss.	140	Harrisburg Miss.	425
New York Miss.	325	Mahanoy City Miss.	325
Newark Miss.	375	Bridesburg Miss.	325
Easton Miss.	250		
Wayne Miss.	250	Total	$3,540

APPOINTMENTS.

PHILADELPHIA DISTRICT—*L. Snyder*, *P. E.*

Philadelphia Sta.—M. Dissinger.
Sth. Philadelphia Sta.—H. Stoetzel.
Germantown Sta.--W. Heim.
Montgomery Cir.—G. B. Fisher and W. H. Weidner.
Norristown and Phoenixville Sta.—Seneca Breyfogel.

Milford Cir.—R. M. Lichtenwalner and A. Leopold.
Kutztown Cir.—J. Zern and B. Moyer.
Bethlehem Cir. — E. Butz and N. Goebel.
Nth. Philadelphia Miss.—J. Kurtz.
Philadelphia Eng. Miss.—J. A. Apgar.
Glassborough Miss.—M. Sindlinger.
Bridesburg Miss.—J. Fry.

LEHIGH DISTRICT—*J. Yeakel, P. E.*
Allentown Sta.—J. Koehl.
Catasauqua Sta.—J. Schell.
New York Sta.—C. B. Fliehr.
Lehigh Cir.—F. Hoffman and L. N. Worman.
Carbon Cir.—G. Knerr and A. Goetschel.
Northampton Cir.—I. E. Knerr and S. B. Brown.
Monroe Cir.—C. Gingrich.
New York Miss.—C. Myers.
Newark Miss.—A. Ziegenfus.
Easton Miss.—I. Hess.
Hazleton Miss.—T. Plattenberger.
Wayne Miss.—T. Harper.

LEBANON DISTRICT—*S. Neitz, P. E.*
Lebanon Sta.—S. S. Chubb.
Reading Sta.—J. Specht.
Lancaster Sta.—E. Ely.
Womelsdorf Cir.—B. F. Bohner.
Fairville Cir.—C. K. Fehr and J. N. Metzgar.
Myerstown Cir.—J. H. Kutz.
Annville Cir.—D. Yingst and A. H. Overholt.

Lancaster Cir.—C. H. Baker and J. C. Hornberger.
Dauphin Cir.—J. M. Saylor.
Chester Cir.—E. B. Miller.
Reading Eng. Miss.—T. Bowman.
Harrisburg Miss.—D. Wieand.

ORWIGSBURG DISTRICT—*G. T. Haines, P. E.*
Schuylkill Haven Sta.—C. S. Haman.
Pottsville Sta.—S. G. Rhoads.
Tamaqua Sta.—J. G. Marquardt.
Orwigsburg Cir.—D. Z. Kembel.
Schuylkill Cir.—A. Schultz.
Cressona Cir.—F. Krecker.
Pinegrove Cir.—J. O. Lehr.
Tremont Cir.—S. P. Reinoehl.
Ashland Cir.—J. Steltzer and D. Hambright.
Mahantongo Cir.—C. Loos and D. Lentz.
Lykens Cir.—J. Adams.
Millersburg Cir.—F. P. Lehr.
Port Carbon Cir.—J. P. Leib.
Mahanoy City Miss.—R. Deisher.
M. Guhl, missionary in California.

1866.

The Twenty-Seventh (59th) Annual Session.

President, Bishop J. Long.
Secretary, Frederick Krecker.
Assistant Secretaries, C. B. Fliehr and Thomas Bowman.

This session of Conference was opened in St. Peter's Evangelical church at Schuylkill Haven, Pa., on Wednesday, Feb. 28th, 1866. The chairman appointed the following committees: On Worship,—The presiding elders and the preacher in charge; On Letters,—J. P.

Leib, F. Hoffman, and J. Schell ; On Statistics,—H. Stoetzel, W. Heim, and R. Deisher; On Boundaries,— The Bishop and the presiding elders; On Finance,— S. G. Rhoads, J. M. Saylor, and C. Loos; On Education,—M. F. Maize, F. Hoffman, and S. P. Reinoehl; On State of Missions,—C. B. Fliehr, C. K. Fehr, and D. Yingst; On Sabbath,—S. Neitz, S. G. Rhoads, H. Stoetzel, T. Bowman, and J. Koehl.

G. W. Wagner, local preacher, withdrew from the church. B. Moyer located during the past year. E. B. Miller received his credentials. J. P. Leib was newly elected, and S. Neitz re-elected to the office of Presiding Elder. Deacons' orders were granted to S. B. Brown, A. H. Overholt, A. Leopold, and S. Ely. The following were licensed as preachers on trial: Henry Oehrle, Jesse Hunsberger, Fr. Leuther, Adam Yeakel, Chas. Burkhardt, Edward Schneider, Wm. Loose, Jacob L. Werner, Benjamin J. Smoyer, Geo. H. Landis, John R. Siegfried, Wm. K. Wieand, and J. S. Scheimer. The brethren J. Laros, S. Ely, J. S. Scheimer, W. K. Wieand, D. Mertz, J. K. Knerr, and B. J. Smoyer were received into the itinerancy ; R. Litzenberger was again received. The widows supported by the Conference are Sisters Hesser and Schnerr.

Sister Spang, of Womelsdorf, offered to give to this Conference two hundred dollars to be applied to church building purposes, provided the Conference agrees to refund the two hundred dollars for a new church in Womelsdorf, in case such a church building be erected within the lifetime of Sister Spang. The offer was accepted and the money paid to the treasurer of the Church Building Society. The advisability of organizing a Church Building Society within the bounds of this Conference was referred to a committee consisting of H. Stoetzel, S. Neitz, and R. M. Lichtenwalner, with instructions to draft a constitution and report at the next annual session.

The subject of spiritualism having been pressed upon the attention of the Conference, the following resolutions were adopted :

Without wishing to decide upon the reality of the intercourse which some claim to hold with the world of spirits, we are, nevertheless, compelled, upon the best evidences presented, to consider such intercourse as unwarranted presumption and deception. Whether such intercourse be true or false, we at all events consider it to be contrary to the Scriptures and in the strongest sense objectionable and sinful; wherefore, we also hold that any one who reveres the name of Christ, and especially every minister of the gospel, should stand aloof from this species of unrighteousness. We, therefore, earnestly warn all those entrusted to us against the detestable evil, and urge them to secure for themselves a rich measure of that Spirit who, according to the promise of Christ, is able to lead us in to all truth, and also direct them to that Word which is a light upon our way and a lamp unto our feet.

Our missionary stationed in the New York (Hudson street) Mission was authorized to devote as much time as possible to the interests of immigrants. The Conference resolved that in the election of presiding elders, no one shall be considered elected who has not received a majority of all the votes cast. The examiners of last year were continued in office for another year.

The stationing committee was instructed to station the preachers, before the Conference assigns the districts to the presiding elders. The book committee was solicited to establish a branch department for our publications in Allentown, Pa., under the charge of Joseph Gross.

BOUNDARIES.

Camden was taken from the South Philadelphia Miss. and annexed to Glassborough Miss.   West Philadelphia was taken up as a mission.   It was ordered that Bridesburg Miss. be served by the preacher in charge of North Philadelphia Miss.   A new mission was located on 54th street, New York, to be known as Central Park Mission.   Union Hill was taken from the New York Hudson street Miss. and in connection with Greenville to constitute Union Hill and Greenville Miss.   Lehigh Ward of Allentown was taken up as a mission and called Allentown Miss.   Fairville was taken from Fairville Cir. and made a station, the name of the circuit being changed to Brownstown.   An English mission was located in the city of Lancaster.   Bethlehem was made a station and the remainder of Bethlehem Cir. called Pleasant Valley Cir.   Norristown and Phoenixville were changed into a mission.   Reading English Mission was changed into a station.   Pinegrove and Manbeck class were constituted a station.   Rausch Creek class was annexed to Tremont.   Zion class in the city of Lebanon was taken from Myerstown Cir. and its members instructed to unite with the various classes in Lebanon Sta.

CHURCH AFFAIRS.

The money for the Harrisburg church was paid to

14

the trustees of that congregation. The sixty dollars
the keeping of Moor Casner of New Jersey were
given to him to be used for his church. The missionaries collecting for church buildings received permission to canvass the entire conference territory.

SABBATH.

The Conference resolved the following: 1st, That
we will use all our influence to uphold the sanctity of
the Sabbath among the people. 2d, That we enter our
solemn protest against all efforts that are made to re-
scind the existing Sabbath laws. 3d, That we respectfully pray the honored senators and representatives of
our legislative assemblies to reject all proposals tending
to lessen the observance of the Lord's Day.

On Sunday forenoon Bishop Long preached the ordination sermon from 2 Tim. 4:5. In the afternoon
the Bishop delivered an address to the candidates for
ordination, after which the brethren elected to the office
were ordained deacons. Preachers and people participated in the celebration of the Lord's Supper. In the
evening T. Bowman preached a missionary sermon from
1 Cor. 6:20, after which the sum of $119.00 was
secured for the missionary cause.

FINANCE.

Received from conference collections..........$363.79
Received from the Charitable Society........ 83.98
Received from the book establishment....... 100.00

Total...............................$547.77
Paid to the conference claimants.......... 547.77

MISSIONARY APPROPRIATIONS.

Hudson St. N. Y. Miss. $500

Central Park N. Y.
  Miss............. 425

Union Hill and Green-
  ville Miss........ 350

Newark Miss....... 300

Easton Miss....... 100

Mahanoy City Miss.. 275

Hazleton Miss...... 200

Harrisburg Miss.... 250

Norristown and Phœ-
  nixville Miss...... $300

Nth. Phila. Miss.... 200

Camden and Glass-
  borough Miss..... 300

W. Philadelphia Miss. 500

Phila. Eng. Miss.... 300

Allentown Miss..... 150
  ────────
Total.........$4,150

APPOINTMENTS.

PHILADELPHIA DISTRICT — S. Neitz, P. E.

Philadelphia Sta.—M. Dissinger.

Sth. Philadelphia Sta.—R. M. Lichten-walner.

Germantown Sta.—E. Butz.

Milford Cir. — A. Leopold and G. Scharf.

Kutztown Cir.—J. Zern.

Montgomery Cir.—W. H. Weidner and J. S. Scheimer.

Norristown Miss.—Seneca Breyfogel.

Nth. Philadelphia Miss.—J. Kurtz.

Philadelphia Eng. Miss.—G. B. Fisher.

West Philadelphia Miss.—H. Stoetzel.

Camden and Glassborough Miss.—N. Goebel.

EASTON DISTRICT—J. Yeakel, P. E.

Catasauqua Sta.—J. Koehl.

Bethlehem Sta.—I. Hess.

New York Sta.—C. B. Fliehr.

Pleasant Valley Cir.—C. Gingrich and S. Ely.

Northampton Cir.—A. Ziegenfus.

Monroe Cir.—L. N. Worman.

Wayne Miss.—T. Harper.

Easton Miss.—D. Mertz.

Newark Miss.—

Union Hill and Greenville Miss.—A. Goetschel.

Hudson Str. N. Y. Miss.—J. G. Marquardt.

Central Park N. Y. Miss.—C. Meyers.

ALLENTOWN DISTRICT—G. T. Haines, P. E.

Allentown Sta.—J. Schell.

Tamaqua Sta.—J. H. Kurtz.

Lehigh Cir. — D. Z. Kembel.

Carbon Cir.—G. Knerr.

Schuylkill Cir.—A. Schultz.

Orwigsburg Cir.—S. B. Brown.

Ashland Cir.—J. Steltzer and W. K. Wicand.

Hazleton Miss.—T. Plattenberger.

Mahanoy City Miss.—R. Deisher.

Allentown Miss.—B. F. Bohner.

READING DISTRICT—L. Snyder, P. E.

Reading Sta.—J. Specht.

Reading Eng. Sta.—C. S. Haman.

Lebanon Miss.—F. Hoffman.

Fairville Miss.—F. Krecker.

Lancaster Miss.—D. Yingst.

Lancaster Cir.—

Brownstown Cir.—C. K. Fehr and M. Sindlinger.

Myerstown Cir.—W. Heim.
Annville Cir.—A. H. Overholt.
Womelsdorf Cir.—J. M. Saylor.
Chester Cir —J. A. Apgar.
Lancaster English Miss.—

POTTSVILLE DISTRICT—J. P. Leib, P. E.
Pottsville Sta.—S. S. Chubb.
Schuylkill Haven Sta.—S. G. Rhoads.

Pinegrove Sta.—T. Bowman.
Tremont Sta.—S. P. Reinoehl.
Dauphin Cir.—D. Hambright.
Millersburg Cir.—F. P. Lehr.
Mahantongo Cir. — C. Loos and D. Lentz.
Port Carbon Cir.—E. Ely.
Cressona Cir.—J. O. Lehr.
Harrisburg Miss.—D. Wieand.

1867.

The Twenty-Eighth (60th) Annual Session.

President, Bishop J. J. Esher.
Secretary, John Koehl.
Assistant Secretary, Reuben Deisher.

The Conference convened in the St. John's Evangelical church, Bethlehem, Pa., on Wednesday, February 27th, 1867, to transact the business of its twenty-eighth annual session. The chairman appointed the following committees: On Worship,—Isaac Hess and the presiding elders; On Letters,—F. Hoffman, C. Meyers, and S. G. Rhoads; On Boundaries,—The Bishop and the presiding elders; On Finance,—C. Loos, R. M. Lichtenwalner, and C. K. Fehr; On Statistics,—A. Schultz, G. B. Fisher, and S. B. Brown; On Education,—F. Krecker, C. S. Haman, H. Stoetzel, S. G. Rhoads, and C. H. Baker.

J. A. Apgar and R. Litzenberger located during the past year. J. Yeakel was re-elected to the office of Presiding Elder. Elders' orders were granted to D. Lentz, W. H. Weidner, A. Getschel, and D. Z. Kembel. Deacons' orders, to L. N. Worman, J. K. Knerr, J. C. Hornberger, J. N. Metzgar, G. Scharf, and Levi Miller.

The following received license as preachers on trial: B. D. Albright, J. P. Schmidt, W. A. Leopold, Franklin Siechrist, I. Zimmerman, H. A. Neitz, Anthony Kindt, J. Schirmeyer, and L. Ruhl. The brethren H. A. Neitz, J. C. Bliem, G. Scharf, W. A. Leopold, J. G. Sands, B. D. Albright, and E. A. Hoffman were received into the itinerancy. Sisters Schnerr and Hesser received support. The Conference organized itself into a Church Building Society. This society did not, however, go into active operation at once. Formerly such preachers who did not reside upon their fields of labor received no rent; this regulation was abolished.

WHEREAS, Our beloved Brother Marquardt, a highly esteemed member and a useful preacher of the East Pa. Conference, has been appointed missionary to the city of San Francisco, Cal., by the executive committee of the board of missions; therefore *Resolved*, That we are deeply sensible of his withdrawal from our midst, that we wish him the protection of the Most High during his perilous journey, and great efficiency in his new field of labor, and that we will remember him in our prayers.

The delegates elected to the General Conference were: S. Neitz, J. P. Leib, J. Yeakel, G. T. Haines, L. Snyder, F. Hoffman, T. Bowman, C. S. Haman, S. G. Rhoads, F. Krecker, J. Koehl, and C. Meyers; alternates, J. Adams, I. Hess, J. M. Saylor, and S. P. Reinoehl.

WHEREAS, It has become customary in our church for our people to engage in picnics, celebrations, exhibitions, and excursions, and because upon such occasions some indulge in frivolous and unbecoming games and amusements which bring reproach upon the cause of Christ ; therefore be it *Resolved*, That we disapprove of such performances, and advise our members to conduct these events in strict accordance with the spirit of the teachings of Christ.

Inasmuch as our Hudson Street Mission in the city of New York is conducted chiefly in the interests of immigrants and therefore intimately connected with our general work in this and in foreign lands; therefore be it *Resolved*, That we request General Conference at its next session, to take charge of the said mission and to supply it with a missionary. C. S. Haman was appointed to take charge of the reception and distribution of the tracts of this Conference. It was resolved that hereafter the money collected for the support of the superannuated preachers, their widows and orphans shall be applied to no other purpose.

BOUNDARIES.

Easton Miss. was changed to a station. That part of Carbon Cir. lying east of the Blue Mountain was formed into a separate charge and called Berlinsville Cir. Manbeck class was taken from Cressona Cir. and annexed to Pinegrove Sta. Trevorton, Fresh Valley, Seven Points, and Hallin Run were taken from Mahantongo Cir. and formed into a mission called Trevorton Mission. The action of F. Hoffman in annexing Zion class to Lebanon Sta. was approved.

CHURCH AFFAIRS.

It was ordered that a church building be erected in the North Philadelphia Miss. during the ensuing year, and that the presiding elder, C. H. Baker, and J. Specht shall constitute a building committee. The erection of a church building in Central Park Miss., New York, was referred to the presiding elder, R. Deisher, and C. Meyers, with permission to build, if advisable. C. B. Fliehr was elected agent to collect throughout the bounds of the Conference for these two mission churches, and to appropriate $4,000 of the money thus collected to the North Philadelphia Miss. and the balance to the Central Park Miss. Each preacher was obligated to do his utmost to assist the collector.

The committee appointed to audit the accounts of Seneca Breyfogel, collector for the Norristown Miss. church, reported the following:

Amount of cash secured..................$3,836.10

Amount expended for the church..........$3,700.00
Amount of traveling and other expenses.....   48.39
Amount of cash on hand.................. $7.71

                                        $3,836.10
Amount of unpaid subscriptions........... $638.35

EDUCATION.

The introduction of parochial schools engaged the attention of the Conference, the deliberations resulting in a resolution to submit the subject to the discretion of the various congregations.

FINANCE.

Receipts:

Conference collections.............$357.81
Charitable Society...............   89.12
Book Establishment............... 150.00
                                 ——————
                                        $596.93

Expenditures:

Paid to conference claimants................$545.95

Balance on hand........................$ 50.98

MISSIONARY APPROPRIATIONS.

Hudson St. N.Y.Miss.	$500	Allentown Miss.....	$225
Central Park N. Y. Miss............	450	Norristown Miss....	200
		Nth. Phila. Miss....	325
Union Hill N. Y.Miss.	325	Phila. Eng. Miss....	450
Newark N. J. Miss...	250	Camden Miss.......	250
Wayne Miss........	225	Bridesburg Miss.....	200
Mahanoy Miss......	275	Trevorton Miss.....	325
Hazleton Miss......	200	Lancaster Miss......	400
Harrisburg Miss.....	200	Total.........$4,800	

SUNDAY SERVICES.

On Sunday forenoon Bishop J. J. Esher preached an appropriate, profound, and powerful ordination sermon from 1 Pet. 5:1-4. Streams of salvation poured in upon preachers and people until shouts of praise ascended. After the sermon the candidates for Deacons' orders were ordained. J. M. Saylor opened the afternoon services, during which the elders were ordained. J. P. Leib delivered the sacramental address, after which the Lord's Supper was administered. The glory of the Lord appeared. It was indeed a baptism of fire. In the evening S. Neitz preached the missionary sermon from Matt. 20:8. During the description of the distribution of the penny wages among the laborers there was another shout of hallelujahs in the congregation. Thus ended a day that will be held in remembrance forever.

Within the recollection of Bishop Esher and the older brethren of the Conference there never had been a day like this at a conference session.

APPOINTMENTS.

PHILADELPHIA DISTRICT — *S. Neitz*, *P. E.*
Philadelphia Sta.—C. H. Baker.
Philadelphia Sta.—J. Kurtz.
Germantown Sta.—E. Butz.
Milford Cir.—C. K. Fehr and S. Ely.
Montgomery Cir.—J. H. Kutz and J. S. Schelmer.
Kutztown Cir.—A. F. Leopold and J. Laros.
Norristown Miss.—T. Harper.
Nth. Philadelphia Miss.—J. Specht.
Philadelphia Eng. Miss.—R. M. Lichtenwalner.
Bridesburg Miss.—G. Scharf.
Camden and Glassborough Miss.—N. Goebel.
West Philadelphia Miss.—(Unsupplied.)

EASTON DISTRICT—*G. T. Haines*, *P. E.*
Catasauqua Sta.—J. Koehl.
Bethlehem Sta.—I. Hess.
Easton Sta.—B. F. Bohner.
New York Sta.—R. Deisher.
Pleasant Valley Cir.—J. C. Bllem and W. A. Leopold.
Northampton Cir.-A. Ziegenfus and J. K. Kuerr.
Monroe Cir.—L. N. Worman.
Wayne Miss.—G. B. Fisher.
Newark Miss.—I. E. Knerr.
Union Hill and Greenville Miss.—A. Goetschel.
Hudson Str. N. Y. Miss.—H. Stoetzel.
Central Park N. Y. Miss.—C. Meyers.

ALLENTOWN DISTRICT—*J. Yeakel*, *P. E.*
Allentown Sta.—M. Dissinger.
Orwigsburg Sta.—S. B. Brown.
Tamaqua Sta.—J. O. Lehr.
Lehigh Cir.—J. Adams.
Berlinsville Cir.—G. Knerr.
Carbon Cir.—J. Stelzer and B. J. Smoyer.

Schuylkill Cir.—C. Loos.
Ashland Cir.—T. Plattenberger and W. K. Wieand.
Allentown Miss.—D. Wieand.
Mahanoy City Miss.—D. Z. Kembel.
Hazleton Miss.—A. Schultz.

READING DISTRICT—*L. Snyder*, *P. E.*
Reading Sta.—J. Schell.
Reading Eng. Sta.—C. S. Haman.
Lebanon Sta.—F. Hoffman and E. A. Hoffman.
Fairville Sta.—J. C. Hornberger.
Lancaster Sta.—D. Yingst.
Lancaster Cir.—J. Zern.
Brownstown Cir. — D. Lentz and M. Sindlinger.
Womelsdorf Cir.—Seneca Breyfogel.
Myerstown Cir.—J. M. Saylor.
Annville Cir.—J. Frey and H. A. Neitz.
Chester Cir.—J. G. Sands.
Lancaster English Miss.—J. N. Metzgar.

POTTSVILLE DISTRICT—*J. P. Leib*, *P. E.*
Pottsville Sta.—S. S. Chubb.
Schuylkill Haven Sta.—S. G. Rhoads.
Pinegrove Sta.—T. Bowman.
Tremont Sta.—S P. Reinoehl.
Dauphin Cir.—D. Hambright.
Millersburg Cir.—A. H. Overholt.
Lykens Cir.—W. H. Weidner and B. D. Albright.
Mahantongo Cir.—F. P. Lehr and D. Mertz.
Port Carbon Cir.—E. Ely.
Cressona Cir.—F. Krecker.
Harrisburg Miss.—W. Heim.
Trevorton Miss.—C. Gingrich.
Agent for church buildings in North Philadelphia and New York.—C. B. Fliehr.

1867.

The General Conference.

Presidents, Bishops J. Long and J. J. Esher.

Secretary, Reuben Yeakel.

Assistant Secretaries, R. Dubs, W. F. Schneider, and S. G. Rhoads.

On Thursday, October 10th, 1867, the delegates representing twelve annual conferences assembled in Pittsburg, Pa., to transact the business of the regular quadrennial session of the General Conference.* Both bishops and eighty-one delegates were in attendance.

The delegates of the East Pa. Conference were all present except G. T. Haines, whose place was filled by J. Adams, an alternate. I. Hess, an alternate, occupied the seat of J. Yeakel during a part of the session. The Conference spent one hour each morning, after the opening of the session, in earnest and importunate prayers for God's blessing upon the daily proceedings and upon the church at large. Charges were preferred against a delegate for persisting in the advocacy of doctrines which are antagonistic to those held by the Evangelical Association. After the complainant and defendant had each addressed the Conference, the question was referred to a committee.

The report of this committee disapproved of certain terms, phrases, and figures employed by the defendant in expounding his views, but unanimously acquitted him of any design to teach doctrines essentially different from those held by the church. The report of the

*See Preface on page 95.

committee was adopted.   Another delegate was charged with having made disparaging remarks concerning others in our church periodicals.   The matter was referred to a committee, whose report was finally laid on the table.   Subsequently the Conference advised the defendant to come to an understanding with the plaintiffs, if possible.

After having declined to publish a monthly magazine, the Conference nevertheless resolved that in case a brother, or several brethren, will undertake to publish a monthly magazine agreeably with the sense and spirit of our church, we will give them our efficient help.   A new conference was formed and called *The Minnesota Conference.*

By a vote of 66 yeas to 11 nays the General Conference adopted the following as a recommendation to the annual conference :

Resolved, That the book agent, the editor of the *Christliche Botschafter,* the editor of the *Evangelical Messenger,* the editor of the S. S. Literature, the corresponding secretary of the missionary society, and the bishops, at the time when they are not in the chair, be members of the General Conference *ex-officio,* provided they are elders, but that the annual conferences to which they may belong, shall not, in making up the number of delegates to be elected by them, count the above named officers of the book establishment.   At the request of the East Pa. Conference the board of missions was authorized to take charge of the immigrant mission in the city of New York and to supply it if possible.

A motion to elect three bishops was defeated.   The elections resulted as follows :   Bishops, J. Long and J.

212 EVANGELICAL LANDMARKS. [1868.

J. Esher; general book agent, S. Neitz; editor of the
Christliche Botschafter, R. Dubs; editor of the *Evangelical Messenger*, T. G. Clewell; editor of the Sunday-
School and Tract Literature, R. Yeakel; corresponding
secretary of the Missionary Society, W. Yost; editor of
the *Evangelische Botschafter* and book agent in Germany, J. G. Wollpert; superintendent of the Ebenezer
Orphan Institute, J. G. Zinser. S. Neitz resigned the
office of general book agent; W. W. Orwig was elected
in his stead.

These are the statistics reported at this session:
Itinerant preachers, 484; local preachers, 379; full
members, 58,225; probationary members, 2,176;
churches, 736; parsonages, 187; Sunday-schools, 808;
officers and teachers, 8,304; scholars, 41,395; catechetical classes, 283; catechumens, 2,772.

1868.
The Twenty-Ninth (61st) Annual Session.

President, Bishop J. Long.
Secretary, S. G. Rhoads.
Assistant Secretaries, C. K. Fehr and J. S. Scheimer.

Conference convened in its twenty-ninth annual session on Wednesday, February 26th, 1868, in the Salem
Evangelical church at Reading, Pa.

The following committees were appointed: On Worship,—The presiding elders and the two preachers stationed in Reading, Pa.; On Letters,—F. Hoffman, F.
Krecker, and G. Knerr; On Boundaries,—The Bishop
and the presiding elders; On Finance,—J. M. Saylor,

T. Bowman, and R. M. Lichtenwalner; On Statistics,—
R. Deisher, L. N. Worman, and G. B. Fisher; On Ed-
ucation,—J. Yeakel, C. Loos, J. Adams, J. N. Metzgar,
and S. S. Chubb; On Last Year's Proceedings,—J.
Koehl, H. Stoetzel, and C. H. Baker; On Auditing,—
D. Wieand, J. C. Hornberger, and S. B. Brown.

C. Loos located on account of family concerns.   A.
Goetschel, desiring to unite with a western conference,
received his credentials.   W. Dewees, a local preacher,
died during the past year.   J. M. Saylor and F. Hoff-
man were elected to the office of Presiding Elder.   B.
F. Bohner, S. Ely, A. F. Leopold, S. B. Brown, A. H.
Overholt, J. C. Bliem, and D. Mertz were ordained
Elders; J. S. Scheimer, J. G. Sands, W. K. Wieand, J.
Laros, E. A. Hoffman, B. J. Smoyer, H. A. Neitz, and
S. Frankenfield, Deacons.   Edw. Schultz, Jonas Schaeffer,
Benj. Wimmer, Isaac Hoch, Simon Licht, W. A. Shoe-
maker, A. M. Stirk, J. K. Lutz, Reuben Dreibelbis,
Samuel Engel, and B. H. Miller were licensed as
preachers on trial.   The supernumerary preachers are
D. Berger, G. T. Haines, D. Wieand, and M. Sind-
linger.   The widows of deceased preachers having claims
upon this Conference for support are Sisters Hesser and
Schnorr.

WHEREAS, A work entitled "*Der Alte Weg*" written
by S. G. Rhoads, has appeared in print, and WHEREAS,
We are convinced that it is both a useful and timely
book; therefore be it *Resolved*, That we hail with joy
its appearance and that we will exert ourselves as much
as possible to secure for it a wide circulation.

G. T. Haines and L. Snyder, ex-presiding elders,
were made advisory members of the stationing com-

mittee. The presiding elders were constituted the committee on missionary appropriations. The Conference adopted the following: Inasmuch as it is clearly in conflict with the rules of our church for any one, without license, to make appointments for preaching or in any other manner offer or announce himself to conduct religious meetings; therefore be it *Resolved*, That we require all our preachers and congregations to act in strict accordance with our Church Discipline, and to extend the aforementioned privileges to such only as are regularly entitled thereto.

WHEREAS, It has already frequently occurred that church members and class leaders have instituted extra prayer meetings and religious gatherings whereby discord and dissension have been engendered in the churches, and occasions given for the neglect of our tried and regular religious meetings, finally resulting in the loss of members and leaders; therefore be it *Resolved*, That we discountenance all such gatherings and exercises with which the preacher in charge and the presiding elder are not in accord, or which they cannot recommend.

Sunday was a blessed day. The Lord was among his people, and jubilant shouts of praise and thanksgiving ascended from his courts. In the forenoon Bishop Long preached an appropriate and powerful ordination sermon to a great gathering of people in our German church. In the afternoon the ordination services took place.

BOUNDARIES.

A new English Mission was located in the city of Allentown. Port Clinton was taken from Schuylkill

Circuit and in connection with Orwigsburg and Auburn called Orwigsburg Circuit.   Mahanoy City Mission was changed to a station.   Dunkelberger's class and Shamokin were taken from Ashland Circuit, the former annexed to Lykens Circuit and the latter, to Trevorton Mission.

CHURCH AFFAIRS.

The auditing committee reported the following as the correct accounts of the North Philadelphia Mission church, C. B. Fliehr, collector, and J. Specht, preacher in charge:

Entire cost of church building.............		$5,170.00
Cash received from C. B. Fliehr's subscriptions................	$3,325.13	
Cash received from the Philadelphia subscriptions	947.96	
		$4,273.09
Entire indebtedness....................		$896.91
Unpaid subscriptions..................		$1,547.77

The congregation of the Salem church on Water street, Lancaster City, received permission to sell their property, upon certain stipulated conditions.   The congregation at Slatedale received permission to sell their church in order to build a more commodious one.   The trustees of our Norristown church were empowered to give a mortgage upon their church property as security for money borrowed.   The preacher in charge of our congregation at Greenville, Hudson Co., N. Y., was authorized to collect money in Newark, Greenville, and New York City for their new church building.   Furthermore, it was resolved that the Con-

ference recognizes N. Sayler, C. Frundt, E. H. Menke,
F. Bose, and J. J. Birmile as the trustees elected according to the rules of our church and considers all other
parties as intruders upon our rights.   C. Meyers was
appointed collector for the Central Park Mission, with
access to the entire conference territory.   The presiding
elder of Easton District, I. E. Knerr, and R. Deisher
were appointed a committee of three to superintend the
erection of a church building.   It was resolved that a
collector be appointed next year to gather funds for a
church in the Philadelphia English Mission.

EDUCATION.

Previously declared opinions of the usefulness and
desirability of higher institutions of learning were reasserted.   The brethren also solemnly obligated themselves to continue the catechetical classes already formed
and to organize new ones wherever practicable.   The
examiners of junior preachers were continued in office.

FINANCES.

Receipts:

From balance on hand.......................$ 52.00
From the conference collections.............. 398.00
From the Charitable Society................. 100.00

                                            $550.00

Expenditures :

Paid to two claimants...................... 250.00

Balance in Treasury......................$300.00

MISSIONARY APPROPRIATIONS.

Phila. Eng. Miss....$450
Nth. Phila. Miss.... 225
Camden and Glass-
  borough Miss..... 200
Bridesburg Miss..... 275
Norristown Miss..... 75
Central Park Miss... 450
Union Hill and Green-
  ville Miss. 325
Newark Miss....... 275

Allentown Ger. Miss.$200
Allentown Eng. Miss. 300
Hazleton Miss...... 150
Harrisburg Miss..... 150
Trevorton Miss..... 275
Lancaster Eng. Miss. 400
Wayne Miss........ 200

Total..........$3,950

APPOINTMENTS.

PHILADELPHIA DISTRICT—*S. Neitz, P. E.*
Philadelphia Sta.—C. H. Baker.
Sth. Philadelphia Sta.—J. Kurtz.
Germantown Sta.—R. M. Lichten-
  walner.
Montgomery Cir.—F. P. Lehr and B.
  D. Albright.
Milford Cir.—C. K. Fehr and J. Fry.
Kutztown Cir.—A. F. Leopold and F.
  Siechrist.
Norristown Miss.—E. Butz.
Nth. Philadelphia Miss.—J. Specht.
Philadelphia Eng. Miss.—T. Bowman.
Bridesburg Miss.—N. Goebel.
Camden and Glassborough Miss.—J. S.
  Scheimer.

EASTON DISTRICT—*F. Hoffman, P. E.*
Catasauqua Sta.—J. O. Lehr.
Bethlehem Sta.—J. Adams.
Easton Sta.—C. B. Fliehr.
New York Sta.—R. Deisher.
Pleasant Valley Cir.—J. C. Bliem and
  T. Plattenberger.
Northampton Cir.—H. Stoetzel and L.
  N. Worman.
Monroe Cir.—D. Hambright and W. A.
  Leopold.
Wayne Miss.—G. B. Fisher.
Newark Miss.—D. Yingst.

Union Hill and Greenville Miss.—G.
  Scharf.
Central Park Miss.—I. E. Knerr.

ALLENTOWN DISTRICT—*J. Yeakel, P. E.*
Allentown Sta.—M. Dissinger.
Tamaqua Sta.—W. K. Weand.
Mahanoy City Sta.—J. C. Hornberger.
Orwigsburg Cir.—T. Harper.
Lehigh Cir.—S. Ely and J. K. Seyfrit.
Berlinsville Cir.—G. Knerr.
Carbon Cir.—J. Steltzer and A. Kindt.
Schuylkill Cir.—A. Ziegenfus.
Ashland Cir.—D. Z. Kembel.
Hazleton Miss.—A. Schultz.
Allentown Ger. Miss.—E. Ely.
Allentown Eng. Miss.—S. S. Chubb.

READING DISTRICT—*J. M. Saylor, P. E.*
Reading Ger. Sta.—J Schell.
Reading Eng. Sta.—S. G. Rhoads.
Lebanon Sta.—S. B. Brown.
Fairville Sta.—E. A. Hoffman.
Lancaster Sta.—J. Koehl.
Lancaster Cir.—J. Zern and A. M. Stirk.
Brownstown Cir.—D. Lentz and D.
  Mertz.
Womelsdorf Cir.—I. Hess.
Myerstown Cir.—L. Snyder.
Chester Cir.—J. G. Sands.

15

Annville Cir.—J. Loras and I. E. Zimmerman.

Lancaster Eng. Miss.—J. N. Metzgar.

POTTSVILLE DISTRICT—J. P. Leib, P. E.
Pottsville Sta.—L. H. Gehman.
Schuylkill Haven Sta.—S. P. Reinoehl.
Pinegrove Sta.— C. S. Haman.
Tremont Sta.—H. A. Neitz.
Dauphin Cir.—J. K. Knerr.
Millersburg Cir.—A. H. Overholt.

Lykens Cir.—W. H. Weidner and J. Schaeffer.

Mahantongo Cir.—B. F. Bohuer and B. J. Smoyer.

Port Carbon Cir.—Seneca Breyfogel.
Cressona Cir.—F. Krecker.
Harrisburg Miss.—W. Heim.
Trevorton Miss.—C. Gingrich.
Collector for Central Park Miss., N. Y.—C. Meyers.

1869.

The Thirtieth (62d) Annual Session.

President, Bishop J. J. Esher.

Secretary, Jesse Yeakel.

Assistant Secretaries, C. B. Flichr and J. C. Bliem.

The members of the East Pa. Conference assembled in the Salem Evangelical church on Second Street, Philadelphia, on Wednesday, February 24th, 1869, Bishop J. J. Esher presiding. The Bishop appointed the following standing committees:

On Worship,—The presiding elders; On Letters,—G. Knerr, F. Krecker, and W. Heim; On Finance,—S. G. Rhoads, L. N. Worman, and J. K. Knerr; On Statistics,—G. B. Fisher, ——; On Boundaries,—The presiding elders; On Education,—J. Kochl, C. S. Haman, H. Stoetzel, A. Schultz, and J. Schell; On Quarterly Conference Records,—G. T. Haines, L. Snyder, C. Meyers, J. Adams, and J. Steltzer; To Audit Accounts of Collectors,—J. Kurtz, D. Z. Kembel, and J. N. Metzgar; On Temperance,—J. S. Scheimer, A. H. Overholt, and E. Butz.

The name of a traveling preacher was stricken from

the records.   It was announced that a local preacher
had been expelled during the year.   W. C. Detweiler,
a local preacher, withdrew from the church.   E. A.
Hoffman received credentials.   J. Frey located on
account of ill health.   A. Saylor, I. Deppen, and L.
Ruehl died during the year.   Elders' orders were granted
to J. N. Metzgar, J. K. Knerr, L. N. Worman, J. C.
Hornberger, G. Scharf, and L. H. Gehman ; and Dea-
cons' orders to J. K. Seyfrit, I. E. Zimmerman, B. D. Al-
bright, H. E. Oehrle, W. A. Leopold, and F. Siechrist.
The following were licensed as preachers on trial :   M.
Canzler, N. Heil, N. Kaufman, A. Weaver, A. Light,
F. B. Lutman, W. W. Hambright, S. L. Wiest, and W.
Wagner.   E. Bast was again received as preacher on
trial.   L. Schmidt was again received as elder, the
relation which he held at the time of his withdrawal.
The supernumerary preachers were D. Berger, G. T.
Haines, D. Wicand, M. Sindlinger, J. S. Scheimer, A.
H. Overholt, and S. P. Reinoehl.   The conference
claimants were G. T. Haines, M. Sindlinger, D. Wicand,
S. P. Reinoehl, and Sisters Schnerr and Hesser.

L. Scheuerman addressed the Conference in the interests of our Orphans' Home, after which he secured the
sum of $130.22 in subscriptions, and $400 in endowment
notes.   The preachers were instructed to report their
collections for the orphan cause in the annual statistics
hereafter.   The Conference endorsed the publication of
an English translation of S. G. Rhoads' German work,
" *Der Alte Weg.*"

A committee was appointed to investigate and
report such preachers who neglect to perform their
duty in the missionary cause.   The chairman having

informed the Conference that Bishop J. Long has been greatly afflicted for some time, and that he sends to this Conference his cordial greetings and blessing, it was resolved that we herewith reciprocate the friendly greetings of our highly esteemed Bishop Long, and that we wish him a speedy recovery, long life, and peace. The presiding elders were instructed to select the most suitable persons from among the candidates for the itinerancy, in order that all vacancies may be properly supplied, the brethren thus selected to serve under the charge of the presiding elders.

BOUNDARIES.

Allentown German Mission was changed to a station. Freemansburg was taken from Pleasant Valley Circuit and constituted a station. An English mission was located in Easton. Jefferson and Sterling classes were taken from Wayne Mission and annexed to Monroe Circuit. A new mission was formed in Wayne Co. and called Kellytown Mission.

CHURCH AFFAIRS.

With reference to the Central Park Mission in New York City it was resolved that a lot be secured in another location and that a frame chapel be erected at a cost of about $3,000; and inasmuch as there still remains a deficit of $2,500 to pay for the ground alone, for which deficit no provision has been made, and as this Conference finds it impossible to do more for that mission at present; and futhermore, in view of the fact that New York City is the chief landing place for immigrants to this country and our work there has been

the means of strengthening the churches in other conferences, thus investing it with the importance of a
general church interest, it was resolved that an appeal
be made through our highly esteemed bishops to the
various conferences to permit our collector to solicit
contributions in such fields of labor as the respective
conferences may see proper to open for this purpose.
The following is a summary of the account of C.
Meyers, collector for the mission during the past year:

Cash secured..........................$4,150.02
Expenses, salary, and rent................   796.52

Total...............................$3,354.50
Unpaid subscriptions.....................   544.80

In response to an appeal from the Immanuel congregation of Philadelphia, it was resolved that each
preacher take a collection on his field of labor during
the months of May and June of the current year, to be
applied to the erection of a new church edifice for the
use of the said congregation. It was resolved that
$6,000 be collected, as soon as practicable, for the
erection of a new church edifice for the English mission
in Philadelphia, and that T. Bowman shall serve as collector for this purpose during the ensuing year. The
trustees of the Phoenixville congregation received permission to borrow $1,000 for their new church edifice.
The class in the vicinity of the "Albright Church"
received permission to sell lots for the purpose of liquidating the debt still burdening the church. It was
resolved that the stationing committee appoint an agent
for a new church edifice in the English Mission in Lancaster City.

EDUCATION.

The training of the young should be considered one of the most important commissions given to the church of Christ; and this subject challenges our most earnest attention, the more because of the great injury to which our youth are exposed by the reading of novels and such other frivolous publications which have a tendency to destroy their taste for pure literature as well as to impair their moral and christian culture. The attention of our Association is also directed to the fact that many of the books which answer to the foregoing description appear in our Sunday-school libraries. So-called stories, which have no foundation in fact, are not adapted to produce the desired results. It is also our belief that all theatrical representations and such picnics which are not conducted according to strict christian principles are injurious, and we therefore recommend that, if possible, these degenerate practices be suppressed and uprooted.

TEMPERANCE.

The following was adopted: As a Conference we rejoice to hear of the organization of the Pennsylvania State Temperance Union, whose object is to secure co-operation on the part of all the churches and temperance societies of this State for the overthrow of the liquor traffic. We agree to open our churches at all suitable times to the preachers sent by the Union for the purpose of preaching or lecturing on the subject of temperance and will use our influence with all our members to become total abstainers from all intoxicating drinks.

FINANCE.

Receipts :

Balance on hand from 1868........$105.07
Conference collections........... 596.58
Charitable Society.............. 400.00
Book establishment............. 150.00
                              ———— $1,251.65
Paid to conference claimants.............. 1,218.00

                                  $ 33.65

MISSIONARY APPROPRIATIONS.

Phila. Eng. Miss....$550	Easton Eng. Miss...$350
Nth. Phila. Eng Miss. 200	Allentown Eng. Miss. 325
Camden and Glass-	Hazleton Miss...... 250
borough Miss..... 300	Kellytown Miss..... 75
Bridesburg Miss..... 275	Lancaster Miss...... 400
Norristown Miss.... 50	Harrisburg Miss.... 400
Central Park Miss... 500	Trevorton Miss..... 350
Union Hill Miss..... 250	————
Newark Miss...... 225	Total.........$4,500

APPOINTMENTS.

PHILADELPHIA DISTRICT—*S. Neitz, P. E.*
Philadelphia Sta.—I. Hess.
Sth. Philadelphia Sta. — T. Platten-
 berger.
Germantown Sta. — R. M. Lichten-
 walner.
Montgomery Cir.—F. P. Lehr and B.
 D. Albright.
Milford Cir.—J. Schell and ————.
Kutztown Cir.—F. Sicchrist and A.
 Kindt.
Norristown Miss.—E. Butz.
Nth. Philadelphia Miss.—J. Kurtz.
Philadelphia Eng. Miss.—T. Bowman.
Bridesburg Miss.—N. Goebel.
Camden and Glassborough Miss.—H. E.
 Oehrle.

EASTON DISTRICT—*F. Hoffman, P. E.*
Catasauqua Sta.—J. O. Lehr.
Bethlehem Sta.—J. Adams.
Freemansburg Sta.—J. C. Bliem.
Easton Sta.—C. B. Fliehr.
New York Sta.—I. E. Knerr.
Pleasant Valley Cir.—A. Schultz and
 J. L. Werner.
Northampton Cir.—H. Stoetzel and I.
 E. Zimmerman.
Monroe Cir.—D. Hambright and W. A.
 Leopold.
Kellytown Miss.—G. B. Fisher.
Newark Miss.—D. Yingst.
Union Hill Miss.—G. Scharf.
Central Park Miss.—R. Deisher.
Easton Eng. Miss.—L. N. Worman.

ALLENTOWN DISTRICT—*J. Yeakel, P. E.*
Allentown Sta.—C. H. Baker.
East Allentown Sta.—E. Ely.
Tamaqua Sta.—W. K. Wieand.
Mahanoy City Sta.—J. C. Hornberger.
Lehigh Cir.—S. Fly and J. K. Seyfrit.
Berlinsville Cir.—J. Steltzer.
Carbon Cir.—M. Dissinger and ——-.
Schuylkill Cir.—A. Ziegenfus.
Orwigsburg Cir.—T. Harper.
Ashland Cir.—D. Z. Kembel.
Hazleton Miss.—C. Meyers.
Allentown Eng. Miss.—J. G. Sands.

READING DISTRICT.—*J. M. Saylor, P. E.*
Reading Sta.—G. Knerr.
Reading Eng. Sta.—S. G. Rhoads.
Lebanon Sta.—S. B. Brown.
Fairville Sta.—C. K. Fehr.
Lancaster Sta.—J. Koehl.
Lancaster Cir.—J. Specht and A. M. Stirk.

Brownstown Cir.—J. Zern and D. Mertz.
Womelsdorf Cir.—A. F. Leopold.
Myerstown Cir.—D. Lentz.
Annville Cir.—J. Laros and ——.
Chester Cir.—H. H. Landis.
Lancaster Eng. Miss.—J. N. Metzgar, agent for Church Building.

POTTSVILLE DISTRICT—*J. P. Leib, P. E.*
Pottsville Sta.—L. H. Gehman.
Schuylkill Haven Sta.—B. J. Smoyer.
Pinegrove Sta.—C. S. Haman.
Tremont Sta.—F. Krecker.
Dauphin Cir.—J. K. Knerr.
Millersburg Cir.—L. Snyder.
Lykens Cir.—W. Heim and S. L. Wiest.
Mahantongo Cir.—B. F. Bohner and W. H. Weidner.
Port Carbon Cir.—Seneca Breyfogel.
Cressona Cir.—H. A. Neitz.
Harrisburg Miss.—C. Gingrich.
Trevorton Miss.—S. S. Chubb.

1870.

The Thirty-First (63d) Annual Session.

President, Bishop J. J. Esher.
Secretary, Jesse Yeakel.
Assistant Secretaries, C. K. Fehr and S. B. Brown.

The members of the East Pa. Conference assembled in annual session in the Emanuel Evangelical church at Catasauqua, Pa., February 23d, 1870. The following committees were appointed: On Worship,—The five presiding elders, J. O. Lehr, and C. H. Baker; On Letters,—A. Schultz, F. Krecker, and M. Dissinger; On Quarterly Conference Proceedings,—L. Snyder, C. Meyers, C. S. Haman, H. Stoetzel, and J. Koehl; On Statistics,—I. E. Knerr, C. B. Fliehr, and J. K. Seyfrit; On Finances,—S. G. Rhoads, J. K. Knerr, and

W. K. Wieand; On Education,—T. Bowman, J. Kurtz, R. Deisher, S. S. Chubb, and J. Steltzer; To Audit Accounts,—D. Z. Kembel, Seneca Breyfogel, and R. M. Lichtenwalner.

It was reported that a preacher on trial had been expelled during the past year. J. S. Scheimer located on account of bodily infirmities. E. Ely was permitted to rest one year. The supernumerary preachers were D. Berger, G. T. Haines, D. Wieand, M. Sindlinger, S. P. Reinoehl, A. H. Overholt, and H. Stoetzel. The widows Hesser and Schnerr received support from the Conference.

S. Neitz was re-elected, and C. S. Haman was newly elected to the office of Presiding Elder. H. A. Neitz, B. J. Smoyer, W. K. Wieand, J. Loras, and J. G. Sands were ordained to the office of Elder; A. M. Stirk, A. Kindt, J. L. Werner, J. Savitz, and G. Miller, to the office of Deacon. The following received license as preachers on trial: S. F. Dundor, J. M. Soliday, A. Straub, E. Gammer, J. A. Fegar, I. W. Yeakel, D. S. Stauffer, M. Trumbore, and M. N. Bernhart. The Conference received H. K. Funk, formerly a local preacher in the M. E. Church, as preacher on trial. The brethren S. L. Wiest, J. Savitz, W. A. Shoemaker, J. L. Werner, and R. Dreibelbies were received into the itinerancy. The Church Building Society was located in the city of Reading. T. Bowman resigned the position of collector for the Philadelphia English Mission. S. L. Wiest was elected the traveling agent of the Church Building Society. Inasmuch as difficulties are constantly arising in the various congregations in which the people worship in both the German and English languages; therefore be it *Resolved*, That it is the sense of this Conference that all questions arising out of this subject shall be decided by the presiding elder, the preacher in charge, and the majority of the respective congregations. The following were appointed to examine the junior preachers in their studies: F. Hoffman, J. M. Saylor, S. Neitz, J. Yeakel, and G. B. Fisher.

BOUNDARIES.

Rising Sun was taken from Germantown Station and attached to the North Philalelphia Mission. Trappe Circuit was formed by taking Schwenksville, Limerick, and Trappe from Montgomery Circuit. Sterling and Jefferson classes were taken from Monroe Circuit and called Wayne Circuit. Manch Chunk, Mahanoy, etc., were organized into Manch Chunk Circuit. Parryville Circuit was formed of Parryville, Millport, Big Creek, etc. Adamstown Circuit was made up of Mohnsville, Mohnshill, Adamstown, and Reamstown. Trevorton Mission was changed to a circuit. The name of Central Park Mission was changed to New York Mission, 53d Street. New Village and Roxburg were taken from Northampton Circuit and called Bangor Circuit. Little Mahanoy was taken from Mahantongo Circuit and annexed to Trevorton Circuit. Dunkelberger's class was transferred from Lykens Circuit to Mahantongo, and Mahantongo was divided into two fields, the upper to retain the old name and the lower to be called Uniontown Circuit. Tremont and Ransch Creek were annexed to Lykens Circuit. The following appointments were made stations: Norristown, Weissport and Lehighton, and Harrisburg Mission. New missions were located at Phœnixville and Pottstown, Reading, Harrisburg, and South Bethlehem; the last two to be English missions.

CHURCH AFFAIRS.

The committee appointed at the last annual session reported that a lot had been purchased on 53d St., New York (Central Park Mission), and a substantial one-story brick church erected, and that the entire property is worth $16,000.00, encumbered by a debt of $7,100.00. R. Deisher, the collector for this church, made a report which was audited and approved. T. Bowman, collector for the Philadelphia English Mission, reported that he had collected $2,976.24 in cash and subscriptions. The congregations at Cressona and Berne received permission to sell their church properties in order to erect new churches. J. M. Saylor, J. Koehl, S. Neitz, F. Hoffman, and S. P. Reinoehl were appointed a committee to locate the new mission in Reading, Pa.

EDUCATION.

Prof. D. Denlinger addressed the Conference in the interests of Union Seminary, whereupon it was resolved to recommend that institution to our people. Inasmuch as a number of preachers manifested a certain indifference to the Sunday-school cause, it was resolved that a Sunday-school Convention be held within the bounds of the Conference this year.* T. Bowman, S. G. Rhoads, J. Koehl, J. M. Miller, of Philadelphia, and F. G. Boas, of Reading, were appointed a committee to carry out this purpose.

---

*This was the origin of those famous annual Sunday-school Conventions which exerted such an immeasurable influence for good upon the Sunday-schools of the East Pa. Conference.—S. C. B.

MEMORIALS.

WHEREAS, It has pleased Almighty God, the Archbishop and Shepherd of our souls, who has the command over life and death, to take from our midst during the past year our esteemed and useful bishop, J. Long, and to translate him from the church militant to the church triumphant; therefore be it

Resolved, That we erect to him the following memorial: As a superintendent over us he was an upright, candid man, fully consecrated to the work of God, a useful laborer in the vineyard of the Lord, a man full of faith and of the Holy Ghost, and mighty in the Scriptures. His preaching consisted not of words only, but was accompanied by the demonstration of the Spirit and of power. We extend to his bereaved family our sincere sympathy, and humbly acknowledge and bow to the divine will in this occurrence.

MISSIONARY APPROPRIATIONS.

Phila. Eng. Miss.....$550	New York,53d st.Miss.$450
Nth. Phila. Miss.... 150	Easton Eng. Miss.... 250
Camden and Glass-	Bethlehem Eng. Miss. 200
borough Miss...... 300	Hazleton Eng. Miss.. 250
Bridesburgh Miss... 200	Allentown Eng. Miss. 250
Phœnixville and	Lancaster Eng. Miss. 600
Pottstown Miss... 300	Harrisburg Eng. Miss. 500
Newark Miss....... 275	Reading Miss....... 450
Union Hill Miss..... 275	
	Total..........$5,000

APPOINTMENTS.

PHILADELPHIA DISTRICT—*C. S. Haman*, *P. E.*
Philadelphia Sta.—I. Hess.
South Philadelphia Sta.—T. Plattenberger.
Germantown Sta —J. P. Lieb.
Norristown Sta.—J. O. Lehr.
Montgomery Cir.—H. Kempfer and M. Trumbore.
Trappe Cir.—T. Harper.
Milford Cir.—F. Siechrist and R. Dreibelbies.
Kutztown Cir.—C. Gingrich and A. Kindt.
North Philadelphia Miss.—J. Schell.
Bridesburg Miss.—M. Sindlinger.
Philadelphia Eng. Miss.—S. G. Rhoads.
Camden and Glassborough Miss.—D. Yingst.
Phoenixville and Pottstown Miss.—E. Butz.

EASTON DISTRICT—*F. Hoffman*, *P. E.*
Catasauqua Sta.—C. B. Fliehr.
Bethlehem Sta.—C. Meyers.
Freemansburg Sta.—S. B. Brown.
Easton Sta.—G. Scharf.
New York Sta.—I. E. Knerr.
Bangor Sta.—(To be supplied).
Pleasant Valley Cir.—H. Stoetzel and M. N. Bernhart.
Northampton Cir.—W. A. Leopold and W. Hambright.
Monroe Cir.—I. E. Zimmerman.
Wayne Cir.—G. B. Fisher.
New York, 53d St. Miss.—R. Deisher.
Newark Miss.—J. Kurtz.
Union Hill, &c., Miss.—N. Goebel.
Easton, Eng. Miss.—L. N. Worman.
South Bethlehem Eng. Miss.—D. Hambright.

ALLENTOWN DISTRICT—*J. Yeakel*, *P. E.*
Allentown Sta.—C. H. Baker.
East Allentown Sta.—S. Ely.
Tamaqua Sta.—Seneca Breyfogel.
Mahanoy City Sta.—B. J. Smoyer.

Weissport Sta.—M. Diesinger.
Lehigh Cir.—A. Shultz.
Berlinsville Cir.—J. Steltzer.
Parryville Cir.—D. Z Kembel.
Mauch Chunk Cir.—A. Ziegenfus.
Schuylkill Cir.—J. Werner.
Orwigsburg Cir.—J. K. Seyfrit.
Ashland Cir.—J. Savitz.
Hazleton Miss.—W. K. Wieand.
Allentown Eng. Miss.—J. G. Sands.

READING DISTRICT—*J. M. Saylor*, *P. E.*
Reading Sta.—G. Knerr.
Reading Eng. Sta.—S. P. Reinoehl.
Lebanon Sta.—J. C. Bliem.
Fairville Sta.—C. K. Fehr.
Lancaster Sta.—J. Adams.
Lancaster Cir.—J. Specht and W. A. Shoemaker.
Brownstown Cir.—J. Zern.
Adamstown Cir.—J. Loras.
Womelsdorf Cir.—A. Leopold.
Myerstown Cir.—D. Lentz.
Annville Cir.—A. M. Stirk and D. Mertz.
Chester Cir.—B. D. Albright.
Lancaster Eng. Miss —F. P. Lehr.
Reading Miss.—J. Koehl.

POTTSVILLE DISTRICT—*S. Neitz*, *P. E.*
Pottsville Sta —R. M. Lichtenwalner.
Schuylkill Haven Sta.—T. Bowman.
Pinegrove Sta.—J. C. Hornberger.
Harrisburg Sta.
Dauphin Cir.—J. N. Metzgar.
Millersburg Cir.—L. Snyder.
Lykens Cir.—J. K. Knerr and D. S. Stauffer.
Mahantongo Cir.—W. Heim.
Uniontown Cir.—W. H. Weidner.
Cressona Cir.—H. A. Neitz.
Trevorton Cir.—S. S. Chubb.
Port Carbon Cir.—F. Krecker.
Harrisburg Eng. Miss.—L. H. Gehman.
Agent for the Church Building Society, S. L. Wiest.

1871.

The Thirty-Second (64th) Annual Session.

President, Bishop J. J. Esher.
Secretary, John Koehl.
Assistant Secretaries, R. Deisher and I. E. Knerr.

The East Pa. Conference convened in its thirty-second annual session in the Immanuel Evangelical church, Lebanon, Pa., Wednesday, Feb. 22d, 1871. The standing committees were appointed as follows: On Worship,—The presiding elders and J. C. Bliem; On Letters,—L. Snyder, C. H. Baker, and C. Meyers; On Quarterly Conference Proceedings,—G. T. Haines, A. Schultz, H. Stoetzel, F. Krecker, and M. Dissinger; On Statistics,—C. K. Fehr, R. M. Lichtenwalner, and S. B. Brown; On Church Affairs,—J. Kurtz, Seneca Breyfogel, and H. A. Neitz; On Education,—A. Schultz, S. G. Rhoads, W. Heim, J. Adams, and G. Knerr; On Finance,—T. Bowman, S. S. Chubb, and J. K. Knerr. The committees of investigation reported that two traveling elders had been deposed from the ministry and expelled from the church during the year for immoral conduct. The reports were adopted. E. Ganmer, a local preacher, resigned his license. S. Dundore, a local preacher, died during the year. B. F. Bohner was retained in the itinerancy one year without an appointment. D. Mertz was placed in a local relation.

J. Yeakel was re-elected, and T. Bowman, newly elected to the office of Presiding Elder. W. A. Leopold, J. K. Seyfrit, I. E. Zimmerman, F. Sechrist, and

B. D. Albright were elected to the office of Elder; W. A. Shoemaker, S. L. Wiest, J. Kurtz, O. L. Saylor, R. Dreibelbis, J. Moyer, D. Lehman, and J. Painter, to the office of Deacon. The following brethren received license as preachers on trial: Enos J. Miller, William Minsker, M. Steckley, A. A. Delong, Adam Hofsomer, Jordan F. Wohlfarth, Uriah H. Hershey, Jeremiah K. Fehr, S. S. Young, W. W. Weaver, and S. H. Dunkelberger. A. Markley, a local preacher of the M. E. church, was received. The supernumerary preachers were D. Berger, G. T. Haines, D. Wieand, S. P. Reinoehl, E. Ely, and H. Stoetzel. The widows Hesser and Schnerr received support. The following were received into the itinerancy: D. S. Stauffer, A. A. Delong, E. J. Miller, J. K. Fehr, I. W. Yeakel, B. H. Miller, M. Guhl, and U. H. Hershey. R. Mott, of the Pittsburg Conference, was received into the itinerancy on condition that he bring credentials.

The Conference passed a resolution endorsing a work on Christian Baptism written by J. Koehl and recommending it to preachers and people. Information having come to the Conference that at least one annual conference had established a special fund for the support of its claimants, it was resolved, that we ask of the next General Conference that if it is lawful for a conference to establish a separate fund, that the Charitable Society be disbanded and our share of the funds restored to us. J. P. Leib was elected treasurer of the Conference.

The majority and minority reports of the committee on the proceedings of the board of publication with reference to the ex-editor of the *Evangelical Messenger*.

The majority report: WHEREAS, We learn from the published proceedings of the board of publication that that body had an extra session on Jan. 11th of this year, in Cleveland, O., for the purpose of investigating the editor of the *Evangelical Messenger;* AND WHEREAS, The editor, who had been repeatedly elected by the General Conference, and who had fulfilled the duties of his office with acknowledged ability and to almost universal satisfaction, was induced by this action, to resign his office, we cannot let the opportunity pass without expressing our opinion on this affair. But while thus giving expression to our opinion we do not wish to charge the board of publication with impure motives, nor to dispute its jurisdiction over the official management of the book establishment in general. But inasmuch as this affair of the editor is in many respects a peculiar one, and our Church Discipline prescribes no specific direction how to proceed against an official of the book establishment in such a case; therefore be it *Resolved,* That we herewith instruct our delegates to the General Conference to represent our view before that body and to present these reasons why we consider the action of the board premature: 1st, Because the principal points contained in the charge, so far as doctrines are in question, should have been urged against him by his complainants, who were present, in the investigation at the last General Conference, which, however, was not done. 2d, Because, notwithstanding the fact that his views upon a most important doctrine had become familiarly known through a controversy held in the *Evangelical Messenger*, the General Conference re-elected him editor of the *Evangelical Messenger*.

3d, Because a diversity of opinion has existed among us from the beginning on the doctrines involved, which also appears from the proceedings of the last General Conference, where an effort was made to reconcile these differences by the adoption of a series of resolutions, although the delegates differed in less important particulars. 4th, Because, although we deem it of the highest importance that there should exist unanimity in the essentials of this doctrine, we, however, also consider it of equal importance that forbearance and love should prevail with reference to the less important details of the doctrine so long as redemption from all sin in this life is believed and taught. 5th, Although not desiring to approve of his language and the judiciousness of his proposals, in his editorial entitled "Our Articles of Faith," yet we do not discover anything therein to convict him of revolutionary intentions against the Association. 6th, Because it is our opinion, after mature and impartial deliberation, based upon the official report of the investigation, that the board should have presented its charges—as far as they relate to doctrine and the aforementioned editorial—to the Pittsburg Conference, or else deferred action until the next General Conference.

The minority report is as follows: *Resolved*, 1st, That we express our inmost regret concerning the recent occurrences in our book establishment, with reference to the editorship of the *Evangelical Messenger*. 2d, That in view of the moral character, and the ripe official experience of the members of the board of publication, we repose in them the confidence that they gave the subject mature reflection and acted according

16

to their best judgment, and all the more because of the fact that they are responsible to the General Conference and through that body to the entire church for their conduct.

The majority report was adopted with the following addition: Inasmuch as the majority of this Conference, in its instructions to the delegates to the next General Conference, has freely expressed its opinion on the Cleveland affair, and inasmuch as the Conference cannot justify the conduct of the editor of the *Evangelical Messenger* in every particular; therefore be it *Resolved*, 1st, That we heartily deplore and decidedly disapprove of the conduct of the editor in appealing to the civil courts, however justifiable (and we will not impugn his motives) he may have regarded his course under the peculiar circumstances, because it has deeply grieved the brethren and has given the enemies of the church occasion for rejoicing. 2d, That by this action we do not desire to cast any reflection upon those who have been appointed by the board to edit the *Evangelical Messenger* in the meantime, nor to discourage them in the least, inasmuch as we have the confidence that they will endeavor to do their best under the circumstances, and hope, therefore, that none of our members or well-wishers will withdraw their support from that periodical.

The following is the protest of Bishop Esher against the majority report: Against the foregoing report I record my decided protest: 1st, Because I hold to the conviction that the contents of the report could not come before this Conference or be acted upon legally. 2d, Because the report criticises the regular disciplinary action of one of the official boards of the church in dealing with a transgressing official, and thereby, in an indirect manner, takes the transgressor under protection before the affair has been properly and regularly investigated by the Conference. 3d, Because this report treats the violation of our Church Discipline and the casting of suspicion upon our Articles of Faith as an indifferent matter, since it expresses censure upon a regular action which called to account an official who had made himself guilty of the aforementioned transgression. 4th, Because the delegates of this Conference, who, with the delegates of other annual conferences, are to sit as judges in lawful decision over the said investigation, are instructed beforehand by this report how they are to pronounce judgment in the case and what decision they are to render.

The following were elected delegates to the General Conference: S. Neitz, J. M. Saylor, J. P. Leib, C. S. Haman, T. Bowman, J. Yeakel, S. G. Rhoads, L. Snyder, F. Hoffman, and G. Knerr. The alternates were: C. H. Baker, J. Koehl, and J. O. Lehr.

BOUNDARIES.

North Philadelphia Mission was changed to a station. Bath and Nazareth were called Bath Circuit. Bangor Station was discontinued. Bushkill, Plainfield, Windgap, Ackermantown, Bangor, Miller's class, and Roxburg constituted Northampton Circuit. South Bethlehem Mission was discontinued. White Haven was transferred from Hazleton to Mauch Chunk Circuit. Rush Valley and Locust Valley were taken from Tamaqua and annexed to Schuylkill Circuit. Berrysburg

Circuit was formed of the following appointments: Berrysburg, Gratztown, Oakdale, Dunkelberger's class, and Webers class. Millersburg was made a station. Halifax, Fishersville, and Matimoras and vicinity were constituted a mission. Harrisburg Station was discontinued, and the English Mission connected with the German church. Mahantongo, Uniontown, and a part of Trevorton Circuit were formed into Mahantongo Circuit. New missions were located at the following places: Wilkesbarre and Scranton, Newmanstown, Shamokin, Williams Valley, Tremont, Hellertown, and Hamburg. The conference territory was divided into six presiding elder districts.

CHURCH AFFAIRS.

The South Philadelphia congregation received permission to send a collector throughout the bounds of the Conference. The agent of the Church Building Society reported that he had collected $3,813.85, from which were deducted $925.93 for his salary, rent, and traveling expenses. The trustees of Salem church, Williams Valley Mission, were authorized to sell their church property and to apply the proceeds for the erection of a new church. It was resolved that hereafter the Sunday services in the Germantown and Norristown churches shall be German in the forenoon and English in the evening. The affairs of the Hatfield church were referred to the presiding elder and preacher in charge of the congregation.

EDUCATION.

Resolved, That we are highly gratified with the decided success of the Annual Sunday-school Convention held in the city of Reading, Pa., in October, 1870, and that we rejoice over the announcement that another convention is to be held at Allentown during the current year. S. G. Rhoads, T. Bowman, C. K. Fehr, C. S. Haman, and H. Stoetzel were appointed examiners for the next year.

FINANCE.

Balance on hand from last year............$ 32.35
Received from conference collections....... 628.27
      "   "   the book establishment....... 200.00
      "   "   the Charitable Society....... 265.50

                                          $1,126.12
Paid to claimants..................... 847.50

Balance...... ....$ 278.62

MISSIONARY APPROPRIATIONS.

Philadelphia Miss...$500	Tremont Miss... ...$200
Camden Miss....... 275	Williams Valley Miss. 300
Bridesburg Miss..... 250	Shamokin Miss...... 400
Pottstown and Phœ-	Harrisburg Miss..... 400
nixville Miss...... 400	Lancaster Miss...... 550
Easton Miss........ 350	Reading Miss....... 450
Newark Miss....... 275	Halifax Miss........ 325
New York Miss..... 450	Allentown Miss..... 250
Union Hill and	Hamburg Miss...... 100
Greenville Miss... 275	
Newmanstown Miss.. 150	$6,100
Hazleton Miss...... 200	

APPOINTMENTS.

PHILADELPHIA DISTRICT—*C. S. Haman*, *P. E.*
Philadelphia, 4th St. Sta.—J. Steltzer.
South Philadelphia Sta.—I. Hess.
Philadelphia Eng. Miss.—S. G. Rhoads.
Germantown Sta.—R. M. Lichtenwalner.
Norristown Sta.—J. O. Lehr.
Montgomery Cir.—A. Kindt.
Trappe Cir.—T. Harper.
Milford Cir. — R. Deisher and A. Weaver.
Bridesburg Miss.—M. Sindlinger.
Camden Miss.—D. Yingst.
Phoenixville and Pottstown Miss. — H. Stoetzel.

READING DISTRICT—*J. M. Saylor*, *P. E.*
Reading Sta.—C. H. Baker.
Reading Eng. Sta.—J. G. Sands.
Reading Miss.—J. Koehl.
Kutztown Cir.—C. Gingrich and B. H. Miller.
Adamstown Cir.—J. Loras.
Womelsdorf Cir.—I. E. Knerr.
Brownstown Cir.—A. Schultz.
Fairville Sta.—J. Specht.
Lancaster Sta.—J. Adams.
Lancaster Eng. Miss.—F. P. Lehr.
Lancaster Cir.—W. H. Weidner and U. H. Hershey.
Chester Cir.—B. D. Albright.

HARRISBURG DISTRICT—*F. Hoffman*, *P. E.*
Lebanon Sta.—J. C. Bliem.
Myerstown Cir.—J. F. Wohlfarth.
Newmanstown Miss.—D. Lentz.
Annville Cir.—A. M. Stirk and F. P. Lehr.
Dauphin Cir.—J. A. Feger.
Harrisburg Miss.—C. K. Fehr.
Halifax Miss.—W. Hein.
Millersburg Sta.—S. S. Chubb.
Berrysburg Cir.—J. K. Knerr.
Williams Valley Miss.—R. Dreibelbis and A. A. DeLong.
Mahontongo Cir.—J. L. Werner and D. S. Stauffer.
Shamokin Miss.—R. Mott.

POTTSVILLE DISTRICT —*T. Bowman*, *P. E.*
Pottsville Sta.—H. A. Neltz.
Schuylkill Haven Sta.—L. Snyder.
Cressona Cir.—L. N. Worman.
Pine Grove Sta.—J. C. Hornberger.
Tremont Miss.—J. P. Leib.
Ashland Cir.—J. Savitz.
Mahanoy Sta.—B. J. Smoyer.
Tamaqua Sta —Seneca Breyfogel.
Port Carbon Sta.—F. Krecker.
Orwigsburg Cir.—J. K. Seyfrit.
Schuylkill Cir.—H. Kempfer and A. Hoffsomer.
Schuylkill Haven Miss.—(To be supplied.)
Hazleton Miss.—W. K. Wieand.
Hamburg Miss.—G. Knerr.

ALLENTOWN DISTRICT—*S. Neitz*, *P. E.*
Allentown Sta.—M. Dissinger.
East Allentown Sta.—S. Ely.
Allentown Eng. Miss.—J. N. Metzgar.
Berlinsville Cir.—E. Butz.
Parryville Cir.—D. Z. Kembel.
Weissport Sta.—A. F. Leopold.
Mauch Chunk Cir.—A. Ziegenfus.
Wilkesbarre and Scranton Miss.—(To be supplied.)
Catasauqua Sta.—C. B. Flichr.
Lehigh Cir.—F. Secarist (and one to be supplied).

EASTON DISTRICT—*J. Yeakel*, *P. E.*
Easton Sta.—G. Scharf.
Freemansburg Sta.—S. B. Brown.
Bethlehem Sta.—C. Meyers.
Northampton Cir.—G. B. Fisher and I. W. Yeakel.
Monroe Cir.—I. E. Zimmerman and E. J. Miller.
New York Miss.—T. Plattenberger.
Union Hill and Greenville Miss.—N. Goebel.
New York Sta.—J. Kurtz.
New York 53d St. Miss.—M. Guhl.
Easton Eng. Miss.—S. L. Wiest.
Wayne Cir.--W. A. Shoemaker.
Pleasant Valley Cir.—J. Zern and D. Hambright.

Bath and Nazareth Cir.—W. A. Leopold.

Hellertown Miss.—(To be supplied.)

J. G. Marquardt in the service of the Missionary Society at San Francisco, California.

1871.

The General Conference.

Presidents, Bishops J. J. Esher and R. Yeakel.

Secretary, Jesse Yeakel.

Assistant Secretaries, C. A. Thomas and S. Smith.

The delegates of the various annual conferences assembled in the Zion Evangelical church, Naperville, Ill., on Thursday, October 12th, 1871.* Fourteen conferences and the publishing house were represented by seventy-eight delegates. The delegates of the East Pa. Conference were all present. The following was adopted:

WHEREAS, The ex-editor of the *Evangelical Messenger* has submitted to this body a document containing an appeal in reference to the disciplinary proceedings of the board of publication in regard to his official conduct as editor of the *Evangelical Messenger*; therefore be it *Resolved*, That he has no disciplinary right to an appeal in the above named document, because he has resigned his office and has called to his aid the civil courts, whereby he has forfeited his right to appeal to the higher ecclesiastical courts of our church; and that the documents in question be returned again to the author.

The committee on the proceedings of the board of the publication reported the following, which was adopted: That, notwithstanding the fact that the board in regard to the particulars in its action against the ex-

*See Preface on page 98.

editor of the *Evangelical Messenger*, as in the represen-
tation of the charges, may have varied from the usual
custom of conducting church trials, we cannot see, considering the incomplete directions given in the book of
discipline concerning the trial of officers of the establishment, and as no precedent existed, how they could
have acted otherwise in order to guard the interests of
the establishment.

A recommendation, permitting a preacher to serve
three years instead of two on the same field of labor,
was adopted by 66 votes. The Conference decided that
the yearly allowance of itinerant preachers shall be left
to the various annual conferences for their own regulation, to decide upon the allowance at their annual sessions, or, if they see proper, to refer the matter to the
several quarterly conferences.

The proceedings of the East Pa. Conference of
1871, in regard to the action of the board of publication in the *Evangelical Messenger* affair, were
declared illegal. The subject of a union between the
Evangelical Association and the Methodist Episcopal
Church having been presented anew by three delegates
from the M. E. General Conference, a series of resolutions was adopted declaring it unadvisable to recommend such a union, however desirable, because it could
not be accomplished with the general consent of our
ministry and membership at present. The subject of
changing the name of the Evangelical Association was
indefinitely postponed.

The elections resulted as follows: Bishops, J. J.
Esher and R. Yeakel; general book agent, W. F.
Schneider; editor of the *Christliche Botschafter*, R.

Dubs; editor of the *Evangelical Messenger*, J. Hartzler; editor of the *Magazin* and *Kinderfreund*, W. Horn; editor of the *Living Epistle* and the *S. S. Messenger*, J. Young; corresponding secretary of the Miss. Society, W. Yost; treasurer of the Miss. Society, W. W. Orwig; superintendent of the Ebenezer Orphan Institute, C. Hammer; editor of the *Evangelische Botschafter*, J. Kaechele; editor of the *Evangelische Kinderfreund*, J. Fuessele; delegate to the board of publication from the East Pa. Conference, T. Bowman; trustees of the Charitable Society, J. Freehoefer and Dr. O. L. Saylor.

The following statistics of the general church were reported: Itinerant preachers, 655; local preachers, 479; full members, 76,191; churches, 977; parsonages, 281; Sunday-schools, 1,165; officers and teachers, 13,080; scholars, 68,648; catechetical classes, 497; catechumens, 5,186.

1872.

The Thirty-Third (65th) Annual Session.

President, Bishop J. J. Esher.

Secretary, Thomas Bowman.

Assistant Secretaries, W. K. Wieand and I. E. Knerr.

The members of the East Pa. Conference assembled in the St. Paul's Evangelical church at Pine Grove, Pa., on Wednesday, February 28th, 1872. The president appointed the following committees: On Worship,— The presiding elders and J. C. Hornberger; On Letters,—J. P. Leib, G. T. Haines, and C. Meyers; On Boundaries,—The president and the presiding elders;

On Finance,—S. G. Rhoads, J. C. Bliem, S. S. Chubb, G. Knerr, and R. M. Lichtenwalner; On Statistics,— C. K. Fehr, J. Kurtz, and B. J. Smoyer; On Education,—J. Koehl, F. Krecker, J. C. Hornberger, S. B. Brown, and J. K. Knerr; On Quarterly Conference Proceedings,—J. P. Leib, G. T. Haines, C. Meyers, and C. B. Flichr; On Church Affairs,—L. Snyder, C. B. Flichr, and Seneca Breyfogel.

H. R. Funk, local preacher, withdrew from the Association. W. Heim, D. Hambright, and I. W. Yeakel were retained in the itinerancy without an appointment. Samuel Brown, local preacher, died during the past year. The supernumeraries were: J. Schell, C. Gingrich, D. Wieand, E. Ely, S. Ely, S. P. Reinoehl, D. Berger, H. Stoetzel, and M. Sindlinger. Sisters Hesser and Schnerr received support. J. M. Saylor was re-elected, and G. T. Haines, newly elected to the office of Presiding Elder. The following were ordained to the office of Elder: J. L. Werner, J. Savitz, A. M. Stirk, and A. Kindt; and these to the office of Deacon: I. W. Yeakel, J. A. Fegar, B. H. Miller, D. S. Stauffer, A. A. Delong, E. J. Miller, and J. K. Fehr. The brethren, Daniel A. Medlar, Calvin Bliem, James M. Oplinger, Joshua Wilson, H. Rudolph Yost, Christian Pfeifle, Titus A. Hess, Christian S. Brown, Jacob S. Newhart, and William Nicholas received license as preachers on trial. J. A. Fegar, J. F. Wohlfarth, T. A. Hess, J. M. Oplinger, and O. L. Saylor were received into the itinerancy.

The support of the preachers was referred to the stewards and quarterly conferences of the various charges, with the condition that the salary of a traveling preacher during his first and second years shall not be less than $250.00 a year, and thereafter not less than $500.00 a year.* The following was adopted: WHEREAS, A request has been presented for permission to conduct a "holiness" campmeeting; and WHEREAS, In our judgment the Discipline distinctly indicates under whose authority campmeetings are to be held; therefore be it *Resolved*, That we respectfully refer the request back to the petitioners.

BOUNDARIES.

Southwark Mission was formed of Bridesburg and Philadelphia 5th St. Station. Norristown was changed into a mission. Hellertown Mission was discontinued. Nazareth was transferred from Bath Circuit to Northampton, and Bath was made a mission. Port Jervis Mission was formed of Port Jervis, Sparrow Bush, and Shoholo Valley. Wesnersville, Kistler's Valley, and Bolich's class were taken from Kutztown Circuit and annexed to Hamburg Mission. Ringtown and Fetherolf's class were taken from Ashland Circuit and called Ringtown Station. Mt. Carmel was taken up as a mission. Ashland Mission was formed of Ashland, Gordon, and Mahanoy Plane. Newmanstown Mission was annexed to Myerstown Circuit. Shamokin Mission was changed to a station. Hepler's class, Union Church, and Dunkelberger's class were organized into Mahantongo Circuit, the remainder of the old Mahantongo Circuit to be called Uniontown Circuit. Pine Swamp and Bethel were taken from Chester Circuit and to-

---

*This was amended the following year so as to fix the minimum salary for the third and fourth years at $375.00.

gether with Birdsboro called Birdsboro Mission. Allentown Mission was changed to a station. Kutztown Circuit was called Fleetwood.

CHURCH AFFAIRS.

The church affairs at Halifax were referred to a committee. The preacher in charge of Richmond was instructed to secure articles of incorporation for the congregation there and to secure the deed by legal process if necessary. The English congregation at Lancaster and the congregation at Berlinsville received permission to sell their churches and to erect new ones. The quarterly conference of Pleasant Valley Circuit was authorized to sell the church property called Grover's Church and to apply the proceeds for the erection of a new church at Flint Hill. In answer to a petition from the congregation, the preacher in charge at Schuylkill Haven was advised to conduct the Sunday forenoon services in the German language and the evening services in the English language, the remaining services to be conducted according to his best judgment.

EDUCATION.

The committee on education reported that the Sunday-schools throughout the entire conference district were in a flourishing condition, as a result of the annual Sunday-school conventions. It was also the opinion of the committee that the Sunday-schools, as conducted in many congregations, had taken the place and partially, if not fully, superseded the necessity of catechetical instructions. The erection of a college with a biblical institute was declared to be both necessary and timely, but because such an undertaking is connected with great expense and requires the establishment of a fund, it was resolved that Thomas Bowman be authorized to confer with our well to do members during the year and to ascertain how much they are willing to contribute to such an object. The following examiners were appointed: For the fourth year class, S. G. Rhoads, T. Bowman, and C. S. Haman; for the third year class, C. Myers, R. Mott, and C. K. Fehr; for the second year class, S. B. Brown, I. E. Knerr, and J. C. Hornberger; for the first year class, W. K. Wieand, S. P. Reinoehl, and H. A. Neitz. The examiners were instructed to present a written report at each annual session.

FINANCE.

Receipts :

Balance from last year	$278.00
From conference collections	668.66
" the book establishment	250.00
" the Charitable Society	161.00
	———$1,357.66

Expenditures :

Paid to conference claimants	854.27
Balance on hand	$ 503.39

MISSIONARY APPROPRIATIONS.

Phila. Eng. Miss.	$525	Union Hill and Greenville Miss.	$250
Norristown Miss.	125	Newark Miss.	250
Camden Miss	250	New York 53d Str. Miss.	425
Phoenixville and Pottstown Miss.	200		
Birdsboro Miss.	300	Easton Eng. Miss.	425

Bath Miss.........$175
Mauch Chunk and
    Wilkesbarre Miss.. 400
Hamburg Miss.... 350
Ashland Miss....... 300
Mt. Carmel Miss.... 100
Hazleton Miss...... 200
Tremont Miss....... 100
Reading Miss....... 350

Lancaster Miss......$500
Harrisburg Miss.... 400
Williams Valley
    Miss........... 250
Newmanstown Miss.. 125
Southwark Miss..... 200
         ————
Total.........$6,200

APPOINTMENTS.

PHILADELPHIA DISTRICT—*C. S. Haman,* P. E.
Philadelphia 4th St. Sta.—J. Steltzer.
Philadelphia 6th St. Sta.—F. Hoffman.
Germantown Sta.—J. K. Knerr.
Montgomery Cir.—A. Kindt and J. M. Oplinger.
Milford Cir.—R. Deisher and T. A. Hess.
Trappe Cir.—Fred. Krecker.
Philadelphia Southwark Miss.—Isaac Hess.
Philadelphia Eng. Miss.—S. G. Rhoads.
Camden Miss.—D. Yingst.
Norristown Miss.—J. O. Lehr.
Phoenixville and Pottstown Miss.—J. P. Leib.
Birdsboro Miss.—I. E. Zimmerman.

READING DISTRICT—*G. T. Haines,* P. E.
Reading Sta.—C. H. Baker.
Reading Eng. Sta.—J. G. Sands.
Lancaster Sta.—Jacob Adams.
Fairville Sta.—J. Specht.
Fleetwood Cir.—M. Dissinger.
Adamstown Cir.—J. Loras.
Womelsdorf Cir.—I. E. Knerr.
Brownstown Cir.—A. Schultz.
Lancaster Cir.—W. H. Weidner and U. H. Hershey.
Chester Cir.—B. D. Albright.
Reading Miss.—John Koehl.
Lancaster Miss.—F. P. Lehr.

HARRISBURG DISTRICT—*J. M. Saylor,* P. E.
Lebanon Sta.—J. C. Bliem.
Millersburg Sta.—S. S. Chubb.
Shamokin Sta.—R. Mott.
Myerstown Cir. and Newmanstown Miss.—J. K. Seyfrit, with one to be supplied.
Annville Cir.—B. J. Smoyer and J. K. Fehr.
Dauphin Cir.—J. A. Fegar.
Berrysburg Cir.—J. C. Hornberger.
Mahantongo Cir.—D. Lentz.
Uniontown Cir.—J. L. Werner and J. F. Wohlfarth.
Harrisburg Miss.—C. K. Fehr.
Williams Valley and Halifax Miss.—R. Dreibelbis and W. A. Shoemaker.

ALLENTOWN DISTRICT—*S. Neitz,* P. E.
Allentown Sta.—C. B. Fliehr.
East Allentown Sta.—R. M. Lichtenwalner.
Allentown Eng. Sta.—J. N. Metzgar.
Catasauqua Sta.—Geo. Knerr.
Weissport Sta.—A. F. Leopold.
Lehigh Cir.—F. Sechrist and C. Bliem.
Berlinsville Cir.—E. Butz.
Parryville Cir.—A. Ziegenfus.
Mauch Chunk and Wilkesbarre Miss.—B. F. Bohner and D. A. Medlar.

POTTSVILLE DISTRICT—*Thos. Bowman,* P. E.

Pottsville Sta.—H. A. Neitz.
Schuylkill Haven Sta.—Lewis Snyder.
Pine Grove Sta.—A. M. Stirk.
Tamaqua Sta.—Seneca Breyfogel.
Mahanoy City Sta.—W. K. Wieand.
Ringtown Sta.—Thos. Harper.
Cressona Cir.—L. N. Worman.
Port Carbon Cir.—D. S. Stauffer.
Schuylkill Cir.—H. Kempfer.
Orwigsburg Cir.—A. A. Deloug.
Tremont Miss.—O. L. Saylor.
Ashland Miss.—
Hamburg Miss.—B. H. Miller.
Hazleton Miss.—D. Z. Kembel.
Mt. Carmel Miss.—(To be supplied.)

EASTON DISTRICT—*Jesse Yeakel, P. E.*
Easton Sta.—G. Scharf.

Bethlehem Sta.—C. Myers.
Freemansburg Sta.—S. B. Brown.
New York Sta.—J. Kurtz.
Northampton Cir.—G. B. Fisher and H. R. Yost.
Monroe Cir.—E. J. Miller and J. S. Newhart.
Wayne Cir.—J. Savitz.
Pleasant Valley Cir.—J. Zern. (One to be supplied).
Newark Miss.—T. Plattenberger.
Union Hill and Greenville Miss.—N. Goebel.
New York 53d St. Miss.—M. Guhl.
Easton Eng. Miss.—S. L. Wiest.
Bath Miss.—W. A. Leopold.
Port Jervis Miss.—(To be supplied.)

1873.

The Thirty-Fourth (66th) Annual Session.

President, Bishop J. J. Esher.
Secretary, Thomas Bowman.
Assistant Secretaries, C. K. Fehr, A. M. Stirk, and H. A. Neitz.

On Wednesday, February 26th, 1873, the members of the Conference assembled at Tamaqua, Pa., in their thirty-fourth annual session. Inasmuch as Bishop Esher was prevented by a railroad accident from being present, S. Neitz, at the request of the secretary, opened the session, after which he was elected president. He appointed T. Bowman secretary. The following are the standing committees: On Worship,—T. Bowman and Seneca Breyfogel; On Boundaries,—The Bishop and the presiding elders; On Letters,—J. P. Leib, C. B. Fliehr, and J. Specht; On Finance,—J. C. Bliem,

W. K. Wieand, and I. E. Knerr; On Statistics,—S. S.
Chubb, R. Mott, and U. H. Hershey; On Education,—
S. G. Rhoads, J. Koehl, J. C. Hornberger, J. K. Knerr,
and J. N. Metzgar; On Quarterly Conference Records,—
L. Snyder, A. Schultz, and J. Steltzer; On Church Af-
fairs,—J. O. Lehr, J. Kurtz, and R. M. Lichtenwalner;
On Memorials,—F. Krecker, S. B. Brown, and D.
Wieand; On Temperance,—J. C. Hornberger, C. H.
Baker, and B. J. Smoyer.

Bishop Esher appeared in the Conference and took
the chair.   R. Mott received an honorable dismissal from the Conference.   John Dick, local preacher,
withdrew from the Association.   A. H. Overholt
located on account of bodily infirmities,   C. Meyers, itinerant, and C. Wolf, local preacher, died during
the year.   The supernumeraries were: D. Wieand, M.
Sindlinger, S. P. Reinoehl, S. Ely, J. Shell, C. Gingrich, E. Ely, D. Berger, H. Stoetzel, and I. E. Zimmerman.   The conference claimants were: D. Wieand, M.
Sindlinger, S. P. Reinoehl, J. Shell, H. Stoetzel, and
C. Gingrich.   Father John P. Leib, on account of the
many years of service which he had rendered, was retained in the itinerancy without an appointment and
with a support equal to that of the other beneficiaries.
W. A. Shoemaker, S. L. Wiest, and R. Dreibelbis were
ordained to the office of Elder, and J. F. Wohlfarth, U.
H. Hershey, J. M. Oplinger, Wm. Loos, and G. H.
Landis, to the office of Deacon.   The following received
license as preachers on trial: William Miller, Aldus
W. Warfel, Joseph Moyer, Joseph M. Rinker, Emanuel
Glaeser, Daniel Schnebel, J. F. Weidner, Joseph Workman, John J. High, Frank B. Copp, Samuel Butter-

week, William B. Romig, William L. Black, Lewis E. Leslie, George H. Laury, James Bowman, William Webber, Sylvanus C. Breyfogel, and E. Wilson.

The Conference expressed profound sympathy with Bishop R. Yeakel because of the heavy hand of affliction upon him and his family, by which he was prevented from attending this session and presiding over its deliberations. W. F. Schneider, General Book Agent, addressed the Conference. It was resolved that hereafter certificates given by the East Pa. Conference to preachers, or by preachers to members, shall in no case be valid longer than three months, except where it was impossible for the holders to deposit them sooner. The Conference expressed its joy over the large increase in the circulation of our church periodicals and gave words of good cheer to the editors. C. Hammer delivered an address in the interests of the Orphans' Home.

BOUNDARIES.

Richmond class was transferred from Southwark Mission to the Fourth Street Philadelphia Station. Fleetwood and Lyons were made a station and the name of Fleetwood Circuit changed to Kutztown. Shoemakersville was taken from Kutztown Circuit and annexed to Hamburg Mission. The name of Chester Circuit was changed to Conestoga. Sterling was attached to Wayne Circuit. Port Jervis Mission was discontinued and joined to Wayne Circuit. East Allentown Mission was changed to a station. Howertown was taken from Lehigh Circuit and annexed to Bath Mission. Newmanstown Mission was joined to Myerstown Circuit and

17

Brickersville appointment was annexed to Brownstown Circuit. Williams Valley Mission was changed to a circuit. Barnesville Circuit was formed of Barnesville, Locust Valley, and Quakake Junction, which were taken from Schuylkill Circuit. Orwigsburg and Schuylkill circuits were united, and Wesnersville, Bolich's class, and Kistler's Valley were transferred from Hamburg Mission to Schuylkill Circuit. A new mission was located in Shenandoah City, to be served by the missionary at Mahanoy City. Coaldale was taken from Tamaqua and annexed to Barnesville Circuit. Point Philips was taken from Bath Mission and annexed to Northampton Circuit. Missions were located at the following places: Greenville, Emaus, Scranton, Lebanon (English), and Mauch Chunk.

CHURCH AFFAIRS.

The Conference decided that the religious services in the East Allentown congregation shall be held alternately in the German and English languages. This congregation also received permission to borrow money. The Bernville congregation received permission to borrow $1,000 on their church property, and the Leesport congregation, $600. The trustees of Greenville Mission were authorized to sell their church if they see proper. The Conference approved of the sale of the church at Conestoga Centre.

EDUCATION.

T. Bowman was re-appointed to cultivate a school sentiment among our wealthier members. S. G. Rhoads, T. Bowman, and C. S. Haman were appointed to examine junior preachers for four years; C. K. Fehr, J.

C. Bliem, and W. H. Weidner, for three years; I. E. Knerr, J. C. Hornberger, and S. B. Brown, for two years; and H. A. Neitz, W. K. Wieand, and R. M. Lichtenwalner, for one year.

MEMORIALS.

Of the late brother C. Meyers the Conference gave expression as follows: He was a man of sound abilities and of deep spirituality, true to his high calling, one who feared God, a workman that needed not to be ashamed.   Through the Word which he preached and by means of his Christian character he led many precious souls to the Head of the Church.

TEMPERANCE.

The Conference *Resolved*, 1st, That it is the duty of every legal voter among our members to vote against the granting of license for the sale of intoxicating liquors.   2d, That in the name of the membership which we represent we earnestly protest against the repeal of the present Local Option Law.

FINANCE.

Balance on hand from 1872.........$515.39
Received from the book establishment. 250.00
   "   "   "   Charitable Society. 363.75
   "   "   conference collections.. 792.20
   "   "   a collection from Bishop
Yeakel............................. 18.64
          ————$1,939.98
Paid to conference claimants........ 1,939.98

MISSIONARY APPROPRIATIONS.

Phila. 5th Str. Miss.	$200	Mt. Carmel Miss....	$300
Phila. Eng. Miss....	425	Hazleton Miss......	200
Camden Miss.......	225	East Allentown Miss.	275
Norristown Miss....	200	Emaus Miss.......	200
Phœnixville and		Mauch Chunk Miss..	100
Pottstown Miss...	325	Wilkesbarre and	
Birdsboro Miss.....	200	Scranton Miss....	400
Reading 9th Str. Miss.	300	Easton Eng. Miss....	375
Lancaster Eng. Miss.	400	Bath Miss.........	300
Lebanon Eng. Miss..	325	Newark Miss.......	250
Harrisburg Miss.....	400	New York 53d Str.	
Halifax Miss.......	300	Miss...........	400
Schuylkill Haven		Union Hill Miss.....	250
Eng. Miss........	300	Greenville Miss.....	100
Tremont Miss.......	150		
Hamburg Miss......	350	Total.........$7,450	
Ashland Miss......	200		

APPOINTMENTS.

PHILADELPHIA DISTRICT—*C. S. Haman*, P. E.

Philadelphia 4th St. Sta.—Jos. Steltzer.
"   6th St. Sta.—Isaac Hess.
"   8th St. Miss.—S. S. Chubb.
"   5th St. Miss.—F. Hoffman.
Camden Miss.—R. Deisher.
Germantown Sta.—J. K. Kuerr.
Norristown Miss.—S. G. Rhoads.
Montgomery Cir.—J. M. Oplinger and J. J. High.
Trappe Cir.—A. Kindt.
Milford Cir.—G. Scharf.
Phoenixville and Pottstown Miss.—E. Ely.
Birdsboro Miss.—U. H. Hershey.

READING DISTRICT.—*G. T. Haines, P. E.*

Reading 8th St. Sta.—C. H. Baker.
"   Chestnut St. Sta.—J. G. Sands.
"   9th St. Miss.—E. Butz.
Fleetwood Sta.—M. Dissinger.
Kutztown Cir.—J. Specht.
Womelsdorf Cir.—J. Koehl.
Adamstown Cir.—J. Adams.
Brownstown Cir.—R. Dreibelbis.
Conestoga Cir.—J. N. Metzgar.
Fairville Sta.—A. A. Delong.
Lancaster Sta.—A. Schultz.
Lancaster Miss.—B. D. Albright.
Lancaster Cir.—J. Loras and W. L. Black.

HARRISBURG DISTRICT.—*J. M. Saylor*, P. E.

Lebanon Sta.—C. K. Fehr.

Lebanon Miss.—(To be supplied).
Myerstown Cir.—W. H. Weidner.
Annville Cir.—D. Lentz and J. F. Wohlfarth.
Harrisburg Miss.—F. P. Lehr.
Dauphin Cir.—J. A. Feger.
Halifax Miss.—C. Gingrich.
Millersburg Sta.—H. A. Neitz.
Williams Valley Sta.—W. A. Shoemaker.
Berrysburg Cir.—J. C. Hornberger.
Uniontown Cir.—J. L. Werner and G. H. Landis.
Mahantongo Cir.—B. H. Miller.
Shamokin Sta.—B. J. Smoyer.

POTTSVILLE DISTRICT. — Thos. Bowman, P. E.
Pottsville Sta.—I. E. Knerr.
Schuylkill Haven Sta.—J. K. Seyfrit.
Schuylkill Haven Miss.—Jas. Bowman.
Cressona Cir.—F. Krecker.
Tremont Miss.—O. L. Saylor.
Pinegrove Sta.—A. M. Stirk.
Hamburg Miss.—J. Shell.
Schuylkill Cir.—H. Kempfer and J. S. Newhart.
Tamaqua Sta.—J. C. Bliem.
Barnesville Cir.—S. C. Breyfogel.
Mahanoy Sta.—W. K. Wieand.
Shenandoah Miss.—H. R. Yost.
Ringtown Sta.—T. Harper.
Ashland Miss.—I. W. Yeakel.
Mt. Carmel Miss.—L. N. Worman.
Hazleton Miss.—D. Z. Kembel.

ALLENTOWN DISTRICT—S. Neitz, P. E.
Allentown Sta.—C. B. Fliehr.
Allentown Eng. Sta.—J. O. Lehr.
East Allentown Miss.—R. M. Lichtenwalner.
Emaus Miss.—S. Ely.
Lehigh Cir—F. Sechrist.
Catasauqua Sta.—Geo. Knerr.
Berlinsville Cir.—D. Yingst.
Parryville Cir.—A. Ziegenfus.
Weissport Sta.—A. F. Leopold.
Mauch Chunk Sta.—B. F. Bohner.
Wilkesbarre and Scranton Miss.—J. K. Fehr and D. A. Medlar.

EASTON DISTRICT—J. Yeakel, P. E.
Easton Sta.—Seneca Breyfogel.
Easton Miss.—S. L. Wiest.
Freemansburg Sta.—W. A. Leopold.
Pleasant Valley Cir.—J. Zern and Geo. H. Laury.
Bethlehem Sta.—S. B Brown.
Bath Miss.—L. Snyder.
Northampton Cir.—G. B. Fisher and J. M. Rinker.
Monroe Cir.—E. J. Miller and T. A. Hess.
Wayne Cir.—J. Savitz.
Newark Miss.—N. Goebel.
New York 24th St. Sta.—J. Kurtz.
New York 53d St. Miss.—M. Guhl.
Union Hill Miss.— T. Plattenberger.
Greenville Miss.—E. Glaeser.
J. P. Leib to travel at pleasure within the bounds of the Conference.

1874.

The Thirty-Fifth (67th) Annual Session.

President, Bishop R. Yeakel.
Secretary, Thomas Bowman.
Assistant Secretaries, J. C. Hornberger, M. Guhl, B. J. Smoyer, J. K. Knerr, and H. A. Neitz.

The members of the East Pa. Conference met in the

Salem Evangelical church of Allentown, Pa., on Wednesday, February 25th, 1874. J. C. Hornberger was appointed to record the minutes in the English language. The presiding Bishop appointed the following committees: On Worship,—C. B. Flichr, J. O. Lehr, and R. M. Lichtenwalner; On Boundaries,—The Bishop and the presiding elders; On Letters,—The presiding elders; On Finance,—J. Steltzer, J. Koehl, and C. H. Baker; On Statistics,—G. Scharf, H. A. Neitz, and W. K. Wieand; On Education,—S. S. Chubb, C. K. Fehr, I. E. Knerr, B. J. Smoyer, and Seneca Breyfogel; On Quarterly Conference Proceedings,—S. G. Rhoads, J. C. Hornberger, J. C. Bliem, A. Schultz, and D. Z. Kembel; On Church Affairs,—R. Deisher, J. K. Seyfrit, and A. M. Stirk; On Memorials,—S. G. Rhoads, J. K. Knerr, and M. Guhl; On Temperance,—L. Snyder, J. N. Metzgar, and J. C. Hornberger.

I. E. Zimmerman was placed in a local relation. J. L. Lutman, a local preacher, withdrew from the church. Ephraim Ely, itinerant, and David Thomas, David Light, and Edward Snyder, local preachers, died during the year. G. T. Haines resigned his presiding eldership. C. S. Haman was re-elected, and S. G. Rhoads and C. K. Fehr were newly elected to the office of Presiding Elder. The following named brethren were elected and ordained to the office of Elder: B. H. Miller, D. S. Stauffer, A. A. Delong, I. W. Yeakel, J. K. Fehr, E. J. Miller, O. L. Saylor, and J. A. Feger; and these to the office of Deacon,—J. S. Newhart, Jas. Bowman, D. A. Medlar, H. R. Yost, A. Markley, and E. Glaeser. The following were licensed as preachers on trial: Joshua Hollenbach, Isaac J. Reitz, Henry

D. Shultz, and Augustus Dilabar. The brethren, L. E. Leslie, S. C. Breyfogel, G. H. Laury, J. M. Rinker, A. W. Warfel, H. D. Shultz, A. Dilabar, A. Markley, and J. J. High, were received into the itinerancy. John Dooley, local deacon of the Ohio Conference, was received into this Conference in the same relation. Geo. D. Sweigert, local preacher on trial in the M. E. church, was received into our church in the same relation. The supernumeraries were N. Goebel, D. Wieand, M. Sindlinger, S. P. Reinoehl, D. Berger, H. Stoetzel, J. Shell and Jos. Gross. The conference claimants were D. Wieand, M. Sindlinger, S. P. Reinoehl, H. Stoetzel, J. P. Leib, and the widows Schnerr, Hesser, and Myers.

It was resolved that hereafter local preachers, who make application for ordination, shall be required to pass the examinations of junior preachers two years previous. The Conference decided that no congregation has the right to appropriate missionary money for any other purpose than that for which it was collected. All the congregations were requested to make the necessary preparations to pay their preachers monthly.

BOUNDARIES.

Camden and Southwark missions were discontinued and the two congregations united into one charge. Boyertown and Berlin were taken from Milford Circuit and annexed to Pottstown Mission. Orwigsburg was taken from Schuylkill Circuit and made a station. Bolich's class, Wesnersville, and Kistler's class were taken from Schuylkill Circuit and with Lynnville and the surrounding country constituted Wesnersville

Mission. Port Clinton was taken from Schuylkill Circuit and annexed to Hamburg Mission. Roaring Creek Valley and Brandonville were annexed to Ringtown Station, and called Ringtown Circuit. Tremont and Mauch Chunk missions were changed into circuits. Slatington and Slatedale were taken from Berlinsville Circuit and constituted a station. Northampton Circuit was divided as follows: Nazareth, Plainfield, Windgap, and Bushkill were formed into Nazareth Circuit; Ackermantown, Miller's, Roxburg, and McCracken, into Mt. Bethel Circuit. Monroe Circuit was divided as follows: Altimose's, Snydersville, St. John's, Mechanicsville, Middlecreek, and Pine Swamp were continued as Monroe Circuit; Paradise, Sterling, Puddytown, and Middle Valley were formed into Sterling Circuit. Crum's class was taken from Dauphin Circuit and annexed to the Harrisburg German Mission. Ashland and Hazleton missions were changed into stations. Annville was taken from Annville Circuit and made a mission, and the remainder of the circuit called Mt. Nebo Circuit. New missions were established at the following places: Reading (southeastern part), Harrisburg (English), Frackville and Mahanoy Plane, Scranton, Lehighton, Allentown (northern part), Bangor, and Mauch Chunk (English).

CHURCH AFFAIRS.

The congregations at Pottsville, Eighth St. Reading, Bethlehem, and Bangor were authorized to sell their old church properties upon the condition that the deeds of the new churches be made in accordance with the directions of our Church Discipline. The affairs of

the church at Halifax, Pa., were referred to a committee.   The legal official members of our church at
Mechanicsville, Monroe Co., Pa., were advised to institute legal proceedings against the persons who unlaw-
fully hold the deed of that church.   It was decided that
the persons making claims against the church at Hatfield shall institute legal proceedings to recover the
same, whenever they see proper.   The Central Pa.
Conference was kindly requested to grant permission to
our missionary on the Harrisburg English Mission to
collect money within the bounds of that conference.
The trustees of the various churches which are not
properly deeded, were requested to take the necessary
steps to have the deeds made according to the directions of our Church Discipline.   It was resolved that
the Sabbath services at Wilkesbarre, Pa., be held in
German in the forenoon and in English in the evening.

Permission to collect throughout the Conference was
granted to the following congregations: Scranton Mission, New York 53d St. Mission, Bernville, and Harrisburg English Mission.

EDUCATION.

The Conference appointed a committee of seven to
take active steps this year in the location of an institution of learning, and an agent to secure funds toward
the erection and endowment of such an institution.
Thomas Bowman was elected agent, and T. Bowman, J.
Yeakel, C. S. Haman, C. K. Fehr, Moses Schadt, F. G.
Boas, and D. R. Miller were appointed as the committee.   All the preachers were instructed to preach at
least once during the year at every appointment on the
importance of education, and to take up a collection for

the education of indigent young men studying for the ministry.

In case junior preachers absent themselves from the annual examination without a satisfactory excuse, or are not able to pass the prescribed studies, their ordination shall be deferred according to the judgment of the Conference. B. J. Smoyer, A. M. Stirk, and J. K. Knerr were appointed examiners.

MEMORIALS.

Suitable memorials were erected to the following brethren: Ephraim Ely, an itinerant, a diligent and faithful laborer in the church, departed this life, giving a clear testimony of the hope of eternal life. He was beloved wherever he labored, and was instrumental in leading many to the Shepherd of souls. His preaching was spiritual and full of unction. David Thomas, once in active service, but for fifty years a blameless and useful local preacher, finished his course in a triumphant death. The departed brethren, David Light and Edward Snyder, were both active laborers for God. We appreciate their services and believe that they reap with joy what they sowed with tears.

TEMPERANCE.

The following was resolved: 1st, That we would consider the repeal of the Local Option Law as highly unjust, inasmuch as the practical operation of the law has not been sufficiently tested. 2d, That we see the hand of God in the so-called Woman's Crusade against intemperance, and that we heartily wish them God-speed, and would call upon the women in the entire land to arise and to call into action all the power and influence

with which God has endowed them, to drive the demon
of intemperance from the land.

FINANCE.

Receipts :

From conference collections	$ 799.55
From the Charitable Society	280.00
From the publishing house	250.00
	$1,329.55

Expenditures :

Paid to conference claimants	1,315.33
Balance on hand	$ 14.22

MISSIONARY APPROPRIATIONS.

Philadelphia 8th St. Miss	$400	North Allentown Miss	$400
Norristown Miss	100	Lehighton Miss	
Pottstown Miss	250	Wilkesbarre Miss	200
Reading Miss	250	Scranton Miss	400
Lancaster Miss	400	Easton Miss	350
Lebanon Miss	450	Bath Miss	300
Annville Miss	250	Bangor Miss	250
Halifax Miss	125	Newark Miss	250
Schuylkill Haven Miss	300	New York Miss	350
Hamburg Miss	250	Union Hill Miss	250
Wesnersville Miss	375	Greenville Miss	250
Shenandoah Miss	300	Harrisburg Miss	250
Frackville Miss	300	Harrisburg Eng. Miss	500
Mt. Carmel Miss	350	East Reading Miss	25
East Allentown Miss	275	Birdsboro Miss	200
Emaus Miss	150		$8,500

APPOINTMENTS.

PHILADELPHIA DISTRICT. — *S. G. Rhoads, P. E.*
Philadelphia 4th St. Sta.—F. Hoffman.
" 6th St. Sta.—I. Hess.
" 8th St. Miss.—S. S. Chubb.
Southwark Sta.—J. Steltzer.
Germantown Sta.—J. K. Knerr.
Norristown Miss. — R. M. Lichtenwalner.
Montgomery Cir.—W. A. Shoemaker and J. J. High.
Trappe Miss.—J. A. Feger.
Pottstown Miss.—J. M. Oplinger.
Milford Cir.—G. Scharf.
Birdsboro Miss.—U. H. Hershey.
Bridesburg Miss.—

READING DISTRICT—*C. S. Haman, P. E.*
Reading, 8th St., Sta.—S. Neitz.
" Chestnut St. Sta.—George B. Fisher.
Reading, Ninth St. Miss.—E. Butz.
East Reading Miss.—
Fleetwood Sta. - J. Zern.
Kutztown Cir —F. Sechrist.
Womelsdorf Cir.—J. Koehl.
Adamstown Cir.—J. Adams.
Brownstown Cir.—R. Dreibelbis.
Conestoga Cir.—J. N. Metzgar.
Fairville Sta.—A. A. Delong.
Lancaster Sta.—A. Schultz.
" Miss. B. D. Albright.
" Cir. - J. Laros and A. Markley.

HARRISBURG DISTRICT—*C. K. Fehr, P. E.*
Lebanon Sta.—J. Specht.
" Miss.—J. G. Sands.
Myerstown Cir.—W. H. Weidner.
Annville Miss.—E. J. Miller.
Mt. Nebo Cir.—D. Lentz and A. W. Warfel.
Harrisburg Miss.—F. P. Lehr.
" Eng. Miss.—J. C. Hornberger.
Dauphin Cir.—L. E. Leslie.
Halifax Miss.—(To be supplied).
Millersburg Sta.—H. A. Neitz.
Williams Valley Cir.—J. F. Wohlfarth.

Berrysburg Cir.—J. P. Leib.
Uniontown Cir.—S. L. Wiest and H. D. Shultz.
Mahantongo Cir.—B. H. Miller.
Shamokin Sta —B. J. Smoyer.

POTTSVILLE DISTRICT—*T. Bowman, P. E*
Pottsville Sta.—I. E. Knerr.
Schuylkill Haven Sta —J. K. Seyfrit.
" " Miss.—J. Bowman.
Cressona Cir.—F. Krecker.
Tremont Cir.—J. S. Newhart.
Pinegrove Sta.—W. K. Wieand.
Hamburg Miss. - H. Kempfer.
Wesnersville Miss.—Wm. Heim.
Orwigsburg Sta.—A. Dilabar.
Schuylkill Cir.—A. F. Leopold.
Port Carbon Cir.—W. L. Black.
Tamaqua Sta.—J. C. Bilem.
Barnesville Cir.—S. C. Breyfogel.
Mahanoy City Sta.—A. M. Stirk.
Shenandoah City Miss.—H. R. Yost.
Frackville Miss.—G. H. Laury.
Ringtown Cir.—D. S. Stauffer.
Mt. Carmel Miss.—L. N. Worman.
Ashland Sta.—I. W. Yeakel.
Hazleton Sta.—D. Z. Kembel.

ALLENTOWN DISTRICT—*J. M. Saylor, P. E.*
Allentown Linden St. Sta. — C. B. Fliehr.
Allentown Turner St. Sta.—J. O. Lehr.
East Allentown Miss.—C. H. Baker.
North Allentown Miss.—J. Schell.
Emaus Miss.—S. Ely.
Lehigh Cir.—J. L. Werner.
Catasauqua Sta.—Geo. Knerr.
Berlinsville Cir.—D. Yingst.
Slatington Sta.—R. Deisher.
Parryville Cir.—A. Ziegenfus.
Weissport Sta.—G. T. Haines.
Lehighton Miss.—A. Krecker.
Mauch Chunk Cir.—B. F. Bohner.
Wilkesbarre Miss.—J. K. Fehr.
Scranton Miss.—D. A. Medlar.

EASTON DISTRICT—*Jesse Yeakel, P. E.*
Easton Sta.—Seneca Breyfogel.

Easton Miss.—O. L. Saylor.
Freemansburg Sta.—W. A. Leopold.
Pleasant Valley Cir.—Moses Dissinger.
Bethlehem Sta.—S. B. Brown.
Bath Miss.—L. Snyder.
Nazareth Cir.—T. Harper.
Mt. Bethel Cir.—J. M. Rinker.
Bangor Miss.—C. Gingrich.

Monroe Cir.—A. Kindt.
Sterling Cir.—T. A. Hess.
Wayne Cir.—J. Savitz.
Newark Miss.—N. Goebel.
New York Sta.—M. Guhl.
New York Miss.—John Kurtz.
Union Hill Miss.—T. Plattenberger.
Greenville Miss.—E. Glaeser.

1875.

The Thirty-Sixth (68th) Annual Session.

President, Bishop J. J. Esher.
German Secretary C. B. Fliehr.
English Secretary, J. C. Hornberger.
Assistant Secretaries, G. Scharf and B. J. Smoyer.

The Conference convened in the St. Matthew's Evangelical church at Millersburg, Dauphin Co., Pa., on Wednesday forenoon, February 24th, 1875. The following committees were appointed: On Worship,—C. K. Fehr, H. A. Neitz, and J. P. Leib; On Letters and Boundaries,—The Bishop and the presiding elders; On Finance,—R. Deisher, J. Steltzer, and D. Z. Kembel; On Statistics,—W. K. Wieand, J. K. Knerr, A. M. Stirk, O. L. Saylor, and E. Butz; On Education,—I. E. Knerr, U. H. Hershey, B. J. Smoyer, G. B. Fisher, and B. F. Bohner; On Quarterly Conference Records,—S. Neitz, A. Schultz, G. T. Haines, F. Krecker, and J. C. Bliem; On General Conference Recommendations,—J. Kochl, S. S. Chubb, S. B. Brown, J. P. Leib, and F. Hoffman; On Church Affairs,—S. Ely, R. M. Lichtenwalner, G. Knerr, Seneca Breyfogel, and J. N. Metzgar; On Memorials,—J. K. Seyfrit, J. O. Lehr, and W. A. Leopold.

Nathan Kaufman, B. Wimmer, and G. H. Landis, local preachers, withdrew from the church. An elder and a local preacher were deposed from the ministry and the former expelled from the church. Levi Miller and G. F. Weidner resigned their licenses as local preachers. The announcement was made that R. Dreibelbis, itinerant, and Isaac Overholser, Christopher Yeakel, and G. Reich, local preachers, had died. T. Bowman was re-elected, and S. Neitz, newly elected to the office of Presiding Elder. U. H. Hershey, J. F. Wohlfarth, and J. M. Oplinger were ordained Elders; T. A. Hess, W. L. Black, L. E. Leslie, S. C. Breyfogel, J. J. High, G. H. Lanry, J. M. Rinker, A. Straub, A. W. Warfel, and C. S. Brown, Deacons. The following received license as preachers on trial: J. C. E. Waehlte, J. D. Campbell, M. L. Custer, J. A. Transue, Henry J. Glick, Franklin E. Erdman George W. Gross, Augustus Krecker and Sylvester T. Leopold. The following were received into the itinerancy: I. J. Reitz, A. Krecker, G. W. Gross, S. T. Leopold, H. J. Glick, M. L. Custer, W. C. Kantner, J. R. Workman, C. S. Brown, and A. Straub.

The supernumeraries were N. Goebel, D. Wieand, M. Sindlinger, D. Berger, H. Stoetzel, J. Schell, J. Gross, S. P. Reinoehl, C. Gingrich, and J. P. Leib. The conference claimants were S. P. Reinoehl, H. Stoetzel, M. Sindlinger, D. Wieand, N. Goebel, and Sisters Hesser, Schnerr, and Meyers. The following were elected delegates to the General Conference: T. Bowman, C. S. Haman, S. G. Rhoads, C. K. Fehr, S. Neitz, J. M. Saylor, J. Yeakel, J. P. Leib, L. Snyder, J. Koehl, J. O. Lehr, F. Hoffman, and J. C. Hornberger; alternates, G. T. Haines, F. Krecker, I. E. Knerr, and S. B. Brown.

The committee on quarterly conference records reported the following, which was adopted: "We find in a number of records that substitutes, sent by presiding elders to hold quarterly meetings, presided at the quarterly conferences, which we consider illegal." The following was adopted: WHEREAS, We understand that some of our congregations prohibit their pastors from lifting such collections as are authorized by Conference; therefore be it *Resolved*, 1st, That we most emphatically disapprove of such action and declare it to be a violation of our church rules and contrary to the spirit of true Christianity. 2d, That no congregation supplied by this Conference has any right to prohibit such collections nor to appropriate them, or any part of them, for their own use and purpose. It was made the imperative duty of every presiding elder and preacher in charge to see to it that the churches built on their fields of labor are deeded in accordance with the provision of our Discipline.

BOUNDARIES.

Bath Mission was made a station. Mahoning Valley was annexed to Lehighton Mission. Sterling Circuit was discontinued; Paradise and Union Church were annexed to Monroe Circuit; and Sterling and Middle Valley, to Wayne Circuit. A German mission was located in the vicinity of New York City, the presiding elder of the district and the missionary to select the specific locality. Camden was taken from Southwark Station, Camden and Glassborough to form a circuit. Richmond was annexed to Bridesburg. Link's class on Birdsboro Mission was annexed to the Reading 8th Str.

congregation. Leesport was taken from Womelsdorf
Circuit and annexed to Hamburg Mission. Crum's
church was taken from Harrisburg Mission and an-
nexed to Dauphin Circuit. Mountville, Jonestown, and
Fredericksburg were taken from Mt. Nebo Circuit and
annexed to Myerstown Circuit; Mt. Nebo, Steelstown,
Hanover, and Conewago to constitute Mt. Nebo Circuit.
Palmyra and Campbellstown were annexed to Annville
Mission. Coaldale and Ashton (Lansford) were taken
from Barnesville Circuit, and Summit Hill from Mauch
Chunk Circuit, these three appointments to constitute
Coaldale Circuit. New missions were located at Mauch
Chunk and White Haven, Sparrow Bush, N. Y., South-
wark (Philadelphia), Phoenixville, Lititz and Manheim,
and Fleetwood.

CHURCH AFFAIRS.

A committee of five was appointed to consider the
necessity of changing the location of Newark Mission,
with authority to sell the old church property and to
erect a new church edifice in another part of the city.
The Mt. Carmel congregation received permission to
sell a lot from their church property. The congregation at Fredericksburg, Pa., received permission to sell
a part of their church lot and to purchase an adjoining
piece of ground. The members of the Conference
made an effort to liquidate the indebtedness of $954.25
on the church at Halifax by personal contributions;
$668 were immediately secured. The trustees of our
church at Pine Grove were authorized to sell their old
church property. Permission was given to the proper
persons to sell the parsonage of the old Northampton

Circuit, providing the proceeds of such sale be applied for the purpose for which the money was first given. Permission was given to Lehighton Mission to apply a certain sum of money in their possession toward building a church at Lehighton, and to Flint class on Pleasant Valley Circuit, to remove the Gruber Church to Flint Hill.

EDUCATION.

WHEREAS, The standing committee on education have not yet determined on a location for the founding of a higher institution of learning, nor received any endowments therefor, but are convinced that the Conference should press the project to a successful issue as soon as the depressed state of business and the finances of our country and other circumstances make it practicable; therefore be it *Resolved*, That the same committee be continued. Cedar Hill Seminary, of Mt. Joy, Pa., under the supervision of Prof. D. Denlinger, was commended for its excellencies. The Conference created the office of Treasurer of the Educational Fund, whose duty it shall be to report to Conference annually. He shall have power to purchase any books prescribed in our course of study for the use of indigent young preachers traveling in our Conference, upon the presentation of an order from their presiding elders. The money thus expended shall be refunded into the treasury as soon as the recipient of the books is able. J. C. Bliem was elected educational treasurer. District ministerial conventions were commended as a valuable means for the development of our ministerial efficiency. I. E. Knerr, S. B. Brown, and J. C. Hornberger were appointed to examine junior preachers. W. K. Wieand

18

and J. K. Seyfrit were appointed to examine applicants for the itinerancy.

MEMORIALS.

The ranks of the ministry were diminished during the past year by the decease of four brethren. Reuben Dreibelbis, an itinerant, was a diligent laborer in the church of his choice and was instrumental in leading many souls to the Great Shepherd of the flock. His sermons were sound, evangelical, and full of divine unction. His life was devoted and his walk consistent. Isaac Overholser, once in the active ministry, but of recent years a local preacher, lived a useful life and died a triumphant death. His sermons were spiritual and his life blameless. Father Christopher Yeakel was perhaps the oldest veteran of the cross among the local preachers of our Conference. He walked with God. In his day he suffered much from persecution, but his confidence in God remained unshaken. Father George Reich, a local deacon, passed away during the past year in the hope of a blissful immortality.

TEMPERANCE.

We thank God and take courage from the fact that in spite of the violent efforts of the liquor dealers, the Local Option Law remains unrepealed, and from the fact that through the prayers and labors of self-denying Christian women the church and the friends of order have been aroused against the foe, as has never before been witnessed in our country.

FINANCE.

Received from conference collections....... $1,208.38
Received from the book establishment....... 300.00
Received from the Charitable Society....... 255.00

$1,763.38
Paid to conference claimants.............. 1,758.98

Balance on hand.................. ....$ 4.40

MISSIONARY APPROPRIATIONS.

Phila. 8th Str. Miss.	$400	Mt. Carmel Miss....	$400
Norristown Miss....	100	Nth. Allentown Miss.	350
Phoenixville Miss...	200	East Allentown Miss.	275
Pottstown Miss.....	250	Emans Miss........	100
Birdsboro Miss.....	300	Lehighton Miss.....	300
Reading 9th Str. Miss.	100	Mauch Chunk Miss..	
Fleetwood Miss.....		Wilkesbarre Miss....	200
Lititz and Manheim		Scranton Miss......	350
Miss............	100	Easton Eng. Miss...	300
Lancaster Miss.....	300	Bangor Miss........	250
Hamburg Miss......	200	Sparrowbush Miss...	300
Wesnersville Miss...	350	New York 53d Str.	
Lebanon Miss.......	425	Miss............	350
Annville Miss.......	150	Union Hill Miss.....	250
Harrisburg Ger. Miss.	250	Greenville Miss.....	400
Harrisburg Eng.Miss.	500	Newark Miss.......	250
Halifax Miss.......	100	New York vicinity	
Schuylkill Haven		Miss............	550
Miss............	275	Additional for last	
Shenandoah Miss....	200	year, North Allen-	
Frackville Miss	350	town Miss...	100

The $25 appropriated to East Reading at the last session was applied to Lehighton Miss. for last year.

APPOINTMENTS.

PHILADELPHIA DISTRICT. — *S. G. Rhoads, P. E.*
Philadelphia 4th St. Sta.—C. B. Fliehr.
    "   5th St. Sta.—F. Hoffman.
    "   6th St. Sta.—J. Yeakel.
    "   8th St. Miss.—S. S. Chubb.
Germantown Sta.—J. O. Lehr.
Camden and Glassborough Cir.—N. Goebel.
Norristown Miss. — R. M. Lichtenwalner.
Phoenixville Miss.—J. P. Leib.
Trappe Cir.—J. A Feger.
Montgomery Cir.—W. A. Shoemaker and H. J. Glick.
Milford Cir.—G. Scharf.
Pottstown Miss.—J. M. Oplinger.
Birdsboro Miss.—G. B. Fisher.
Bridesburg and Richmond.—M. Sindlinger.

READING DISTRICT.—*C. S. Haman, P. E.*
Reading 8th St. Sta.—B. F. Bohner.
Reading Chestnut St. Sta.—U. H. Hershey.
Reading 9th St. Miss.—E. Butz.
Fleetwood Miss.—J. Zern.
Kutztown Cir.—A. Ziegenfus.
Womelsdorf Cir.—D. Z. Kembel.
Adamstown Cir.—F. Sechrist.
Brownstown Cir.—W. Heim.
Conestoga Cir.—J. N. Metzgar.
Fairville Sta.—W. L. Black.
Lititz and Manheim Miss.—C. S. Brown.
Lancaster Cir.—A. A. Delong and A. Markley.
Lancaster Sta.—A. Shultz.
Lancaster Miss.—B. D. Albright.
Hamburg Miss.—H Kempfer.
Wesnersville Miss.—W. H. Weidner.

HARRISBURG DISTRICT.—*C. K. Fehr, P. E.*
Lebanon Sta.—J. Specht.
Lebanon Miss.—J. G. Sands.

Myerstown Cir.—D. Lentz and M. L. Custer.
Annville Miss.—E. J. Miller.
Mt. Nebo Cir.—A. W. Warfel.
Harrisburg Ger. Miss.—J. Laros.
Harrisburg Eng. Miss.—J. C. Hornberger.
Dauphin Cir.—F. P. Lehr.
Halifax Miss.—I. J. Reitz.
Millersburg Sta.—H. A. Neitz.
Williams Valley Cir.—J. F. Wohlfarth.
Berrysburg Cir.—J. S. Newhart.
Uniontown Cir.—S. L. Wiest and S. T. Leopold.
Mahanongo Cir.—B. H. Miller.
Shamokin Sta.—W. A. Leopold.

POTTSVILLE DISTRICT.—*S. Neitz, P. E.*
Pottsville Sta.—I. E. Knerr.
Schuylkill Haven Sta.—J. K. Seyfrit.
Schuylkill Haven Miss.—Jas. Bowman.
Cressona Cir.—D. A. Medlar.
Tremont Cir.—W. C. Kantner.
Pine Grove Sta.—W. K. Wieand.
Orwigsburg Sta.—G. W. Gross.
Schuylkill Cir.—A. F. Leopold.
Port Carbon Cir.—J. R. Workman.
Barnesville Cir.—A. Krecker.
Coaldale Cir.—L. E. Leslie.
Tamaqua Sta.—J. K. Knerr.
Mahanoy City Sta.—A. M. Stirk.
Shenandoah Miss.—H. R. Yost.
Frackville Miss.—G. H. Laury.
Ringtown Cir.—A. Dilabar.
Mt. Carmel Miss.—L. N. Worman.
Ashland Sta.—D. S. Stauffer.

ALLENTOWN DISTRICT—*J. M. Saylor, P. E.*
Allentown, Linden St. Sta.—J. Steltzer.
    "   East Miss.—C. H. Baker.
    "   North Miss—John Shell.
Emaus Sta.—Solomon Ely.
Lehigh Cir.—J. L. Werner.

Catasauqua Sta.—Jacob Adams.
Berlinsville Cir.—D. Yingst.
Slatington Sta.—R. Deisher.
Parryville Cir.—Seneca Breyfogel.
Weissport Sta.—G. T. Haines.
Lehighton Miss.—J. C. Bliem.
Mauch Chunk Miss.—John Koehl.
Wilkesbarre Miss.—J. K. Fehr.
Scranton Miss.—J. M. Rinker.
Hazleton Sta.—F. Krecker.

EASTON DISTRICT—*T. Bowman, P. E.*
Easton German Sta.—Isaac Hess.
"   English Miss.—O L. Saylor.
Freemansburg Sta.—Lewis Snyder.
Bethlehem Sta.—S. B. Brown.

Allentown Eng. Miss.—B. J. Smoyer
Bath Cir.—S. C. Breyfogel.
Nazareth Cir.—Thomas Harper.
Mount Bethel Cir.—J. J. High.
Bangor Miss.—I. W. Yeakel.
Monroe Cir.—A. Kindt.
Pleasant Valley Cir.—M. Dissinger and
   H. D. Shultz.
Wayne Cir.—T. A. Hess.
Sparrow Bush Miss.—J. Savitz.
New York, 24th St. Sta.—G. Knerr.
"   53d St. Miss.—John Kurtz.
Union Hill Miss.—T. Plattenberger.
Greenville Miss.—M. Guhl.
New York & Vicinity Miss.—E. Glaeser.
Newark Miss.—A. Straub.

1875.

The General Conference.

Presidents, Bishops J. J. Esher, R. Yeakel, R. Dubs, and T. Bowman.

Secretary, H. Huelster.

Assistant Secretaries, R. Mott, E. J. Schultz, J. C. Hornberger, H. B. Hartzler, and S. Smith.

The members of the General Conference met in the Emanuel Church, Philadelphia, Pa., on Thursday, October 14th, 1875, and continued in session nineteen days. Besides the eight *ex-officio* delegates, there were ninety delegates, representing fourteen annual conferences, in attendance. All the representatives of the East Pa. Conference were present except the late Father J. P. Leib, whose seat was occupied by F. Krecker, alternate. In the examination of the officials appointed by the General Conference, and of the delegates, no charges were preferred.   After two days of discussion the following was adopted by a vote of 76 to 14: *Resolved*, That a German conference shall be constituted, embracing the following fields of labor: New York Station, New York Mission, Newark Mission, Union Hill Mission, Greenville Mission, Easton Station, Fifth Street Station (Philadelphia), Bridesburg and Richmond, Camden Mission, and Harrisburg Mission, of the East Pa. Conference; Green Street Station and East Baltimore Station in Baltimore, York Station, and the German Station in Williamsport, of the Central Pa. Conference; and Washington Mission.   This conference shall be called the *Atlantic Conference*, and shall be organized at the next session of the East Pa. Conference.

The Conference adopted suitable resolutions relative to the death of J. P. Leib, a delegate of the East Pa. Conference.   A memorial service was held in which W. W. Orwig, E. Kohr, and S. Neitz made appropriate addresses.

On Tuesday, the 19th day of Oct., in the year of our Lord 1875, the first heathen mission of the Evangelical Association was established by the adoption of the following: WHEREAS, We as a church are undoubtedly called to preach the Gospel to the heathen; and many contributions for such a mission have been received, and a considerable fund has already been secured; and the board of missions has for several years had this subject under earnest and favorable consideration; and of late the desire of the church for the establishment of such a mission seems to have grown in strength; and men, whom we believe have the necessary qualifications, have offered their services in this direction; and we believe that the establishment of such a mission will not, as some fear, interfere with contributions for other missionary purposes, but, on the contrary, will develop the spirit of missions and increase the contributions for other benevolent purposes; therefore, *Resolved*, 1st, That a mission among the heathen be established forthwith.   2d, That we consider Japan as the most favorable country for such a mission, and that it be established in said country.   3d, That the board of missions be instructed to take the necessary steps that this mission be supplied with at least two suitable men as soon as possible.   These resolutions were unanimously adopted amid profound feeling and great enthusiasm.

The elections resulted as follows: Bishops, J. J. Esher, R. Yeakel, R. Dubs, and T. Bowman; general book agent, W. F. Schneider; editor of the *Christliche Botschafter*, M. Lauer; editor of the *Evangelical Messenger*, J. Hartzler; editor of the *Evangelische Magazin* and German S. S. Literature, W. Horn; editor of the *Living Epistle* and English S. S. Literature, H. J. Bowman; corresponding secretary of the Missionary Society, J. Young; treasurer of the Missionary Society, W. Yost; superintendent of the Orphans' Home, Jacob Dreisbach; editor of the *Evangelische Botschafter*, J. Kaechele; editor of the *Kinderfreund*, G. Fuessele; book agent in Germany, J. Walz.

The following statistics were reported: Itinerant preachers, 836; local preachers, 503; members, 95,253; churches, 1,233; parsonages, 324; Sunday-schools, 1,509; officers and teachers, 16,875; scholars, 90,090; catechetical classes, 509; catechumens, 6,186.

1876.

The Thirty-Seventh (69th) Annual Session.

President, Bishop R. Yeakel.
Secretary, W. K. Wieand.
Assistant Secretaries, S. L. Wiest and B. J. Smoyer.

The thirty-seventh annual session of the Conference was held in the St. Peter's Evangelical Church, at Schuylkill Haven, Pa., beginning on Wednesday, February 23d, 1876. The Bishop appointed the following Committees: On Public Worship,—J. K. Seyfrit, J. Bowman, D. A. Medlar, and I. E. Knerr; On Letters, —The presiding elders and J. Yeakel; On Boundaries, —The Bishop and the presiding elders; On Quarterly Conference Records,—A. Schultz, G. T. Haines, Seneca Breyfogel, J. Adams, C. H. Baker, M. Dissinger, and H. Stoetzel; On Statistics,—B. J. Smoyer, J. O. Lehr, W. A. Leopold, J. G. Sands, S. C. Breyfogel, and I. W. Yeakel; On Education,—S. S. Chubb, J. K. Knerr, O. L. Saylor, A. M. Stirk, and H. A. Neitz; On Church Affairs,—F. Krecker, L. Snyder, S. Ely, R. Deisher, J. Koehl, and J. N. Metzgar; On Temperance and Sabbath,—J. C. Hornberger, S. L. Wiest, A. Kindt, E. J. Miller, J. Specht, and F. P. Lehr; On the Centennial,—I. E. Knerr, J. C. Bliem, R. M. Lichtenwalner, J. L. Werner, and J. N. Metzgar; On Memorials,—J. Yeakel, F. Hoffman, S. B. Brown, U. H. Hershey, and B. F. Bohner; On Finance,—C. B. Fliehr, J. Specht, T. Harper, D. A. Medlar, and B. D. Albright; On Conference Claimants,—S. Neitz, H. Kempfer, and D. Z. Kembel. A Reportorial Committee was appointed consisting of J. F. Wohlfarth, J. C. Hornberger, and S. C. Breyfogel.

The resignation of Nathan Heil as local preacher was accepted. Simon Frankenfield and Wm. Webber, local preachers, withdrew from the church. The announcement was made that J. P. Leib and S. G. Rhoads, itinerants, and John Eckert, local elder, had died during the year. J. M. Saylor was re-elected, and J. O. Lehr and I. E. Knerr were newly elected to the office of Presiding Elder. J. Bowman, H. R. Yost, A. Markley, E. Glaeser, J. S. Newhart, and D. A. Medlar were ordained Elders; S. T. Leopold, H. D. Shultz, I. J. Reitz, A. Dilabar, A. Krecker, and G. D. Sweigert, Deacons. The following received license as preachers on trial: Jonas H. Shirey, John W. Woehrle, Galen W. Hoover, Dr. Fred. Krecker, John R. Hensyl, and Samuel H. Dunkelberger. The supernumeraries were: N. Goebel, D. Wieand, J. Gross, M. Sindlinger, D. Berger, H. Stoetzel, S. P. Reinoehl, C. Gingrich, W. Heim, S. Ely, and J. Kurtz. The conference claimants were, S. P. Reinoehl, C. Gingrich and wife, M. Sindlinger and wife, D. Wieand and wife, H. Stoetzel, D. Berger, J. P. Leib, and the widows Schnerr, Hesser, and Myers. The name of Samuel Miesse was recorded on the list of local elders. C. H. Egge, of the Iowa Conference, and N. B. Shirk, of the Central Pa. Conference, were received into this Conference in the same relation which they sustained in the respective conferences from which they brought credentials. The former was also received into the itinerancy. Rev. L. N. Worman received permission to remain in the itinerancy one year without an appointment, his intention being to make a journey to Palestine. W. C. Kantner having received and accepted a call from the executive committee of the Missionary

Society to go as a missionary to Oregon, the Conference granted him an honorable dismissal and a favorable recommendation to our brethren on the Pacific coast. At his request the Conference granted to M. Guhl a letter of dismissal and a recommendation to the Erie Conference. J. A. Transue, local preacher, also received a letter of dismissal.

The following was adopted: WHEREAS, General Conference has taken from our midst our beloved brother, Thomas Bowman, by choosing him one of the bishops of our church; therefore be it *Resolved*, That, although we keenly feel his absence, we will humbly submit to this decision of the General Conference and always pray that the Lord may fully qualify him for his honorable position, and that we will always welcome Bishop Bowman in our midst and regard him as one of our number.

The following members of this Conference connected themselves with the ATLANTIC CONFERENCE: Jesse Yeakel, Geo. Knerr, R. Deisher, J. Steltzer, J. Koehl, G. Scharf, T. Plattenberger, A. F. Leopold, E. Glaeser, A. Straub, M. Sindlinger, and C. B. Fliehr. J. Steltzer, of the *Atlantic Conference*, read a fraternal address, whereupon it was *Resolved*, That we have heard the address with pleasure, and that we will ever remember these brethren in our prayers and welcome them in our midst.

OUR NATIONAL CENTENNIAL.

The General Conference of the Evangelical Association having expressed its opinion in regard to the celebration of the Centennial, the East Pa. Conference resolved that the occasion be observed in an appropriate manner, and appointed the second day of July for thanksgiving services in our churches and other places of public worship. It was ordered that subscriptions be secured for educational purposes.

BOUNDARIES.

Shamrock was taken from Milford Circuit and annexed to Lehigh Circuit. Boyertown was transferred from Pottstown Mission to Milford Circuit. Birdsboro Mission was changed to a circuit. Lykens, Dayton, and Wiconisco were taken from Williams Valley Circuit and formed into Lykenstown Circuit. Seven Points, Irish Valley, and Fisher's Ferry were taken from Uniontown Circuit, and together with Sunbury were formed into Sunbury Mission. Bangor Mission was discontinued; and Bangor, Miller's Church, and Roxburg were formed into Bangor Circuit. Ackermanville, Wind Gap, Plainfield, Bushkill, and Bartholomew's class were formed into Ackermanville Circuit. Nazareth was annexed to Bath Station. Sparrowbush Mission was discontinued and annexed to Wayne Circuit. Paradise and Union were taken from Monroe Circuit and Sterling from Wayne Circuit and formed into Sterling Circuit. St. Peter's, St. John's, Mechanicsville, Woehrle's, Snydersville, East Stroudsburg, Middlecreek, and Albrightsville were formed into Hamilton Circuit. Fredericksburg, Mountville, Jonestown, and Union were taken from Myerstown Circuit and annexed to Mt. Nebo Circuit. Coaldale was annexed to Port Carbon Circuit. Stemton was taken from Bath Circuit and annexed to Catasauqua Station. Phœnixville was annexed to Pottstown Mission. The Conference was divided into six presiding elder districts.

The following congregations received permission to collect on their respective presiding elder districts: Bernville, Frackville, Leesport, Port Clinton, Myerstown, and Shenandoah City. The affairs of the Port Clinton church were submitted to a committee. The request of the Myerstown church to sell their old property and to apply the proceeds toward the erection of a new church in a more suitable part of the town, was referred to a committee. The congregation at Wescoesville received permission to sell or move their church and to apply the proceeds to build at a more suitable place, upon condition that they retain their present burial ground. The trustees of the Millerstown church received permission to exchange part of a lot of ground for other ground which will make the church lot more valuable and suitable. Hamburg church being burdened with a debt of $876.24, demanding prompt payment, it was resolved to raise the claim at this session, if possible. Our friends of the Germantown congregation were requested to build a new church edifice in order better to promote the work of Christ and the honor of the Evangelical Association. The trustees of the Bolich church were requested to borrow a sufficient amount of money in order to secure the deed of their property. The Lebanon English Mission was authorized to collect funds within the bounds of the Conference during the coming year to aid in the erection of a house of worship. After due investigation it was found that the claim of Christ Church, Philadelphia, upon the Conference is $561.21, and on the Church Building Society $65; it was resolved, therefore, that the Church Building Society grant said church a loan of $65, and that the Conference permit the missionary stationed at Philadelphia to collect $561.21 within the bounds of the East Pa. Conference. The trustees of Christ Church also received permission to grant to D. Focht a mortgage of $3,250 for five years upon their church. The Church Building Society was instructed to grant a loan of $300 to the Phœnixville congregation.

EDUCATION.

The Central Pa. Conference having sent delegates to this Conference with instructions to suggest the propriety of the Pennsylvania conferences uniting in one grand effort to secure an endowment and found a college in one of the said conferences, we recognize the great importance and necessity of prompt action in this matter. Be it therefore *Resolved,* That we will join with our brethren of the Central Pa. and the Pittsburg conferences in taking immediate steps towards the establishment of a college, and that we will secure an endowment fund of at least *one hundred thousand dollars,* towards which no subscription shall be considered binding until seventy-five thousand dollars of the amount are secured. That the subscriptions to this fund shall be payable as follows: One-tenth at the time when the seventy-five thousand dollars have been secured, and the balance in four equal payments; the first within two years, the second within four years, the third within six years, and the fourth within eight years, with notes bearing lawful interest from the time

the subscriptions become binding until paid.   Rev. H.
A. Neitz was appointed agent to secure funds within
the bounds of this Conference.   Revs. S. S. Chubb, C.
K. Fehr, C. S. Haman, and Messrs. D. R. Miller and
M. B. Shadt were appointed a committee to consult
with, and secure the co-operation of similar committees
from the Central Pa. and the Pittsburg conferences.
The following were appointed examiners: Of Applicants,—S. S. Chubb, W. A. Leopold, and U. H. Hershey; of the First Year's Class,—W. K. Wieand, J.
K. Seyfrit and S. L. Wiest.

MEMORIALS.

To the memory of J. P. Leib, J. Shell, and S. G.
Rhoads the Conference erected the following tribute:
They were men of fine intellectual and social qualities,
of varied and useful attainments, exemplary piety, and
rich spiritual experience.   In their walk and conversa-
tion they were characterized by punctuality, fidelity,
and entire devotion to the Master's cause; serving the
church in important positions of trust with untiring
energy and the most cheerful self-sacrificing zeal.   Because of their thoroughly evangelical principles, their
usefulness, and their powerful and eloquent preaching
they won many souls to Christ, and endeared themselves
to the ministry and laity.   In this bereavement we
humbly submit to the divine will.   John Eckert, a local
preacher, but formerly in the itinerancy, was a successful worker.   His last will and testament gave ample
proof of his love for the church of his choice.

FINANCE.

Receipts:

Conference collections.. ....$1,092.46
Book establishment............. 300.00
Charitable Society............ 338.25
$1,730.71

Expenditures:

Paid to conference claimants... .... 1,730.71

MISSIONARY APPROPRIATIONS.

Phila. 8th Str. Miss..$350
Norristown Miss.... 100
Pottstown Miss..... 250
Reading 9th Str. Miss. 100
Fleetwood Miss..... 100
Lititz and Manheim
Miss............ 125
Lancaster Miss..... 200
Hamburg Miss...... 100
Wesnersville Miss... 325
Lebanon Miss....... 450
Annville Miss....... 200
Harrisburg Miss..... 500
Halifax Miss....... 25
Schuylkill Haven
Miss............ 250

Shenandoah City
Miss............ 100
Frackville Miss...... 350
Mt. Carmel Miss.... 300
Nth. Allentown Miss. 200
East Allentown Miss. 250
Emaus Miss........ 50
Lehighton Miss..... 225
Mauch Chunk Miss.. 200
Wilkesbarre Miss.... 250
Scranton Miss...... 350
Easton Miss........ 275
Sunbury Miss....... 200

Total.........$5,825

APPOINTMENTS.

PHILADELPHIA DISTRICT—*J. M. Saylor*, *P. E.*
Philadelphia Eng. Miss.—J. Bowman.
Germantown Sta —J. K. Seyfrit.

Norristown Miss.—F. Hoffman.
Trappe Cir.—J. A. Feger.
Pottstown Miss.—T. Harper.
Birdsboro Cir.—L. E. Leslie.

Montgomery Cir.—W. A. Shoemaker and H. J. Glick.
Milford Cir.—D. Lentz.
Conestoga Cir.—J. J. High.
Kutztown Cir.—A. Ziegenfus.
Fairville Sta.—W. L. Black.
Fleetwood Miss.—J. Zern.

READING DISTRICT—*C. S. Haman, P. E.*
Reading 8th St. Sta.—B. F. Bohner.
Reading 9th St. Miss.—I. Hess.
Reading Chestnut St. Sta. — U. H. Hershey.
Adamstown Cir.—F. Sechrist.
Brownstown Cir.—H. Kempfer.
Lititz and Manheim Miss.—J. M. Oplinger.
Lancaster Sta.—H. R. Yost.
   "   Eng. Miss.—Dr. F. Krecker.
   "   Cir.—A. A. Delong and A. Markley.
Womelsdorf Cir.—D. Z. Kembel.
Myerstown Cir.—C. S. Brown.
Schuylkill Cir.—E. Butz.
Hamburg Miss.—C. Gingrich.
Wesnersville Miss.—W. H. Weidner.

HARRISBURG DISTRICT—*C. K. Fehr, P. E.*
Lebanon Sta.—J. Specht.
   "   Eng. Miss.—J. G. Sands.
Annville Miss.—E. J. Miller.
Mt. Nebo Cir.—A. W. Warfel.
Harrisburg Eng. Miss.—J. C. Hornberger.
Dauphin Cir.—F. P. Lehr.
Halifax Miss.—I. J. Reitz.
Millersburg Sta.—W. K. Wieand.
Williamstown Cir.—J. F. Wohlfarth.
Lykenstown Cir.—G. H. Laury.
Berrysburg Cir.—J. S. Newhart.
Uniontown Cir.—B. H. Miller and J. H. Shirey.
Sunbury Miss.—(To be supplied).
Shamokin Sta.—W. A. Leopold.
Mahantongo Cir.—S. T. Leopold.
Tremont Miss.—(To be supplied).

POTTSVILLE DISTRICT—*I. E. Knerr, P. E.*
Pottsville Sta.—A. M. Stirk.

Schuylkill Haven Sta.—S. B. Brown.
   "   Eng. Miss.—Chas. H. Egge.
Cressona Cir.—D. A. Medlar.
Pine Grove Sta.—S. S. Chubb.
Orwigsburg Sta.—G. W. Gross.
Port Carbon and Coaldale Cir.—J. R. Workman.
Tamaqua Sta.—B. J. Smoyer.
Mahanoy City Sta.—S. L. Wiest.
Frackville Miss.—J. N. Metzgar.
Ashland Sta.—D. S. Stauffer.
Shenandoah City Miss.—A. Krecker.
Barnesville and Ringtown Cir.—A. Dilabar.
Mt. Carmel Miss.—N. B. Shirk.
Hazleton Sta.—F. Krecker.

ALLENTOWN DISTRICT—*S. Neitz, P. E.*
Allentown Linden St. Sta.—R. M. Lichtenwalner.
Allentown Turner St. Sta.—B. D. Albright.
East Allentown Miss.—C. H. Baker.
North Allentown Miss.—J. Laros.
Lehigh Cir.—*J. L. Werner.*
Slatington Cir.—M. Dissinger.
Parryville Cir.—Seneca Breyfogel.
Weissport Sta.—J. K. Knerr.
Lehighton Miss.—J. C. Bliem.
Mauch Chunk Miss.—I. W. Yeakel.
Wilkesbarre Miss.—A. Kindt.

BETHLEHEM DISTRICT—*J. O. Lehr, P. E.*
Easton Eng. Miss.—O. L. Saylor.
Freemansburg Sta.—J. K. Fehr.
Bethlehem Sta.—L. Snyder.
Pleasant Valley Cir.—D. Yingst and M. L. Custer.
Bangor Cir.—G. B. Fisher.
Bath Cir.—S. C. Breyfogel.
Ackermanville Cir.—T. A. Hess.
Hamilton Cir —H. D. Shultz.
Sterling Cir.—J. W. Woehrle.
Wayne Cir.—J. Savitz.
Berlinsville Cir.—A. Schultz.
Catasauqua Sta.—J. Adams.
Emaus Miss.—G. T. Haines.
Scranton Miss.—J. M. Rinker.

1877.

The Thirty-Eighth (70th) Annual Session.

President, Bishop Thomas Bowman.

Secretary, S. B. Brown.

Assistant Secretaries, S. C. Breyfogel and H. A. Neitz.

The thirty-eighth annual session of the East Pa. Conference was held at Shamokin, Pa., beginning on Wednesday, February 28th, 1877. The president announced the following committees: On Public Worship,—C. K. Fehr and W. A. Leopold; On Boundaries,—The Bishop and the presiding elders; On Letters,—F. Hoffman, G. T. Haines, and A. Schultz; On Finance,—J. K. Knerr, B. D. Albright, and E. J. Miller; On Quarterly Conference Records,—F. Krecker, J. Zern, E. Butz, A. Ziegenfus, F. Sechrist, and B. F. Bohner; On Statistics,—O. L. Saylor, J. A. Feger, J. M. Oplinger, J. Bowman, J. N. Metzgar, and D. A. Medlar; On Education,—J. C. Hornberger, B. J. Smoyer, A. M. Stirk, J. K. Seyfrit, and H. A. Neitz; On Church Affairs,—S. S. Chubb, W. H. Weidner, L. N. Worman, C. H. Baker, and B. H. Miller; On Memorials,—U. H. Hershey, J. S. Newhart, and H. R. Yost; On Sabbath and Temperence,—W. K. Wieand, J. G. Sands, J. M. Rinker, C. H. Egge, and D. S. Stauffer; On Conference Claimants,—I. Hess, I. W. Yeakel, and J. L. Werner. S. B. Brown was appointed to report the proceedings for the *Christliche Botschafter*, and S. C. Breyfogel, for the *Evangelical Messenger*. A reportorial committee was appointed, consisting of

19

G. W. Gross, A. Krecker, U. H. Hershey, D. A. Medlar, and S. L. Wiest.

Credentials were granted to N. B. Shirk and M. L. Custer. J. K. Workman located on account of ill health. H. A. Neitz was retained in the itinerancy with permission to rest one year. Seneca Breyfogel, G. B. Fisher, J. Frey, F. P. Lehr, and C. Gingrich took a super numerary relation. J. J. High died during the year. Elders' orders were granted to A. W. Warfel, L. E. Leslie, W. L. Black, T. A. Hess, C. S. Brown, J. M. Rinker, and S. C. Breyfogel; and Deacons' orders, to Dr. F. Krecker, G. W. Gross, H. J. Glick, M. L. Custer, and N. B. Shirk. The following were licensed as preachers on trial: C. J. B. Cole, Henry M. Wingert, Albert M. Sampsel, Ferdinand Smith, A. V. Hirst, Daniel W. Bicksler, J. S. Dissinger, Geo. Wagner, Cyrus Y. Weidenhammer, G. W. Moore, and Edward Fordman. J. W. Woehrle, J. H. Shirey, and G. D. Sweigert were received into the itinerancy.

BOUNDARIES.

Cresswell, Conestoga Centre, and Pittsburg were taken from Lancaster Circuit and formed into Creswell Circuit, the remainder of that field to be called Millersville Circuit. Wesnersville was discontinued as a mission and annexed to Schuylkill Circuit. Port Clinton was detached from Hamburg Mission and annexed to Schuylkill Circuit. Pricetown, Friedensburg, Pleasantville, Blandon, and Lyons were formed into Friedensburg Circuit. Fleetwood Mission was changed into a station. Steelstown and The Forge were detached from Mt. Nebo Circuit and annexed to Annville Station. Palmyra was taken from Annville and annexed to Mt. Nebo Circuit. Sunbury and Fisher's Ferry were placed under the charge of Shamokin Station. Seven Points was taken from Sunbury Mission and annexed to Uniontown Circuit. Barnesville, Quakake, and Locust Valley were taken from Barnesville and Ringtown Circuit and annexed to Tamaqua Station. Ringtown and Brandonville were annexed to Shenandoah Station. Port Carbon was connected with Pottsville Station. Coaldale, Summit Hill, Mahoning, West Penn, and Centreville were organized into Mahoning Circuit. Mt. Carmel Mission was placed under the charge of Ashland Station. Kutztown, Shamrock, Richmond, Moselem, Shoemakersville, and Hamburg were called Kutztown Circuit. Nazareth was taken from Bath Circuit and annexed to Ackermanville Circuit. Bushkill and Bartholomew's were taken from Ackermanville Circuit and annexed to Bath Circuit. Stroudsburg, Snydersville, St. John's, Woehrle's, Paradise, and Union Church were organized into Stroudsburg Circuit. Saylorsburg, Mechanicsville, and Albrightsville were called Middlecreek Circuit. Sterling was annexed to Wayne Circuit. Miller's Church was transferred from Bangor to Ackermanville Circuit. Scranton was put under the charge of Wilkesbarre Mission.

CHURCH AFFAIRS.

The accounts of the Frackville Mission Church were audited and reported as follows: The total cost of church, including interest, is $3,015.46; the total amount collected, $695.00; the present indebtedness,

$2,320.46. The following congregations received permission to borrow money and to give mortgages on their churches: Leesport, $800.00; Shenandoah, $1,000.00; and Hamburg, $600.00. The congregation at Bernville received permission to collect on Reading District. The congregations at East Allentown and at Bath were permitted to collect on Allentown and Bethlehem districts. The church affairs in the Tower City, Trevorton, and Barnesville congregations were referred to their respective presiding elders and preachers in charge. The trustees at Coaldale were instructed to have their church incorporated as soon as practicable and to secure their creditors. The congregation at Plymouth was requested to defer the completion of their church for the present unless the required sum can be collected at home. The trustees at Shenandoah were instructed to secure their church in a legal manner. Permission to collect over the entire conference district for a new church edifice was granted to the congregation at Germantown, Pa.

EDUCATION.

In view of the depression in financial circles, and inasmuch as the Conference could not agree to send out a college agent during this year, it was resolved that the secured subscriptions be regarded as valid in the future, and that it is the continued purpose of the Conference to carry the college project to a successful issue. It was furthermore resolved that although the soliciting of subscriptions be suspended during the present year, it shall again be resumed at our next annual session and urged forward with all possible energy and increased zeal. An executive committee was appointed to confer with similar committees from other conferences. The committee were: Revs. S. S. Chubb, B. J. Smoyer, J. C. Hornberger, H. A. Neitz, and Messrs. Jno. Swab, F. G. Boas, and M. B. Shadt. The committee appointed to audit the accounts of the college agent for the past year, reported the following: Salary, rent and expenses of agent, $1,235; total amount of cash collected, $803.85; borrowed from the educational fund, $173.93; amount due the agent, $257.22; total amount secured by subscriptions during the year, $10,392.58. C. S. Haman, C. K. Fehr, and D. A. Medlar were appointed examiners for five years.

MEMORIALS.

During the past year J. J. High, a member of this Conference, was taken from our ministerial ranks. He was a man of deep piety, of gentle demeanor, and of winning qualities of character, sweetly singing, preaching, and confessing a full salvation from all sin through the blood of the Lamb. We rejoice that the gospel he preached, abundantly supported him in his dying hour.

THE SABBATH.

WHEREAS, Efforts have recently been made to pass a bill in the Legislature of Pennsylvania, the effects of which would have been to abolish our Sabbath laws; and WHEREAS, The Christian sentiment of the Legislature prevented the passage of said bill; therefore *Resolved*, That we express our hearty approval.

TEMPERANCE.

It is the sense of this Conference that the Church

Discipline forbids any of our church members to rent or to permit the use of any of their property for the purpose of manufacturing or selling spirituous or malt liquors, and that wherever and whenever any of our members are guilty of the above named offence they shall be dealt with as if they were actually engaged in selling intoxicating drinks; and in case they refuse to withdraw their property from such unrighteous purposes, they shall be excluded from the church.

FINANCE.

Receipts :

From the conference collections..... $765.52
" " publishing house......... 120.71
" " Charitable Society........ 356.40
———— $1,242.63

Expenditures :

Amount paid to conference claimants.   1,242.36

MISSIONARY APPROPRIATIONS

Philadelphia 8th St.
    Miss.......... ....$350
Norristown Miss.... 75
Pottstown Miss..... 200
Reading 9th St. Miss. 100
Lititz and Manheim
    Miss............. 100
Lancaster Miss...... 350
Lebanon Miss....... 400
Harrisburg Miss..... 450
Halifax Miss........ 50
Sunbury Miss....... 200
Schuylkill Haven
    Miss............. 225

Frackville Miss..... $350
Mt. Carmel Miss.... 275
North Allentown
    Miss............. 250
East Allentown Miss. 300
Emaus Miss........ 100
Lehighton Miss..... 225
Mauch Chunk Miss.. 100
Wilkesbarre Miss.... 300
Easton Miss........ 250
————
$4,650

APPOINTMENTS.

PHILADELPHIA DISTRICT.—*J. M. Saylor,* **P. E.**

Philadelphia 8th St. Miss.—J. Bowman.
Germantown Sta.—J. K. Seyfrit.
Norristown Miss.—F. Hoffman.
Trappe Cir.—J. G. Sands.
Pottstown Miss.—Thomas Harper.
Birdsboro Cir.—L. E. Leslie.
Montgomery Cir.—A. Ziegenfus and F. Smith.
Milford Cir.—D. Lentz.
Conestoga Cir.—G. D. Sweigert.
Friedensburg Cir —J. Zern.
Fleetwood Sta.—A. Shultz.
Reading Chestnut St. Sta.—C. H. Hershey.

READING DISTRICT.—*C. S. Haman,* **P. E.**
Reading 8th St. Sta.—B. F. Bohner.
Reading 9th St. Miss.—Isaac Hess.
Adamstown Cir —F. Sechrist.
Brownstown Cir.—H. Kempfer.
Lititz and Manheim Miss.—J. M. Oplinger.
Lancaster Sta.—H. R. Yost.
Lancaster Miss.—O. L. Saylor.
Creswell Cir.—Jos. Spech:.
Millersville Cir.—A. A. Delong.
Fairville Sta.—A. W. Warfel.
Womelsdorf Cir.—W. L. Black.
Myerstown Cir.—C. S. Brown.
Schuylkill Cir.—E. Butz.

HARRISBURG DISTRICT.—*C. K. Fehr,* **P. E.**
Lebanon Sta.—J. C. Hornberger.
Lebanon Miss.—A. M. Stirk.
Annville Sta.—A. Krecker.
Mt. Nebo Cir.—J. K. Fehr.
Harrisburg Miss.—J. A. Feger.
Dauphin Cir.—A. Markley.
Halifax Miss.—D. W. Bicksler.
Millersburg Sta.—W. K. Wieand.
Williamstown Cir.—L. N. Worman.
Lykens Cir.—J. R. Hensyl.
Berrysburg Cir.—J. S. Newhart.
Uniontown Cir.—B. H. Miller and J. H. Shirey.
Sunbury Miss.—G. W. Moore.
Shamokin Sta.—W. A. Leopold.

Mahantongo Cir.—S. T. Leopold.
Tremont Cir.—E. Fordman.

POTTSVILLE DISTRICT—*I. E. Knerr,* **P. E.**
Pottsville Sta.—D. A. Medlar.
Schuylkill Haven Sta.—S. B. Brown.
Schuylkill Haven Miss.—C. H. Egge.
Cressona Cir.—W. A. Shoemaker.
Pine Grove Sta.—S. S. Chubb.
Orwigsburg Sta.—F. Krecker.
Mahanoy City Sta.—S. L. Wiest.
Frackville Miss.—J. N. Metzgar.
Ashland Sta.—A. Dilabar.
Shenandoah Sta.—E. J. Miller.
Mt. Carmel Miss.—A. M. Sampsel.
Tamaqua Sta.—B. J. Smoyer.
Mahoning Cir.—I. J. Reitz.
Hazleton Sta.—J. M. Rinker.

ALLENTOWN DISTRICT—*S. Neitz,* **P. E.**
Allentown Linden St. Sta. — R. M. Lichtenwalner.
Allentown Turner St. Sta.—B. D. Albright.
North Allentown Miss.—J. Laros.
Emaus Miss.—G. T. Haines.
Lehigh Cir.—C. H. Baker.
Slatington Cir.—M. Dissinger.
Parryville Cir.—J. L. Werner.
Weissport Sta.—J. K. Knerr.
Lehighton Miss.—J. C. Bllem.
Mauch Chunk Miss.—I. W. Yeakel.
Kutztown Cir.—D. S. Stauffer.

BETHLEHEM DISTRICT—*J. O. Lehr,* **P. E.**
Bethlehem Sta.—L. Snyder.
Freemansburg Sta.—F. P. Lehr.
Easton Miss.—S. C. Breyfogel.
Pleasant Valley Cir.—D. Yingst and J. W. Woehrle.
Bangor Cir.—H. J. Glick.
Bath Cir.—G. W. Gross.
Ackermanville Cir.—T. A. Hess.
Middle Creek Cir.—F. E. Erdman.
Stroudsburg Cir.—H. D. Shultz.
Wayne Cir.—J. Savitz.
Catasauqua Sta.—J. Adams.
Berlinsville Cir.—W. H. Weidner.
Wilkesbarre Miss.—A. Kindt.
East Allentown Miss.—D. Z. Kembel.

1878.

The Thirty-Ninth (71st) Annual Session.

President, Bishop J. J. Esher.
Secretary, J. C. Hornberger.
Assistant Secretaries, B. J. Smoyer and G. W. Gross.

The East Pennsylvania Conference met in the Salem Evangelical church, Reading, Pa., February 27th, 1878, to hold its thirty-ninth annual session. The president appointed the following standing committees: On Public Worship,— C. S. Haman, J. M. Saylor, B. F. Bohner, U. H. Hershey, and Isaac Hess; On Letters,—Tho Bishop, G. T. Haines, A. Shultz, D. Z. Kembel, A. Ziegenfus, D. Yingst, and F. Hoffman; On Quarterly Conference Records,—F. Hoffman, F. Krecker, J. Adams, J. Specht, H. Stoetzel, E. Butz, and J. M. Metzgar; On Boundaries,—The Bishop and the presiding elders; On Finance,—B. J. Smoyer, C. H. Egge, J. Bowman, J. M. Oplinger, and D. S. Stauffer; On Statistics,—S. L. Wiest, D. A. Medlar, H. R. Yost, J. M. Rinker, S. T. Leopold, and A. A. Delong; On Education,—S. S. Chubb, J. K. Knerr, J. C. Bliem, J. K. Seyfrit, A. M. Stirk, O. L. Saylor, and B. H. Miller; On Ways and Means,—L. Snyder, C. H. Baker, Seneca Breyfogel, A. Kindt, W. A. Leopold, M. Dissinger, F. P. Lehr, and W. H. Weidner. A reportorial committee was appointed, consisting of W. K. Wieand, J. H. Shirey, J. A. Feger, H. J. Glick, and A. Krecker.

Credentials were granted to J. F. Wohlfarth, F. E. Erdman, and L. E. Leslie. Joseph Moyer, local preacher, withdrew from the church. An itinerant minister was deposed, and excluded from the church, and a local preacher suspended from all his official functions for one year.   J. Adams and F. P. Lehr changed their relation from supernumerary to active.   S. Neitz resigned his presiding eldership.   C. S. Haman and C. K. Fehr were re-elected to the office of Presiding Elder. S. T. Leopold, A. Krecker, H. D. Shultz, I. J. Reitz, G. D. Sweigert, and A. Dilabar were ordained to the office of Elder; J. H. Shirey, J. W. Woehrle, F. E. Erdman, W. Minsker, and W. Wagner, to the office of Deacon.   The following received license as preachers on trial: Jacob Keller, Nathan A. Barr, James M. Shoop, Albert D. Light, James D. Woodring, A. S. Steltz, A. L. Yeakel, and Charles W. Snyder.   The supernumeraries were: N. Goebel, D. Wicand, J. Gross, D. Berger, H. Stoetzel, W. Heim, S. P. Reinoehl, C. Gingrich, S. Ely, J. Fry, G. B. Fisher, and Seneca Breyfogel.   The conference claimants were: G. B. Fisher, N. Goebel, H. Stoetzel, J. Gross, S. P. Reinoehl, D. Wicand, C. Gingrich, Sisters Schnerr, Rhoads, Hesser, Meyers, and Schell, and two children of J. J. High.   Bishops Reuben Yeakel and Thomas Bowman were cordially welcomed by the Conference.

It was decided that it is within the power of the quarterly conference to confirm or reject the amount of salary agreed upon by the stewards, provided such action is in harmony with a resolution of annual Conference adopted at Tamaqua in 1873.

The following was adopted: WHEREAS, According to our Church Discipline the gain of our book establishment, not needed for carrying on the business, shall be devoted to the support of indigent preachers,

and the widows and orphans of deceased preachers ; and,
WHEREAS, Ten thousand dollars of this money has been
loaned to the Germany Conference for the purpose of
erecting a publishing house in Germany; therefore, be it

Resolved, That we regard the action of the board of
publication in giving this loan as illegal, and that we,
as a Conference, demand our share of the said ten thousand dollars for the use of our supernumeraries, and the
widows and orphans of deceased preachers.

BOUNDARIES.

The Conference was divided into five presiding elder
districts.   Landsdale was taken from Plymouth Mission
and annexed to Montgomery Circuit.   Tower City,
Reiner City, and Salem were transferred from Williams Valley Circuit to Tremont Circuit, and Williamstown, Dayton, Wiconisco, and Lykens retained
the of name Williamstown Circuit.   Halifax Mission
was annexed to Berrysburg Circuit.   Mt. Carmel Mission was placed under the charge of Shamokin Station,
to be supplied if practicable.   Port Carbon was taken
from Pottsville Station and annexed to Orwigsburg Station.   Barnesville was taken from Tamaqua Station and
annexed to Mahanoy City Station.   Emaus Mission
was changed into a station, and Vera Cruz class was
taken from Milford Circuit and annexed to Emaus Station.   Williams Township was taken from Pleasant Valley Circuit and annexed to Easton Mission.   Miller's
class was taken from Pleasant Valley Circuit and annexed to Freemansburg Station.   East Stroudsburg,
Union Church, and Paradise were constituted a mission,
to be called Stroudsburg Mission.   Snydersville, St

John's, and Woehrle's classes were annexed to Middle
Creek Circuit.   Mauch Chunk and Weissport were con-
stituted one field of labor, to be called Weissport and
Mauch Chunk Station.   Ackermantown Circuit and
Bath were united into one field of labor, called Bath
Circuit.   Lyons was transferred from Friedensburg Cir-
cuit to Kutztown Circuit.   White Haven was taken
from Mauch Chunk and annexed to Wilkesbarre Mis-
sion.   Sunbury Mission was connected with Uniontown
Circuit.

CHURCH AFFAIRS.

The Conference appointed C. K. Fehr, J. O. Lehr,
A. Kindt, J. K. Seyfrit, and B. D. Albright, a committee to investigate the affairs of the Scranton Mission.
The Church Building Society was requested to loan to
the congregation at Shenandoah the amount in the hands
of the treasurer.   The quarterly conference of Creswell Circuit received permission to sell the Washington
church and to apply the proceeds to pay the debt on
the Pittsburg church.   The quarterly conference of
Womelsdorf Circuit received permission to dispose of
the Strausstown church and to apply the proceeds
wherever most needed on the circuit.   The church at
Ackermanville being a union church without a deed or
legal agreement, it was recommended that this church
be sold by the sheriff so that whoever desires to purchase it can procure a sheriff's deed.   There being a
debt on the church at Summit Hill of $115.00, which
must be paid by April 1st, 1878, the church was recommended to the favor of the members of Mahoning Circuit with the expectation that they pay the debt.   Conference sanctioned the sale of the Leesport church to

ten brethren, who promised to hold the property for five years, to be redeemed at no advance in price. The affairs of the Harrisburg Mission church were referred to a committee of three, consisting of C. S. Haman, J. A. Feger, and J. C. Hornberger. The financial troubles of the Hamburg Mission church were referred to a committee of three, consisting of I. E. Knerr, Bishop Bowman, and the preacher in charge. The treasurer of the Missionary Society was instructed to pay the interest on the debt of the church at East Allentown, upon condition that the money be paid back out of the funds collected throughout the bounds of the Conference for the liquidation of the debt. The preacher in charge and the presiding elder are to be held responsible for the management of the finances of this church in the future. Plymouth church, Montgomery Circuit, received permission to collect money on Philadelphia district. It was decided that the parsonage at Millersville, Lancaster Co., Pa., is the property of Lancaster Circuit as it was constituted in April, 1864. The following named churches received permission to borrow money toward the payment of church debts: Albany, Schuylkill Circuit, $350.00; Tower City, $150.00; Blandon, $350.00; Drehersville, $250.00; and Shamrock, $691.00.

EDUCATION.

It having come to the knowledge of the Conference that there is a property, suitable for a higher institution of learning, situated in Mt. Carmel, and that the same might be obtained gratis by our church for such purpose, a committee of five was appointed to inquire whether the above mentioned property can be procured for such purpose, and so as not to place the Conference under any monetary obligations; committee, C. S. Haman, I. E. Knerr, S. S. Chubb, J. C. Hornberger, and A. M. Stirk. This committee was empowered to organize and conduct a school, provided that it will not cost more than $1,000; that this amount be pledged by the members of Conference; and that one or more neighboring conferences will co-operate in *word* and *deed* so that a faculty of three efficient teachers can be employed. This committee, or a representative of the same, was instructed to lay the matter before the Central, Atlantic, and Pittsburg conferences. B. J. Smoyer, A. M. Stirk, and J. K. Knerr were elected examiners for five years.

FINANCE.

Receipts:

From conference collections.........$757.69
"   the publishing house 375.00
"   "   Charitable Society......... 331.65
                                   ————$1,464.34

Expenditures:

Paid to conference claimants.........   1,464.34

The Conference obligated itself to raise funds for the conference claimants at the rate of ten cents for every church member within the bounds of the East Pa. Conference.

MISSIONARY APPROPRIATIONS.

Philadelphia Miss...$350
Norristown Miss.... 100
Plymouth Miss...... 125
Pottstown Miss..... 175
Reading 9th St. Miss.$ 75
Lititz and Manheim
    Miss............. 100
Lancaster Miss...... 350

Lebanon Miss.......$350	East Allentown Miss.$300
Harrisburg Miss.... 400	Lehighton Miss..... 200
Schuylkill Haven Miss............. 225	Wilkesbarre Miss... 225
Frackville Miss..... 350	Easton Miss........ 200
Nth. Allentown Miss. 225	Stroudsburg Miss.... 150

$3,900

APPOINTMENTS.

PHILADELPHIA DISTRICT—*J. O. Lehr*, P. E.

Phila. 'th St. Miss.—J. K. Knerr.
Germantown Sta.—H. A. Neitz.
Norristown Miss.—B. F. Bohner.
Plymouth Miss.—J. H. Shirey.
Trappe Cir.—J. G. Sands.
Milford Cir.—D. Lentz.
Montgomery Cir.—A. Ziegenfus and F. Smith.
Pleasant Valley Cir.—D. Yingst.
Bethlehem Sta.—L. Snyder.
Freemansburg Sta.—F. P. Lehr.
Easton Miss.—S. C. Breyfogel.
Bath and Ackermantown Cir.—G. W. Gross and J. W. Woehrle.
Bangor Cir.—H. J. Glick.
Middle Creek Cir.—I. W. Yeakel.
Stroudsburg Miss.—H. D. Shultz.
Wayne Cir.—J. Savitz.

ALLENTOWN DISTRICT—*C. K. Fehr*, P. E.

Allentown Linden St. Sta.—R. M. Lichtenwalner.
Allentown Turner St. Sta.—J. Bowman.
Allentown Liberty St. Miss.—J. Laros.
Allentown 1st Ward Miss.—D. Z. Kembel.
Lehigh Cir.—C. H. Baker.
Emaus Sta.—F. Hoffman.
Catasauqua Sta.—G. T. Haines.
Slatington Sta.—M. Dissinger.
Berlinsville Cir.—W. H. Weidner.
Parryville Cir.—J. L. Werner.

Weissport and Mauch Chunk.—J. K. Seyfrit.
Lehighton Miss.—B. D. Albright.
Hazleton Sta.—J. M. Rinker.
Mahoning Cir.—L. J. Reitz.
Wilkesbarre Miss.—A. Kindt.

READING DISTRICT—*J. M. Saylor*, P. E.

Reading 8th St. Sta.—S. Neitz.
Reading Chestnut St. Sta.—W. A. Leopold.
Reading 9th St. Miss.—I. Hess.
Friedensburg Cir.—J. Zern.
Pottstown Miss.—T. Harper.
Birdsboro Cir.—T. A. Hess.
Adamstown Cir.—H. R. Yost.
Fairville Sta.—A. W. Warfel.
Brownstown Cir.—H. Kempfer.
Lititz and Manheim Miss.—J. M. Oplinger.
Lancaster Sta.—J. Adams.
Lancaster Miss.—O. L. Saylor.
Millersville Cir.—U. H. Hershey.
Creswell Cir.—J. Specht.
Conestoga Cir.—G. D. Sweigert.

HARRISBURG DISTRICT—*C. S. Haman*, P. E.

Lebanon Sta.—J. C. Hornberger.
Lebanon Miss.—A. M. Stirk.
Myerstown Cir.—C. S. Brown.
Womelsdorf Cir.—F. Sechrist.
Kutztown Cir.—D. S. Stauffer.
Fleetwood Sta.—A. Schultz.
Annville Sta.—A A. Delong.
Mt. Nebo Cir.—J. K. Fehr.
Dauphin Cir.—A. Markley.*

*In the Fall of 1878 this appointment became vacant and J. W. Hoover was appointed to fill the place of A. Markley until the next annual session.

Harrisburg Miss.—J. A. Feger.
Millersburg Sta.—W. K. Wieand.
Berrysburg Cir.—W. L. Black.
Williamstown Cir.—J. S. Newhart.
Tremont Cir.—L. N. Worman.
Pine Grove Sta.—S. S. Chubb.

POTTSVILLE DISTRICT—*I. E. Knerr*, *P. E.*
Pottsville Sta.—D. A. Medlar.
Schuylkill Haven Sta.—S. B. Brown.
Schuylkill Haven Miss.—C. H. Egge.
Cressona Cir.—W. A. Shoemaker.

Orwigsburg and Port Carbon Cir.—F. Krecker.
Schuylkill Cir.—E. Butz.
Tamaqua Sta.—B. J. Smoyer.
Mahanoy City Sta.—S. L. Wiest.
Shenandoah City Sta.—E. J. Miller.
Ashland Sta.—A. Dilabar.
Frackville Miss.—J. N. Metzgar.
Shamokin Sta.—J. C. Bliem.
Mt. Carmel Miss.—N. A. Barr.
Uniontown Cir. and Sunbury Miss.—B. H. Miller and A. Krecker.
Mahantongo Cir.—S. T. Leopold.

1879.

The Fortieth (72d) Annual Session.

President, Bishop R. Dubs.

Secretary, J. C. Hornberger.

Assistant Secretaries, B. J. Smoyer and G. W. Gross.

The Conference met in the Linden Street Evangelical church, Allentown, Pa., February 26th, 1879. The president appointed the following standing committees: On Letters,—The Bishop, G. T. Haines, A. Schultz, T. Harper, A. Ziegenfus, D. Yingst, and F. Hoffman; On Public Worship,—C. K. Fehr, R. M. Lichtenwalner, J. Bowman, J. Laros, and D. Z. Kembel; On Boundaries,—The Bishop and the presiding elders; On Quarterly Conference Records,—S. Neitz, F. Hoffman, F. P. Lehr, J. Specht, A. Kindt, and F. Sechrist; On Finance,—J. K. Knerr, C. H. Egge, B. F. Bohner, J. G. Sands, S. C. Breyfogel, and S. T. Leopold; On Statistics,—S. L. Wiest, W. A. Leopold, H. A. Neitz, O. L. Saylor, J. M. Rinker, and H. R. Yost; On Church Affairs,—J. C. Bliem, C. H. Baker, D. Yingst, Isaac Hess, W. H. Weidner, J. L. Werner, and E. Butz; On

Education,—S. S. Chubb, J. K. Seyfrit, U. H. Hershey,
J. M. Oplinger, J. S. Newhart, and J. A. Feger; On
Sabbath and Temperance,—A. M. Stirk, W. A. Shoe-
maker, J. N. Metzgar, E. J. Miller, and D. S. Stauffer;
On Memorials,—F. Krecker, S. B. Brown, L. N. Wor-
man, H. Stoetzel, B. D. Albright, and A. A. Delong.

F. B. Copp, local preacher, withdrew from the
church. A. Markley located on account of bodily infirmities. A. Schultz was retained in the itinerancy one
year without an appointment. G. B. Fisher changed
his relation from supernumerary to active. Credentials
were granted to L. Snyder, M. Dissinger, W. H. Bachman, G. W. Moore, and C. W. Snyder. S. P. Reinoehl, H. Kempfer, J. Breidenstein, and W. Heim, itinerants, and J. Bertolet and I. Dissinger, local preachers, died during the past year. G. W. Gross, H. J.
Glick, and Dr. F. Krecker were ordained to the office of
Elder; F. Smith and A. M. Sampsel, to the office of
Deacon, and received into the itinerancy. The follow-
ing were licensed as preachers on trial: George
Swartz, A. E. Gobble, John W. Hoover, Howard H.
Romberger, Jacob L. Guinther, and William H. Rinek.
J. S. McNutt, a local preacher on trial in the M. E.
Church, was received into our church in the same rela-
tion. The supernumeraries were N. Goebel, D. Wieand,
H. Stoetzel, J. Gross, D. Berger, C. Gingrich, S. Ely,
J. Frey, and Seneca Breyfogel.

The following were reported as *conference claimants:*
N. Gœbel, H. Stoetzel, J. Gross, D. Wieand, C. Gingrich, Sisters Schnerr, Hesser, Rhoads, Meyers, Shell,
Kempfer, and the two children of J. J. High. On behalf of Sister Heim, W. K. Wieand presented to the

Conference the library of her deceased husband, Rev. W. Heim, whereupon a suitable resolution of thanks was adopted. Among the recommendations to General Conference were the following: 1st, With reference to preachers being connected with oath-bound societies— affirmative, 3; negative, 81. 2d, With reference to assistant class-leaders—affirmative, 0; negative, 80. The following rules for the examination of junior preachers were adopted: A uniform method shall be observed by all examiners; the degree of merit of each student shall be indicated by the figures 1 to 100; no one shall be passed from a lower to a higher class, or be ordained, who has a less average than 75; all applicants for license shall be present for examination in the studies of the first year; the different examining committees shall report each year in writing; the stationing committee shall select from such applicants only as are favorably reported by the respective committees. On motion of H. A. Neitz, the preachers in charge were instructed to report their annual conference statistics to the first quarterly conference of the year, and in case there is no regular church record on the charge, to record the statistics in the quarterly conference minutes. S. B. Brown having asked for a letter of dismissal, in order to join the Kansas Conference, and A. Krecker having been appointed by the executive committee of the board of missions to labor on the Pacific Coast, the Conference expressed its deep regret at parting with these brethren, and granted to them the desired certificates of dismissal. S. S. Chubb was elected conference treasurer.

The following were elected delegates to the General

20

Conference: C. S. Haman, I. E. Knerr, S. Neitz, J. O. Lehr, C. K. Fehr, J. M. Saylor, J. C. Hornberger, and B. F. Bohner; alternates, S. S. Chubb, B. J. Smoyer, and C. H. Baker. It was resolved that a collection be taken up in the month of June at each appointment, to defray the expenses of the delegates to General Conference. W. F. Schneider, General Book Agent, addressed the Conference in the interests of our publishing house. T. G. Clewell, formerly a member of this Conference, was introduced and delivered an address.

The Conference resolved to raise forty cents per member for the missionary cause and eight cents per member for our superannuated preachers this year. Each ministerial district convention was instructed to apportion the sum total of the district among the several charges. The pastors of stations and missions were instructed to devote at least one Sabbath to the missionary cause. To merely lift a basket collection was declared insufficient. The preachers on circuits were urged to organize a missionary auxiliary at each appointment. It was made the duty of the presiding officer of the Conference to inquire of each member, during the investigation, whether he has done his duty in reference to the benevolent collections.* The delegates were instructed to ask General Conference to so change our Church Discipline as to secure a more equitable distribution of the proceeds of the book establishment and of the Charitable Society. The Conference decided that a preacher in charge may secure votes in private for any purpose

---

*These resolutions, with some changes and amendments, have continued in force to the present time.

pertaining to church building, provided a public meeting orders him to do so. A committee was appointed to secure and to put in order the grave of Rev. J. Walter.

BOUNDARIES.

Miller's class and Ackermantown were taken from Bath Circuit and annexed to Bangor Circuit. Howertown was detached from Bath Circuit and annexed to Berlinsville Circuit. Mauch Chunk was taken from Weissport Station and attached to Mahoning Circuit, the whole to be called Mauch Chunk Circuit. Turkey Hill was taken from Conestoga Circuit and connected with Fairville Station. Fleetwood Station was annexed to Friedensburg Circuit. Halifax was taken from Berrysburg Circuit and annexed to Millersburg Station. Mt. Carmel Mission was annexed to Ashland Station. Trevorton, Little Mahanoy, Mahanoy, Fisher's Ferry, Sunbury, Seven Points, and Irish Valley were taken from Uniontown Circuit and formed into a new charge, called Trevorton Circuit. Barnesville was transferred from Mahanoy City to Tamaqua.

CHURCH AFFAIRS.

The Trustees of the Allentown Turner St. church received permission to grant a new mortgage of $1,100, and a second mortgage of $500. Conference confirmed the giving of a certain mortgage on the church at Pequea. Zion church, Mt. Nebo Circuit, received permission to sell lots on their burial ground, the proceeds to be applied to church purposes. The financial difficulties of the churches at Summit Hill and Ackermantown were referred to their respective presiding elders and the preachers in charge. The society at Bolich's church was instructed to pay the claims of W. H. Weidner forthwith. The financial difficulties of the church at Shenandoah City were referred for adjustment to a committee consisting of I. E. Knerr, C. K. Fehr, and J. O. Lehr, providing the trustees of said church enter into a written agreement to surrender the affairs into the hands of this committee. The Bishop of the district, the presiding elders of the Conference, the preacher in charge of the mission, and the preacher in charge of Germantown Station, were appointed a committee on the Philadelphia Mission. This committee was empowered to authorize the trustees to dispose of the church property, and with the proceeds locate and erect a church building in a more suitable and advantageous place, whenever they have an opportunity to do so. The Conference ordered that the proceeds from the sale of the Strausstown church be placed into the hands of the presiding elder and given to Bernville church as a loan. Permission was given to churches to borrow money and give security as follows: Lyons, Kutztown Circuit, $300; Catasauqua, $1,300; Schuylkill Haven Mission, $900; Wilkesbarre, $750; and Eighth Str., Philadelphia, $500. The following congregations received permission to collect for their churches: Coaldale, in Pottsville District, for a debt of $630; East Greenville and Bath, in Philadelphia District. It was resolved that German preaching in the church at Germantown, Pa., shall not be dispensed with so long as ten votes out of one hundred members desire by a vote at a special meeting to continue German preaching.

EDUCATION.

The Conference resolved to organize an Educational Society to be duly incorporated for the purpose of advancing our educational interests. District ministerial and Sunday-school conventions were urgently recommended in the place of the annual Sunday-school convention, which was discontinued. The International Series of Lessons was commended to all the Sunday-schools of the Conference as a most efficient method of Bible study. The teachers and workers of our schools were requested to procure the Sunday-school literature of our church.

S. C. Breyfogel, I. E. Knerr, and J. C. Hornberger were elected examiners for five years. B. F. Bohner, J. G. Sands, and H. A. Neitz were elected to examine applicants for the itinerancy.

MEMORIALS.

The following memorial was erected to the memory of our departed brethren:

Father John Breidenstein was one of our oldest pioneer preachers. He was very eloquent, and possessed the happy gift of fascinating large congregations for hours during his discourses, so that it was a common occurrence that hundreds of souls were melted to tears, many of whom fell prostrate before the Lord, and cried for mercy and pardon.

Wm. Heim, an old veteran of the cross, was one of the pioneer preachers of the East Pennsylvania Conference. He bore hardships like a faithful soldier of our Lord, and preached the everlasting gospel in and out of season to the salvation of many precious souls.

S. P. Reinoehl passed through many severe bodily afflictions, and very reluctantly retired from active service. He was a man of brilliant intellectual qualities, of rich and useful attainments, a deep thinker, original in his discourses, and whose preaching was universally appreciated.

H. Kempfer was a devoted man of God, an effectual preacher, and a faithful worker. He served the church as a local and itinerant preacher for the space of twenty-six years, leading many souls to Christ.

J. Bertolet, a local preacher, labored with success and acceptability for many years. His godly life exerted a salutary influence on all with whom he came in contact.

SABBATH AND TEMPERANCE.

The Conference took the usual high moral ground upon the questions of the Sabbath and temperance. It was resolved that no person addicted to the use of tobacco shall hereafter be received into the itinerancy.

FINANCE.

Receipts:

Collections.......................$ 843.65
Book establishment....................... 555.55
Charitable Society....................... 248.40

$1,647.60

Expenditures:

Paid to bishops and conference claimants.... . 1,644.25

Balance in treasury....................$ 3.35

MISSIONARY APPROPRIATIONS.

Philadelphia Miss... $400
Norristown Miss.... 50
Plymouth Miss. 175
Pottstown Miss..... 100
Reading Miss...... 100
Lancaster Miss..... 325
Lititz and Manheim Miss............ 75
Lebanon Miss....... 350
Harrisburg Miss..... 350
Schuylkill Haven Miss............ 200

Frackville Miss...... $350
Nth. Allentown Miss. 150
East Allentown Miss. 325
"   "   (Interest)........... 100
Lehighton Miss..... 175
Wilkesbarre Miss.... 325
Easton Miss........ 150
Stroudsburg Miss.... 200

Total..........$3,900

APPOINTMENTS.

PHILADELPHIA DISTRICT—*J. O. Lehr*, *P. E.*
Phila. 8th Street Miss.—J. K. Knerr.
Germantown Sta.—H. A. Neitz.
Norristown—B. F. Bohner.
Plymouth—J. H. Shirey.
Trappe—J. N. Metzgar.
Montgomery—A. Ziegenfus, N. A. Barr.
Milford—H. J. Glick.
Pleasant Valley—W. H. Weidner.
Bethlehem—R. M. Lichtenwalner.
Freemansburg—J. D. Woodring.
Easton—S. C. Breyfogel.
Bath--G. W. Gross.
Bangor—A. Kindt.
Middle Creek—G. D. Sweigert.
Stroudsburg—G. B. Fisher.
Wayne— J. W. Woehrle.

ALLENTOWN DISTRICT—*C. K. Fehr*, *P. E.*
Allentown, Linden Street—D. Yingst.
    "   Turner "   —J. Bowman.
    "   First Ward—W. K. Wieand.
    "   Liberty Street—B. H. Miller.

Lehigh—C. H. Baker.
Emaus—F. Hoffman.
Catasauqua—G. T. Haines.*
Slatington—J. C. Bliem.
Berlinsville—D. Lentz.
Parryville—E. Butz.
Weissport—J. K. Seyfrit.
Mauch Chunk--H. D. Shultz.
Lehighton—B. J. Smoyer.
Hazleton—J. M. Rinker.
Wilkesbarre—J. Savitz.

READING DISTRICT—*J. M. Saylor*, *P. E.*
Reading Eighth Street—S. Neitz.
Reading Chestnut St.—W. A. Leopold.
Reading Ninth Street—F. P. Lehr.
Friedensburg—J. Zern.
Pottstown—F. Krecker.
Birdsboro—T. A. Hess.
Adamstown—H. R. Yost.
Fairville—A. W. Warfel.
Brownstown—F. Sechrist.
Lititz and Manheim—J. Specht.
Lancaster Sta.—J. Adams.
Lancaster Miss.—O. L. Saylor.

*In the latter part of this year G. T. Haines died, and Seneca Breyfogel was appointed to take his place.

Millersville—U. H. Hershey.
Creswell—T. Harper.
Conestoga—F. Smith.

HARRISBURG DISTRICT—C. S. Haman, P. E.
Lebanon Sta.—J. C. Hornberger.
Lebanon Miss.—A. M. Stirk.
Myerstown—B. D. Albright.
Womelsdorf—I. Hess.
Kutztown—D. S. Stauffer.
Annville—A. A. Delong.
Mt. Nebo—C. S. Brown.
Dauphin—J. W. Hoover.
Harrisburg—J. A. Feger.
Millersburg—S. S. Chubb.
Berrysburg—W. L. Black.
Williamstown—J. S. Newhart.
Tremont—A. M. Sampsel.
Pine Grove—J. M. Oplinger.

POTTSVILLE DISTRICT—I. E. Knerr, P. E.
Pottsville—D. A. Medlar.
Schuylkill Haven Sta.—S. L. Wiest.
Schuylkill Haven Miss.—J. G. Sands.
Cressona—I. J. Reitz.
Orwigsburg and Port Carbon—J. R. Hensyl.
Schuylkill—J. Laros.
Tamaqua—C. H. Egge.
Mahanoy City—S. T. Leopold.
Shenandoah—E. J. Miller.
Ashland—A. Dilabar.
Frackville—L. N. Worman.
Shamokin—W. A. Shoemaker.
Uniontown—J. K. Fehr.
Trevorton—D. Z. Kembel.
Mahantongo—J. L. Werner.

1879.

The General Conference.

Presidents, Bishops J. J. Esher, R. Yeakel, R. Dubs, and T. Bowman.

Secretary, C. A. Thomas.

Assistant Secretaries, J. C. Hornberger, M. Stamm, M. Pfitzinger, S. Smith, and C. W. Anthony.

Seventy-seven delegates, representing twenty-one annual conferences, and nine *ex-officio* delegates assembled in General Conference session in the city of Chicago, Illinois, on Thursday, October 2d, 1879.* The representatives of the East Pa. Conference were all in attendance.

It was resolved that two book agents be elected, who shall have equal power, rights, and prerogatives, and be equally responsible for the management of the publish-

*See Preface on page 93.

ing house. The agent first elected shall be the senior in the firm and shall be a member *ex-officio* of General Conference in accordance with the provisions of the Discipline. The editors of the *Christliche Botschafter* and the *Evangelical Messenger* each received an annual allowance of $250.00 for correspondence; the editors of the *Evangelische Magazin* and the *Living Epistle*, each, $150.00. The bishops and editors were appointed a committee to publish an English hymn book with notes. Appropriate and touching memorial resolutions were adopted with reference to the death of S. G. Rhoads of the East Pa. Conference, C. A. Schnake of the Wisconsin Conference, and W. F. Schneider, General Book Agent. The elections resulted as follows: Bishops, J. J. Esher, R. Dubs, and T. Bowman; general book agents, M. Lauer and W. Yost; editor of the *Christliche Botschafter*, W. Horn; editor of the *Evangelical Messenger*, H. B. Hartzler; editor of the *Evangelische Magazin* and German Sunday-school Literature, C. A. Thomas; editor of the *Living Epistle* and English Sunday-school Literature, H. J. Bowman; corresponding secretary of the Missionary Society, S. L. Wiest; editor of the *Evangelische Botschafter* and *Kinderfreund;* G. Fuessele; general book agent of our publishing house in Germany, J. Walz; superintendent of the Orphans' Home, J. Driesbach. S. Neitz was elected to represent the East Pa. Conference in the board of publication. T. Linder, G. Moyer, and G. Boyer were elected trustees of the Charitable Society. J. C. Hornberger was appointed fraternal delegate to the General Conference of the United Brethren Church.

The following statistics of the entire church were reported: Itinerant preachers, 909; local preachers, 636; members, 109,773; churches, 1,434; parsonages, 449; Sunday-schools, 1,918½; officers and teachers, 20,553; scholars, 118,640; catechetical classes, 646; catechumens, 8,455.

1880.

The Forty-First (73d) Annual Session.

President, Bishop Thomas Bowman.

Secretary, J. C. Hornberger.

Assistant Secretaries, W. A. Leopold and S. C. Breyfogel.

The forty-first annual session of the East Pa. Conference was held in the Evangelical church at Weissport, Pa., beginning on Wednesday, February 25th, 1880.

The following were the standing committees: On Letters,—F. Hoffman, J. Adams, A. Ziegenfus, Jos. Specht, and Thomas Harper; On Public Worship,—C. K. Fehr, J. K. Seyfrit, and B. J. Smoyer; On Boundaries,—The Bishop and the presiding elders; On Quarterly Conference Records,—S. Neitz, Isaac Hess, J. Zern, E. Butz, D. Z. Kembel, F. Sechrist, and J. Laros; On Finance,—C. H. Baker, A. Kindt, B. D. Albright, E. J. Miller, G. B. Fisher, and C. S. Brown; On Statistics,—S. L. Wiest, H. A. Neitz, J. G. Sands, J. M. Rinker, D. S. Stauffer, S. T. Leopold, and A. A. Delong; On Church Affairs,—S. S. Chubb, J. C. Bliem, B. F. Bohner, O. L. Saylor, W. A. Shoemaker, and J. A. Feger; On Education,—W. K. Wieand, A. M.

Stirk, J. N. Metzgar, D. Lentz, H. R. Yost, J. S. New-hart, and J. K. Fehr; On Sabbath and Temperance,— J. K. Knerr, J. N. Metzgar, D. Lentz, H. R. Yost, J. S. Newhart, and J. K. Fehr; On Memorials,—F. Krecker, F. P. Lehr, D. Yingst, L. N. Worman, J. L. Werner, and W. H. Weidner; Reporters,—W. K. Wieand, A. M. Stirk, H. A. Neitz, W. L. Black, O. L. Saylor, D. A. Medlar, and W. H. Rinck. Geo. Swartz, local preacher, withdrew from the church. J. R. Workman resigned his license as local preacher. W. H. Weidner and D. Yingst were retained in the itinerancy one year without appointments. Samuel Ganmer and G. T. Haines died during the year. I. E. Knerr and J. O. Lehr were re-elected, and J. C. Hornberger was newly elected to the office of presiding elder. J. W. Woehrle and J. H. Shirey were ordained to the office of Elder; N. A. Barr and J. R. Hensyl, to the office of Deacon. The following received license as preachers on trial: William H. Stauffer, F. G. Stauffer, James C. Krause, H. M. Capp, William F. Heil, and J. Weidel. H. S. Clemens was received from the M. E. Church as a local preacher on trial. T. G. Clewell and G. C. Knobel presented their credentials and were received into the Conference as elders. T. G. Clewell, J. D. Woodring, N. A. Barr, and J. R. Hensyl were received into the itinerancy. The super-annuated preachers were,—N. Goebel, D. Wieand, J. Gross, D. Berger, H. Stoetzel, C. Gingrich; the super-numeraries,—S. Ely, J. Fry, Seneca Breyfogel, J. M. Oplinger, W. H. Weidner, and J. Savitz. The follow-ing were reported as conference claimants: N. Goebel, H. Stoetzel, J. Gross, D. Wieand, C. Gingrich, Sisters

Schnerr, Hesser, Rhoads, Meyers, Shell, Kempfer, and Haines, and three children of J. J. High.

The necessary grade in the examination of applicants for the ministry was reduced from 75 to 60. O. L. Saylor was elected treasurer of the educational fund, S. S. Chubb, treasurer of the Conference, and J. G. Sands, statistical secretary. The bishops and the presiding elders were constituted a judiciary committee to decide questions of law. The members of the Conference obligated themselves to solicit contributions for the orphan cause, and to report them in the annual statistics. Prof. A. E. Gobble, Principal of Union Seminary, addressed the Conference in the interests of that institution. On motion of A. M. Stirk the following was adopted: *Resolved*, That the Conference protests against the introduction into our churches or societies of all questionable measures, such as fairs, festivals, cake walks, bazaars, oyster suppers, etc. It was resolved that no member shall be reported expelled unless such expulsion has occurred in accordance with the Church Discipline; that no member shall be reported withdrawn unless he sever his connection with the church; and that those who move away, either with or without certificate, shall be reported as moved away.

Brother S. L. Wiest having been elected to the office of corresponding secretary of the Missionary Society, the Conference adopted resolutions congratulating the church upon this choice, wishing him the help of the Lord in his arduous work, and bidding him always welcome in our midst. W. Yost, Junior Book Agent, addressed the Conference. The presiding elders were instructed to see to it that each charge is supplied with a good

church record.   C. S. Haman, conference librarian,
reported 65 volumes in the library.

Among the General Conference recommendations
acted upon were the following :   With reference to
stewards reporting pastors' salary to Quarterly Conference: Affirmative, 83.   To expunge the clause to
license exhorters: Affirmative, 83.   With reference to
locating inefficient ministers :   Affirmative, 83.   To expunge the clause relating to probationary members :
Affirmative, 82 ; negative, 1.   *Ex-officio* members of
General Conference : Affirmative, 81 ; negative, 2.
To change the church name: Affirmative, 9 ; negative,
74.   It was resolved that hereafter all ministers who
claim support from the Conference shall be placed upon
the list of superannuated preachers.

BOUNDARIES.

Quakertown was taken from Montgomery Circuit,
Williams Township from Easton Mission, and Miller's
class from Freemansburg, and annexed to Pleasant
Valley Circuit.   Vera Cruz was taken from Emaus and
annexed to Milford Circuit.   West Penn, Hunsicker's,
and Centreville were taken from Mauch Chunk Circuit
and annexed to Schuylkill Circuit.   Lansford and Coaldale were taken from Mauch Chunk Circuit, and
Barnesville and Locust Valley from Tamaqua Station,
and formed into a new field called Barnesville Circuit.
Mahoning Valley was taken from Mauch Chunk Circuit
and annexed to Lehighton Mission.   Reamstown was
transferred from Adamstown to Brownstown Circuit.
Lykens, Wiconisco, and Dayton were detached from
Williamstown Circuit and called Lykens Circuit; Williamstown, Tower City, and Reiner City to remain as

Williamstown Circuit. Herndon was transferred from Uniontown Circuit to Trevorton Circuit. Norristown Mission was made a station. Mauch Chunk, Mt. Carmel, Lansdale and Hatfield, and Emaus and Salisbury were taken up as missions.

CHURCH AFFAIRS.

The following congregations received permission to collect: Germantown, within the bounds of the Conference; Lykens, on Berrysburg and Tremont Circuits, for a debt of $290; Bethlehem, in Philadelphia District and in Allentown District south of the Blue Mountain, for a new church; Frackville, in Pottsville District, for a debt of $1,070; Reading Ebenezer, in Reading District, for a debt; Quakertown, on Pleasant Valley and Montgomery Circuits, for a new church. Permission to give mortgages on their churches was granted to the congregations at the following places: Germantown, Fredericksburg for $625, and Palmyra for $85.10. The financial affairs of the churches at Dauphin, Bernville, and Port Clinton were referred to their respective presiding elders and preachers in charge. The trustees of Seven Points church received permission to sell a part of their church lot, the proceeds to be applied toward liquidating their church debt. The trustees of Bethlehem church received permission to sell eight feet of their church lot on one side and to purchase additional ground on the other side. The former committee to manage the financial affairs of the church at Shenandoah City was continued. Salem church, in Porter Township, Schuylkill County, Pa., was ordered to be sold, the proceeds to be applied to the church at Tower City. WHEREAS, There is danger of losing our church property at Bath, Pa., because of a pressing debt; therefore be it *Resolved*, That if the members of Bath will obligate themselves to raise $1,250 on Bath Circuit, we, the East Pennsylvania Conference, will obligate ourselves to raise $1,250, this amount to be equally apportioned to the five presiding elder districts, the presiding elders of the districts to collect their apportionments during the conference year. The congregation of the Chestnut Street church at Reading received permission to sell their church property and to apply the proceeds to the erection of a new church. It was resolved that the deed of our church at Pine Grove be placed in the hands of the presiding elder of the district.

EDUCATION.

All moneys, books, etc., in the possession of Conference or placed into the hands of others as a loan, were transferred to the East Pennsylvania Conference Educational Society. Union Seminary, at New Berlin, Pa., and Northwestern College, at Naperville, Illinois, were recommended to the favorable consideration of all contemplating a scientific, classical, or theological course. On motion it was resolved that the committee to examine applicants for the itinerancy be made a permanent one, whose duty it shall be to inquire into the call to the ministry and moral character of such candidates; the other committees to examine into the literary qualifications of their respective classes. J. K. Seyfrit, W. K. Wieand, and G. W. Gross were elected examiners for five years.

MEMORIALS.

Resolved, That we erect to the memory of our departed brethren the following memorial: Rev. Samuel Gamner served the church for 13 years as an itinerant, after which he sustained a local relation unto the end of his life. His gentlemanly and Christian demeanor towards all those with whom he came in contact is worthy of imitation.

Father G. T. Haines, a veteran of the cross, was born October 12, 1809. After his conversion, which occurred at the age of twenty, he felt and finally obeyed an inward call to the ministry. His active service covers a period of more than 42 years. During his late illness he left a clear testimony of his entrance into heaven. In his last hours he said several times: "When I die, I shall go from labor to reward."

THE SABBATH.

Should the sanctity of the Sabbath be displaced by a simple holiday of the European pattern, our surest stronghold against the assaults of socialistic and communistic influences will fall into the hands of those who are the enemies of the Christian family and Christian marriage. As Christian ministers and friends of the laborer, we appeal to those industrial classes, especially who are in the employ of powerful corporations, to use their utmost endeavor to counteract the despotism of consolidated capital, which, by offering extra compensation for Sabbath work, would bribe the workingmen into a surrender of this boon—*a day of rest on the Christian Sabbath.*

TEMPERANCE.

We commend the proposed Temperance Law to the members of our Church and others, and ask them to secure, by petition and all other honorable means, its enactment by the Legislature of our State.

FINANCE.

Receipts:

Conference collections........... $1,188.65
Charitable Society.............. 296.60
Book establishment............. 421.00
                                  ——— $1,906.25

Expenditures:

Paid to conference claimants............. 1,795.12

Balance in treasury................ $111.13

MISSIONARY APPROPRIATIONS.

Allentown Liberty Str. Miss. for last year........... $100
Philadelphia 8th Str. Miss............ 250
Philadelphia 8th Str. Miss. (ground rent) 150
Plymouth Miss...... 75
Lansdale and Hatfield Miss........ 75
Easton Miss........ 200
Stroudsburg Miss.... 225
Allentown 1st ward Miss............ 300
Allentown Liberty Str. Miss........ 275
Emaus Miss........ 75

Lehighton Miss..... $150
Mauch Chunk Miss.. 250
Wilkesbarre Miss.... 325
Reading 9th Str. Miss. 150
Pottstown Miss..... 75
Lititz and Manheim Miss........... 75
Lancaster Miss...... 325
Lebanon Miss....... 325
Harrisburg Miss..... 350
Schuylkill Haven Miss............ 200
Frackville Miss..... 350
Mt. Carmel Miss.... 250
Wesnersville Miss... 50
                        ———
                        $4,600

21

APPOINTMENTS.

PHILADELPHIA DISTRICT—*J. C. Hornberger, P. E.*

Philadelphia 8th Street—S. C. Breyfogel.

Germantown—H. A. Neitz.

Norristown—B. F. Bohner.

Plymouth—J. C. Krause.

Trappe—J. N. Metzgar.

Montgomery—G. D. Sweigert.

Lansdale and Hatfield—W. F. Hell.

Milford—S. Ely.

Pleasant Valley—A. Ziegenfus and W. H. Rinck.

Bethlehem—R. M. Lichtenwalner.

Freemansburg—J. D. Woodring.

Easton—A. M. Stirk.

Bath—W. L. Black.

Bangor—A. Kindt.

Stroudsburg—G. B. Fisher.

Middle Creek—J. L. Gilther.

Wayne—J. S. Newhart.

ALLENTOWN DISTRICT — *C. K. Fehr, P. E.*

Allentown Linden Street—H. R. Yost.

Allentown Turner Street—Jas. Bowman.

Allentown First Ward—W. K. Wieand.

Allentown Liberty Street—B. H. Miller.

Lehigh—E. Butz.

Emaus- F. Hoffman.

Kutztown—A. L. Yeakel.

Catasauqua—Seneca Breyfogel.

Slatington—J. C. Bliem.

Berlinsville—D. Lentz.

Parryville—G. W. Gross.

Weissport—E. J. Miller.

Lehighton—B. J. Smoyer.

Mauch Chunk—D. S. Stauffer.

Hazleton—J. K. Seyfrit.

Wilkesbarre—H. D. Shultz.

Wesnersville—A. M. Hartman.

READING DISTRICT—*I. E. Knerr, P. E.*

Reading 8th Street—S. Neitz.

Reading Chestnut Street—W. A. Leopold.

Reading 9th Street—F. P. Lehr.

Friedensburg—Jacob Adams.

Pottstown—F. Krecker.

Birdsboro—J. W. Hoover.

Adamstown—J. M. Saylor.

Fairville—A. M. Sampsel.

Brownstown—F. Seehrist and D. W. Bleksler.

Lititz and Manheim—Jos. Specht.

Lancaster Water Street—J. Zern.

Lancaster Mulberry Street — J. A. Feger.

Millersville—U. H. Hershey.

Creswell—Thos. Harper.

Conestoga—F. Smith.

HARRISBURG DISTRICT—*C. S. Haman, P. E.*

Lebanon Chestnut Street—J. K. Knerr.

Lebanon 8th Street—J. H. Shirey.

Myerstown—B. D. Albright.

Womelsdorf—Isaac Hess.

Annville—N. A. Barr.

Mt. Nebo—C. S. Brown.

Harrisburg—A. W. Warfel.

Dauphin—H. M. Capp.

Millersburg—S. S. Chubb.

Berrysburg—A. Dilabar.

Williamstown—H. J. Glick.

Uniontown—J. K. Fehr.

Tremont—H. H. Romberger.

Pine Grove- D. A. Medlar.

Lykens—A. A. Delong.

POTTSVILLE DISTRICT—*J. O. Lehr, P.E.*

Pottsville—O. L. Saylor.

Schuylkill Haven St. Peters—C. H. Baker.

Schuylkill Haven Trinity — J. G. Sands.

Cressona—I. J. Reitz.

Orwigsburg and Port Carbon—J. R. Hensyl.

Schuylkill—J. Loras.

Tamaqua—C. H. Egge.

Barnesville—I. E. Zimmerman.

Mahanoy City—S. T. Leopold.

Shenandoah—J. M. Rinker.

Ashland—T. A. Hess.

Frackville—L. N. Worman.

Shamokin—W. A. Shoemaker.

Mt. Carmel—J. W. Woehrle.
Trevorton—D. Z. Kembel.
Mahantongo—J. L. Werner.

S. L. Wiest, corresponding secretary Missionary Society.
T. G. Clewell, assistant editor *Evangelical Messenger*.

1881.

The Forty-Second (74th) Annual Session.

President, Bishop J. J. Esher.

Secretary, B. J. Smoyer.

Assistant Secretaries, W. A. Leopold and S. C. Breyfogel.

The East Pa. Conference met in annual session in the Evangelical church at Millersburg, Pa., on February 23d, 1881. The Bishop appointed the following committees: On Worship,—C. S. Haman and S. S. Chubb; On Letters,—J. M. Saylor, F. Hoffman, J. Adams, A. Ziegenfus, and Thomas Harper; On Quarterly Conference Records,—S. Neitz, Isaac Hess, J. N. Metzgar, E. Butz, D. Z. Kembel, F. Sechrist, J. Laros, S. Ely, J. K. Knerr, and J. C. Bliem; On Boundaries, —The Bishop and the presiding elders; On Statistics,— H. A. Neitz, J. G. Sands, J. M. Rinker, D. S. Stauffer, S. T. Leopold, and G. W. Gross; On Finance,—C. H. Baker, B. D. Albright, E. J. Miller, G. B. Fisher, C. S. Brown, and J. S. Newhart; On Education,—W. K. Wieand, D. A. Medlar, C. H. Egge, S. C. Breyfogel, and O. L. Saylor; On Church Affairs,—S. S. Chubb, B. F. Bohner, Jas. Bowman, A. Kindt, J. A. Feger, and J. K. Fehr; On Sabbath and Temperance,—A. M. Stirk, U. H. Hershey, J. K. Seyfrit, G. D. Sweigert, and J. H. Shirey; On Memorials,—F. Krecker, Seneca Breyfogel, H. R. Yost, F. P. Lehr, H. D. Shultz, W.

L. Black, and F. Smith; To Audit Accounts of Collectors,—D. Wieand, H. D. Shultz, and H. R. Yost; Reportorial Committee,—W. K. Wieand, O. L. Saylor, W. H. Rinek, H. M. Capp, and W. F. Heil.

A local preacher and a traveling deacon were deposed from office and expelled from the church during the past year. D. Berger, W. L. Reber, Jacob Snyder, and Jonathan Kurtz died during the year. Credentials were granted to J. S. McNutt and Wm. Loose, who desired to withdraw from the church; to A. E. Gobble and to T. G. Clewell in order to unite with the conferences within the bounds of which they reside; and to I. E. Zimmerman, to unite with another conference. F. Smith and A. M. Sampsel were ordained to the office of Elder; D. W. Bicksler, J. W. Hoover, J. D. Woodring, and H. S. Clemens, to the office of Deacon. The following were licensed as preachers on trial: Rudolph Roessel, Jas. R. Teter, Daniel G. Reinhold, John S. Overholser, Israel F. Heisler, Joseph Fox, and Webster C. Weiss. The brethren W. H. Rinek, W. F. Heil, H. M. Capp, J. L. Guinther, J. W. Hoover, H. H. Romberger, and J. C. Krause were received into the itinerancy. W. C. Kantner was received with credentials from the Oregon Conference. The supernumeraries were,—S. Ely, J. Fry, and Seneca Breyfogel; the superannuated,—N. Goebel, Daniel Wieand, J. Gross, H. Stoetzel, J. M. Oplinger, J. Savitz, and C. Gingrich. Solomon Neitz was retained in the itinerancy one year without an appointment.

On motion of J. O. Lehr it was *Resolved*, 1st, That all applicants for the itinerancy must study and be examined in the German language for four years. 2d,

That we will hereafter not receive any preachers into the itinerancy of this Conference, unless they exercise in both the German and English languages.

M. Lauer, Senior Book Agent, addressed the Conference. J. G. Sands was elected statistical secretary; S. S. Chubb, conference treasurer; and O. L. Saylor, treasurer of the educational fund. It was made the duty of the preacher, officiating at the funeral of a member of Conference, to furnish all possible information for the preparation of memorials at the annual session. On motion of D. A. Medlar it was resolved that in recognition of the divine approval of our Christian endeavor in the work of foreign missions, we will urge our members to remember the parent treasury by special contributions, large gifts, and bequests. The following delegates were appointed to attend the State Temperance Convention at Harrisburg: B. J. Smoyer, S. C. Breyfogel, J. K. Knerr, J. G. Sands, A. W. Warfel, H. M. Capp, and L. N. Worman. Bishop J. J. Esher, A. M. Stirk, and G. W. Gross were elected delegates to the National Temperance Convention to meet at Saratoga. In a fitting resolution the Conference expressed its appreciation of a sermon preached at this session by H. B. Hartzler, editor of the *Evangelical Messenger*, and wished him God-speed in his arduous work.

BOUNDARIES.

Stroudsburg Mission was discontinued. Bangor was constituted a station, and Roxburg, Miller's church, and Ackermanville were annexed to Bath Circuit. Tower City and Reiner City were taken from Williamstown Circuit, and together with Tremont constituted a mis-

sion called Tremont Mission.   Williamstown was made
a station.   Ringtown was taken from Shenandoah City
Station and annexed to Barnesville Circuit.

CHURCH AFFAIRS.

The following resolutions were adopted: WHEREAS,
Christ Church, of Philadelphia, has been suffering under a burdensome debt of $10,000, greatly hindering its
prosperity and endangering its future existence; and
WHEREAS, The sum of $6,000 has been secured among
the members of that church toward the liquidation of
the debt, with a fair prospect of being able to secure
an additional thousand in the City of Philadelphia;
therefore be it *Resolved*, 1st, That this Conference
grant permission to their preacher to canvass the entire
Conference district to secure the balance of the $10,-
000; 2d, That we will use our influence in word and
deed in carrying out this undertaking.   The trustees of the Lancaster English Mission received permission to sell the Eden church, the proceeds to be applied to the liquidation of the debt on the mission
church.   Of the claim of Brother Alspach against the
Scranton church, $400 were assumed by the Confer-
ence upon condition that if after a thorough investigation
by a committee, consisting of C. K. Fehr and J. C.
Hornberger, the facts substantiate the claim as presented, each traveling preacher shall send his *pro rata*
share of the amount to the committee.   The congregations at Hellertown, Trevorton, and Friedensburg
received permission to sell their church properties and
to apply the proceeds to the erection of new churches.

The congregations at Quakertown and Bernville were
authorized to sell portions of their church lots and to
apply the income toward the payment of their church
debts. The financial difficulties of the churches at Port
Clinton and Hamburg were referred to the respective
presiding elders and preachers in charge. The affairs
at Shenandoah were continued under the former arrangement. The difficulties existing between Creswell
and Millersville circuits concerning the parsonage of
Lancaster Circuit, were referred to the presiding elder
of Reading District for adjustment by arbitration.
The sale of the Myerstown parsonage was sanctioned,
and Brother Stoner's claim of $50 submitted for inves-
tigation. The financial difficulties at Bainbridge were
referred to Rev. C. H. Baker, to dispose of the property
to the best advantage of all parties. The members of
Mahantongo Circuit were urged to accept the offer of
Elias Hepler and to purchase his church for $1,000.
Permission was given to the members of Wayne Circuit
to collect on Middle Creek Circuit for the payment of
their parsonage debt. The trustees of the church at
Wind Gap were authorized to effect a loan of $1,000
by giving a mortgage on their church property. Concerning the unsecured balance of $125 in Pottsville
District for the Bath church debt, it was ordered that
one-half be again apportioned to that district and the
other half equally divided among the remaining districts. The Linden Street congregation, of Allentown,
having submitted to the Conference the question of language in their Sunday services, it was ordered that
there be English preaching every other Sunday evening.

In the following resolutions, presented by the committee on education, *Schuylkill Seminary* was born:

WHEREAS, The desire for an educational institution in our Conference is daily becoming stronger; and WHEREAS, This desire is founded upon a manifest need which we can no longer afford to disregard; therefore be it *Resolved*, That this Conference locate an educational institution in the city of Reading upon the following plan, viz: 1, That this institution shall afford opportunities for such as desire an academic course, and also for lower grades of instruction. 2, That some competent man of our own church be chosen principal. 3, That a building affording the proper accommodations be secured. 4, That this institution be encouraged in a natural growth to a collegiate grade. 5, That an executive committee be appointed, consisting of seven ministers and two laymen, which shall have full power to execute the plan submitted in these resolutions.

Resolved, That we will endeavor to raise at least five cents per member for educational purposes, and that these contributions be gathered and sent to the treasurer of the educational fund before August 1, 1881.

The following were appointed the Committee on Institution of Learning: Bishop T. Bowman, I. E. Knerr, J. C. Hornberger, S. S. Chubb, A. M. Stirk, W. K. Wieand, S. C. Breyfogel, J. G. Mohn, and F. G. Boas. S. S. Chubb, J. O. Lehr, and W. A Leopold were elected examiners for five years.

MEMORIALS.

Jacob Snyder served the church of his choice acceptably as a local preacher till the end of his pilgrimage.

He was a friend of the missionary cause, and a man of exemplary Christian character.

D. Berger was one of our pioneer preachers. God blessed him with a strong constitution, a fine intellect, a genial disposition, and varied and useful attainments, which, with a strict morality, practical judgment, and sound theological views qualified him to fill the most important fields of labor. He served long and faithfully as a traveling preacher and died in the triumphs of faith.

W. L. Reber was one of the early preachers of our Conference, having served important charges for twenty-two years. He was considered a good preacher, sound in his theological views, and an efficient disciplinarian.

Jonathan Kurtz was indeed a diligent and faithful laborer in the church, beloved by all who knew him, and a great help to the itinerant preachers. He died triumphantly.

TEMPERANCE.

The president and secretary of the Conference were instructed to petition the Legislature of Pennsylvania in behalf of this body to pass the " temperance law" and take the preliminary steps to submit to the people a constitutional amendment prohibiting the sale and manufacture of spirituous and malt liquors for other than medicinal, mechanical, and scientific purposes.

FINANCE.

Receipts.

Conference collections............$1,177.23	
Charitable Society................	318.50
Book establishment...............	500.00
Bal. in treasury last year.........	68.84
	————$2,064.57

Expenditures:

Paid to conference claimants.............1,957.00

Balance in treasury...................$ 107.57

MISSIONARY APPROPRIATIONS.

Philadelphia, Eighth
St. Miss..........$250
Philadelphia, Eighth
Str. (ground rent).. 150
Plymouth Miss...... 300
Lansdale and Hatfield Miss....... 75
Easton Miss........ 225
Allentown First Ward
Miss............. 275
Allentown Liberty St.
Miss............. 275
Emaus Miss........ 100
Lehighton Miss..... 200
Mauch Chunk Miss.. 225
Wilkesbarre Miss.... 350
Wesnersville Miss... 300
Reading, Ninth Str.
Miss............. 150

Pottstown Miss.....$ 75
Lititz and Manheim
Miss............. 75
Lancaster Miss...... 200
Lebanon Miss...... 300
Harrisburg Miss.... 200
Schuylkill Haven
Miss............. 300
Frackville Miss..... 350
Mt. Carmel Miss.... 350
Reading Southeast
Miss............. 350
Reading Southeast
Miss. (rent)....... 150
Tremont Miss....... 100
Williamstown Miss.. 50

$5,375

APPOINTMENTS.

PHILADELPHIA DISTRICT—*J. C. Hornberger*, P. E.
Philadelphia 8th St.—S. C. Breyfogel.
Germantown—R. M. Lichtenwalner.
Norristown—W. L. Black.
Plymouth—J. N. Metzgar.
Trappe—U. H. Hershey.
Montgomery—G. D. Sweigert.

Lansdale and Hatfield—W. F. Heil.
Milford—S. Ely.
Pleasant Valley—D. Lentz, F. G. Stauffer.
Bethlehem—J. D. Woodring.
Freemansburg—J. L. Guinther.
Easton—A. M. Stirk.
Bath—W. H. Weidner, W. H. Stauffer.

Bangor—A. Kindt.
Middle Creek—G. B. Fisher.
Wayne—J. S. Newhart.

ALLENTOWN DISTRICT—*C. K. Fehr*, P. E.
Allentown Linden St.—B. F. Bohner.
Allentown Turner St.—J. A. Feger.
Allentown First ward—W. K. Wieand.
Allentown Liberty St.—B. H. Miller.
Lehigh—E. Butz.
Emaus—J. Adams.
Catasauqua—Seneca Breyfogel.
Slatington—J. C. Bliem.
Berlinsville—H. R. Yost.
Parryville—G. W. Gross.
Weissport—E. J. Miller.
Lehighton—B. J. Smoyer.
Mauch Chunk—D. S. Stauffer.
Hazleton—J. K. Seyfrit.
Wilkesbarre—H. D. Shultz.
Wesnersville—J. M. Saylor.

READING DISTRICT—*I. E. Knerr*, P. E.
Reading 8th St.—S. S. Chubb.
Reading Chestnut St.—J. Bowman.
Reading 9th St.—F. P. Lehr.
Reading S. E. Miss.—W. A. Leopold.
Friedensburg—T. Harper.
Pottstown—F. Krecker.
Birdsboro—D. W. Bicksler.
Adamstown—A. W. Warfel.
Fairville—A. M. Sampsel.
Lititz and Manheim—J. Specht.
Lancaster Water St.—J. Zern.
Lancaster Mulberry St.—J. C. Kranse.
Brownstown—F. Sechrist, D. G. Reinhold.
Millersville—J. W. Hoover.
Creswell—W. C. Kantner.
Conestoga—F. Smith.

HARRISBURG DISTRICT—*C. S. Haman*, P. E.
Lebanon Chestnut St.—J. K. Knerr.
Lebanon 8th St.—J. H. Shirey.
Myerstown—B. D. Albright.
Womelsdorf—Isaac Hess.
Annville—N. A. Barr.
Mt. Nebo—C. S. Brown.
Harrisburg—W. H. Rinek.
Dauphin—H. M. Capp.
Millersburg—H. A. Neitz.
Berrysburg—A. Dilabar.
Williamstown—H. J. Glick.
Uniontown—J. K. Fehr.
Tremont—F. Hoffman.
Pine Grove—D. A. Medlar.
Lykens—A. A. Delong.

POTTSVILLE DISTRICT—*J. O. Lehr*, P. E.
Pottsville—O. L. Saylor.
Schuylkill Haven St. Peter's—C. H. Baker.
Schuylkill Haven Trinity—J. G. Sands.
Cressona—I. J. Reitz.
Orwigsburg and Port Carbon—J. R. Hensyl.
Schuylkill—J. Laros.
Kutztown—A. Ziegenfus.
Tamaqua—C. H. Egge.
Barnesville—H. H. Romberger.
Mahanoy City—S. T. Leopold.
Shenandoah—J. M. Rinker.
Ashland—T. A. Hess.
Frackville—L. N. Worman.
Shamokin—W. A. Shoemaker.
Mt. Carmel—J. W. Woehrle.
Trevorton—D. Z. Kembel.
Mahantongo—J. L. Werner.
F. Krecker, Jr., Missionary, Tokio, Japan.

1882.

The Forty-Third (75th) Annual Session.

President, Bishop R. Dubs.
Secretary, B. J. Smoyer.

Assistant Secretaries, S. S. Chubb and D. A. Medlar.

The Conference met in annual session in the St. John's Evangelical church, Bethlehem, Pa., on Wednesday, February 22d, 1882. The Bishop appointed the following standing committees: On Worship,—J. C. Hornberger and J. D. Woodring; On Letters,— J. M. Saylor, F. Hoffman, A. Ziegenfus, T. Harper, Seneca Breyfogel, D. Wieand, C. Gingrich, J. M. Oplinger, and N. Goebel; On Quarterly Conference Proceedings,— Solomon Neitz, Isaac Hess, J. N. Metzgar, E. Butz, D. Z. Kembel, F. Sechrist, J. Laros, S. Ely, and J. C. Bliem; On Boundaries,—The Bishop and the presiding elders; On Statistics,—H. A. Neitz, J. G. Sands, J. M. Rinker, D. S. Stauffer, B. D. Albright, G. W. Gross, W. C. Kantner, G. D. Sweigert, and J. W. Woehrle; On Finance,—O. L. Saylor, C. S. Brown, W. H. Weidner, A. Kindt, A. A. Delong, F. Smith, I. J. Reitz, A. M. Sampsel, and H. D. Shultz; On Education,—S. S. Chubb, U. H. Hershey, J. Specht, D. A. Medlar, J. H. Shirey, G. B. Fisher, C. H. Baker, J. A. Feger, and L. N. Worman; On Church Affairs,—W. K. Wieand, R. M. Lichtenwalner, J. K. Seyfrit, C. H. Egge, H. J. Glick, J. K. Fehr, B. H. Miller, and N. A. Barr; On Sabbath and Temperance,—A. M. Stirk, S. C. Breyfogel, W. A. Shoemaker, J. R. Hensyl, A. W. Warfel, E. J. Miller, A. Dilabar, J. W. Hoover, and J. S. Newhart; On Memorials,—F. Krecker, F. P. Lehr, J. L. Werner, D. Lentz, W. A. Leopold, and H. R. Yost; To Audit Accounts,—J. H. Shirey, S. T. Leopold, and E. J. Miller; Reportorial Committee,—W. K. Wieand, W. H. Rinek, W. F. Heil, O. L. Saylor, and J. H. Shirey.

W. K. Wieand was appointed to report the proceedings of the Conference for the *Christliche Botschafter*, and D. A. Medlar for the *Evangelical Messenger*. A. V. Hirst and A. Weaver, local preachers, withdrew from the church. The latter withdrew in 1880. Jacob Adams and Abraham Shultz died during the year. C. S. Haman and C. K. Fehr were re-elected to the office of Presiding Elder. J. R. Hensyl and N. A. Barr were ordained to the office of Elder; W. F. Heil, J. L. Guinther, J. C. Krause, H. M. Capp, and W. H. Rinek, to the office of Deacon. The following received license as preachers on trial: Charles D. Dreher, Thomas L. Wentz, J. R. Hashinger, H. M. Harris, Hirakawa Toyotsura, and Mikuma Uyeno. I. E. Zimmerman, elder, was received with credentials. W. L. Black took a local relation. J. Bowman, D. Yingst, and J. K. Knerr, took a supernumerary relation. S. B. Brown, of the Kansas Conference, was again received into this Conference upon condition that he present the proper credentials. The brethren D. W. Bicksler, W. H. Stauffer, F. G. Stauffer, and Hirakawa Toyotsura of Tokio, Japan, were received into the itinerancy. The conference claimants were: N. Goeble and wife, D. Wieand and wife, C. Gingrich and wife, H. Stoetzel, J. Gross and wife, J. M. Oplinger and wife, J. Savitz and wife, Sisters Schnerr, Hesser, Myers, Schell, Heim, Haines, Sister Rhoads and one child, Sister Kempfer and one child, and three children of J. J. High. The conference claimants were instructed to present their financial circumstances in figures to their respective presiding elders and preachers in charge, who shall submit these reports to the committee on finance and recommend what in their estimation such claimants ought to have. W. Yost, Book Agent, and Treasurer of the Orphans' Home, Prof. W. E. Walz, Principal of Schuylkill Valley Seminary, and Mrs. Annie Wittenmeyer, organizer of the State Prohibition movement, addressed the Conference. J. G. Sands was re-elected statistical secretary, and S. S. Chubb, conference treasurer.

S. C. Breyfogel, A. M. Stirk, J. Bowman, G. W. Gross, and A. Kindt were appointed to prepare resolutions on Speculative Life Insurance Companies and the Mormon question. The following is an abstract of their report: *Resolved*, That we consider all speculative (commonly known as death-bed and graveyard) insurance business, a species of gambling which has already carried great harm into the communities, and to the individuals engaged in it; that we consider it a traffic of chance in the lives of those insured, which has a strong tendency to obliterate all feelings of love and respect, thus rending the strongest and tenderest ties of humanity; and that we as a Church, and especially as ministers, will do all in our power to suppress it, considering it a moral offence to be dealt with according to our Discipline.

WHEREAS, The Latter Day Saints are fostering the degrading doctrine and practice of polygamy in order to gain civil strength and power; therefore be it *Resolved*, That we consider it an offence against humanity, the purity of our civil institutions, the welfare of the church and State, and that we hail with delight the growing sentiment of the people, and the advanced action taken by the Senate and House of Representatives of these United States, and would herewith, as a

Conference, urge the speedy enactment of such laws as may be necessary to extirpate this corrupt doctrine and practice.

Father J. M. Saylor, the oldest traveling preacher in our church, having asked for a superannuated relation, his request was granted and the following adopted: *Resolved*, That we duly appreciate the past services which he has rendered to the church in the days when the itinerancy was connected with many sacrifices and privations, as well as during the later years of his ministry, and trust that the evening of a well spent life may be pleasant and full of joy in waiting for the coming of his Master.

H. Stoetzel, S. L. Wiest, W. Yost, F. Krecker, and S. Neitz were appointed to prepare greetings to our brethren in Japan. They made a report of which the following is an abstract: This Conference having received a communication from Rev. Jacob Hartzler, the esteemed Superintendent of our Japan Mission, with papers from the class and quarterly conference of Tokio, recommending Hirakawa Toyotsura and Uyeno Mikuma as proper persons to preach the gospel, we gratefully acknowledge the hand of the infinitely loving God in according to us as a Conference the honor and privilege of licensing these brethren to proclaim the message of life to a people sunken in idolatry and heathenism. It seems to us but fitting that the oldest Conference, honored with the oldest missionary society in the church, and the first to send out missionaries to proclaim the everlasting gospel to the neglected of other states and countries, should also open her ministerial ranks to receive the first fruits of our first heathen mission. In the name of our common Master we greet these newly licensed brethren, and all our missionaries, with the whole church of Japan. We also highly appreciate the successful labors of our beloved Dr. F. Krecker and family, and of sister Rachel Hudson, who has labored much for the Lord, and bid these Christian workers from our own ranks a hearty God speed.

On motion of S. C. Breyfogel the following question was inserted in the statistical blank of the Conference : "What is the entire amount of indebtedness on this field of labor ?" It was resolved that itinerant preachers and their families shall be permitted to hold their membership where they see fit. On motion of D. A. Medlar it was resolved that we hold a Conference Pentecostal meeting sometime during the fall of the year, and that Bishop R. Dubs be requested to preside. The Bishop and the presiding elders were instructed to appoint the time and place.

BOUNDARIES.

Coplay, Stemton, Whitehall, Laury's, and vicinity were formed into Lehigh Valley Mission. Wesnersville Mission was transferred to Pottsville District, to be supplied by the preachers on Kutztown Circuit. Barnesville and Schuylkill circuits were united into one field.

CHURCH AFFAIRS.

These congregations received permission to collect for church debts within certain prescribed limits as follows: Frackville, in Pottsville and Allentown districts ; Mt. Carmel, in Pottsville District ; Harrisburg, in Harrisburg District ; White Haven, in Allentown District ;

Eighth Str., Philadelphia, in such charges which the collector has not yet visited; Hellertown, in Allentown District and within the bounds of Pleasant Valley Circuit, for a new church. Bishop Bowman was authorized to collect within the bounds of the Conference for the Hamburg church. The preachers in charge of the congregations at Port Carbon and Cressona were urged to collect within their respective fields and to pay off the debts on those churches. The affairs of the churches at Port Clinton and Leesport were referred to their respective presiding elders and preachers in charge. The affairs at Bolich's church were referred to the presiding elders of the Conference, and the finances of the church at Coaldale, to the presiding elder, the preacher in charge, and the trustees of the congregation. The committee to audit the accounts of J. M. Rinker reported that the church debt at Shenandoah City had been reduced $363.80 during the past year, and that the remaining indebtedness was $2,405.54. The financial management of the past year was continued. The committee appointed to assess the traveling preachers, in order to reimburse John Alspach for the loss he sustained in the church at Scranton, reported that $400 had been paid to him. It was resolved that the resolutions of 1878, making the presiding elder of the district and the preacher in charge of East Allentown Mission responsible for the financial management of that congregation, be considered no longer in force. The Conference treasurer was instructed to refund $20.00 to B. D. Albright, the amount which he advanced to save the church at Summit Hill from the hands of the sheriff. I. E. Knerr, S. B. Brown, S. S. Chubb, J. N. Metzgar, J.

22

G. Mohn, Geo. Hendel, and Wm. Laubenstine were appointed a committee to take charge of the finances of
the Southeast Mission at Reading.   The five presiding
elders were instructed to locate the South-East Reading
Mission.   J. O. Lehr, C. J. Warmkessel, and D. Z. Kembel were appointed to dispose of the old church property
at Trevorton and to erect a new church in a more suitable locality.   The Hepler church affair on Mahantongo
Circuit was referred to the Bishop, the presiding elder,
and the preacher in charge.   C. K. Fehr, C. S. Haman,
and I. E. Knerr were instructed to visit the members at
Bernville, and if said members obligate themselves to
raise the amount which, in the judgment of the committee
they ought to raise, the preacher in charge shall have
the privilege of collecting the balance in the Reading
and Philadelphia districts.   It was resolved that a certain amount of missionary money be appropriated to
pay the interest on the church debt at Harrisburg.   The
congregation at Kulpsville received permission to give
a mortgage for $500.00 on their church property.

EDUCATION.

The long cherished desire for an educational institution in our Conference having at last been realized by
the establishment of Schuylkill Valley Seminary at
Reading, Pa., the Conference gratefully acknowledged
the goodness of God in making us to abound in this
grace.   The Conference also commended the work of
the Educational Committee in securing a gifted and
efficient faculty for the seminary, and their economic
and highly satisfactory administration of the finances
of the school.   It was agreed that an earnest effort

be made to raise at least five cents per member for educational purposes this year. Conference authorized the trustees of the seminary to elect their treasurer. The name of the institution was changed to Schuylkill Seminary and the charter presented by the trustees was adopted by a rising vote. It was resolved that if the trustees of Schuylkill Seminary should find that verbal changes may become necessary in the charter adopted by this Conference, or that changes may be necessary by legal enactments of the State, these changes shall be considered as binding as if adopted by the Conference.

The following were appointed trustees: Revs. Thos. Bowman, I. E. Knerr, J. C. Hornberger, S. S. Chubb, A. M. Stirk, W. K. Wieand, S. C. Breyfogel, and Bros. J. G. Mohn, F. G. Boas, D. Gensemer, and J. A. Medlar.

The last Sunday of June in each year was set apart as our Annual Sunday-school Day. C. S. Haman, C. K. Fehr, and D. A. Medlar were appointed examiners for five years.

SABBATH AND TEMPERANCE.

The Conference reasserted the principles of temperance maintained and observed by our church from the beginning, and recognized in suitable words the loyalty of our ministers and laymen to the principles of total abstinence. "The Temperance Lesson Book," by Dr. Richardson, was recommended to the faculty of Schuylkill Seminary to be used as a text book in the school. Former resolutions on the Sabbath were reaffirmed.

MEMORIALS.

Jacob Adams was born at Adamstown, Lancaster

Co., Pa., July 9th, 1815. He was a fine theologian, a faithful worker, and an earnest advocate of the abolition of slavery, rum, and tobacco. He was fearless and outspoken on all public questions, yet kind-hearted and sympathetic. His sun set in peace and splendor.

Abraham Shultz was born on the 5th day of January, 1810, in Milford, Bucks Co., Pa. Brother Shultz was a profound theologian and at times preached with great power and unction. His last work on earth was to pray with a family. When but a few rods from the house the summons suddenly came and the spirit took its flight to fairer climes.

FINANCE.

Receipts:

From conference collections........$1,180.66
From the Charitable Society.......   267.00
From the book establishment......   750.00
Balance from last year... ....   97.00
                                  ————$2,294.66

Expenditures:

Paid to conference claimants.............. 2,102.00

    Balance on hand................... $192.66

On motion of C. K. Fehr, it was resolved that hereafter the treasurer shall receive the dividend from the book establishment, report the same in his annual statement to this body, and pay the amount to the finance committee which they need to satisfy the claims of the conference claimants, and keep the balance, if any, in the treasury.

MISSIONARY APPROPRIATIONS.

Phila. 8th Str. Miss.	$250
Phila. 8th Str. Miss. ground rent	150
Plymouth Miss	250
Lansdale and Hatfield Miss	250
Easton Miss	225
Hall rent in South Easton	50
Allentown First Ward Miss	175
Allentown Liberty Str. Miss	275
Emaus Miss	200
Lehighton Miss	200
Mauch Chunk Miss	350
Wilkesbarre Miss	350
Lehigh Valley Miss	300
Reading 9th Str. Miss	150
Reading South East Miss	350
Reading South East Miss., house rent	150
Pottstown Miss	$ 75
Pottstown Miss., house rent	100
Lititz and Manheim Miss	75
Lancaster Mulberry Str. Miss	300
Lebanon 8th Str. Miss	300
Harrisburg Miss	200
Harrisburg—for interest	125
Williamstown Miss	50
Tremont Miss	200
Schuylkill Haven Miss	300
Frackville Miss	350
Mt. Carmel Miss	325
Wesnersville Miss	100
To F. Hoffman, for last year	100
	$6,150

APPOINTMENTS.

PHILADELPHIA DISTRICT—*J. C. Hornberger*], *P. E.*
Philadelphia 8th St.—S. C. Breyfogel.
Germantown—W. A. Leopold.
Norristown—F. P. Lehr.
Plymouth—H. M. Capp.
Trappe—U. H. Hershey.
Montgomery—G. D. Sweigert.
Lansdale and Hatfield—F. Krecker.

Milford—J. K. Fehr.
Pleasant Valley—D. Lentz and F. G. Stauffer.
Bethlehem—J. D. Woodring.
Freemansburg—C. D. Dreher.
Easton—A. M. Stirk.
Bath—W. H. Weidner and W. H. Stauffer.
Bangor—W. F. Heil.

Middle Creek—H. H. Romberger.
Wayne—J. S. Newhart.

**ALLENTOWN DISTRICT—*C. S. Haman,
P. E.***
Allentown Linden St.—B. F. Bohner.
Allentown Turner St.—J. A. Feger.
Allentown First Ward—J. C. Bliem.
Allentown Liberty St.—J. Specht.
Lehigh—E. Butz.
Emaus—B. H. Miller.
Catasauqua—R. M. Lichtenwalner.
Slatington—G. W. Gross.
Berlinsville—H. R. Yost.
Parryville—A. Kindt.
Weissport—A. A. Delong.
Lehighton—W. K. Wieand.
Mauch Chunk—D. S. Stauffer.
Hazleton—J. K. Seyfrit.
Wilkesbarre—H. D. Shultz.
Lehigh Valley—D. Yingst.

READING DISTRICT—*I. E. Knerr, P. E.*
Reading 8th St.—S. S. Chubb.
Reading Chestnut St.—J. N. Metzgar.
Reading 9th St.—S. Neitz.
Reading South East—S. B. Brown.
Friedensburg—Thomas Harper.
Pottstown—I. J. Reitz.
Birdsboro—L. N. Worman.
Adamstown—A. W. Warfel.
Fairville—A. M. Sampsel.
Lititz and Manheim—B. D. Albright.
Lancaster Water St.—J. Zern.
Lancaster Mulberry St.—J. C. Krause.
Brownstown—J. L. Werner and I. F. Heisler.
Millersville—J. W. Hoover.
Creswell—W. C. Kantner.
Conestoga—J. G. Sands.

**HARRISBURG DISTRICT—*C. K. Fehr,
P. E.***
Lebanon Chestnut St.—B. J. Smoyer.

Lebanon 8th St.—J. H. Shirey.
Myerstown—E. J. Miller.
Womelsdorf—D. W. Bicksler.
Annville—J. L. Guinther.
Mt. Nebo—R. Deisher.
Harrisburg—W. H. Rinek.
Dauphin—G. B. Fisher.
Millersburg—H. A. Neitz.
Berrysburg—A. Dilabar.
Williamstown—H. J. Glick.
Uniontown—C. S. Brown.
Tremont—F. Hoffman.
Pine Grove—D. A. Medlar.
Lykens—N. A. Barr.

**POTTSVILLE DISTRICT — *J. O. Lehr,
P. E.***
Pottsville—O. L. Saylor.
Schuylkill Haven St. Peter's—C. H. Baker.
Schuylkill Haven Trinity—F. Smith.
Cressona—C. H. Egge.
Orwigsburg—D. G. Reinhold.
Port Carbon—H. M. Wingert.
Schuylkill and Barnesville—A. Ziegenfus and W. C. Weiss.
Kutztown and Wesnersville—J. Laros and J. S. Overholser.
Tamaqua—S. T. Leopold.
Mahanoy City—W. A. Shoemaker.
Shenandoah—J. M. Rinker.
Frackville—J. R. Hensyl.
Ashland—T. A. Hess.
Mt. Carmel—J. W. Woehrle.
Shamokin—D. Z. Kembel.
Trevorton—C. J. Warmkessel.
Mahantongo—Fr. Sechrist.
Dr. F. Krecker, Missionary, Tokio, Japan.
Hirakawa Toyotsura, Missionary, Tokio, Japan.

1883.

The Forty-Fourth (76th) Annual Session.
President, Bishop Thomas Bowman.
Secretary, B. J. Smoyer.

Assistant Secretaries, S. S. Chubb, D. A. Medlar, and J. H. Shirey.

The Conference met in Christ Church, Philadelphia, Pa., on Wednesday, February 28th, 1883. The following standing committees were appointed:

On Worship,—J. C. Hornberger, S. C. Breyfogel, and W. A. Leopold; On Letters,—F. Krecker, F. Hoffman, J. M. Saylor, J. N. Metzgar, T. Harper, and J. Zern; On Quarterly Conference Minutes,—S. Neitz, F. P. Lehr, C. H. Baker, E. Butz, J. K. Fehr, J. Specht, and B. D. Albright; On Boundaries,—The Bishop and the presiding elders; On Finance,—C. H. Egge, B. H. Miller, A. W. Warfel, A. Dilabar, W. A. Shoemaker, A. A. Delong, and H. J. Glick; On Statistics,—F. Sechrist, J. G. Sands, J. A. Feger, L. N. Worman, S. T. Leopold, J. H. Shirey, and H. D. Shultz; On Education,—S. S. Chubb, W. K. Wieand, S. B. Brown, O. L. Saylor, D. A. Medlar, J. D. Woodring, U. H. Hershey, G. C. Knobel, and G. W. Gross; On Church Affairs,—B. F. Bohner, J. K. Seyfrit, D. Z. Kembel, J. L. Werner, D. Lentz, J. M. Rinker, and E. J. Miller; On Sabbath and Temperance,—A. M. Stirk, W. H. Weidner, G. D. Sweigert, D. S. Stauffer, and A. M. Sampsel; On Memorials,—J. C. Bliem, H. A. Neitz, H. R. Yost, G. W. Gross, C. S. Brown, F. Smith, and G. B. Fisher; Reportorial Committee,—O. L. Saylor, J. D. Woodring, W. F. Heil, W. H. Rinek, W. A. Shoemaker, W. C. Kantner, I. J. Reitz, J. M. Rinker, W. H. Stauffer, and F. G. Stauffer; To Audit Accounts,—W. A. Leopold, A. M. Sampsel, and F. Smith. The tellers of the Conference were H. R. Yost, F. Smith, J. W. Woehrle, J. C. Krause, and G. D. Sweigert.

J. M. Oplinger, itinerant, and W. W. Hambright and
Jeremiah Rhoads, local preachers, died during the year.
The name of the late Moses Dissinger was referred to
the committee on memorials.   A. M. Hartman with-
drew from the church.   Galen W. Hoover resigned his
office as local preacher and returned his license.   F. G.
Stauffer received credentials to unite with the Ohio
Conference.   D. W. Bicksler, J. W. Hoover, and J. D.
Woodring were ordained to the office of Elder; and W.
H. Stauffer, F. G. Stauffer, H. H. Romberger, and D.
G. Reinhold, to the office of Deacon.   The following
received license as preachers on trial: William E.
Walz, John Stermer, F. DeLong Geary, A. Benfield,
Andrew B. Saylor, M. Manshardt, William Schuler,
Alfred S. Kline, and William H. Medlar.   The brethren,
C. D. Dreher, I. F. Heisler, R. Deisher, C. J. Warm-
kessel, H. M. Wingert, J. S. Overholser, F. E. Erd-
man, and D. G. Reinhold were received into the itinerancy.   R. Deisher, of the Atlantic Conference, and F.
E. Erdman, of the Michigan Conference, were received
into this Conference as elders.   J. Derone was received
as a local preacher on trial.   R. Yeakel, J. N. Metzgar,
H. A. Neitz, J. L. Werner, and C. H. Baker were retained in the itinerancy one year.   J. Zern, T. Harper,
and J. Laros took a supernumerary relation.

The presiding elders were instructed to report all
investigations of preachers held in their respective districts.   The Conference resolved that hereafter all applicants for the itinerancy shall be received by ballot
only, and in private session.   W. Yost, Junior Publishing Agent, and Treasurer of the Orphans' Home, addressed the Conference.   Prof. W. E. Walz, Principal

of Schuylkill Seminary, delivered an address after which the Conference expressed its appreciation of the abilities which he had consecrated to that institution and congratulated the board of missions upon having secured his services as a missionary of the church to Japan. The following were elected delegates to the General Conference : C. K. Fehr, C. S. Haman, J. C. Hornberger, J. O. Lehr, I. E. Knerr, S. Neitz, B. J. Smoyer, and S. S. Chubb ; alternates, A. M. Stirk, S. C. Breyfogel, and B. F. Bohner.   W. W. Orwig's Book of Sermons was recommended to the favorable consideration of the members of Conference.

It was resolved that hereafter basket collections only shall be lifted at our annual Conference missionary meetings. Two additional questions were inserted into the annual statistical blank : "What is the amount contributed on this field of labor toward the support of its preacher or preachers?" and "What is the amount contributed on this field of labor toward the support of the presiding elder ?"

BOUNDARIES.

Norristown was changed to a mission. Quakertown was detached from Pleasant Valley Circuit and with the surrounding country constituted a mission. Williams Township was taken from Pleasant Valley Circuit, South Easton Class from Easton, and the two formed into a mission. Miller's class was transferred from Pleasant Valley Circuit to Fremansburg Station. White Haven was detached from Wilkesbarre and with the surrounding country called White Haven Mission. Howertown was taken from Berlinsville Circuit and annexed to Lehigh Valley Mission. Trevorton was changed to a mission. Hamburg and Shoemakersville were taken from Kutztown Circuit and annexed to Wesnersville Mission. Barnesville was attached to Tamaqua, and Locust Valley to Mahanoy City. Orwigsburg was constituted a mission. Tower City and Reiner City were detached from Tremont and annexed to Lykens Circuit. Coaldale and Lansford were transferred from Schuylkill Circuit to Port Carbon.

CHURCH AFFAIRS.

The trustees of the Miller's and Roxburg churches, Bath Circuit, received permission to appropriate the money realized from the sale of the parsonage of Northampton Circuit to erect a new church at Miller's, and to repair the church at Roxburg. W. C. Weiss having saved our church at Coaldale from financial disaster, the Conference gratefully acknowledged his services and accepted his kind offer to secure, if possible, the remaining debt of $210. These congregations received permission to collect, as follows: Port Clinton, on Schuylkill and Kutztown circuits; Frackville, in the uncanvassed portions of Pottsville and Allentown districts; Myerstown, in Harrisburg District, for a church debt of $1,000.00; Manheim, in Reading District, for a new church; and Leesport, in Philadelphia District, for a debt of $985.25, provided the presiding elder and the preacher in charge find that the members at Leesport, Berne, and Centreport will obligate themselves to raise a just portion of the amount. The congregation at Wilkesbarre received permission to give a mortgage of $1,000 on a house and lot about to be purchased for a parsonage. The Conference recommended a continuation of last year's committee and of the same financial arrangement at Shenandoah City. Inasmuch as the congregation at Manheim proposed to build a Seybert Memorial Church, the Conference, on motion of I. E. Knerr, resolved to encourage this praiseworthy project by word and deed, and granted them permission to sell their old church property and to apply the proceeds towards the new church. The Conference extended an invitation to all the friends of the sainted Bishop Seybert, throughout the church, to participate in the erection of this memorial. In view of the fact that the church at Shamokin was burdened with a debt of $650, and in need of repairs, the congregation was exempted from outside collectors. The urgent financial needs of the new church at Trevorton were recommended to the favorable consideration of the Church Building Society, and the trustees were instructed to give a first mortgage to D. Z. Kembel, Jos. Kline, Wm. Knapp, and C. J. Warmkessel as security for money advanced by these brethren. It was resolved that hereafter such committees to whom the erection of church edifices is entrusted, shall be duly instructed as to the manner of building and the amount of money to be invested. The auditing committee reported that they had found the accounts of S. C. Breyfogel, collector for the Philadelphia Eighth Street church, correct, and that the entire debt of ten thousand dollars was paid.

EDUCATION.

The presiding elders were instructed to preach a sermon on the subject of education at each appointment, and to collect an amount equal to at least $10 for every charge on their respective districts for educational purposes. The Conference expressed its approbation of the prudent and economical administration of the finances of Schuylkill Seminary, the success of the trustees, and the efficiency of the faculty. It was mutually agreed that at least five cents per member be raised on the various charges for the support of the seminary.

WHEREAS, The citizens of Millersburg, Pa., and Fredericksburg, Pa., have submitted liberal financial offers and urgent invitations for the location of the seminary in their midst; therefore be it

Resolved, That we highly appreciate these generous offers, and that the trustees of Schuylkill Seminary are hereby directed to visit the several proposed localities and such others as may be brought to their notice, during the year, to determine the advantages and disadvantages thereof, and report to the Conference at its next session. The following were elected trustees of the seminary: Revs. I. E. Knerr, T. Bowman, and C. S. Haman, and Messrs. J. G. Mohn and H. G. Moyer for three years; Revs. J. C. Hornberger and S. S. Chubb, and Mr. J. R. Carl for two years; Revs. A. M. Stirk and S. C. Breyfogel, and Mr. P. Kellmer for one year. C. S. Haman, J. O. Lehr, and W. K. Wieand were appointed a visiting committee to attend the commencement exercises of Schuylkill Seminary. B. J. Smoyer, A. M. Stirk, and J. K. Knerr were elected examiners of junior preachers for five years. The necessary average grade in the examination of applicants for license was reduced from 60 to 50.

MEMORIALS.

Moses Dissinger, late of the Kansas Conference, was an itinerant preacher of this Conference for many years. He was an extraordinary man, possessing more than ordinary physical energy and a peculiar intellectual originality which made him a powerful preacher. His memory is held dear.

J. M. Oplinger was converted to God and united with the Evangelical Association at an early age. He was an earnest worker in God's vineyard, a man of holy boldness, and of unshaken firmness.

Jeremiah Rhoads, a local preacher, was a faithful son of the gospel, and an old and valiant champion of the cross.

W. W. Hambright, a son of Father Davis Hambright, was a useful local preacher of the Conference. He was taken away in the prime of his life and usefulness.

SABBATH AND TEMPERANCE.

Resolved, That we give our united and unqualified support to the civil authorities in their laudable efforts to suppress all violations of the Sabbath laws, and that we unanimously disapprove of all trafficking at campmeetings on Sunday.

Resolved, That we will continue to sow the seeds of total abstinence in our Sunday-schools and families by the circulation of healthful temperance literature.

FINANCE.

Receipts:

Balance on hand	$156.01
From conference collections	966.19
From the book establishment	800.00
From the Charitable Society	257.85
	$2,180.05

Expenditures:

Paid to conference claimants.......$2,163.00
Paid for conference expenses.......   14.72
———$2,177.72

Balance in treasury................. $2.33

MISSIONARY APPROPRIATIONS.

Philadelphia Eighth Street...........$225	Pottstown and Phœnixville..........$175
Plymouth.......... 300	Pottstown, house rent 100
Norristown........ 100	Lititz and Manheim.. 75
Quakertown 75	Lancaster........... 300
Easton............. 275	Lebanon............ 250
Sth. Easton and Williams Township... 200	Harrisburg......... 200
Lansdale and Hatfield 250	Harrisburg, interest. 60
Allentown 1st Ward. 160	Williamstown....... 75
do. Liberty St. 300	Tremont........... 200
Emans............. 200	Schuylkill Haven... 350
Lehighton.......... 200	Frackville........ 50
Mauch Chunk...... 225	Mt. Carmel........ 325
Wilkesbarre........ 350	Trevorton.......... 300
Lehigh Valley...... 225	Orwigsburg........ 200
White Haven....... 175	Wesnersville........ 350
Reading 9th Street.. 200	$6,770

APPOINTMENTS.

PHILADELPHIA DISTRICT—*J. C. Hornberger*, P. E.
Philadelphia 8th St.—J. D. Woodring.
Germantown—W. A. Leopold.
Norristown—F. P. Lehr.
Plymouth—H. M. Capp.
Trappe—U. H. Hershey.
Montgomery—J. S. Newhart.
Milford—J. K. Fehr.

Lansdale and Hatfield—F. Krecker.
Quakertown—F. D. Geary.
Pleasant Valley—J. K. Seyfrit.
Bethlehem—O. L. Saylor.
Freemansburg—C. D. Dreher.
Easton—J. G. Sands.
South Easton and Williams Tp.—W. H. Stauffer.
Bath—W. H. Weidner and W. Schuler.

Bangor—W. F. Heil.
Middle Creek—H. H. Romberger.
Wayne—D. G. Reinhold.

ALLENTOWN DISTRICT—*C. S. Haman,
P. E.*
Allentown Linden St.—B. F. Bohner.
Allentown Turner St.—J. A. Feger.
Allentown First Ward—J. C. Bliem.
Allentown Liberty St.—J. Specht.
Lehigh—A. W. Warfel.
Emaus—B. H. Miller.
Catasauqua—R. M. Lichtenwaluer.
Lehigh Valley—D. Yingst.
Slatington—G. W. Gross.
Berlinsville—F. E. Erdman.
Parryville—A. Kindt.
Weissport—A. A. Delong.
Lehighton—W. K. Wieand.
Mauch Chunk—H. R. Yost.
Hazleton—D. S. Stauffer.
White Haven—A. S. Kline.
Wilkesbarre—J. W. Woehrle.

READING DISTRICT—*I. E. Knerr, P. E.*
Reading 8th St.—S. S. Chubb.
Reading Chestnut St.—S. C. Breyfogel.
Reading 9th St.—S. Neitz.
Reading South East—To be supplied.
Friedensburg—H. J. Glick.
Pottstown—J. J. Reitz and one to be
supplied.
Birdsboro—J. R. Hashinger.
Adamstown—A. Dilabar.
Fairville—W. C. Kantner.
Lititz and Manheim—B. D. Albright.
Lancaster Water St.—E. Butz.
Lancaster Mulberry St.—L. N. Wor-
man.
Brownstown—A. Ziegenfus and A. B.
Saylor.

Millersville—J. W. Hoover.
Creswell—T. A. Hess.
Conestoga—J. C. Krause.

HARRISBURG DISTRICT—*C. K. Fehr,
P. E.*
Lebanon Chestnut St.—B. J. Smoyer.
Lebanon 8th St.—J. M. Rinker.
Myerstown—E. J. Miller.
Womelsdorf—D. W. Bicksler.
Annville—J. L. Guinther.
Mt. Nebo—R. Deisher.
Harrisburg—W. H. Rinek.
Dauphin—G. B. Fisher.
Millersburg—D. A. Medlar.
Berrysburg—G. D. Sweigert.
Williamstown—A. M. Sampsel.
Uniontown—C. S. Brown.
Tremont—F. Hoffman.
Pine Grove—S. B. Brown.
Lykens—N. A. Barr.

POTTSVILLE DISTRICT—*J. O. Lehr, P.E.*
Pottsville—J. H. Shirey.
Schuylkill Haven St. Peters—A. M.
Stirk.
Schuylkill Haven Trinity—F. Smith.
Cressona—C. H. Egge.
Orwigsburg—T. Harper.
Port Carbon—H. M. Wingert.
Schuylkill—J. Savitz.
Tamaqua—S. T. Leopold.
Mahanoy City—W. A. Shoemaker.
Shenandoah—H. D. Shultz.
Frackville—J. R. Hensyl.
Ashland—I. E. Zimmerman.
Mt. Carmel—J. S. Overholser.
Shamokin—D. Z. Kembel.
Trevorton—C. J. Warmkessel.
Mahantongo—F. Sechrist.
Kutztown—J. L. Werner.
Wesnersville—D. Lentz.

1883.

The General Conference.

Presidents, Bishops J. J. Esher, R. Dubs, and T.
Bowman.

Secretary, W. Horn.

Assistant Secretaries, R. Mott, G. Heinmiller, S. P. Spreng, and U. F. Swengel.

The delegates of the General Conference assembled in the Linden Street Evangelical church, Allentown, Pa., Oct. 4th, 1883.* Eighty-seven delegates, representing twenty-two annual conferences, and nine *ex-officio* delegates were in attendance. A. M. Stirk, alternate, took the seat of S. Neitz, a delegate of the East Pa. Conference, who was absent on account of sickness. S. C. Breyfogel and B. F. Bohner, alternate delegates of the East Pa. Conference, served temporarily and at different times as alternates for S. S. Chubb. The chairman announced the recent decease of J. G. Zinser, and Bishop Bowman read a telegram announcing the death of J. M. Sindlinger.

Father H. Stoetzel was invited to deliver an address on the origin of the Evangelical Association, inasmuch as the General Conference was holding its daily sessions near the birthplace and in the very cradle of the church. This address was of the highest interest. The women of our church having presented a petition, asking permission to organize a Woman's Missionary Society of the Evangelical Association, the General Conference granted the petition upon certain prescribed conditions. The Conference recommended the publication of a monthly missionary paper in pamphlet form. Harrisburg, Pa., was transferred from the Atlantic Conference to the East Pa. Conference. The presiding bishop and the presiding elder of Harrisburg District were instructed to supply North Mission, Harrisburg,

*See Preface on page 98.

with a preacher. The board of publication was instructed to publish a new English family magazine as soon as sixteen hundred subscribers have been secured. Appropriate memorial resolutions upon the death of Dr. F. Krecker, late missionary to Japan, were adopted. An expression of sympathy was sent to S. Neitz in his severe bodily affliction.

The elections resulted as follows: Bishops, J. J. Esher, R. Dubs, and T. Bowman; publishing agents, M. Lauer and W. Yost; editor of the *Christliche Botschafter*, W. Horn; editor of the *Evangelical Messenger*, H. B. Hartzler; editor of the *Evangelische Magazine* and German Sunday-school Literature, C. A. Thomas; editor of the *Living Epistle* and English Sunday-school Literature, P. W. Raidabaugh; corresponding secretary of the Missionary Society, S. Heininger; treasurer of the Missionary Society, S. L. Wiest; book steward of the publishing house in Germany, J. Walz; editor of the *Evangelische Botschafter* and Sunday-school Literature of Germany, G. Fuessle; superintendent of the Ebenezer Orphan Institute, E. Kohr. S. P. Spreng was elected fraternal delegate to the General Conference of the United Brethren in Christ. C. S. Haman was elected to represent the East Pa. Conference in the board of publication.

The following were the statistics of the Evangelical Association: Itinerant preachers, 1,053; local preachers, 618; total membership, 120,231; church buildings, 1,622 1-6; estimated value, $3,577,883; parsonages, 501; estimated value, $507,205; Sunday-schools, 2,131; officers and teachers, 22,646; scholars, 135,795; catechetical classes, 641; catechumens, 8,233.

23

The Forty-Fifth (77th) Annual Session.

President, Bishop J. J. Esher.

Secretary, S. C. Breyfogel.

Assistant Secretaries, D. A. Medlar, J. H. Shirey, and G. W. Gross.

The East Pa. Conference met in annual session in the Emanuel (Chestnut St.) Evangelical church at Lebanon, Pa., on Wednesday, February 27th, 1884. The president announced the following standing committees:

On Worship,—C. K. Fehr, B. J. Smoyer, J. M. Rinker, and J. L. Guinther; On Letters,—E. Butz, T. Harper, F. P. Lehr, J. L. Werner, J. Specht, and G. B. Fisher; On Quarterly Conference Records,—S. S. Chubb, F. Sechrist, J. C. Bliem, A. Ziegenfus, L. N. Worman, U. H. Hershey, C. S. Brown, and G. D. Sweigert; On Boundaries,—The Bishop and the presiding elders; On Finance,—A. M. Stirk, B. F. Bohner, D. Z. Kembel, S. T. Leopold, A. M. Sampsel, F. Smith, and N. A. Barr; On Statistics,—J. A. Feger, J. G. Sands, E. J. Miller, A. Dilabar, H. R. Yost, J. W. Hoover, and H. H. Romberger; On Education,—S. B. Brown, J. K. Seyfrit, O. L. Saylor, J. K. Knerr, C. H. Egge, W. C. Kantner, W. A. Leopold, H. J. Glick, J. D. Woodring, and G. C. Knoble; On Church Affairs,—A. Kindt, W. H. Weidner, D. Lentz, I. J. Reitz, H. D. Shultz, B. D. Albright, D. W. Bicksler, and J. C. Krause; On Sabbath and Temperance,—J. N. Metzgar, A. W. Warfel, J. K. Fehr, A. A. Delong, J. W. Woehrle, J. R. Hensyl, and H. M. Capp; On Memorials,—F. Krecker, R. Deisher, B. H. Miller, J. S. Newhart, D. S. Stauffer, W. A. Shoemaker, and T. A. Hess; Reportorial Committee,—W. K. Wieand, W. A. Leopold, W. H. Rinck, W. F. Heil, W. C. Kantner, and F. E. Erdman; To Audit Accounts,—I. J. Reitz, S. T. Leopold, and J. M. Rinker; Tellers,—J. R. Hensyl, H. M. Capp, C. D. Dreher, and H. A. Neitz. W. K. Wieand was appointed to report the proceedings for the *Christliche Botschafter.*

W. Nicholaus, a local preacher, resigned his license, and A. M. Manshardt, a local preacher, withdrew from the church. Joseph Gross, Dr. Fred. Krecker, J. B. Cole, and Samuel Miesse died during the past year. Reuben Yeakel and J. R. Hashinger received credentials. J. C. Hornberger was re-elected, and B. J. Smoyer and A. M. Stirk were newly elected, to the office of Presiding Elder. J. C. Krause, H. M. Capp, W. H. Rinek, J. L. Guinther, W. F. Heil, and Hirakawa Toyotsura were elected to the office of Elder; and C. D. Dreher, H. M. Wingert, I. F. Heisler, J. S. Overholser, and C. J. Warmkessel, to the office of Deacon. The following were licensed as preachers on trial: E. B. Manger, Horace A. Smith, Charles C. Speicher, Cyrus M. Rothermel, William W. Yost, John P. Miller, Augustus H. Snyder, G. Holzapfel, and Irvin U. Royer. The name of M. Steckley was added to the list of local deacons. M. W. Harris was reinstated as local elder, and J. R. Hensyl took a supernumerary relation. The relation of J. Savitz was changed from supernumerary to active. R. M. Lichtenwalner, C. H. Baker, J. L. Werner, S. Neitz, H. A. Neitz, and H. M. Capp were retained in the itinerancy one year without an appointment. A. B. Saylor, F. D. Geary, J. Stermer,

W. Schuler, and A. S. Kline were received into the
itinerancy. The supernumerary preachers were: Sen-
eca Breyfogel, Isaac Hess, S. Ely, J. Fry, Jas. Bow-
man, D. Yingst, J. Zern, T. Harper, J. Laros, and J.
R. Hensyl; the superannuated, N. Goebel, D. Wieand,
C. Gingrich, II. Stoetzel, J. K. Knerr, and J. M. Say-
lor. The conference claimants were: N. Goebel and
wife, D. Wieand and wife, C. Gingrich and wife, II.
Stoetzel, J. M. Saylor and wife, J. Gross and wife, and
Sisters Schnerr, Rhoads, Meyers, Shell, Shultz, and
Heim, Sister Kempfer and one child, one child of J.
Adams, and two children of J. J. High.

The preachers were instructed to report the salaries
received on their respective fields of labor hereafter. A
letter from W. E. Walz, Missionary in Tokio, Japan,
was read, to which the secretaries were instructed to
send an answer. II. R. Yost was elected statistical
secretary, and S. S. Chubb, re-elected Conference treasurer. W. Yost, Junior Publisher, and J. F. Crowell,
Principal of Schuylkill Seminary, addressed the Conference. The brethren pledged their continued prayers
and support to the publishing interests of the church.
On motion of G. W. Gross the members of Conference,
and our people in general, were cautioned to be careful
in their recognition of strangers as evangelists. The
Conference expressed profound sympathy with brother
S. Neitz, who had been severely stricken in health during the past year.

BOUNDARIES.

Miller's class was taken from Freemansburg and annexed to Pleasant Valley Circuit. Schnecksville was
transferred from Lehigh Circuit to Lehigh Valley Mis-

sion. Millersville, New Danville, and vicinity were organized into Millersville Mission. Mt. Joy, Reich's class, and Milton Grove were taken from Millersville Circuit and called Mt. Joy Mission. The name of Fairville Station was changed to Terre Hill. Coaldale and Lansford were detached from Port Carbon and constituted a mission. Ringtown was taken from Shenandoah Station and called Ringtown Station. The church affairs at Harrisburg were referred to a committee, consisting of the presiding elder of the district, the preacher in charge of Harrisburg Mission, C. K. Fehr, and one member of each of the congregations at Harrisburg. The trustees of both churches were authorized, if so decided by this committee, to sell either or both church properties and to apply the proceeds of such sale to the erection of a new church. Annville and Dauphin circuits were constituted missions.

CHURCH AFFAIRS.

The trustees of the church at Shenandoah received permission to give a mortgage of $350.00 in place of two old mortgages of $500.00. During the past year the debt upon this church was reduced $821.00, leaving an indebtedness of $1,768.00. The church at Leesport being burdened with a debt of between five and six hundred dollars, the Church Building Society was advised to grant a loan of $300.00 at the end of the year, provided the congregation raise the balance of the entire claim.

These congregations received permission to collect money within certain prescribed limits, as follows: Pen Argyl, in Philadelphia and Allentown districts for a new church; South Easton, in Philadelphia District for a new church; Manheim, Seybert Memorial, in Reading District; Lancaster English Mission, $600 in Reading District toward liquidating a debt of $1,600; Myerstown, in Harrisburg District; Hamburg, throughout the bounds of the Conference. The trustees of Easton Mission were authorized to give an additional mortgage for $300, thus increasing their debt to $2,300. The church at Irish Valley, Trevorton Circuit, being in a very dilapidated condition and without trustees or members, the preacher in charge of the circuit was instructed to have trustees elected from the Trevorton class, who shall be empowered to dispose of the church building and to apply the proceeds to the improvement of the cemetery connected with the same. The trustees at Ashland were authorized to sell their church property and to apply the proceeds to the erection of a new church in a more suitable locality. The General Conference having ordered that a collection be taken in all our churches for the erection and completion of a Seybert Memorial Church at Manheim, Pa., the brethren were urgently requested to act at once and to forward their collections.

On motion of J. C. Hornberger, the following was adopted: WHEREAS, The Church Building Society of this Conference has loaned the Philadelphia 8th St. Mission $3,000; AND WHEREAS, Said loan was accepted by the trustees of the congregation in lieu of the same amount which had been promised them by the East Pennsylvania Conference; AND WHEREAS, It would in our opinion be prejudicial to our interests as a Conference and injurious to the above charge to insist upon the payment of said amount; therefore, be it *Resolved*, That the East Pennsylvania Conference assume said debt, and that the debt to the Church Building Fund be paid by such annual appropriations from the Missionary Treasury as the Conference may feel able to make until the whole is cancelled.

The quarterly conference of Germantown Station unanimously petitioned the annual conference to order English preaching one Sunday morning of each month; the appeal was granted.

EDUCATION.

Col. J. H. Lick, of Fredericksburg, Lebanon Co., having made a liberal offer to the trustees of Schuylkill Seminary upon the conditions that the institution be transferred to Fredericksburg and that the seminary be developed into a college as soon as possible, the board of trustees presented the following which was adopted: WHEREAS, It is necessary to raise $7,000 in order to meet the offer of Col. J. H. Lick for the erection of suitable college buildings and the appropriate furnishing of the same, and an additional $1,500 in order to defray the current school expenses of the year; therefore, be it *Resolved*, 1st, That we expect the citizens of Fredericksburg to furnish $2,000 of this amount. 2d, That we most cordially urge the ministers of the East Pa. Conference to raise the sum of $2,000 as their personal contributions. 3d, That the balance be secured by an apportionment made upon the different fields of labor, the presiding elders and the preachers in charge to be held jointly responsible for the amount; the apportionments and subscriptions to be paid in one

year in four installments. The preachers subscribed
$2,225.00. The board of trustees were instructed to
secure the services of a good architect and to appoint a
building committee. The Conference gave expression
in suitable words to its appreciation of Col. J. H. Lick's
generous proposal. The last Sunday in September
was appointed as Seminary Day. S. C. Breyfogel
and S. B. Brown were appointed to visit the Atlantic
Conference and enlist their co-operation in the interests
of Schuylkill Seminary. A. M. Stirk, S. C. Breyfogel,
and P. Kellmer were re-elected trustees of the seminary for three years. C. K. Fehr, J. O. Lehr, and W.
K. Wieand were re-appointed a visiting committee to
attend the closing exercises.

It was resolved that the examinations of junior
preachers of the first and third years may be held orally
at the option of the examiners. S. C. Breyfogel, I. E.
Knerr, and J. C. Hornberger were re-appointed examiners. J. G. Mohn, Treasurer of Schuylkill Seminary,
reported that the receipts of that institution during the
year were $2,817.82, and the expenditures, $1,938.30.

MEMORIALS.

Dr. Frederick Krecker, Jr., was converted to God at
the early age of eight years. Thirteen years of his life
were devoted to the practice of medicine, during which
time he was an active and successful worker in the
church and Sunday-school. In 1876 he was licensed to
preach the gospel and was appointed by the board of
missions as a missionary to Japan, arriving in that country in the month of October of the same year. He and
his companion devoted themselves to their calling with

true heroism and labored in the Spirit of the Lord with good success. Joseph Gross was converted in the year 1837 and united with our church as soon as it had gained a foothold in the city of Allentown. He was licensed to preach in 1841. Brother Gross was the author of several books.

James B. Cole, a faithful local preacher, an earnest Sunday-school worker, and a strong advocate of temperance, died in peace at Allentown. Samuel Miesse was converted in early life and labored as an itinerant preacher for a number of years. His last words were "Jesus, bless my soul."

SABBATH AND TEMPERANCE.

The Conference resolved to make more determined efforts to maintain the sanctity of the Sabbath and to give united and unqualified support to all civil authorities in their laudable efforts to suppress every violation of the Sabbath laws.

Temperance campmeetings and the distribution of temperance literature were commended as efficient means to educate the people on this subject. Constitutional prohibition for the state and nation were re-affirmed.

FINANCE.

Receipts:

Balance from last year	$ 2.03
From the Charitable Society	213.00
From the book establishment	800.00
Total	$1,015.03

Expenditures:

To Conference claimants and for expenses	$ 943.83
Balance in treasury	$ 71.20

MISSIONARY APPROPRIATIONS.

Phila., 8th Street..$175.00	Lancaster.......$300.00
Philadelphia...... 250.00	Lebanon........ 250.00
Norristown...... 100.00	Harrisburg....... 250.00
Plymouth........ 325.00	Harrisburg, int... 60.00
Lansdale and Hat-	Mount Joy....... 250.00
field.......... 250.00	Trevorton....... 300.00
Quakertown..... 200.00	Trevorton....... 160.79
Easton.......... 275.00	Williamstown.... 75.00
South Easton..... 350.00	Tremont........ 200.00
Allentown, 1st	Schuylkill Haven. 350.00
Ward......... 225.00	Frackville....... 350.00
Allentown, Lib-	Mt. Carmel..... 375.00
erty Street..... 300.00	Orwigsburg...... 200.00
Emaus.......... 200.00	Wesnersville..... 300.00
Lehighton....... 250.00	Annville........ 150.00
Mauch Chunk.... 225.00	Dauphin........ 100.00
Wilkesbarre...... 350.00	Coaldale........ 200.00
White Haven..... 175.00	Ashland........ 300.00
Lehigh Valley.... 400.00	F. Hoffman, for last
Reading, 9th St... 200.00	year.......... 75.00
Pottstown and	———
Phœnixville.... 175.00	Total......$8,745.79
Lititz and Manheim 75.00	

APPOINTMENTS.

PHILADELPHIA DISTRICT—*C. K. Fehr*, *P. E.*
Philadelphia 8th St.—J. D. Woodring.
Germantown—W. A. Leopold.
Norristown—F. P. Lehr.
Plymouth—C. H. Hershey.
Trappe—W. H. Rinck.
Montgomery—J. S. Newhart.
Milford—J. K. Fehr.
Lansdale and Hatfield—G. C. Knobel.

Quakertown—F. Krecker.
Pleasant Valley—J. K. Seyfrit.
Bethlehem—O. L. Saylor.
Freemansburg—I. U. Royer.
Easton—J. G. Sands.
South Easton and Williamstown—W. H. Stauffer.
Bath—R. Deisher and W. Schuler.
Bangor—W. F. Heil.
Middle Creek—C. C. Speicher.

Wayne—D. G. Reinhold and H. A. Smith.

ALLENTOWN DISTRICT—C. S. Haman, P. E.

Allentown Linden St.—J. C. Bliem.
Allentown Turner St.—J. W. Hoover.
Allentown First Ward—J. O. Lehr.
Allentown Liberty St.—J. Specht.
Lehigh Circuit—A. W. Warfel.
Emaus—B. H. Miller.
Catasauqua—B. F. Bohner.
Lehigh Valley—D. Lentz.
Slatington—G. W. Gross.
Berlinsville—F. E. Erdman.
Parryville—H. M. Wingert.
Weissport—A. A. Delong.
Lehighton—S. S. Chubb.
Mauch Chunk—H. R. Yost.
Hazleton—D. S. Stauffer.
White Haven—A. S. Kline.
Wilkesbarre—J. W. Woehrle.

READING DISTRICT—J. C. Hornberger, P. E.

Reading 8th St.—W. K. Wieand.
Reading Chestnut St.—S. C. Breyfogel.
Reading 9th St.—I. J. Reitz.
Friedensburg—H. J. Glick.
Pottstown and Phoenixville—I. F. Heisler and F. D. Geary.
Birdsboro—C. D. Dreher.
Adamstown—A. Dilabar.
Terre Hill—W. C. Kantner.
Conestoga—J. C. Krause.
Lititz and Manheim—B. D. Albright.
Brownstown—A. Ziegenfus and C. Rothermel.
Lancaster Water St.—E. Butz.
Lancaster Mulberry St.—L. N. Worman.
Millersville—A. B. Saylor.
Creswell—T. A. Hess.

HARRISBURG DISTRICT—A. M. Stirk, P. E.

Lebanon Chestnut St.—I. E. Knerr.
Lebanon 8th St.—J. A. Feger.
Myerstown—E. J. Miller.
Womelsdorf—J. L. Guinther and F. Hoffman.
Annville—A. Kindt.
Mt. Nebo—H. H. Romberger.
Mt. Joy—D. W. Bicksler.
Harrisburg—J. N. Metzgar.
Dauphin—G. B. Fisher.
Millersburg—D. A. Medlar.
Berrysburg—G. D. Sweigert.
Uniontown—C. S. Brown.
Trevorton—C. Warmkessel.
Lykens—J. S. Overholser.
Williamstown—A. M. Sampsel.
Tremont—To be supplied.
Pine Grove—S. B. Brown.

POTTSVILLE DISTRICT—B. J. Smoyer, P. E.

Pottsville—J. H. Shirey.
Schuylkill Haven St. Peter's—J. M. Rinker.
Schuylkill Haven Trinity—F. Smith.
Cressona—C. H. Egge.
Orwigsburg—T. Harper.
Port Carbon—J. P. Miller.
Schuylkill Circuit—J. Savitz.
Kutztown—W. H. Weidner and J. Sterner.
Coaldale and Lansford—A. H. Snyder.
Tamaqua—S. T. Leopold.
Mahanoy City—W. A. Shoemaker.
Shenandoah City—H. D. Shultz.
Ringtown—To be supplied.
Frackville—N. A. Barr.
Ashland—I. E. Zimmerman.
Mt. Carmel—J. R. Hensyl.
Shamokin—D. Z. Kembel.
Mahantongo—F. Sechrist.

1885.

The Forty-Sixth (78th) Annual Session.

President, Bishop R. Dubs.
Secretary, S. C. Breyfogel.

Assistant Secretaries, D. A. Medlar, J. II. Shirey, and G. W. Gross.

The members of the Conference assembled in the Emanuel Evangelical church at Catasauqua, Pa., on Wednesday, February 25th, 1885. The president appointed the following standing committees:

On Worship,—C. S. Haman and B. F. Bohner; On Letters,—E. Butz, J. Specht, F. Sechrist, T. Harper, F. P. Lehr, J. L. Werner, G. B. Fisher, A. Ziegenfus, J. S. Newhart, and W. II. Rinek; On Quarterly Conference Records,—S. B. Brown, J. C. Bliem, W. F. Heil, W. C. Kantner, W. A. Shoemaker, E. J. Miller, W. II. Weidner, A. W. Warfel, and B. II. Miller; On Education,—I. E. Knerr, S. S. Chubb, D. A. Medlar, B. D. Albright, J. II. Shirey, O. L. Saylor, U. II. Hershey, S. T. Leopold, and G. C. Knobel; On Boundaries,—The Bishop and the presiding elders; On Finance,—W. K. Wieand, D. Z. Kembel, C. S. Brown, R. Deisher, J. M. Rinker, A. Dilabar, G. W. Gross, F. Smith, and I. J. Reitz; On Church Affairs,—S. S. Chubb, J. K. Seyfrit, A. Kindt, II. D. Shultz, II. J. Glick, J. K. Knerr, C. II. Egge, J. K. Fehr, and D. Lentz; On Statistics,—J. A. Feger, H. R. Yost, J. G. Sands, J. L. Guinther, N. A. Barr, J. S. Overholser, T. A. Hess, J. W. Hoover, and J. R. Hensyl; On Sabbath and Temperance,—J. N. Metzgar, B. F. Bohner, W. A. Leopold, A. M. Sampsel, F. E. Erdman, D. W. Bicksler, D. S. Stauffer, II. D. Shultz, and J. C. Krause; On Memorials,—F. Krecker, J. O. Lehr, F. Hoffman, J. Savitz, G. D. Sweigert, J. W. Woehrle, W. II. Stauffer, A. A. Delong, and II. II. Romberger; Reportorial Committee,—O. L. Saylor, C. D. Dreher, J.

R. Hensyl, W. Schuler, D. W. Bicksler, L. N. Worman, I. F. Heisler, and F. E. Erdman; To Audit Accounts,—H. D. Shultz, W. F. Heil, and W. H. Rinck. G. C. Knobel was appointed to report the proceedings for the *Christliche Botschafter*, and D. A. Medlar for the *Evangelical Messenger*.

A. H. Overholt, D. Hambright, and Seneca Breyfogel died during the past year. A. D. Light received credentials. E. B. Manger withdrew from the church during the past year. C. H. Baker took a superannuated and J. R. Hensyl, an active relation. Isaac Hess, R. M. Lichtenwalner, S. Neitz, D. S. Stauffer, J. N. Metzgar, J. L. Werner, H. M. Capp, and J. O. Lehr were retained in the itinerancy one year without an appointment. H. H. Romberger, D. G. Reinhold, and W. H. Stauffer were ordained to the office of Elder; and J. Sterner, F. D. Geary, A. B. Saylor, A. S. Kline, W. Schuler, and W. E. Walz, missionary to Japan, to the office of Deacon. The following received license as preachers on trial: Edwin R. Scip, D. J. Ebert, Benjamin C. Krupp, Alfred J. Brunner, Stephen Bantz, William J. Johnson, Albert E. Williams, W. W. Fetter, David S. Manning, and A. H. Doerstler. The brethren A. Krecker, of the Oregon Conference, and J. M. Longsdorf, of the Central Pa. Conference, were received into this Conference in the same relation which they sustained to the above named conferences, upon condition that their credentials be presented as soon as possible. A. F. Leopold was received into this Conference in the same relation which he sustained to the Atlantic Conference. A. Krecker, G. C. Knobel, J. M. Longsdorf, J. P. Miller, A. H. Snyder, W. E.

Walz, and I. U. Royer were received into the itinerancy.
The supernumerary preachers were: S. Ely, J. Fry, J.
Bowman, D. Yingst, J. Zern, T. Harper, and J. Laros.
The superannuated preachers and conference claim-
ants were: N. Goebel and wife, D. Wieand and wife,
C. Gingrich and wife, J. M. Saylor and wife, J. K.
Knerr and wife, C. H. Baker and wife, F. Hoffman and
wife, H. Stoetzel, Sisters Schnerr, Rhoads, Myers, Kemp-
fer, Gross, Schell, Heim, Sister Adams and one child, and
one child of J. J. High.

W. Yost, junior publisher, addressed the Conference
in the interests of our publishing house. The Conference adopted resolutions of sympathy with the brethren,
S. Neitz, D. S. Stauffer, and H. M. Wingert, who were
suffering under severe bodily affliction. On motion of
W. K. Wieand the president and the secretary of the
Conference were instructed to sign a petition addressed
to the Legislature of Pennsylvania, earnestly requesting
that honorable body to approve a bill now on file in the
House of Representatives and having reference to a
marriage license law. The question, "What is the
amount contributed for house rent or interest on parsonage?" was inserted into the Annual Conference statistical form. H. R. Yost was elected statistical secretary and S. S. Chubb was re-elected Conference treasurer. On motion of H. D. Shultz it was resolved that
the brethren appointed by the Conference to collect for
churches shall be required to present to the auditing
committee all books and papers used in the canvass.
The following was adopted: It is our opinion that no
meetings of any kind, except the usual regular divine
services, shall be held in any of our churches, except by

consent of the presiding elder, the preacher in charge, and the trustees.

Some of our unordained preachers having of late taken upon themselves the right to perform marriage ceremonies and administer the sacrament of holy baptism, the Conference declared such actions a violation of the spirit of our church Discipline.

A letter addressed to the Conference from Bishop J. J. Esher and dated Tokio, Japan, January 24th, 1885, was read. In this communication the Bishop refers to the ordination of Hirakawa Toyotsura, missionary at Hinoyeki, Japan, and a member of this Conference, to the office of deacon. This was the first ordination by our church in heathen lands and of a convert from heathendom.

BOUNDARIES.

A mission was located in the State of Florida. Freemansburg, Reddington, and vicinity, were taken up as a mission. Hellertown Mission was connected with Pleasant Valley Circuit. Turkey Hill and Mt. Zion were taken from Terre Hill and with Bowmansville, Red Run, and Denver, were constituted a mission. Reiner City and Tower City were taken from Lykens Circuit and constituted a mission. Lykens, Wiconisco, and Dayton were called Wiconisco Mission. Fredericksburg, Union, and Lickdale were taken from Mount Nebo Circuit and called Fredericksburg Mission. Port Carbon was changed into a mission. It was resolved that Ashland Mission and Ringtown Station be served together. The East Reading Chapel was placed under the charge of the Reading Eighth Str. Station. Lancaster Water Str. Station and Port Carbon were changed into missions.

CHURCH AFFAIRS.

Lancaster English Mission received permission to collect in Reading District, with the exception of the city of Reading, for a church debt; Coplay class, in Allentown District, for a new church; the Kutztown congregation, in Pottsville District south of the Blue Mountain, in the city of Reading, and on Fleetwood Circuit, for the erection of a new church edifice; the South Easton congregation, in Allentown District, for a debt of $1,931.50; Kulpsville class, in Philadelphia District, for a debt of $868.45; the congregation at Pen Argyl, in Philadelphia District, for a new church. The last named congregation was instructed not to finish the second story of the church until they are able to pay for it. The congregation at Ringtown was instructed to accept the offer of Enoch Manbeck to cancel his claim of $569.60 against that church in exchange for $1\frac{1}{2}$ acres of ground for which the congregation paid $85 per acre. The practicability of erecting a church at Harrisburg was referred to the presiding elder, the preacher in charge, J. N. Metzgar, and two lay members of the society, to be selected by the presiding elder, who shall constitute a building committee. This committee was instructed to proceed to build, provided the present indebtedness of two thousand dollars shall not be increased more than one thousand dollars additional. Permission was granted to the trustees of the Shamrock church to give a mortgage of $525 on their church property. The financial difficulties of our church at Leesport were referred to the presiding elder and preacher in charge. The requests of the churches at Hellertown and Frackville were referred to the Church

Building Society for favorable consideration. E. J. Miller, collector, reported that during the past year $960.46 had been secured and paid on the church debt at Myerstown, leaving a deficit of $257.80. H. D. Shultz, financial agent at Shenandoah, reported that $825.13 had been expended for repairs and $364.43 towards the liquidation of the debt, leaving an indebtedness of $1,403.57. The following is a summary of the accounts of the Seybert Memorial Church: The cost of lot and building was $10,079.34; cash received at home and throughout the Conference, $5,526.89; from collections ordered by the General Conference, $862.06; for old church property, $942.80; material sold, $84.43; total cash receipts, $7,416.18; present indebtedness, $2,663.16; amount unsecured, $203.79.

EDUCATION.

The report of Thos. S. Stein, Acting Principal of Schuylkill Seminary, was characterised as able, practical, and encouraging in its tone. Fifteen hundred dollars were apportioned among the presiding elder districts to defray the current expenses for the ensuing year, the presiding elders and preachers in charge to be held jointly responsible for the amount. The Conference instructed the trustees to secure the amount necessary for the contingent expenses of the college building. B. J. Smoyer, J. D. Woodring, and D. A. Medlar were appointed a visiting committee to attend the closing exercises of the seminary.

S. C. Breyfogel, one of the delegates appointed by this Conference to visit the Atlantic Conference in the interests of Schuylkill Seminary, reported (owing to

24

sickness, his colleague, S. B. Brown, was not able to go,) that the conference thus visited indicated, both by resolution and by public individual expression, a deep interest in the projected college ; that they appointed a committee to attend the commencement exercises of the school; and that in the opinion of the delegates, a further continuance of such fraternal relations upon the subject, would be of vital importance to our educational interests.

I. E. Knerr was appointed to represent the interests of the seminary at the next session of the Atlantic Conference. J. C. Hornberger, S. S. Chubb, and J. R. Carl were elected trustees of the seminary for three years. The committee on education was instructed hereafter to nominate the examiners for applicants for license, and that the examiners for the itinerancy are to serve three years, one to be appointed each year by the same committee. J. K. Seyfrit, B. F. Bohner, and J. G. Sands were appointed examiners of applicants for the itinerancy; and W. K. Wieand, G. W. Gross, and J. D. Woodring to examine junior preachers for five years.

The preachers were again urged to organize catechetical classes wherever practicable. To expedite the carrying out of this resolution, it was suggested that where the people are not friendly to such a course, a decided position on the part of the pastor, tempered with prudence, patience, and perseverance, will soon overbear all such objections.

J. G. Mohn, treasurer of Schuylkill Seminary, reported that the receipts of that institution during the past Conference year were $3,224.59, including the Conference apportionment; the expenditures, $2,240.70. The trustees of the seminary through their secretary reported the following, which was referred to the presiding elders: "*Resolved*, That it is the opinion of the trustees of the seminary, that the East Pennsylvania Conference should at this session locate a mission at Fredericksburg, with the understanding that the missionary appointed there, shall be a member of the building committee."

MEMORIALS.

Davis Hambright was born in Lancaster County, Pa., January 3, 1810. He was converted early in life, when the work of the Lord was despised, and God's people treated with contempt in the place of his nativity. Soon after his conversion he experienced a call to the ministry, to which he faithfully responded. His spirit of self-denial was great, being willing to go wherever sent, and work for the salvation of souls. By his great zeal and fiery pulpit efforts, he laid the ground work of religion in the hearts of many who call him their spiritual father.

Seneca Breyfogel was born in Berks County, Pa., February 18, 1823. As a preacher Brother Breyfogel was original, clear, and eminently Scriptural, his sermons manifesting a deep and constant study of God's Word. He was an earnest defender of the doctrine of Christian Perfection, as taught by the Evangelical Association, and his life was in beautiful accord with the doctrine he so fearlessly preached, and so humbly professed. He was especially successful as a revivalist, the last year of his ministry, having been conspicuously blessed with a gracious revival of religion. His influence as a preacher and pastor is felt to-day on every charge where he labored. Many pious men and women thank God for his life, and for his private and public ministrations. Under his superintendence, four new churches were built and debts liquidated on a number of others.

Aaron H. Overholt was born in Berks County, Pa., September 25, 1834. He was converted in 1860. He was licensed to preach in 1864, and served as an itinerant for a number of years. From the time of his location up to the time of his death, he held creditably his relation to his Conference as local elder. Brother Overholt was a man of good judgment and wise counsel, and an earnest and faithful worker in the church and Sabbath-school. He died in great peace. A memorial service was held in which addresses were delivered by F. Krecker, Bishop T. Bowman, and C. K. Fehr.

SABBATH AND TEMPERANCE.

In addition to a reassertion of former declarations on Sabbath observance, it was resolved that we are most unqualifiedly opposed to Sunday newspapers and that we will use our influence against them by word and deed.

It was resolved that we are in favor of Constitutional Prohibition and that we consider it a violation of our discipline for any of our members either to sign applications for liquor license or to rent their properties for the sale of liquors.

FINANCE.

Receipts :

Balance in treasury.......................$ 71.20
From the book establishment.............. 1,187.00
From the Charitable Society..............   195.00
From the conference collections.......... 1,252.42

$2,705.62

Expenditures:

Paid to conference claimants and for expenses, $2,489.03

Balance on hand........................$ 216.59

MISSIONARY APPROPRIATIONS.

Philadelphia 8th Str.$175	Denver and Bowmans-
Philadelphia " " 250	ville.............$150
Norristown......... 75	Lancaster Water Str. 50
Plymouth.......... 275	Lebanon 225
Lansdale and Hatfield 300	Harrisburg......... 450
Quakertown........ 250	Harrisburg interest.. 60
Hellertown........ 200	Trevorton to be ap-
Freemansburg...... 150	plied as last year.. 280
Easton............ 275	Mt. Joy........... 250
South Easton and	Fredericksburg...... 300
Williams Twp.... 350	Annville.......... 200
Allentown 1st Ward 225	Wiconisco......... 150
Allentown Liberty St. 300	Dauphin.......... 75
Emaus............ 200	Williamstown....... 75
Lehighton......... 250	Florida............ 500
Mauch Chunk...... 250	Schuylkill Haven... 350
Wilkesbarre....... 350	Frackville......... 350
White Haven....... 250	Mt. Carmel........ 350
Lehigh Valley...... 400	Orwigsburg........ 200
Reading 9th Street.. 175	Wesnersville....... 350
Pottstown and Phœn-	Coaldale.......... 200
ixville.......... 200	Ashland to be applied
Pottstown house rent 150	as last year....... 300
Lancaster Mulberry	Port Carbon....... 100
Street 300	
Millersville........ 75	Total.........$10,465
Lititz and Manheim. 75	

APPOINTMENTS.

PHILADELPHIA DISTRICT—*C. K. Fehr,* P. E.
Philadelphia Sth St.—J. D. Woodring.
Germantown—S. T. Leopold.
Norristown—W. A. Leopold.
Plymouth—W. H. Rinck.
Trappe—F. Smith.
Lansdale and Hatfield—G. C. Knobel.
Montgomery {J. S. Newhart.
Quakertown {F. Krecker.
Milford—F. Sechrist.
Pleasant Valley {W. A. Shoemaker.
Hellertown {C. Rothermel.
Bethlehem—O. L. Saylor.
Freemansburg - I. U. Royer.
Easton—J. G. Sands.
S. Easton and Williams Twp.—W. H. Stauffer.
Bath—R. Deisher and A. E. Williams.
Bangor—A. Krecker.
Middle Creek—D. G. Reinhold.
Wayne—H. A. Smith.

ALLENTOWN DISTRICT—*C. S. Haman,* P. E.
Allentown Linden St.—J. C. Bliem.
Allentown Turner St.—J. W. Hoover.
Allentown First Ward—J. Specht.
Allentown Liberty St.—A. W. Warfel.
Lehigh—D. Yingst.
Emaus—J. Stermer.
Catasauqua—B. F. Bohner.
Lehigh Valley—D. Lentz.
Slatington—A. S. Kline.
Berlinsville—F. E. Erdman.
Parryville—H. M. Wingert.
Weissport—C. H. Egge.
Lehighton—G. W. Gross.
Mauch Chunk—H. R. Yost.
Hazleton—S. B. Brown.
White Haven—W. Schuler.
Wilkesbarre—J. W. Woehrle.

READING DISTRICT—*J. C. Hornberger,* P. E.
Reading Sth St.—W. K. Wieand.
Reading 6th St—S. C. Breyfogel.
Reading 9th St.—I. J. Reitz.
East Reading Chapel—F. Hoffman.
Friedensburg—H. J. Glick.

Pottstown and Phœnixville—I. F. Heisler and B. C. Krupp.
Birdsboro—C. D. Dreher.
Adamstown—B. D. Albright.
Terre Hill—W. C. Kantner.
Denver and Bowmansville—W. W. Fetter.
Conestoga—J. C. Krause.
Lititz and Manheim—A. Dilabar.
Brownstown—A. Ziegenfus and A. J. Brunner.
Lancaster Water St.—E. Butz.
Lancaster Mulberry St.—L. N. Worman.
Millersville—A. B. Saylor.
Creswell—T. A. Hess.

HARRISBURG DISTRICT—*A. M. Stirk* P. E.
Lebanon Chestnut St.—I. E. Knerr.
Lebanon Sth St.—J. A. Feger.
Myerstown—D. Z. Kembel.
Womelsdorf—J. Savitz.
Annville—A. Kindt.
Mt. Nebo—H. H. Romberger.
Mt. Joy—E. J. Miller.
Harrisburg—S. S. Chubb.
Dauphin—D. W. Bicksler.
Millersburg—D. A. Medlar.
Berrysburg—G. B. Fisher.
Uniontown—C. J. Warmkessel.
Trevorton—F. D. Geary.
Wiconisco—J. S. Overholser.
Tremont and Reiner City—W. W. Yost.
Williamstown—G. D. Sweigert.
Pine Grove—A. M. Sampsel.
Fredericksburg—W. F. Heil.
Florida Mission—J. L. Guinther.

POTTSVILLE DISTRICT—*B. J. Smoyer,* P. E.
Pottsville—J. H. Shirey.
Schuylkill Haven St. Peter's—J. M. Rinker.
Schuylkill Haven Trinity—U. H. Hershey.
Cressona—B. H. Miller.
Orwigsburg—T. Harper.
Port Carbon—J. P. Miller.

Schuylkill—N. A. Barr.
Kutztown—W. H. Weidner and C. C. Speicher.
Coaldale and Lansford—A. H. Snyder.
Tamaqua—F. P. Lehr.
Mahanoy City—J. K. Seyfrit.
Shenandoah—H. D. Shultz.

Frackville—J. M. Longsdorf.
Ashland—J. K. Fehr.
Ringtown—E. R. Seip.
Mt. Carmel—J. R. Hensyl.
Shamokin—A. A. Delong.
Mahantongo—C. S. Brown.

1886.

The Forty-Seventh (79th) Annual Session.

President, Bishop Thomas Bowman.
Secretary, S. C. Breyfogel.
Assistant Secretaries. D. A. Medlar, J. H. Shirey, G. W. Gross, and H. D. Shultz.

The forty-seventh annual session of the East Pennsylvania Conference was held in the Immanuel Church, Sixth street, Reading, Pa., beginning Wednesday, February 24th, 1886. The following standing committees were appointed: On Worship,—J. C. Hornberger, S. C. Breyfogel, W. K. Wieand, I. J. Reitz, and F. Hoffman; On Letters and Documents,—J. Specht, A. Ziegenfus, F. P. Lehr, G. B. Fisher, T. Harper, and J. Savitz; On Quarterly Conference Records,—S. B. Brown, B. F. Bohner, J. C. Bliem, R. Deisher, A. Kindt, W. H. Weidner, A. Dilabar, B. H. Miller, A. A. Delong, H. H. Romberger, and C. J. Warmkessel; On Boundaries,—The Bishop and the presiding elders; On Education,—I. E. Knerr, S. S. Chubb, W. K. Wieand, U. H. Hershey, W. C. Kantner, J. D. Woodring, G. C. Knobel, A. M. Sampsel, H. D. Shultz, A. S. Kline, and W. F. Heil; On Finance,—J. K. Seyfrit, W. A. Shoemaker, C. S. Brown, W. H. Rinck, F. Smith, G. D. Sweigert, and A. B. Saylor; On Church

Affairs.—J. M. Rinker, D. Lentz, J. S. Newhart, S. T. Leopold, E. J. Miller, J. C. Krause, and J. S. Overholser; On Statistics,—J. A. Feger, J. G. Sands, F. E. Erdman, N. A. Barr, H. M. Wingert, D. G. Reinhold, and F. D. Geary; On Sabbath and Temperance,—W. A. Leopold, A. W. Warfel, H. J. Glick, J. W. Hoover, A. Krecker, J. K. Fehr, J. W. Woehrle, W. H. Stauffer, and J. M. Longsdorf; On Memorials,—C. S. Haman, F. Krecker, S. Ely, J. M. Saylor, D. Wieand, E. Butz, B. D. Albright, C. H. Baker, F. Sechrist, D. Yingst, and J. N. Metzgar; To Audit Accounts,—C. H. Egge, W. F. Heil, and H. M. Capp; Reportorial Committee,—O. L. Saylor, C. D. Dreher, D. W. Bicksler, L. N. Worman, W. Schuler, J. R. Hensyl, and I. F. Heisler.   G. C. Knobel was appointed to report the proceedings for the *Christliche Botschafter.*   Solomon Neitz, elder, H. C. Major, local deacon, and G. Miller, local preacher, died during the year.   Credentials were granted to D. G. Reinhold and I. E. Zimmerman.   J. R. Teter and I. Wilson, local preachers, withdrew from the church.   D. Yingst took and active relation.   The supernumerary preachers were S. Ely, J. Fry, J. Bowman, J. Zern, J. Laros, and J. L. Werner.   The superannuated preachers and conference claimants were: N. Goebel and wife, D. Wieand and wife, C. Gingrich and wife, J. M. Saylor and wife, J. K. Knerr and wife, C. H. Baker and wife, F. Hoffman and wife, H. R. Yost and wife, J. O. Lehr and wife, H. Stoetzel, Sisters Schnerr, Rhoads, Myers, Kempfer, Gross, Schell, Heim, Haines, Sister Adams and one child, and one child of J. J. High.   The brethren, T. Harper and A. Ziegenfus, took a superannuated relation.   J. N.

Metzgar, H. M. Capp, and H. A. Neitz were retained in the itinerancy without an appointment for one year.

S. C. Breyfogel was newly elected, and C. S. Haman and C. K. Fehr were re-elected to the office of Presiding Elder. H. M. Wingert, J. S. Overholser, C. D. Dreher, I. F. Heisler, and H. A. Smith were ordained to the office of Elder; and J. P. Miller, A. H. Snyder, and I. U. Royer to the office of Deacon. The following received license as preachers on trial: Howard Dutill, A. S. Kresge, W. R. S. Fluck, J. K. Freed, James D. Acker, George A. Knerr, J. Berg Esenwein, Thomas M. Reed, and H. Strunk. The brethren, B. C. Krupp, A. J. Brunner, A. E. Williams, and E. R. Seip were received into the itinerancy.

J. C. Hornberger offered the following, which was adopted unanimously by a rising vote: WHEREAS, Father F. Hoffman, who for the past sixty years has uninterruptedly served in the active itinerant work of this Conference, serving during this long term of years as circuit, station, and mission preacher, as well as for quite a number of years in the office of presiding elder, to the edification of the church and the glory of Christ; AND WHEREAS, On account of his age he has signified his willingness to accept a superannuated relation if the Conference sees fit; therefore *Resolved*, That Brother Hoffman be placed in a superannuated relation, and that he be allowed to travel and preach within the bounds of this Conference as he may see fit.

On motion of A. M. Stirk it was resolved that recommendations for license shall be valid only until the next annual session of the Conference. H. R. Yost having been severely afflicted during the year, and thereby compelled to retire from active work, the Conference expressed sympathy with the brother. The secretary was instructed to prepare suitable answers to letters received from J. L. Guinther, our missionary in Florida, and W. E. Walz, our missionary in Tokio, Japan. On motion of B. J. Smoyer it was resolved that hereafter the members of this Conference in active service and their families be members of the charge where they labor, and that those not in active service shall be members where they reside. On motion of B. F. Bohner the Conference advised that class leaders and exhorters be elected by ballot.

On motion of D. Z. Kembel, it was resolved that it is the sense of this Conference, that a general effort should be made throughout our entire church to raise funds for the purpose of erecting a suitable monument to the memory of our sainted founder, Jacob Albright, whose remains lie at rest within the bounds of this Conference, and that we kindly request our worthy bishops to lay this matter before our conferences, both at home and in foreign lands, for their earnest consideration and action.

WHEREAS, Our beloved sister in the Lord, Mrs. Dr. Krecker, has returned to us for a period of rest from her field of labor in Japan, where she has spent nine years of unwearied diligence and toil in her Master's work; AND WHEREAS, In addition to the ordinary sacrifices incident to missionary work in heathen countries, she has been called upon by the inscrutable Providence of God to lay upon the altar of missions her faithful companion and very successful co-worker in the bonds of the Gospel; therefore be it *Resolved*, That we bid her a most hearty welcome and highly appreciate her faithfulness and devotion to the cause of God and the church, and thank God for the success that has attended her labors as well as the labors of all our missionaries in Japan, and that we continue to pray that He may bless her and her children, and prepare and sanctify them for still greater usefulness in the missionary work of our beloved church.

F. E. Erdman was elected statistical secretary and S. S. Chubb was re-elected treasurer of the Conference. S. Heininger, Corresponding Secretary of the Missionary Society, and W. Yost, Junior Publisher, addressed the Conference, after which the customary resolutions of devotion to the publishing interests and missionary cause of the church were adopted. Thomas S. Stein, Principal *de facto* of Schuylkill Seminary, read the annual report of that institution. It was resolved that hereafter no donations be made to any preacher in active work unless he assume a superannuated relation.

BOUNDARIES.

The Conference territory was divided into six presiding elder districts. Pen Argyl, Ackermanville, Miller's church, and Roxburg were taken from Bath Circuit and called Pen Argyl Mission. New missions were established at the following places: South Bethlehem and Freemansburg, Phœnixville, Lansdale and Quakertown, Tamaqua, and Souderton and Telford; the last named mission to be served in connection with Montgomery Circuit. Kutztown, Lyons, Shamrock, and Virginsville appointments on Kutztown Circuit were formed into Kutztown Mission. Williamstown Mission was changed into a station. Port Clinton was taken from Schuylkill Circuit, and Hamburg and Shoemakersville from Kutztown Circuit and formed into a new field called Hamburg Mission. West Penn and Hunsicker's were taken from Schuylkill Circuit and annexed to Wesnersville Mission. Orwigsburg Mission was discontinued, and Drehersville, New Ringgold, Lewistown, and Centreville appointments on Schuylkill Circuit were annexed to Orwigsburg and called Orwigsburg Circuit. Barnesville was detached from Tamaqua Station, and Locust Valley from Mahanoy City Station, and together with Grier City and Delano were called Barnesville Circuit. Lincoln and Reamstown were detached from Brownstown Circuit and annexed to Denver and Bowmansville Mission. Mohnsville was taken from Adamstown Circuit and constituted a station. Hatfield was transferred from Lansdale and Hatfield Mission to Montgomery Circuit. Lehigh Valley Mission was discontinued; and Coplay connected with Catasauqua, Howertown with Berlinsville Circuit, and Schnecksville with Lehigh Circuit.

CHURCH AFFAIRS.

Permission was given to the members of Birdsboro Circuit to remove the Hay Creek chapel to the California appointment, the latter class agreeing to pay $225 for the property. The church at Lititz having been injured by a storm, the request of the congregation to collect in Reading District was referred to the presiding elder and the preacher in charge. The Conference appointed a committee to superintend the erection of a church at Denver, and the Church Building

Society was requested to grant a loan of $500.00 to the congregation at Bowmansville. The site of the North street property was recommended for the location of our new church at Harrisburg, the Conference instructing the building committee to borrow the money required to complete the building. The advisability of building a church at Coplay was referred to a committee. During the past year the sum of $691.38 was paid on the church debt at Shenandoah City, reducing the entire indebtedness to $766.15. The advisability of erecting a church at Elizabethville, Berrysburg Circuit, was referred to the presiding elder and the preacher in charge. The congregation at Ashland was urged to secure a suitable lot and to build a new church as soon as practicable. An appeal from Lansford asking aid toward the erection of a church was referred to the presiding elder and preacher in charge. These congregations received permission to collect within certain prescribed limits as follows: Denver and Bowmansville, in Reading District; Harrisburg, in Lebanon and Millersburg Districts; Coplay, in Philadelphia District, and at Bath and Bangor, in Allentown District; Kulpsville, at Norristown, Germantown, Plymouth, Lansdale, and on Pleasant Valley and Bath circuits; Pen Argyl, in Pottsville District. The auditing committee reported the following accounts for the past year: 1st, The cash receipts for the South Easton church debt, W. H. Stauffer collector, amounted to $1,006.85, leaving an indebtedness of $1,040.72. 2d, The amount of cash received by D. Lentz, collector for a new church at Coplay, aggregated to $357.61, of which $219.56 was expended. 3d, J. S. Newhart, collector for Kulps-

ville, received $224.30, leaving an indebtedness of
$704.00.   4th, L. N. Worman, collector for Lancaster
English Mission, received $1,780.67 in cash, a sufficient
amount to liquidate the entire indebtedness.   5th, The
entire amount expended for the Pen Argyl church, R.
Deisher collector, was $4,723.95; cash received
$1,555.75, leaving an entire indebtedness of $3,168.20.

EDUCATION.

Whereas, Our Schuylkill Seminary is in a flourishing
condition and the new buildings at Fredericksburg, Pa.,
are rapidly nearing completion, And Whereas, The entire expenditures necessary to the satisfactory completion and equipment of these buildings are $40,000, and
$7,000 of this amount is unprovided for, and it is de-
sirable to adopt a plan promising the gradual removal
of this deficiency; therefore be it *Resolved*, That the
last Sunday of June, recognized as Children's Day by
order of General Conference, be devoted to the raising
of funds for the liquidation of the indebtedness incurred
in the completion of the seminary buildings.   S. S.
Chubb, C. S. Haman, S. C. Breyfogel, W. K. Wicand,
and J. H. Shirey were appointed to arrange a pro-
gramme and to cultivate a seminary sentiment in our
Sunday-schools.   The Conference resolved to raise
$1,500 for the current expenses of the seminary, the
presiding elders and preachers in charge to be held
jointly responsible for the amount.   Revs. Bishop T.
Bowman, I. E. Knerr, and C. S. Haman, and Messrs.
J. G. Mohn and H. G. Moyer were elected trustees of
the seminary for three years.   U. H. Hershey, J. H.
Shirey, and A. M. Sampsel were appointed a visiting
committee to attend the closing exercises of the school.

The trustees of the institution were authorized to meet the deficiency incurred in completing the seminary buildings. J. G. Mohn, the treasurer, reported a cash balance in treasury of $1;121.35. S. B. Brown, J. K. Seyfrit, and B. F. Bohner were appointed to examine applicants for the itineracy, and G. C. Knobel, W. C. Kantner, and W. A. Leopold to examine junior preachers for five years.

MEMORIALS.

Solomon Neitz, a veteran of the cross, was born in 1821, and born again at the age of fourteen. In 1840 he was licensed to preach the gospel. For a number of years he served as presiding elder in the Conference. In 1860 the board of publication selected him to the honorable task of writing the biography of Bishop John Seybert, which he accomplished in the year 1861.

Brother Neitz was a wise counselor and a good organizer, exerting a great influence in his Conference. For a number of years he was the Conference delegate to the board of missions, by which board he was sent to Germany in 1863. He was a member of the first board of publication and of a number since. He was also a member of the General Conference since 1856. Brother Neitz was a great theologian. By eminent divines he was pronounced to be one of the greatest German pulpit orators in this country. Frequently he preached the Word with great power, and in such demonstration of the Holy Ghost that the whole audience was moved to tears and shouts of praise to God. He swayed his congregations to and fro like forest trees under the force of a mighty tempest. His work is done, but we all miss him greatly. He died in perfect peace May 11th, 1885.

Henry C. Major was born in 1810. As far as is known, he was converted when a young man, and labored as an itinerant in our church for several years and then located, and held a local relation to the end of his life. He was a good and effectual preacher.

George Miller was born in 1802, in Germany. He was converted to God when a young man and joined our church. He was a good, practical preacher. Brother Miller bequeathed $200 to the missionary work of the Evangelical Association.

At a memorial service addresses were delivered by C. K. Fehr, F. Krecker, C. S. Haman, and Bishop Thomas Bowman.

TEMPERANCE.

Resolved, That we, the ministers of the East Pennsylvania Conference, do hereby pledge our honor to each other to manfully withstand the efforts of the Liquor Dealers' Protective Association, and that we will do all in our power to sustain existing temperance legislation and aim at nothing short of entire and total prohibition of the manufacture and sale of alcoholic beverages, until we have total abstinence for the individual and prohibition for the state and nation.

FINANCE.

Receipts :

Balance in treasury	$ 216.59
From the book establishment	1,156.00
From the Charitable Society	216.00
From conference collections	1,411.64
From a special collection	226.95
	$3,227.18

Expenditures:

Paid to conference claimants and for conference expenses.......................$3,555.71

MISSIONARY APPROPRIATIONS.

Phila. 8th St	$175	Lititz and Manheim	$175
Phila. " "	250	Denver and Bowmans-	
Norristown	75	ville	50
Plymouth	150	Harrisburg	400
Lansdale and Quaker-		Harrisburg, interest	60
town	300	Trevorton, to be ap-	
Souderton	150	plied as in 1884–'85	280
Hellertown	250	Mt. Joy	300
Freemansburg and		Fredericksburg	300
Sth. Bethlehem	250	Annville	200
Easton	275	Wiconisco	150
South Easton and Wil-		Dauphin	175
liams Twp	325	Schuylkill Haven	300
Allentown 1st Ward	200	Frackville	300
Allentown Liberty St.	300	Mt. Carmel	300
Emaus	200	Wesnersville	350
Lehighton	225	Coaldale and Lansford	200
Mauch Chunk	225	Ashland, salary	125
Wilkesbarre	350	Port Carbon	200
White Haven	225	Florida	500
Reading 9th Street	150	Pen Argyl	200
Pottstown	150	Kutztown	300
Phœnixville	250	Hamburg	200
Lancaster Mulb'y St.	250	Tamaqua	100
" Water St.	50		
Lebanon	225	Total	$10,215
Millersville	50		

25

APPOINTMENTS.

PHILADELPHIA DISTRICT—*C. K. Fehr*, P. E.

Philadelphia 8th St.—D. A. Medlar.
Germantown—S. T. Leopold.
Norristown—W. A. Leopold.
Plymouth—F. Krecker.
Trappe—W. H. Stauffer.
Pottstown—J. S. Newhart.
Phœnixville—B. C. Krupp.
Milford—F. Sechrist.
Lansdale and Quakertown — G. C. Knobel.
Montgomery) T. A. Hess.
Souderton,) J. D. Acker.
Pleasant Valley—I. F. Heisler and T. L. Wentz.
Bethlehem—B. F. Bohner.
Freemansburg and South Bethlehem—O. L. Saylor.
Easton—J. C. Krause.
South Easton—W. H. Rinek.

ALLENTOWN DISTRICT — *S. C. Breyfogel*, P. E.

Allentown Linden St.—J. C. Bliem.
Allentown Turner St.—J. W. Hoover.
Allentown First Ward—J. Specht.
Allentown Liberty St.—A. W. Warfel.
Emaus—E. Butz.
Lehigh—D. Yingst.
Catasauqua—H. J. Glick.
Slatington—A. S. Kline.
Berlinsville—R. M. Lichtenwalner.
Bath—I. U. Royer.
Pen Argyl—C. D. Dreher.
Bangor—A. Krecker.
Monroe—A. E. Williams.
Wayne—H. A. Smith.

READING DISTRICT—*J. C. Hornberger*, P. E.

Reading 8th St.—W. K. Wieand.
Reading 6th St.—J. H. Shirey.
Reading 9th St.—I. J. Reitz.
Reading Chapel—To be supplied.
Friedensburg—R. Deisher.
Kutztown—W. H. Weidner.
Wesnersville—D. Lentz.
Hamburg—J. Stermer.

Birdsboro—N. A. Barr.
Adamstown and Mohnsville—B. D. Albright.
Denver and Bowmansville — A. J. Brunner.
Terre Hill—J. D. Woodring.
Conestoga—F. D. Geary.
Brownstown—J. W. Woehrle.
Florida—J. L. Guinther.

LEBANON DISTRICT—*A. M. Stirk*, P. E.

Lebanon Chestnut St.—I. E. Knerr.
Lebanon Eighth St.—J. A. Feger.
Annville—A. Kindt.
Harrisburg—S. S. Chubb.
Mt. Nebo—H. H. Romberger.
Fredericksburg—W. F. Heil.
Pine Grove—A. M. Sampsel.
Tremont and Reiner City—W. W. Yost.
Williamstown—G. D. Sweigert.
Myerstown—D. Z. Kembel.
Womelsdorf—J. Savitz.
Lititz) A. Dilabar.
Manheim) W. G. Schoepflin.
Lancaster Water St.—Isaac Hess.
Lancaster Mulberry St.—F. Smith.
Millersville—A. B. Saylor.
Creswell—L. N. Worman.
Mt. Joy—E. J. Miller.

POTTSVILLE DISTRICT—*C. S. Haman*, P. E.

Pottsville—W. C. Kantner.
Schuylkill Haven St. Peters—J. M. Rinker.
Schuylkill Haven Trinity—U. H. Hershey.
Cressona—B. H. Miller.
Orwigsburg—W. A. Shoemaker.
Port Carbon—J. P. Miller.
Coaldale and Lansford—A. H. Snyder.
Tamaqua—F. P. Lehr.
Mauch Chunk—F. E. Erdman.
Hazleton—S. B. Brown.
White Haven—W. Schuler.
Wilkesbarre—J. G. Sands.
Lehighton—G. W. Gross.
Weissport—C. H. Egge.
Parryville—H. M. Wingert.

MILLERSBURG DISTRICT—*B. J. Smoyer, P. E.*
Millersburg—H. D. Shultz.
Dauphin—D. W. Bicksler.
Berrysburg—G. B. Fisher.
Wiconisco—J. S. Overholser.
Uniontown—C. J. Warmkessel.
Trevorton—E. R. Scip.
Mahantongo—C. S. Brown.

Shamokin—A. A. Delong.
Mt. Carmel—J. R. Hensyl.
Ashland ⎱ J. K. Fehr.
Ringtown ⎰ G. A. Knerr.
Shenandoah—D. S. Stauffer.
Frackville—J. M. Longsdorf.
Mahanoy City—J. K. Seyfrit.
Barnesville—J. M. Shoop.

1887.

The Forty-Eighth (80th) Annual Session.

President, Bishop J. J. Esher.

Secretary, W. A. Leopold.

Assistant Secretaries, J. H. Shirey, G. W. Gross, W. C. Kantner, H. D. Shultz, and G. C. Knobel.

The members of the East Pennsylvania Conference assembled in annual session in the Salem Evangelical church at Bangor, Pa., on Wednesday, February 23d, 1887. The following standing committees were appointed:

On Worship,—S. C. Breyfogel and A. Krecker; On Letters,—J. C. Bliem, I. Hess, F. P. Lehr, G. B. Fisher, and D. Lentz; On Finance,—B. F. Bohner, A. W. Warfel, D. Yingst, L. N. Worman, J. M. Rinker, C. S. Brown, and F. E. Erdman; On Quarterly Conference Records,—W. K. Wieand, F. Sechrist, J. Specht, R. Deisher, A. Kindt, A. Dilabar, D. S. Stauffer, J. M. Longsdorf, and F. Smith; On Boundaries,— The Bishop and the presiding elders; On Education,— S. B. Brown, S. S. Chubb, W. F. Heil, G. C. Knobel, O. L. Saylor, J. D. Woodring, J. W. Hoover, A. M. Sampsel, and J. C. Krause; On Church Affairs,—J. K.

Seyfrit, W. H. Weidner, J. S. Newhart, B. H. Miller, C. H. Egge, A. A. Delong, E. J. Miller, J. K. Fehr, and J. Stermer; On Statistics,—J. G. Sands, H. J. Glick, G. D. Sweigert, I. F. Heisler, H. M. Wingert, J. P. Miller, F. E. Erdman, T. A. Hess, D. W. Bicksler, C. D. Dreher, and J. S. Overholser; On Temperance and Sabbath,—U. H. Hershey, S. T. Leopold, W. A. Shoemaker, W. H. Stauffer, W. H. Rinek, I. U. Royer, N. A. Barr, and A. H. Snyder; On Memorials,—D. A. Medlar, J. A. Feger, B. D. Albright, H. H. Romberger, F. D. Geary, J. O. Lehr, D. Z. Kembel, I. J. Reitz, and C. J. Warmkessel; Reporterial Committee,—D. A. Medlar, J. R. Hensyl, J. W. Woehrle, A. S. Kline, A. B. Saylor, J. B. Esenwein, G. A. Knerr, and E. H. Romig; To Audit Accounts,—H. A. Neitz, J. N. Metzgar, and J. K. Knerr.

Isaiah E. Knerr, itinerant, Daniel Clouser, local preacher, and Sister Lydia Heim, widow of Rev. W. Heim, died during the past year. Thomas M. Reed returned his license to the Conference. The name of a local preacher was stricken from the record for failing to comply with a resolution of Conference. M. W. Harris and D. J. Ebert received credentials. W. H. Rinek was retained in the itinerancy one year without an appointment. The supernumerary preachers were: S. Ely, J. Fry, J. Bowman, J. L. Werner, and J. Zern. The following were the superannuated preachers and conference claimants: C. H. Baker, H. Stoetzel, N. Goebel, D. Wieand, C. Gingrich, J. M. Saylor, J. O. Lehr, H. R. Yost, A. Ziegenfus, J. K. Knerr, T. Harper, and F. Hoffman; also Sisters Schnerr, Rhoads, Kempfer, Gross, Schell, Adams and one child, one child of J. J. High, and Sister Knerr and three children.

F. D. Geary, C. J. Warmkessel, J. Stermer, A. B.
Saylor, A. S. Kline, W. Schuler, and Hirakawa Toy-
otsura were ordained to the office of Elder; W. W.
Yost, J. M. Shoop, B. C. Krupp, A. J. Brunner, A. E.
Williams, and T. L. Wentz, to the office of Deacon.
The following received license as preachers on trial:
Edwin H. Romig, Stephen A. B. Zuber, Charles E.
Hess, Aaron Souliard, G. E. McCloud, James P. Mal-
seed, and D. F. Kostenbader. The brethren T. L.
Wentz, J. M. Shoop, W. W. Yost, and G. A. Knerr
were received into the itinerancy.

The last Thursday in February, 1888, was appointed
for the opening of the next annual session, the examinations of applicants and junior preachers to begin on
the Tuesday evening previous. The following were
elected delegates to the General Conference: A. M.
Stirk, B. J. Smoyer, C. S. Haman, S. S. Chubb, S. C.
Breyfogel, D. A. Medlar, J. C. Hornberger, R. M.
Lichtenwalner, and J. K. Seyfrit; alternates, C. K.
Fehr, J. D. Woodring, and W. F. Heil. It was decided that the delegates to the General Conference
pay their own traveling expenses. Permission was
granted to J. L. Guinther, our missionary in Florida, to
pay his traveling expenses out of collections taken for
the liquidation of church debts, during his proposed
trip through the Conference in the months of July and
August of the current year. W. Yost, Junior Publisher, addressed the Conference.

On motion of A. M. Stirk the following resolution
having reference to this volume, "LANDMARKS OF
THE EVANGELICAL ASSOCIATION," was adopted: WHEREAS,
S. C. Breyfogel has prepared a manuscript containing

the transactions of this Conference from its origin to the present session, and asks Conference to grant him permission to publish it. Therefore, be it

Resolved, That we grant the required permission, and encourage the publication of the contemplated work in considertion of its value to preachers and people as a book of reference.

On motion of A. M. Sampsel it was *Resolved*, 1st, That the presiding elders of this Conference shall constitute a committee on church building, and that all projects for building new churches or parsonages, or remodeling old ones, where any indebtedness will be incurred, shall be submitted to this committee for its approval.   2d, That any congregation, which by building or otherwise, incurs debts without the approval of this committee, shall not be privileged to collect outside of the bounds of the charge to which it belongs.

The following was adopted: WHEREAS, W. A. Leopold, a member of our Conference, contemplates and is now engaged in writing a work to be entitled, "Our Crowned Defenders," containing a series of biographical sketches of the deceased members of our Conference from the origin of the same, with a brief sketch and pen portraits of the *personnel* of the present East Pennsylvania Conference; therefore, *Resolved*, That we as a Conference will do all in our power to aid and assist Brother Leopold in his work of preparation, and barring all intrusion in this line from other quarters, we will lend our influence and encouragement to circulate the same whenever published.   R. M. Lichtenwalner, treasurer of the Missionary Society, was authorized to borrow the money necessary to meet the claims of the missionaries during the year. In behalf of the stationing committee C. K. Fehr presented the following resolution, which was unanimously adopted: In view of the long, self-sacrificing, as well as acceptable services Father F. Krecker has rendered in the active ministry—this being his year of jubilee—in the East Penna. Conference of the Evangelical Association, and in view of his advanced age, your committee is of the opinion, with which Father Krecker is in cordial agreement, that he take no particular field of labor this year, but be retained in the itinerancy without an appointment, and be allowed to labor and preach wherever he desires.

BOUNDARIES.

Lansdale and Montgomery Circuit was formed of Lansdale, Hatfield, Hilltown, Kulpsville, Worcester, and Perkiomen. Bridgetown, Perkasie, and Quakertown were organized into Quakertown Mission. Coplay, Howertown, and vicinity were formed into Coplay Mission. Reading Ninth Street Mission was changed into a station. A new mission was established in Reading. Rothville and Millway were transferred from Brownstown Circuit to Lititz Mission. It was resolved that Florida Mission be served by two men. Turkey Hill was taken from Bowmansville Mission and annexed to Conestoga Circuit. Adamstown, Mohn's Hill, Reamstown, Mount Zion, and Bowmansville were called Adamstown Circuit. Annville, Steeltown, Palmyra, and Hanover were constituted Annville and Hanover Mission. Conewago was annexed to Mount Joy Mission. Mount Nebo, Mountville, and Fredericksburg were called Fredericksburg and Mount Nebo Mission. Sunbury and Pike appointment were taken up as a mission.

CHURCH AFFAIRS.

These churches received permission to collect within certain prescribed limits, as follows: Wind Gap, in Allentown District, for a debt of $1,200; Lansford, in Pottsville District, for a new church; Topton, in Reading District, for a church debt of $800; Pen Argyl, in Millersburg District, for a church debt of $2,500; Harrisburg, throughout the bounds of the Conference, for a debt of $4,470.96; South Bethlehem, in Philadelphia District, for a new church; Lansdale, in Allentown District, for a debt of $800, provided the members at Lansdale pledge themselves to raise one half of the amount; West Penn, in Reading District, for a new church. Sister Lydia Yeakel's claim of $525 against our church at Shamrock was referred to the presiding elder and the preacher in charge for adjustment, the latter to have permission, if necessary, to collect in Lebanon District. Trinity Mission, Harrisburg, Pa., received permission to effect a loan sufficient to meet the necessary demands and to give a mortgage on the church property for the same. The congregation at Lansford was advised not to build a new church unless they have a guarantee of $800. Frackville Mission received permission to build a parsonage, to effect a loan sufficient for its erection, and to give a mortgage on the building for the amount. Inasmuch as the congregation at Pen Argyl is still making a heroic struggle under a debt of $2,500, the Church Building Society was requested to grant a loan of $600. The members of Birdsboro Circuit received permission to sell Hay Creek chapel and to apply the proceeds toward liquidating the debt of and repairing the old church, instead of removing the chapel to California appointment. The Quarterly Conference of Wayne Circuit was authorized to sell the parsonage at Sterling and to build another in a more suitable part of the circuit. The members at Temple were advised to postpone the erection of a chapel for at least one year. The trustees of the Brownstown church having sold a piece of land opposite their church in order to secure a tract of similar dimensions adjoining their burying ground, their action was approved. The Conference resolved to raise 20 cents per Conference member for the Albany church debt and referred the remaining $200 of the debt to the presiding elder and preacher in charge.

The auditing committee reported the following as the financial condition of the churches for which funds had been collected during the year:—1st, Topton, W. H. Weidner, collector: entire cost of church and lot, $1,714; cash received, $730.65; present indebtedness, $983.35; unpaid subscriptions, $110. 2d, Kutztown, W. H. Weidner, collector: entire cost of church, $5,947.13; total cash receipts, $5,396.30; present indebtedness, $550.83; unpaid subscriptions, $231. 3d, Bowmansville, A. J. Brunner, collector: paid on the debt during the year, $229.98; present indebtedness, $790. 4th, Pen Argyl, C. D. Dreher, collector: paid on debt and cash in hand, $628; actual indebtedness, $2,280.13. 5th, Shenandoah, D. S. Stauffer, financial agent: paid on debt, interest, &c., during the year, $458.14; present indebtedness, $377.46. 6th, Coplay, H. J. Glick, collector: entire cost of church, $1,549.65; cash received, $966.96; present indebtedness, $582.69; unpaid subscriptions, $592.91. 7th, Harrisburg, S. S.

Chubb, collector: total cost of church, $9,708.31; cash paid on debt, $4,779.16; indebtedness, $4,929.15, old debt, $800; loan from the Church Building Society, $358; unpaid subscriptions, $1,616.19.

EDUCATION.

Schuylkill Seminary was strongly recommended as affording excellent advantages for mental culture, safely guarded by a thoroughly Christian environment.

The Conference resolved to raise $1,500 for the current expenses of the seminary during the ensuing year, and apportioned the amount among the presiding elder districts. The treasurer was authorized to borrow money sufficient to cover the present indebtedness of the institution. It was resolved that the money raised on Children's Day be appropriated to the building fund of the seminary. A. M. Stirk, S. C. Breyfogel, and P. Kellmer were elected trustees of the seminary for three years; W. F. Heil was elected to fill the unexpired term of I. E. Knerr, deceased. S. B. Brown, O. L. Saylor, and F. E. Erdman were appointed a visiting committee to attend the closing exercises of the school.

J. G. Mohn, treasurer of Schuylkill Seminary, presented the annual financial report of the trustees, which shows the receipts of the institution from Feb. 26th to July 1st, 1886, to have been $1,615.62; the expenditures, $1,377.15; leaving a balance in the treasury of $238.47. The receipts of the building committee for the erection of the college building were $31,103.-89; the expenditures for the building, furniture, etc., $35,767.46; thus leaving an indebtedness of $4,663.57.

J. A. Feger, S. B. Brown, and J. K. Seyfrit were

appointed to examine applicants for the itinerancy, and
C. K. Fehr, D. A. Medlar, and W. F. Heil to examine
junior preachers for five years.   J. H. Shirey was appointed to fill the vacancy in the examining committee
occasioned by the death of I. E. Knerr.

MEMORIALS.

Isaiah E. Knerr was born November 28th, 1838.
He was an earnest and faithful preacher of the gospel
of Christ.   His sermons, always well prepared, were
clear and logical in their construction and sound in
doctrine.   In imitation of his great Master he largely
employed illustrations, and delighted to unfold the
parables and figurative portions of the Word of God.
Endowed with a noble and majestic frame, robust and
vigorous constitution, and a good voice, he possessed
the natural elements of an orator, which, under the
anointing of the Holy Ghost, enabled him at times to
preach with great eloquence and power.   His ministrations were crowned and blessed of God to the conversion of many souls.   His career as a presiding elder
showed that he was possessed of rare executive abilities
in enforcing the Discipline and administering the
financial affairs of his districts.   He was converted when
young, and associated with his father, brother and son
in the same church, ministry, and Conference.   He was
intensely loyal to the church, and guarded the integrity
of her institutions with a jealous eye.   In 1881 when
the East Penna. Conference contemplated establishing
an institution of learning within her bounds, he was
chosen as one of a committee of organization, and
helped to organize Schuylkill Seminary.   From its or-

ganization he has been the vice-president of the board
of trustees, and also the chairman of the executive
committee, as well as the chairman of the building
committee.

Daniel Clouser was born December 24th, 1813, in
Berks County, Pa. In the year 1833 he was converted to God and united with the Evangelical Association. He was a pious, devoted follower of Christ, and
a very acceptable local preacher, never standing in opposition to the regular pastor. His end was peace. To
the question of the future his invariable answer was,
"all right." His last words were " Jesus! now, now!"

A memorial service was held in which addresses were
delivered by A. M. Stirk, C. S. Haman, and C. K.
Fehr. Bishop Esher presided.

TEMPERANCE.

Resolved, That we utterly condemn the present high
license movement as being in the interest of the saloon
and intended to divide the temperance hosts; and that
we demand constitutional prohibition for the state and
nation, and for the securing of this we solemnly pledge
our influence as gospel ministers, our prayers as Chris-
tians and our ballots as American freemen. *Resolved,*
That the radical and widespread difference of opinion
as to the best method to be employed for the speedy
securing of prohibition is but natural and must always
be expected as the legitimate result of free thought and
free speech on every great question; and therefore we
condemn as un-American and un-Christian the spirit of
intolerance so extensively manifested in this contest.
Resolved, That we rejoice in the fact that the Legisla-

ture of Pennsylvania has taken initiative steps towards securing constitutional prohibition by submitting this question to the votes of the people.

FINANCE.

Receipts:

Balance on hand................$	71.47	
From Charitable Society.........	262.50	
From publishing house..........	1,131.00	
From conference collections......	1,658.77	
		$3,123.74

Expenditures:

Paid to claimants...............$3,025.00		
Conference expenses............	52.57	
		$3,077.57
Balance on hand.................... $	46.17	

MISSIONARY APPROPRIATIONS.

Phila. 8th St.......$150		Allentown 1st Ward.$175	
Plymouth.......... 100		" Liberty St. 300	
Norristown........ 50		Emaus............ 200	
Souderton.......... 150		Pen Argyl......... 275	
Perkasie and Quaker-		Coplay............ 225	
town............ 125		Reading Mission.... 400	
Hellertown........ 250		" house	
Phœnixville........ 150		rent............ 100	
Pottstown.......... 175		Wesnersville....... 375	
South Bethlehem and		Kutztown.......... 275	
Freemansburg.... 275		Hamburg.......... 275	
Easton............. 250		Florida sr. preacher.. 333	
South Easton....... 250		Florida jr. preacher.. 167	
Lansdale and Quaker-		Florida traveling ex-	
town (for last year) 100		penses jr. preacher. 35	

Mauch Chunk	$250	Fredericksburg	$250
Wilkesbarre	350	Annville	100
White Haven	275	Dauphin	175
Coaldale and Lansford	275	Wiconisco	150
Schuylkill Haven	300	Trevorton, to be ap-	
Lehighton	225	plied as last year	280
Port Carbon	250	Sunbury	175
Tamaqua	75	Mount Carmel	300
Lebanon	200	Ashland	125
Lititz	100	Frackville	300
Lancaster Mulb'y St.	300	Phila. 8th St., into	
" Water St.	75	Church Building	
Harrisburg	400	treasury	250
" for interest	180		
Mt. Joy	200	Total	$10,520

APPOINTMENTS.

PHILADELPHIA DISTRICT—*C. K. Fehr*, *P. E.*
Philadelphia 8th St.—D. A. Medlar.
Germantown—S. T. Leopold.
Norristown—W. A. Leopold.
Plymouth—A. Markley.
Trappe—W. H. Stauffer.
Pottstown—J. S. Newhart.
Phœnixville—A. J. Brunner.
Milford—F. Sechrist.
Lansdale and Montgomery—W. W. Yost.
Souderton—J. D. Acker.
Perkasie and Quakertown—T. A. Hess.
Pleasant Valley—I. F. Heisler.
Hellertown Miss.—T. L. Wentz.
Bethlehem—B. F. Bohner.
Freemansburg and South Bethlehem—O. L. Saylor.
Easton—J. C. Krause.
South Easton—B. C. Krupp.

ALLENTOWN DISTRICT—*S. C. Breyfogel*, *P. E.*
Allentown Linden St.—W. K. Wieand.
Allentown Turner St.—A. Krecker.
Allentown First Ward—J. Specht.
Allentown Liberty St.—A. W. Warfel.
Emaus—E. Butz.
Lehigh—W. H. Weidner.
Catasauqua—H. J. Glick.
Coplay—A. E. Williams.
Slatington—A. S. Kline.
Berlinsville—R. M. Lichtenwalner.
Bath—I. U. Royer.
Pen Argyl—C. D. Dreher.
Bangor—J. W. Hoover.
Monroe—D. S. Manning.
Wayne—H. A. Smith.

READING DISTRICT—*J. C. Hornberger*, *P. E.*
Reading 8th St.—J. M. Rinker.
Reading 6th St.—J. H. Shirey.
Reading 9th St.—J. C. Bliem.
Reading Mission—B. D. Albright.
Friedensburg—R. Deisher.
Kutztown—D. Yingst.
Wesnersville—D. Lentz.
Hamburg—J. Stermer.

Birdsboro—N. A. Barr.
Mohnsville—B. H. Miller.
Adamstown—J. K. Fehr.
Terre Hill—J. D. Woodring.
Conestoga—F. D. Geary.
Brownstown—J. W. Woehrle.
Florida—J. L. Guinther and H. Dutill.

LEBANON DISTRICT—*A. M. Stirk*, P. E.
Lebanon Chestnut St.—W. F. Heil.
Lebanon 8th St.—U. H. Hershey.
Annville and Hanover—J. Savitz.
Harrisburg—S. S. Chubb.
Fredericksburg and Mount Nebo—A. M. Sampsel.
Pine Grove—E. J. Miller.
Tremont and Reiner City—A. Souliard.
Williamstown—G. D. Sweigert.
Myerstown—D. Z. Kembel.
Womelsdorf—A. Kindt.
Lititz—A. Dilabar.
Manheim—J. P. Miller.
Lancaster Water St.—I. Hess.
Lancaster Mulberry St.—F. Smith.
Millersville—J. B. Esenwein.
Creswell—H. H. Romberger.
Mt. Joy—A. B. Saylor.

POTTSVILLE DISTRICT—*C. S. Haman*, P. E.
Pottsville—W. C. Kantner.
Schuylkill Haven St. Peter's—I. J. Reitz.

Schuylkill Haven Trinity—J. A. Feger.
Cressona—J. S. Overholser.
Orwigsburg—W. A. Shoemaker.
Port Carbon—F. P. Lehr.
Tamaqua—A. H. Snyder.
Mauch Chunk—F. E. Erdman.
Hazleton—S. B. Brown.
White Haven—W. Schuler.
Coaldale and Lansford—L. N. Worman.
Wilkesbarre—J. G. Sands.
Lehighton—G. W. Gross.
Weissport—C. H. Egge.
Parryville—A. F. Leopold & C. E. Hess.

MILLERSBURG DISTRICT—*B. J. Smoyer*, P. E.
Millersburg—H. D. Shultz.
Dauphin—D. W. Bicksler.
Berrysburg—H. M. Wingert.
Wiconisco—G. B. Fisher.
Uniontown—C. J. Warmkessel.
Trevorton—E. R. Seip.
Sunbury—G. A. Knerr.
Mahantongo—C. S. Brown.
Shamokin—A. A. Delong.
Mt. Carmel—G. C. Knobel.
Ashland—J. K. Seyfrit.
Shenandoah—D. S. Stauffer.
Frackville—J. M. Longsdorf.
Mahanoy City—J. R. Heusyl.
Barnesville—J. M. Shoop.
Ringtown—S. Buntz.

"*Hitherto hath the Lord helped us.*"—I Samuel vii : 12.

Alphabetical Roll of Preachers.

I.—Such Who Have Traveled and Whose Names Appear on the Lists of Appointments.

"Men that have hazarded their lives for the name of our Lord Jesus Christ." Acts xv:26.

In the earlier years the quarterly conferences frequently granted licenses to local preachers, but inasmuch as these transactions are not always recorded in the annual conference books, it is impossible in many instances to determine the exact year in which brethren received license. Where the exact date of licensing is missing, the year in which the name first appears on the annual conference records is substituted. The year 1887 has been counted in computing the number of "years in active service." This item includes the number of years traveled in the East Pa. Conference only. The names marked with a * are still upon the roll of the Conference as Itinerants ; those marked with a † are also still upon the records but not in the Traveling Connection.

Names.	Licensed.	Entered Active Service.	Ordained Deacon.	Ordained Elder.	Years in Active Service.
†Acker J. D.	1886	1886	......	......	2
Adams Jacob.............	1847	1847	1848	1850	33
Aepley Benj......................	1837	1838	1839	......	2
Albright Jacob................	1803	1796	......	1803	12
*Albright B. D..................	1867	1867	1869	1871	21
Allen Joseph.....................	1827	1827	......	......	1
Altimos Solomon.......	1833	1833	1835	......	3
Anstein George......	1831	1831	......	......	2
Apgar J. A......................	1859	1859	1861	1864	8

NAMES.	Licensed.	Entered Active Service.	Ordained Deacon.	Ordained Elder	Years in Active Service.
Bachman Wm. H............	1855	1856	1858	1860	8
*Baker C. H......................	1853	1862	1859	1864	20
Barber James	1817	1817	1818	1820	21
*Barr N. A......................	1878	1878	1880	1882	10
† 1 Bartholomew Daniel....	1856	......	1859	1861	...
Bast Ephraim...................	1844	1844	1845	1847	12
Bauer Moses.....................	1837	1837	......	......	2
Baumgartner Jacob..........	1819	1819	1821	......	6
Baumgartner Samuel........	1832	1832	1834	1836	4
Becker Michael...............	1810	1810	......	......	3
Becker Abraham...............	1822	1822	1824	1826	5
Becker Benjamin.............	1825	1825	......	......	1
Bell Jacob......................	1832	1832	1834	......	2
Berger Daniel...................	1834	1834	1836	1838	20
Bernhart M. N.....	1870	1870	......	......	1
Best Joseph	1839	1839	......	......	1
Betz Matthew...................	1809	1809	1810	1813	5
*Bicksler D. W..............	1877	1877	1881	1883	9
Bixler Benjamin..............	1823	1823	.....	......	3
Bixler Jacob...................	1821	1821	......	......	2
Bisse H. A......................	1850	1850	1851	......	4
†Black W. L.....	1873	1873	1875	1877	9
*Bliem J. C....................	1855	1866	1863	1868	22
†Bliem Calvin A...............	1872	1872	......	......	1
2 Boas Jacob....................	1833	1833	1835	......	3
Boesher Benjamin............	1817	1817	......	......	2
3 Boetzel A...................	1858	1858	1860	1862	7
*Bohner B. F.................	1862	1864	1865	1868	23
Borauf Frederick............	1822	1822	......	......	3
4 Bosch J. G.	1844	1844	1846	1848	5
*5 Bowman Thomas..........	1859	1859	1861	1863	29

1. Traveled ten years in the Indiana Conference where he was ordained Deacon and Elder. 2. Entered the Western Conference in 1836. 3. In later years he traveled in the Atlantic Conference. 4. Entered the N. Y. Conference in 1848. 5. Elected Bishop in 1875, but retained his membership in the East Pa. Conference until the present time.

NAMES.	Licensed.	Entered Active Service.	Ordained Deacon.	Ordained Elder	Years in Active Service.
*Bowman James...............	1873	1873	1874	1876	9
Breidenstein John.....	1818	1818	1820	1822	6
Breyfogel Seneca.............	1859	1862	1863	1865	18
*Breyfogel S. C...............	1873	1873	1875	1877	15
Brickley George..........	1829	1829	1830	1832	10
Brickley Daniel...............	1831	1831	1833	1835	5
Brickley John..................	1835	1835	......	......	1
*1 Brown S. B..................	1861	1864	1866	1868	21
*Brown C. S.....................	1872	1874	1875	1877	14
Bruer Thomas................	1814	1814	1815	......	2
Bruer Jacob....................	1815	1815	1817	1828	8
*Brunner A. J..................	1885	1885	1887	......	3
Buchman Abraham..........	1813	1813	1814	......	3
Buck Thomas.................	1823	1823	1825	1827	18
Bucks Henry...................	1832	1832	1834	1843	15
Buechwalter John......	1812	1812	......	......	1
†Buntz Stephen..............	1885	1887	......	.....	1
Burkhart Jacob..............	1831	1831	1833	1846	8
*Butz Edmund......	1857	1858	1860	1862	30
Campbell John.................	1831	1831	......	......	2
*Capp H. M.....................	1880	1880	1882	1884	4
*Chubb S. S.....................	1859	1860	1862	1864	28
2 Clewell T. G..................	1853	1853	1855	1857	5
3 Custer M. L.	1875	1875	1877	......	2
Danner Fred...............	1840	1840	1841	1843	14
4 Dareich Jacob...........	1841	1841	1843	1845	8
Dehoff John....................	1815	1815	1816	1821	10
Dehoff Moses.................	1816	1816	1818	1820	6
Deibler Michael...............	1812	1812	......	......	2
*5 Deisher Reuben...........	1844	1846	1851	1853	33
Dellinger George.............	1837	1837	......	......	2
*Delong A. A..................	1871	1870	1872	1874	17
Deppen Isaac..................	1833	1833	......	......	1

1. Served three years in Kansas the Conference. 2. Elected editor of the *Evangelical Messenger* in 1857. 3. Entered a western conference in 1877. 4. Entered the N. Y. Conference in 1848. 5. Served six years in the Atlantic Conference.

NAMES.	Licensed.	Entered Active Service.	Ordained Deacon.	Ordained Elder	Years in Active Service.
*Dilabar Augustus............	1874	1874	1876	1878	14
1 Dissinger Moses............. ...	1853	1854	1856	1859	25
Dotterer Franklin.............	1846	1846	......	.....	1
*Dreher C. D...................	1882	1882	1884	1886	6
Dreibelbis Reuben.............	1868	1870	1871	1873	5
Dreisbach John.....	1807	1807	......	1809	14
†Dutill Howard.....…	1886	1887	......	......	1
Ebbert Joseph..................	1829	1829	1835	......	1
Eby Andrew....................	......	1835	......	......	1
Eckert John....................	1844	1845	1846	1848	8
*2 Egge C. H...................	1866	1866	1868	1870	12
Eisenberger John.............	1821	1821	......	......	2
3 Eiss Michael.................	1837	1837	1840	1841	12
Ely Ephraim....................	1852	1852	1854	1856	19
*Ely Solomon......	1856	1866	1866	1868	11
Enders George	1827	1827	1830	......	5
Erb John.....	1808	1808	1810	1812	8
*4 Erdman F. E	1875	1875	1878	1880	7
Erly Jacob....................	1825	1825	......	......	2
†Esenwein J. B...............	1886	1887	......	......	1
Ettinger Adam.....	1816	1816	1817	......	2
Ettinger Benjamin............	1816	1816	1818	1820	7
Farnsworth J. C...............	1843	1843	1844	1846	13
Farry Abraham................	1839	1839	......	......	1
*Feger J. A...................	1870	1871	1872	1874	17
*Fehr C. K....................	1861	1861	1863	1865	27
*Fehr J. K	1871	1870	1872	1874	17
†Fetter W. W.................	1885	1885	.....	......	1
Fisher David..................	1840	1840	1842	1846	9
*Fisher G. B..................	1859	1860	1862	1864	26
Fisher Henry.................	1831	1831	1335	1839	13
5 Fliehr C. B.................	1859	1863	1863	1865	13

1. Entered the Kansas Conference in 1879. 2. Received his license and orders in the Iowa Conference, where he traveled ten years before entering the East Pa. Conference. 3. Entered the N. Y. Conference in 1848. 4. Traveled four years in the Michigan Conference where he was ordained Elder. 5. Entered the Atlantic Conference in 1876.

NAMES.	Licensed.	Entered Active Service.	Ordained Deacon.	Ordained Elder	Years in Active Service.
1 Focht George.	1860	1864	1865	......	1
Fordman Edward.............	1877	1877	......	......	1
Foy Jacob........................	1823	1823	1825	......	3
Frey Abraham.................	1832	1832	1835	......	4
Frey Jacob.	1807	1807	1819	.....	6
*Frey Joshua	1848	1855	1855	1857	14
Friess Samuel..................	1835	1835	......	......	1
Frueh John.....................	1816	1816	1818	1820	4
Gates Peter.....................	1833	1833	......	......	3
Gaumer Samuel...............	1847	1847	1848	1850	13
†Garret William..............	1840	1840	1851	......	1
*Geary F. D....	1883	1883	1885	1887	5
Gehman L. H..................	1863	1868	......	1869	3
*Gingrich Christian..........	1849	1851	1852	1854	24
2 Glaeser E.....................	1873	1873	1874	1876	3
Glasser Frederick.............	1821	1821	1823	.....	7
*Glick H. J.	1875	1875	1877	1879	13
*Goebel Nicholas..............	1851	1851	1853	1856	25
3 Goetschel A...................	1862	1864	1865	1867	4
Gross Joseph....................	1842	1842	1847	1850	17
Gross Jacob...............	1846	1846	1848	1850	9
*Gross G. W..............	1875	1875	1877	1879	13
4 Guhl Matthew......	1857	1857	1859	1861	13
*Guinther J. L.................	1879	1880	1882	1884	8
Haines G. T	1837	1837	1839	1841	36
*Haman C. S..................	1854	1855	1857	1859	33
Hambright Davis.............	1848	1848	1850	1854	21
Hambright W. W.	1869	1870	......	......	1
Hamilton John................	1825	1825	1827	1829	6
5 Hammer Charles............	1830	1830	1831	1833	9
Harlacher Joseph.............	1832	1832	1834	1836	9
*Harper Thomas...............	1852	1860	1860	1864	26

1. Licensed by the Central Conference, was ordained by our Conference, after which he entered the Pittsburg. 2. Entered the Atlantic Conference in 1876. 3. Received credentials to enter a western conference in 1868. 4. Sent as missionary to California in 1864, and entered the Erie Conference in 1876. 5. Elected general book agent in 1839.

NAMES.	Licensed.	Entered Active Service.	Ordained Deacon.	Ordained Elder	Years in Active Service.
Hartman Martin...............	1836	1836	.. ...	......	1
Hartman A. M....................	1880	1880	......	......	1
1 Hashinger J. R...............	1882	1883	......	......	1
Hassler Henry..................	1818	1818	1820	1822	5
*Heil W. F...................	1880	1880	1882	1884	8
Heim Wm.......................	1837	1837	1838	1840	33
*Heisler I. F.....................	1881	1882	1884	1886	5
Henig Adam.....................	1813	1813	1814	......	4
Henneberger Peter..	1836	1836	1837	......	4
*Hensyl J. R.....................	1876	1877	1880	1882	10
*Hershey U. H..................	1871	1871	1873	1875	17
*Hess Isaac.	1848	1848	1850	1852	35
*Hess T. A........................	1872	1872	1875	1877	16
†Hess C. E.........................	1887	1887	......	......	1
Hesser Charles..................	1831	1831	1833	1835	13
High J. J.........................	1873	1873	1875	......	4
Himmelreich J. S.	1830	1830	1832	......	3
*2 Hirakawa Toyotsura....	1882	1882	1885	1887	6
*Hoffman Francis.............	1826	1825	1828	1832	60
Hoffman E. A	1866	1867	1868	......	2
†Hoffsomer A......................	1871	1871	......	......	1
Holl Christian............	1836	1836	1838	1840	11
Hoock Jacob.....................	1828	1828	......	......	1
*Hornberger J. C..............	1865	1865	1867	1869	23
*Hoover J. W....................	1879	1878	1881	1883	9
Hummel Christian...........	1837	1838	1839	1841	16
Hunter R. G	1830	1830	......	......	1
Huth Abraham..................	1812	1812	......	......	1
3 Jacobs J. A....................	1835	1835	1837	1839	5
4 Jacoby Levi...................	1847	1847	......	......	2
Jimeson Alexander...........	1804	1804	......	......	2
Kaltreiter Fred.................	1816	1816	1818	......	3
*5 Kantner W. C...............	1875	1875	1876	1878	8

1. Received credentials in 1884. 2. A native missionary in Japan. 3. Entered the West Pa., Conference in 1839. 4. Entered the N. Y. Conference in 1848. 5. Served five years, 1876–'81, as missionary in Oregon.

NAMES.	Licensed.	Entered Active Service.	Ordained Deacon.	Ordained Elder	Years In Active Service.
Kegel Henry......................	1835	1835	1837	......	5
Kehr Daniel......................	1830	1830	1832	1836	8
1 Kehr Jacob....	1835	1835	1837	1843	10
Kelly Levi........................	1853	1853	1856	......	3
*Kembel D. Z....................	1857	1864	1865	1867	24
Kempfer Herman...............	1851	1860	1858	1874	11
*Kindt Anthony.................	1866	1868	1870	1872	20
Kleinfelter John............ ...	1813	1813	1815	1817	12
Kleinfelter Jacob..............	1813	1813	1815	1817	12
Kleinfelter Adam..............	1817	1817	1819	1821	13
*Kline A. S......................	1883	1883	1885	1887	5
2 Knerr George.................	1849	1850	1852	1854	26
Knerr I. E.......................	1861	1861	1863	1865	26
*Knerr J. K....................	1861	1866	1867	1869	16
*Knerr G. A.....................	1886	1886	......	......	2
*3 Knobel G. C	1871	1874	1875	1878	4
2 Koehl John.	1846	1846	1848	1850	30
4 Koester Henry...............	1853	1854	1856	1858	8
Kopp J. J......	1832	1832	1834	......	4
Krall Samuel........	1838	1838	......	......	1
Kramer John....................	1839	1839	1841	1843	9
*Krause J. C.....................	1880	1880	1882	1884	8
*Krecker Frederick..........	1838	1837	1840	1842	50
5 Krecker Dr. Fred..........	1876	1876	1877	1879	8
*6 Krecker Augustus.........	1875	1874	1876	1878	8
Kring Conrad.............	1823	1823	1825	1827	13
*Krupp B. C.....................	1885	1885	1887	......	3
Kurtz John......................	18‒6	1861	1863	1865	15
Kutz Joseph....................	1856	1858	1861	1864	10
Landis G. H.....................	1866	1869	1873	......	2
Lanz George....................	1820	1820	1820	......	1
†Laros Jesse....................	1864	1865	1868	1870	19

1. Entered the N. Y. Conference in 1848.   2. Entered the Atlantic Conference in 1876.   3. Was licensed and ordained in the Illinois Conference where he traveled before entering this Conference.   4. Entered the Atlantic Conference in 1876.   5. Missionary in Japan from 1876 to the time of his death.   6. Entered the Pacific Conference in 1879 and served there and in the Oregon Conference six years.

NAMES.	Licensed.	Entered Active Service.	Ordained Deacon.	Ordained Elder	Years in Active Service.
1 Lauer Martin................	1844	1844	1846	1848	5
†Laury G. H....................	1873	1873	1875	.....	4
1 Lebn Michael................	1839	1839	1840	1842	10
*Lehr F. P.....................	1853	1853	1855	1858	35
*Lehr J. O.......	1854	1854	1856	1858	31
Leib J. P......................	1821	1831	1833	1835	44
Leitner Christian.............	1831	1831	......	......	2
*Lentz David..................	1862	1862	1864	1867	26
*2 Leopold A. F..............	1865	1865	1866	1868	12
*Leopold W. A............	1867	1867	1869	1871	21
*Leopold S. T.................	1874	1873	1876	1878	14
3 Leslie L. E..................	1873	1874	1875	1877	4
*Lichtenwalner R. M........	1860	1862	1863	1865	24
Liesser Abraham..............	1803	1803	......	......	3
†Litzenberger Reuben.......	1845	1856	1857	1859	8
4 Long Joseph.................	1822	1822	1824	1826	11
Long D. N.....................	1835	1835	......	......	2
5 Longsdorf Alexander......	1838	1838	......	......	2
*6 Longsdorf J. M........	1872	1872	1874	1876	3
†Loos Cornelius..............	1847	1847	1849	1853	12
Lutz John.....................	1832	1833	1835	.....	3
Maize M. F....................	1833	1833	1835	1837	17
Major H. C.....	1851	1852	1853	......	4
†Manning D. A. S.......	1885	1887	......	......	1
Manwiller Daniel.............	1824	1824	1826	1828	6
†7 Markley Abraham.........	1871	1872	1874	1876	6
8 Marquardt J. G.............	1844	1845	1846	1848	20
Mattinger George............	1827	1827	......	1831	8
McCray Robert.....	1812	1812	......	......	2

1. Entered the N. Y. Conference in 1848. 2. Entered the Atlantic Conference in 1876 and after serving there for a number of years returned to this Conference in 1885. 3. Received credentials in 1878. 4. Elected to the office of Bishop in 1843. 5. Entered the W. Pa. Conference in 1839. 6. Licensed and ordained in the Central Pa. Conference, where he traveled 13 years before entering this Conference in 1885. 7. Traveled one year in the Central Pa., Conference. 8. Entered the N. Y. Conference in 1848; returned in 1851; was sent as missionary to California in 1867; returned in 1871. In later years he traveled in the Atlantic Conference.

NAMES.	Licensed.	Entered Active Service.	Ordained Deacon.	Ordained Elder.	Years in Active Service.
McLehn Noah	1848	1848	1850	1852	4
*Medlar D. A	1872	1872	1874	1876	16
†Mertz David	1839	1839	1842	1868	7
* Metzgar J. N	1865	1865	1867	1869	19
Meyers Christian	1841	1841	1842	1844	32
Middlekauf George	1820	1820	1822	......	3
Miesse Samuel	1829	1843	1842	1845	5
1 Miller George	1805	1805	......	1807	5
Miller John W	1822	1822	1825	1827	7
Miller Solomon G	1829	1829	1831	1834	7
Miller Michael	1831	1831	1833	......	3
Miller Frederick	1835	1835	1838	......	
Miller Philip	1846	1846	......	......	1
2 Miller Elias B	1854	1854	1856	1858	11
†Miller J. H	1851	1855	1858	......	1
*Miller B. H	1868	1871	1872	1874	17
*Miller E. J	1871	1871	1872	1874	17
*Miller J. P	1884	1884	1886	......	4
3 Mintz William	1838	1838	1840	1842	11
Moore G. W	1877	1877	......	......	1
4 Mosser Sebastian	1835	1835	1837	1839	5
5 Mott Robert	......	1871	......	......	2
† Moyer Benjamin	1860	1865	......	.....	1
Muck Samuel	1817	1817	1819	......	4
Neitz Solomon	1840	1840	1842	1844	41
*Neitz H. A	1867	1867	1868	1870	14
*Newhart J. S	1872	1872	1874	1876	16
Niebel Henry	1809	1809	1812	1813	17
Noecker John	1834	1834	......	.....	4
Oberholzer Isaac	1848	1858	1856	......	1
Oehrle H. E	1866	1869	1869	......	1

1. In addition to the four or five years spent in active service, Geo. Miller devoted the remainder of his years to preaching as much as his strength would allow, and to valuable literary labors. 2. Received credentials in 1866. 3. Entered the N. Y. Conference in 1848. 4. Entered the West Pa. Conference in 1839. 5. Received from the Pittsburg Conference in 1871, and after traveling two years in this Conference received his credentials.

Names.	Licensed.	Entered Active Service.	Ordained Deacon.	Ordained Elder	Years in Active Service.
Oplinger J. M	1872	1872	1873	1875	8
1 Orwig W. W	1828	1828	1830	1832	9
*Overholser J. S	1881	1882	1884	1886	6
Overholt A. H	1864	1865	1866	1868	4
Peters John	1818	1818	......	......	3
Peters Jacob	1819	1819	......	......	4
Plattenberger Theo	1851	1854	1856	1858	22
Poorman John	1832	1835	......	.....	1
Ramige George.	1839	1839	1841	1843	9
Raus John	1843	1843	......	......	2
Ray William	1829	1829	1831	......	2
Reber W. L.	1843	1843	1845	1847	19
Reich George	1825	1825	1827	......	5
2 Reinhold D. G	1881	1881	1883	1885	5
Reinoehl S. P	1853	1853	1855	1857	16
Reisner J. C	1822	1822	1824	1826	10
*Reitz I. J	1874	1874	1876	1878	14
Rhoads S. G.	1851	1851	1852	1854	25
Rickel John	1816	1816	1818	......	4
Riegel Jacob	1834	1834	1836	1838	11
Riegel John	1834	1834	1836	......	4
*Rinek W. H	1879	1880	1882	1884	6
*Rinker J. M	1873	1873	1875	1877	15
3 Rissman Joseph	1839	1839	......	......	1
Roehrig William	1830	1830	......	.. ...	1
Roessner John	1831	1831	1833	......	4
4 Roland Henry	1839	1839	......	......	1
*Romberger H. H	1879	1880	1883	1885	8
4 Rosenberger John	1838	1838	1840	......	2
†Rothermel C. M	1884	1884	......	......	2
*Royer I. U	1884	1884	1886	......	4
*Sampsel A. M.	1877	1876	1879	1881	11

1. Elected Editor of the *Christliche Botschafter* in 1837. 2. Entered the Kansas Conference in 1886. 3. Entered the West Pa. Conference 1839. 4. Entered the West Pa. Conference in 1839.

NAMES.	Licensed.	Entered Active Service.	Ordained Deacon.	Ordained Elder	Years in Active Service.
*Sands J. G.,	1862	1867	1868	1870	21
Sauer Henry	1842	1842	......	......	2
*Savitz James.	1863	1869	1870	1872	16
*Saylor J. M.	1825	1824	1827	1832	41
Saylor Jacob	1834	1834	1836	1838	8
*Saylor O. L.	1865	1872	1871	1874	16
*Saylor A. B.	1883	1883	1885	1887	5
Schaeffer George	1837	1837	1838	1840	3
Schaeffer J.	1868	1868	......	......	1
Scharfe Frederick.	1843	1843	1845	1847	6
1 Scharfe Gustave	1862	1866	1867	1869	10
Scheiner J. S.	1866	1866	1868	......	3
Schell John	1848	1848	1850	1852	26
Schimpf Jacob	1834	1834	1834	......	2
Schmidt Philip.	1816	1816	......	......	1
Schmidt William	1842	1842	......	......	1
Schmidt G. C	1843	1843	1845	......	3
Schmidt Lewis	1860	1860	1862	1869	4
Schneider George	1825	1825	1829	......	11
2 Schneider Theobald	1843	1843	1845	1847	6
Schneider Jacob.	1851	1859	1859	......	2
Schnerr Jacob	1829	1830	1831	1833	9
Schoepflin W. G.	......	1886	......	......	1
Schreffler John	1833	1833	......	......	1
*Schuler William.	1883	1883	1885	1887	5
Schultz Abraham	1844	1844	1846	1848	29
Schuppert Ludwig	1836	1836	......	......	2
3 Schwilly Philip	1837	1837	1839	1841	6
†Sebold Thomas.	1849	1855	1856	1858	7
*Sechrist Frank	1867	1868	1869	1871	19
Seger George.	1835	1835	......	......	1
*Selp E. R.	1885	1885	......	......	3
Sensel John	1833	1833	1835	1837	18
4 Seybert John	1821	1821	1822	1824	19

1. Entered the Atlantic Conference in 1876. 2. Entered the New York Conference in 1848. 3. Entered the Ohio Conference in 1843. 4. Elected Bishop in 1839.

NAMES.	Licensed.	Entered Active Service.	Ordained Deacon.	Ordained Elder	Years in Active Service.
*Seyfrit J. K.	1866	1867	1869	1871	20
Shauer Frederick	1812	1812	1814	1816	5
Sherk N. B.	1876	1876	1877	.....	1
Shilling John	1816	1816	1818	1820	5
*Shirey J. H	1876	1876	1878	1880	12
*Shoemaker W. A.	1868	1869	1871	1873	19
Sholty William	1822	1822	1823	......	2
*Shoop J. M.	1877	1886	1887	......	2
†Shultz David	1848	1849	......	......	1
*Shultz H. D.	1874	1874	1876	1878	14
Sichley Elias	1832	1832	1834	.....	4
1 Sindlinger J. M	1834	1834	1836	1838	9
2 Sindlinger Michael	1840	1840	1842	1849	29
*Smith Ferdinand.	1877	1877	1879	1881	11
†Smith H. A.	1884	1884	1886	......	4
*Smoyer B. J.	1866	1866	1868	1870	22
3 Snyder Lewis	1849	1851	1852	1856	28
*Snyder A. H	1884	1884	1886	......	4
†Souliard A.	1887	1887	......	......	1
*Specht Joseph.	1858	1858	1860	1862	30
†Speicher C. C	1884	1884	......	......	2
Stambach John	1813	1813	1814	1817	7
Stauffer Henry	1814	1814	......	......	2
*Stauffer D. S	1870	1870	1872	1874	16
*Stauffer W. H	1880	1881	1883	1885	7
4 Stauffer F. G	1880	1881	1883	......	2
Steck Thomas.	1842	1842	1844	......	5
2 Steltzer Joseph	1856	1860	1861	1863	16
*Stermer John	1883	1883	1885	1887	5
*Stirk A. M.	1867	1868	1870	1872	20
*Stoetzel Henry	1837	1837	1839	1858	18
Stoever E	1828	1828	1829	1831	8
Stoever F. L	1849	1849	......	......	1
Stoll John	1821	1821	1823	1825	4

1. Entered the West Pa. Conference in 1843. 2. Entered the Atlantic Conference in 1876. 3. Entered the Kansas Conference in 1879. 4. Entered the Ohio Conference in 1853.

NAMES.	Licensed.	Entered Active Service.	Ordained Deacon.	Ordained Elder	Years in Active Service.
Stoll William	1827	1827	......	......	1
1 Straub Anthony.............	1870	1875	1875	......	1
*Sweigert G. D..	1870	1876	1876	1878	12
Thomas David..................	1815	1815	1816	......	2
Thomas Christian............	1832	1832	......	......	1
2 Thomas Henry..............	1835	1835	1837	......	5
Tobias Samuel..................	1826	1826	1829	.....	6
Tobias Daniel...................	1833	1833	......	......	2
†Trumbore M...................	1870	1870	......	......	1
Vandersal John............... ...	1821	1821	1821	......	2
Van Gundy Samuel	1834	1834	.....	......	2
Vogelbach Jacob..............	1836	1837	1838	1840	4
3 Wagner Philip...............	1822	1822	1824	1826	16
†Wagner William	1831	1831	......	......	1
4 Wagner Jacob..............	1847	1847	......	......	2
5 Walker F. W......	1855	1855	1857	1859	7
Walter John.....................	1802	1802	......	1809	12
Walter, Jr., John.	1813	1813	.....	......	1
Walter Michael................	1814	1814	1816	1820	8
*6 Walz W. E...................	1883	1885	1885	......	...
*Warfel A. W..................	1873	1874	1875	1877	14
*Warmkessel C. J	1881	1882	1884	1887	6
Weaver A.......................	......	1871	......	......	1
Weiand Henry..................	1817	1817	......	......	1
*Weidner W. H...	1858	1864	1865	1867	23
†Weiss W. C....................	1881	1881	.... .	......	2
*Wentz T. L....................	1882	1886	1887	.... .	2
†Werner Joseph..............	1854	1855	1857	1859	5
*Werner J. L..................	1866	1869	1870	1872	15
3 Westhafer Henry...........	1836	1836	1838	......	4
*Wieand Daniel	1844	1845	1847	1849	23
*Wieand W. K..................	1866	1866	1868	1870	22
Wiest Peter....................	1834	1834	......	......	2

1. Entered the Atlantic Conference in 1876. 2. Entered the West Pa. Conference in 1839. 3. Entered the West Pa. Conference in 1839. 4. Entered the N. Y. Conference in 1848. 5. Entered the Illinois Conference in 1862. 6. Missionary to Japan since 1853.

NAMES.	Licensed.	Entered Active Service.	Ordained Deacon.	Ordained Elder	Years in Active Service.
1 Wiest S. L	1869	1869	1871	1873	13
*Williams A. E	1885	1885	1887	......	3
*Wingert H. M	1877	1882	1884	1886	6
Wissler Henry	1824	1824	1826	1828	7
Witt Samuel	1818	1818	1836	......	2
*Woehrle J. W	1876	1876	1878	1880	12
Wohlfarth J. F	1871	1871	1873	1875	6
Wolf Andrew	1816	1816	......	......	1
Wolf David	1819	1819	1820	1822	4
Wolf Christian	1821	1821	1821	......	1
*Woodring J. D	1878	1878	1881	1883	9
Workman J. R	1873	1875	......	......	2
*Worman L. N	1865	1865	1867	1869	22
Wright R.	1856	1856	......	......	2
Yambert J. H	1828	1828	1829	1831	7
Yambert Aaron	1832	1833	......	......	2
2 Yeakel Jesse	1848	1853	1854	1856	23
3 Yeakel Reuben	1853	1854	1855	......	6
Yeakel I. W.	1870	1871	1872	1874	7
4 Yeakel A. L	1878	1880	......	......	1
Yerlitz David	1810	1810	1813	......	5
*Yingst Daniel	1859	1860	1861	1863	25
5 Yost William	1853	1853	1855	1857	12
*Yost H. R	1872	1872	1874	1876	14
*Yost W. W	1884	1885	1887	......	3
6 Young John	1831	1831	1833	1837	9
Young Jesse	1851	1851	1858	......	2
*Zern Jacob	1856	1856	1858	1860	27
*Ziegenfus Andrew	1850	1850	1852	1854	36
Zimmerman Leonard	1811	1811	1813	1816	...
7 Zimmerman I. E	1867	1868	1869	1871	. 8
Zinzer J. G	1829	1829	1831	1833	7

1. Elected corresponding secretary of the Missionary Society in 1879, but did not transfer his membership from the Conference until later. 2. Entered the Atlantic Conference in 1876. 3. Elected corresponding secretary of the Missionary Society in 1859. 4. Subsequently entered the Atlantic Conference. 5. Elected corresponding secretary of the Missionary Society in 1864. 6. Entered the West Pa. Conference in 1839. 7. Received credentials in 1886.

II.—LOCAL DEACONS WHO HAVE NEVER BEEN IN THE ACTIVE WORK.

"*Fellow helpers to the truth.*" 3 John 8.

The names marked with a * are still upon the records of the Conference.

Licensed.	Names.	Licensed.	Names.
1848.	Bertolet Jacob.	1866.	Loos William.
*1862.	Clemens H. S.	1833.	Miesse D. K.
1822.	Conser J. G.	1806.	Miller Solomon.
1832.	Danny Henry.	*1852.	Miller J. H.
1874.	Dooley John.	1862.	Miller Levi.
*1850.	Egge Wm. J.	1859.	Miller George.
1821.	Focht Daniel.	1871.	Minsker W.
1862.	Frankenfleld S.	1860.	Moyer Jos.
1860.	Harm George.	*1859.	Moyer John W.
1823.	Hassel Charles.	*1861.	Painter J.
1820.	Hassler Michael.	1849.	Rhoads Jeremiah.
1828.	Hencky Ludwig.	1831.	Riem Abraham.
1852.	Hinkel Adam.	*1852.	Rogers William.
1824.	Kibler Martin.	1852.	Saylor Abraham.
1827.	Klein Jacob D.	1826.	Seger Samuel.
1849.	Kletzinger Henry.	*1871.	Steckley Matthew.
*1856.	Kneisley B.	1869.	Wagner W.
1839.	Krissinger D. W.	1860.	Werner J.
*1861.	Lehman D.	1851.	Wittmer D.
1851.	Lehr P. H.	1859.	Wolf C.

III.—LOCAL PREACHERS ON TRIAL WHO HAVE NEVER BEEN IN THE ACTIVE WORK.

"*Our fellow-labourers in the gospel of Christ.*" 1 Thess. III: 2.

The names marked with a star (*) are still upon the records of the Conference.

Licensed.	Names.	Licensed.	Names.
*1862.	Alspach William.	*1883.	Benfield A.
1830.	Aubel Christopher.	1835.	Bernsheimer Wm.
1834.	Becker Daniel.	1832.	Bertolet Daniel.

Licensed.	Names.	Licensed.	Names.
1806.	Bisse Charles.	1832.	Fichtner Daniel.
1834.	Boetz Peter.	1859.	Fischer G. H.
1834.	Bolig D.	*1886.	Fluck W. R. S.
1834.	Bolig Wm.	1852.	Foitz Jesse L.
1866.	Boyer Edward.	1877.	Fordman Edward.
1851.	Boyer W. L.	1881.	Fox J.
1851.	Bozzard Joseph.	1832.	Frankenfelter Peter.
1837.	Breidenstein Philip.	*1886.	Freed J. K.
1856.	Brown Samuel.	1832.	Frey Samuel.
1839.	Bruer Moses.	1852.	Fritz J. L.
1866.	Burkhardt C.	1830.	Frueh Conrad.
*1873.	Butterweck S.	1870.	Funk H. K.
1878.	Butz J. K.	1859.	Gaembel D.
*1875.	Campbell J. D.	1870.	Gaumer E.
1869.	Canzler M.	1832.	Gebhart Joseph.
1859.	Clauser Daniel.	1879.	Gobble A. E.
1880.	Cole J. B.	1864.	Guelich H.
1856.	Copp F. B.	1853.	Haberry Adam.
*1882.	Crowell J. F.	*1874.	Hallenbach Joshua.
*1883.	Derone J. B.	1882.	Harris M. W.
1856.	Detweiler W. C.	1837.	Hartman Jacob.
1856.	Detweiler Peter.	1829.	Hassler Jacob.
1851.	Dewies Wm.	1866.	Hawley ——.
1867.	Dick John.	1856.	Hechler D.
1847.	Dieder Emanuel.	1869.	Heil Nathan.
1877.	Dissinger I. S.	1877.	Hirst A. V.
1826.	Dissler Jacob.	1868.	Hoch Isaac.
*1885.	Doerstler A. H.	1843.	Hocka Michael.
1839.	Dressler George.	1860.	Hoehle W.
1870.	Dundore S. F.	*1862.	Hoffman Wm. E.
1876.	Dunkelberger S. H.		Hoffman W. L.
1817.	Dutt John.	1874.	Hollenbach Joshua.
1838.	Ebby Benjamin.	1884.	Holzapfel G.
1854.	Eberhart Levi.	1876.	Hoover Galen W.
1885.	Ebert D. J.	1853.	Hornberger Zach.
1845.	Edel Michael.	*1866.	Hunsberger Jesse.
*1874.	Ely G.	*1885.	Johnson W. J.
1868.	Engel S.	1831.	Kaufman Jacob.
1841.	Eschliman J.	1839.	Kaufman John.
1832.	Ettinger Jacob.	1869.	Kaufman N.

Licensed.	Names.	Licensed.	Names.
1878.	Keller J.	1838.	Miller Samuel.
1860.	Kello Joseph.	1853.	Miller Michael J.
1834.	Kerstetter John.	1859.	Miller J. J.
1828.	Kleinfelter Jacob.	1859.	Miller Jonathan.
1834.	Kleinfelter Peter.	*1877.	Miller Henry.
1835.	Kleinfelter John.	*1877.	Miller L. G.
1834.	Koch Jacob.	*1873.	Miller Wiliiam.
1837.	Kocher George.	*1885.	Mintzger A. H.
1865.	Kolb B. (or L.)	1860.	Moyer B.
1863.	Kooker D.	1873.	Moyer Joseph.
*1887.	Kostenbader D. F.	1872.	Nicholas Wm.
*1886.	Kresge A. S.	1837.	Nies Jacob.
1853.	Kurtz Jonathan.	1835.	Oberdorf Daniel.
1857.	Langhart Jacob.	1872.	Pfeifle Christian.
1831.	Lenhart George.	1806.	Philips J. C.
1866.	Leuther F.	1853.	Plotts P. W.
*1868.	Licht Simon.	1832.	Poorman David.
1848.	Light David.	1837.	Rank Jacob.
1869.	Light A.	1856.	Reber G. H.
*1869.	Light Adam R.	1844.	Reber George.
1878.	Light A. D.	1886.	Reed T. M.
1835.	Long Benjamin.	1865.	Rhoads W. W.
1866.	Ludwig M. F.	1851.	Ripley John.
1869.	Lutman F. B.	*1881.	Roessel R.
1868.	Lutz J. K.	*1873.	Romig W. B.
*1887.	Malseed J. P.	*1887.	Romig E. H.
1883.	Manshardt M.	1867.	Ruehl L.
1884.	Mauger E. B.	*1870.	Sallade J. M.
1833.	McBride Henry.	1856.	Schatz Rudolph.
*1887.	McCloud George.	1845.	Schaug Christian.
*1885.	McCurdy S. O.	*1859.	Schelden L. L.
1879.	McNutt J. S.	1867.	Schirmeyer J.
1855.	Medlar Samuel B.	*1867.	Schmidt J. K.
*1859.	Medlar S. B.	1873.	Schnebel Daniel.
*1883.	Medlar W. H.	1826.	Schneider John.
1834.	Merck George.	1874.	Schneider C.
1816.	Meyer Henry.	1837.	Schreffler Daniel.
1837.	Miesse Henry.	1857.	Schuker Emanuel.
1826.	Miller Peter.	1868.	Schultz Edward.
1826.	Miller John.	1820.	Schwarz John.
1837.	Miller Jacob.	1835.	Schwarz Daniel.

27

Licensed.	Names.	Licensed.	Names.
1860.	Schwarz H.	*1880.	Weidel J.
1861.	Schwerer P.	1877.	Weidenhammer C. Y.
1851.	Sehbold Thomas.	1873.	Weidner J. F.
1830.	Shaefer A. B.	1833.	Wengert Henry.
1856.	Shamo J.	1860.	Wentz Levi.
1835.	Sico Oliver.	1856.	Werner Samuel.
1866.	Siegfried J. R.	1873.	Wilson E.
1878.	Snyder C. W.	*1872.	Wilson Joshua.
1866.	Snyder Edward.	1877.	Wilson I.
1844.	Spohn Samuel.	1856.	Wilson J.
1846.	Stambach Henry.	1868.	Wimmer B.
1878.	Steltz A. S.	1874.	Winsler W.
*1886.	Strunk Henry.	*1867.	Witmer D. L.
1879.	Swartz G.	1875.	Woehlte J. C. E.
1881.	Teter J. R.	1826.	Wunder Matthew.
1851.	Theobald A. H.	1837.	Yeakel Andrew.
1826.	Thomas John.	1842.	Yeakel Christopher.
1875.	Transue J. A.	1845.	Yeakel Christophel.
1880.	Updegraff S.	*1865.	Yeakel D.
*1882.	Uyeno Mikuma.	1866.	Yeakel Adam.
1831.	Vandersal Jacob.	1864.	Yerger J. F.
1837.	Wagner Charles.	*1871.	Young S. S.
*1877.	Wagner George.	1832.	Young Henry.
1860.	Wagner G. W.	1857.	Zuber D.
1871.	Weaver W. W.	*1887.	Zuber S. A.
1873.	Webber William.		

OUR DEAD.

One by one they hang their armour on the tower of David "whereon hang a thousand bucklers, all shields of mighty men."

Year of Death.	Names.	Year of Death.	Names.
1805.	Liesser Abraham.	1819.	Miller Solomon.
1808.	Albright Jacob.	1823.	Peters Jacob.
1813.	Betz Matthew.	1826.	Vandersal John.
1816.	Miller George.	1826.	Schneider John.
1818.	Walter John.	1828.	Stambach John.

Year of Death.	Names.	Year of Death.	Names.
1828.	Kleinfelter Jacob, "the second."	1856.	Gross Jacob.
1829.	Meyer Henry.	1859.	Frey Abraham.
1830.	Manwiller D.	1860.	Seybert Bishop John.
1833.	Frey Samuel.	1863.	Kleinfelter John.
1833.	Wolf Christian.	1864.	Schugar Immanuel.
1833.	Miller John W.	1867.	Barber James.
1833.	Young Henry.	1867.	Dewees W.
1833.	Borauf Frederick.	1869.	Saylor Abraham.
1833.	Wolf Christian.	1869.	Ruehl L.
1834.	Tobias Daniel.	1869.	Deppen Isaac.
1834.	Riem Abraham.	1869.	Long Bishop J.
1837.	Roessner John.	1870.	Wagner Philip.
1837.	Thomas John.	1871.	Dundore S. F.
1837.	Yeakel Andrew.	1871.	Dreisbach John.
1838.	Breidenstein Philip.	1871.	Brown Samuel.
1838.	Ettinger Benjamin.	1871.	Kehr D.
1839.	Dressler George.	1872.	Young John.
1839.	Hammer John.	1873.	Meyers Christian.
1840.	Miesse Henry.	1873.	Wolf Charles.
1840.	Zimmerman Leonhard.	1874.	Ely Ephraim.
1840.	Berkheimer William.	1874.	Thomas David.
1841.	Altimos Solomon.	1874.	Light David.
1842.	Witt Samuel.	1874.	Snyder Edward.
1842.	Strob Abraham.	1875.	Dreibelbis R.
1842.	Shaefer John.	1875.	Overholser Isaac.
1843.	Buck Thomas.	1875.	Yeakel Christopher.
1843.	Hesser Charles.	1875.	Reich George.
1844.	Focht Daniel.	1875.	Leib John P.
1848.	Dieder Emanuel.	1876.	Rhoads S. G.
1848.	Bisse Charles.	1876.	Schell John.
1849.	Schnerr Jacob.	1876.	Longsdorf A.
1850.	Stoever Fred. L.	1876.	Eckert John.
1851.	Shuitz David.	1877.	High J. J.
1851.	Rippley John,	1878.	Kempfer Herman.
1852.	Sensel John.	1878.	Breidenstein John.
1854.	Bisse H. A.	1878.	Heim William.
1854.	Fisher Henry.	1878.	Ettinger Adam.
1855.	Danner Frederick.	1878.	Bertolet Jacob.
		1878.	Dissinger I. S.

Year of Death.	Names.	Year of Death.	Names.
1878.	Dellinger George.	1883.	Dissinger Moses.
1879.	Reinoehl S. P.	1883.	Sindlinger J. M.
1879.	Haines G. T.	1883.	Zinser J. G.
1879.	Gaumer Samuel.	1883.	Miesse Samuel.
1880.	Berger D.	1884.	Gross Joseph.
1880.	Reber W. L.	1884.	Hambright Davis.
1880.	Schneider Jacob.	1884.	Breyfogel Seneca.
1880.	Kurtz Jonathan.	1884	Overholt A. H.
1881.	Adams Jacob.	1884.	Boas Jacob.
1881.	Shultz Abraham.	1885.	Neitz Solomon.
1881.	Snyder Lewis.	1885.	Fliehr C. B.
1882.	Oplinger J. M.	1885.	Miller George H.
1882.	Hambright W. W.	1885.	Major H. C.
1882.	Rhoads Jeremiah.	1886.	Knerr I. E.
1883.	Krecker Dr. Frederick.	1887.	Hammer Charles.
1883.	Farnsworth J. C.	1887.	Clouser Daniel.
1883.	Cole J. B.		

STATISTICAL TABLES.

Prior to the year 1861 no regular statistical tables appear upon the records of the Conference. The following tables up to that time are, therefore, a compilation rather than a transcript, a compilation made from reliable data occurring incidentally upon the minutes. Much time and the most exacting pains were taken to make these statistics minutely accurate and thoroughly reliable. It was impossible to compile trustworthy figures of local preachers before the year 1848, because of the fragmentary and indefinite sources of information.

I.—THE EARLY DAYS.

YEAR.	Newly Converted.	Newly Received.	Whole No. of Members.	Elders and Deacons in the Traveling Connection.	Traveling Preachers on Trial.	Preachers in Active Service.	General Salary Fund.	Subsidiary Collection.	Presiding Elder Districts.	Fields of Labor.
1800			*			1	$	$		1
1801	*	†	‡20			1				1
1802		20			1	2				1
1803			40	1	2	3				1
1804			60	1	3	4	61.00			2
1805		‡35	75	2	3	5				2
1806			120	3		3				2
1807			220	3	2	5				2
1808				4	2	6		44.00		2
1809			426	3	3	5		42.72		2
1810	78	114	528	5	3	7	159.33	30.80		3
1811	72	112	740	6	3	8	283.00	51.97		3
§1812	160	202	761	6	8	13	344.96	113.68		6
1813	101	129	796	8	9	15	414.61	65.36		6
1814	196	304	1016	11	5	13	588.38	59.69	1	7
1815	235	266	1108	14	5	15	553.00	171.80	2	7
1816	330	392	1401	15	10	21	700.40	206.93	2	12
1817	224	306	1493	16	12	21	769.73	354.30	2	13
1818	267	396	1707	23	7	21	935.58	362.15	2	12
1819	273	355	1895	23	7	21	938.66	174.55	2	12
1820	303	343	1992	27	3	22	708.28	177.85	2	12
1821	208	258	1974	28	6	21	611.64	149.62	2	11
1822	204	215	1936	30	10	23	642.97	160.31	2	12
1823	175	205	1854	33	8	19	637.06	137.83	3	10
1824	179	200	1878	36	8	22	676.70	108.86	3	10
1825	231	265	2039	35	9	23	616.16	97.63	3	11
1826	254	345	2207	42	6	21	775.89	123.46	3	10

* "Several." † "A few." ‡ History of the Evangelical Association. § The totals of the statistics for 1812, as given on page 23, were transposed in some unaccountable manner. They are correct as given in this table.

II.—THE EASTERN AND WESTERN CONFERENCES.

Year.	Newly Converted.	Newly Received.	Whole No. of Members.	Elders and Deacons in the Traveling Connection.	Preachers on Traveling Trial.	Preachers in Active Service.	General Salary Fund.	Subsidiary Collections.	Presiding Elder Districts.	Fields of Labor.
* 1827............	346	478	2567	46	16	23	$817.15	$105.40	3	12
" Eastern.......	293	293	2044	32	5	18	704.59	105.40	2	8
1828............	382	458	2677	46	16	22	935.29	200.82	3	11
" Eastern.......	320	373	2176	33	6	16	796.41	185.88	2	8
1829	366	435	2862	40	18	26	932.06	272.37	3	12
" Eastern.......	246	271	2214	35	7	20	790.55	252.82	2	9
1830............	632	720	3245	53	23	25	1275.08	302.36	3	13
" Eastern.......	381	438	2373	36	9	19	1065.66	266.45	2	10
1831............	555	663	3580	56	15	34	1428.79	453.93	4	14
" Eastern.......	446	521	2617	40	10	26	1133.14	424.91	3	11
1832............	697	808	3925	53	21	39	1633.99	513.04	4	17
" Eastern.......	546	627	2792	35	14	30	1360.45	464.91	3	13
1833............	606	762	4252	63	20	44	2157.49	340.19	5	21
" Eastern.......	471	560	3026	42	13	33	1808.43	269.41	4	16
1834............	717	906	4689	66	21	44	2543.80	487.19	5	21
" Eastern......	561	707	3377	41	15	33	2064.41	404.61	4	16
1835............	723	970	5119	72	21	53	2540.17	636.92	5	25
" Eastern.......	508	698	3630	47	17	42	2011.87	475.70	4	19
1836	948	943	5628	...	...	55	....	....	7	28
† " Eastern........	464	617	3379	40	13	30	1833.66	505.04	4	16
1837............	1168	1420	6665	...	...	64	....	....	7	30
" Eastern.......	644	747	3677	45	18	37	2168.37	811.28	4	18
1838	....	....	7309	...	...	70	....	....	8	33
" Eastern.......	512	664	3954	51	12	41	3090.37	794.45	5	19
1839............	....	....	7859	...	...	82	....	....	9	36
" Eastern........	603	711	4206	50	15	43	3607.89	713.10	5	22

* From 1827 to 1840 double statistics will be given. The upper row of figures opposite each year indicate the total statistics for both the Eastern and Western Conferences; the lower row, the statistics of the Eastern Conference only.

† The General Conference of 1835 transferred three circuits to the Western Conference. This accounts for the decrease in the ministry and membership of the Eastern.

III.—THE EAST PENNSYLVANIA CONFERENCE.

Year.	Newly Converted.	Newly Received.	Whole No. of Members.	Elders and Deacons in the Traveling Connection.	Traveling Preachers on Trial.	Local Elders and Deacons.	Local Preachers on Trial.	*Preachers in Active Service.	General Salary Fund.	Subsidiary Collection.	†Salary Received.	Presiding Elder Districts.	Fields of Labor.
1840	525	...	...	...	...	...	...	21	$	$	48.60	3	12
1841	476	618	2723	40	6	...	...	29	2406.82	553.02	60.00	3	15
1842	796	982	3439	44	9	...	...	29	2751.41	779.20	60.00	3	19
1843	1175	1371	4372	44	14	...	...	35	3090.89	475.08	52.80	3	20
1844	575	696	4407	43	20	...	...	37	2922.19	898.48	48.00	4	22
1845	667	833	4747	42	23	...	...	39	...	...	58.20	4	25
1846	557	736	4790	53	6	...	...	41	...	...	56.16	4	26
1847	523	638	4930	50	17	...	...	43	4831.89	432.44	56.90	5	28
1848	703	1041	5169	37	8	19	12	46	4369.54	951.57	54.72	6	28
‡1849	530	620	3910	28	6	12	14	30	...	...	89.50	3	18

Year.	Newly Converted.	Newly Received.	Whole No. of Members.	Elders and Deacons in the Traveling Connection.	Traveling Preachers on Trial.	Local Elders and Deacons.	Local Preachers on Trial.	Preachers in Active Service.	General Salary Fund.	Subsidiary Collection.	Salary Received.	Presiding Elder Districts.	Fields of Labor.	Sunday-Schools.	Officers and Teachers.	Scholars.	Volumes in Library.
1850	487	691	4087	32	4	11	11	33	...	...	$80.00	3	21	35	254	2003	4862
1851	750	875	4538	33	7	12	23	31	...	...	...	3	21	41	444	2363	5727
1852	735	878	4829	36	6	11	21	37	...	...	95.00	3	24	42	507	2036	5949
1853	824	960	5293	38	7	9	15	37	...	...	94.00	3	23	47	527	3030	7638
1854	738	865	5701	35	11	10	..	48	...	...	96.00	3	29	58	647	3646	8880
1855	905	1038	5967	41	10	19	..	46	6665.07	547.78	100.00	3	30	65	717	3947	10206
1856	750	766	6000	43	7	21	25	47	...	...	97.00	3	32	70	725	4136	10972
1857	858	1002	6145	45	3	20	4	48	...	324.67	96.00	3	33	67	618	4532	8147
1858	1286	1543	7009	..	..	..	..	45	...	...	...	3	32	75	900	5000	17007
1859	1209	1397	7564	48	5	21	42	50	...	...	87.00	3	36	86	1630	5552	17466
1860	1071	1251	7863	47	8	21	42	51	...	...	89.00	3	37	80	964	5295	12140

* From this time forth the number of preachers in active service is taken from the list of appointments of the year previous, that is, the number on the list of appointments in 1839, is placed on record as reported in 1840, thus bringing this part into harmony with the rest of the statistics of the East Pa. Conference. † The amount of salary here given is that of an unmarried preacher. An equal amount additional was allowed for the wife of a married preacher, and one-fourth additional for each child under a certain age. ‡ The decrease in the statistics of this year is accounted for by the fact that the New York Conference had been separately organized.

The East Pennsylvania Conference.

(CONTINUED.)

Year.	Died.	Expelled.	Withdrawn.	Moved Away.	Newly Converted.	Newly Received.	Received with Certificates.	Whole Number of Members.	Adults Baptized.	Infants Baptized.	Elders and Deacons in the Traveling Connection.	Traveling Preachers on Trial.	Local Elders and Deacons.	Local Preachers on Trial.	Preachers in Active Service.	Churches.	Probable Value.	Parsonages.
1861	75	377	165	178	....	1537	48	8299	102	756	53	5	23	42	58	103	$171900	9
1862	88	218	177	428	....	1113	120	8633	145	743	52	6	27	45	58	108	177600	10
1863	100	283	193	576	....	1155	123	8755	78	756	57	2	29	44	59	109	176850	10
1864	...	407	136	535	....	1095	121	8793	83	765	55	..	34	..	64	117	200100	10
1865	123	287	140	389	....	1242	175	8775	85	807	60	..	32	..	67	125	225950	13
1866	115	375	184	542	....	1718	130	9000	136	801	64	5	30	23	63	129	264100	12
1867	108	422	228	404	....	1562	226	9507	96	970	67	9	32	46	76	123	309600	12
1868	118	303	221	490	....	1535	276	9854	119	1006	72	8	31	46	77	138	336750	17
1869	121	271	120	537	....	1766	243	10335	223	1009	76	2	33	47	75	158	324700	19
1870	103	247	189	729	1303	1563	211	11060	229	1036	79	3	33	49	81	153	536900	22
1871	103	202	181	623	2929	1655	364	11297	146	1003	84	7	41	53	87	154	545900	27
1872	150	298	365	455	2188	2212	287	12470	127	1062	90	4	39	55	86	177	516600	25
1873	178	230	216	477	2196	2012	227	13475	182	1378	92	6	49	61	94	177	531300	31
1874	148	299	390	763	3005	2649	290	14491	144	1404	97	10	49	54	100	186	653200	31
1875	208	402	551	974	2512	2464	559	14730	252	1401	105	10	35	48	108	195	716700	32
1876	167	329	320	834	3253	2883	458	15959	231	1498	98	4	31	48	91	205	788495	34
1877	153	355	379	895	2741	2177	281	14799	227	1223	102	3	28	53	90	190½	623600	27
1878	147	276	452	896	2763	2365	387	14998	243	1150	98	..	30	56	85	191½	574890	28
1879	127	290	416	945	2007	1928	373	14790	128	1229	91	..	28	56	82	195½	525250	30
1880	156	189	476	943	2225	2027	357	14863	178	1202	94	1	29	59	90	192½	529275	31
1881	183	135	469	839	1549	1590	307	14805	151	1166	93	7	25	54	90	194	554000	30
1882	207	122	377	1014	1719	1782	324	14367	187	1257	94	4	23	65	93	191½	554840	32
1883	171	107	398	757	1926	1884	325	15275	214	1221	101	6	22	53	90	193½	582900	34
1884	196	76	431	1140	1913	2188	282	15472	132	1153	102	5	24	46	95	201	607685	36
1885	183	114	414	766	1682	1742	316	15763	176	1211	111	4	23	56	100	203	645445	35
1886	183	103	427	746	2207	2152	270	16456	219	1234	113	4	21	59	100	206½	676990	37
1887	205	100	468	869	2062	2146	434	16933	262	1352	117	1	21	63	103	210½	702280	35

The East Pennsylvania Conference.

(CONCLUDED.)

Probable Value.	Indebtedness.	Superannuated.	Missionary.	Sunday-School and Tract Union.	Orphan.	Educational.	Building Society.	Sunday-Schools.	Officers and Teachers.	Scholars.	Volumes in Library.	Catechetical Classes.	Catechumens.
			Collections.										
$ 8975 .$......	$......	$186.06	$1620.22	$ 2.00	$......	$......	$......	79	1071	5467	16825	6	92
12975	......	165.08	2204.61	44.11				84	1308	5838	17431	15	172
11380	......	170.90	1881.41	56.20				86	1162	5898	18473	11	122
12200	......	218.27	3113.15	152.34				95	1389	6687	17643	3	24
20400	......	326.17	4562.32	257.96				97	1350	6770	19656	3	76
22450	......	363.66	7284.78	268.16				104	1480	7622	20928	5	124
21900	......	357.81	3418.49	293.34				112	1811	8587	22062	10	162
34100	......	398.00	4540.23	293.34				115	1620	8677	23179	30	457
38900	......	548.97	4950.52	295.21	52.00			129	1672	8972	36096	18	253
54150	......	596.92	8255.41	325.22				143	2196	10946	33068	8	120
57800	......	607.18	5924.33	238.60	9.75			146	2343	11618	25516	10	119
63200	......	667.14	7707.60	343.98	260.67			149	2604	12849	38636	7	118
89300	......	812.95	8289.21	336.54				160	2555	14745	36295	6	139
92900	......	813.60	7831.49	358.33				174	3034	16500	46336	6	153
95300	......	1215.45	7370.54	354.73				184	3205	17507	35602	10	202
83900	......	1089.88	7411.63	313.42				200	3396	19148	35914	4	93
55900	......	747.27	6516.69	220.58				178	3022	17729	29071	...	...
51400	......	748.94	4739.01	192.01		12.49	21.70	191	3124	18174	28470	1	23
44150	......	853.71	4272.79	174.56		87.77	110.49	191	3147	18889	26290	2	42
47900	......	1198.10	7385.35	202.86		101.89	164.29	189	3258	20083	25157	6	99
47500	......	1177.24	8264.99	407.36	257.96	136.66	185.17	193	3258	19900	24100	5	88
50950	......	1170.65	8705.93	219.25	337.23	586.48	186.66	187	3242	20740	24390	2	42
54750	49315.00	966.19	14246.82	231.11	465.86	633.06	209.05	183	3215	20921	21252	..	...
57800	49280.48	1229.76	12048.15	205.86	451.05	1298.77	288.19	189	3256	22356	19815	2	41
57100	49377.27	1252.26	11182.56	201.67	1788.72	5497.49	225.42	189	3234	22865	20396	2	51
60950	57607.50	1563.88	10446.47	198.79	401.29	1536.04	284.25	184½	3244	22504	19683	15	232
60250	55572.77	1615.85	13183.75	192.22	344.55	2554.91	260.6	185½	3437	23569	18067	7	133

INDEX.

Verlag von Ig. Kohler

911 Arch Straße, • = = Philadelphia, Pa.

Die Bibel.

Für Kirche, Schule und Haus, enthaltend sämmtliche Schriften des alten und neuen Testaments, nach Dr. Martin Luther's Uebersetzung. Groß Quart-Format mit großem Druck. Mit einem neuen Zusatz der ganzen Schnorr'schen Bibel in 240 Bildern.

Ferner: Die Zerstörung Jerusalems: ein merkwürdiger Beweis aus der Geschichte für die Wahrheit göttlicher Weissagung, zugleich enthaltend eine Erzählung des großen Elends, welches als ein Gottesgericht über das jüdische Volk hereinbrach.

Und: Nachrichten über die zehn Stämme Israels: gesammelt aus hebräischen, englischen, französischen und holländischen Quellen.

No. 1. Billige Ausgabe mit 2 Stahlstichen schön in Leder gebunden, $6 00
No. 2. Mit 240 Bildern, ebenso gebunden.................... 7.00
No. 3. " " in Marocco mit Goldschnitt, Rücken und
Decken vergoldet.............................. 9.00

Volks-Bilder-Bibel, kleine,

Oder die ganze heilige Schrift des alten und neuen Testaments, nach der deutschen Uebersetzung Dr. Martin Luther's. Mit 200 schönen eingedruckten Abbildungen von Julius Schnorr von Carolsfeld und 2 Stahlstichen, auf feines weißes Papier gedruckt. Groß Octav.

No. 1. Gut in Leder gebunden...........................$3.00

Arndt, J.

Sechs Bücher vom wahren Christenthum, nebst dem Leben des seligen Autors und dissen Paradiesgärtlein; auch die Sonn- und Feiertags-Evangelien und Episteln. Mit 66 Holzschnitten. Quarto.

No. 1. Billige Ausgabe, gut gebunden....................$3.50

Goßner, Johannes.

Schatzkästchen, enthaltend biblische Betrachtungen, mit erbaulichen Liedern auf alle Tage im Jahre, zur Beförderung häuslicher Andacht und Gottseligkeit. Klein Quarto.

In Leinwand mit Goldtitel $1.00, in Lederband...... ....$1.25

Hofacker, M. Ldw.

Predigten für alle Sonn-, Fest- und Feiertage, nebst einigen Bußtagspredigten und Grabreden. Mit dem Bildnisse des Verfassers und erweiterten Mittheilungen aus seinem äußeren und inneren Lebensgange, nebst einem Anhange von 8 nachgelassenen Predigten. Groß Royal-Octav.

Schön in Leinwand gebunden...........................$2.50

P. S.—Vollständige Kataloge werden auf Verlangen gratis versandt.

☞ Agenten werden verlangt.

MUTUAL LIFE INSURANCE

AS PRESENTED BY THE

KEYSTONE

MUTUAL

BENEFIT

Association.

Home Office :

ALLENTOWN, PA.

Incorporated February 7th, 1878.

DR. W. H. HARTZELL, President; JOHN E. LENTZ, Vice-President; DR. A. R. HORNE, Secretary; A. D. DRESHER, Treasurer; J. L. MOYER, General Superintendent; DR. WM. A. HASSLER, Medical Adviser.
REV. BISHOP THOS. BOWMAN, B. D. KECK, Esq., T. J. SCHMEYER, Esq., and DR. H. S. CAMPBELL, Directors.

THE KEYSTONE MUTUAL BENEFIT ASSOCIATION

is, as is shown by the Annual Reports of Insurance Commissioner of Pennsylvania, one of the most successful of the Assessment Companies, and ranks as first-class among its competitors. Among a healthy class of people the death-rate is, as a matter of course, much lower than in a class surrounded by or given to conditions unfavorable to health. Consequently, an association of such healthy persons has a rate of mortality considerably lower than among a body of men selected without due regard to soundness of health or safety of habits.

Why the Keystone is Preferred.

1. Because it is cheap. 2. Because its affairs are economically managed. 3. Because it pays its losses promptly. 4 Because it pays all legitimate claims in full. 5. Because it is careful in taking risks. 6. Because its directors are well known, careful, conscientious men. 7. Because it has never allowed any speculation. 8. Because its officers are gentlemanly and polite. 9. Because it is straightforward and reliable in all its transactions.

A large number of the ministers of the Evangelical denomination are insured in this Association, among others Revs. W. A. Leopold, R. M. Lichtenwalner, C. H. Baker, J. C. Bleim, D. Yingst, J. S. Newhardt, D. Lentz, D. A. Medlar, I. U. Royer, J. W. Hoover, S. B. Brown, C. H. Egge, etc.

Special reductions made to ministers. A new $5,000 policy is now issued on very low terms. Write for particulars.

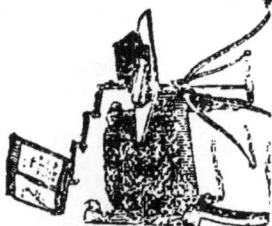

www.ingramcontent.com/pod-product-compliance
Lightning Source LLC
Chambersburg PA
CBHW032302280326
41932CB00009B/662